THE CAMBRIDGE
COMPANION TO
TRAVEL WRITING

EDITED BY

PETER HULME
University of Essex

AND

TIM YOUNGS
The Nottingham Trent University

CAMBRIDGE
UNIVERSITY PRESS

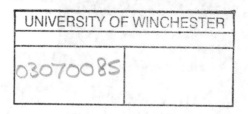
CAMBRIDGE UNIVERSITY PRESS
Cambridge, New York, Melbourne, Madrid, Cape Town, Singapore, São Paulo, Delhi

Cambridge University Press
The Edinburgh Building, Cambridge CB2 8RU, UK

Published in the United States of America by Cambridge University Press, New York

www.cambridge.org
Information on this title: www.cambridge.org/9780521786522

First published 2002
Fourth printing 2008

Printed in the United Kingdom at the University Press, Cambridge

A catalogue record for this publication is available from the British Library

Library of Congress Cataloguing in Publication data

The Cambridge companion to travel writing / edited by
Peter Hulme and Tim Youngs.
p.   cm. – (Cambridge companions to literature)
Includes bibliographical references and index.
ISBN 0 521 78140 X – ISBN 0 521 78652 5 (pb.)
1. Travelers' writings, English – History and criticism.   2. Travelers' writings,
American – History and criticism.   3. English prose literature – History and criticism.
4. British – Foreign countries – Historiography.   5. Voyages and travels – Historiography.
6. Travel in literature.   7. Travelers – History.   I. Title: Companion to travel writing.
II. Hulme, Peter.   III. Youngs, Tim.
PR756.T72 C36   2002
820.9'491 – dc21   2002023425

ISBN 978-0-521-78652-2 paperback

CONTENTS

Contents

LIST OF ILLUSTRATIONS

NOTES ON CONTRIBUTORS

SUSAN BASSNETT is Professor in the Centre for Translation and Comparative Cultural Studies at the University of Warwick. She is the author of over twenty books, including *Translation Studies*, which first appeared in 1980. Her recent books include *Studying British Cultures: An Introduction* (1997), *Constructing Cultures* (1998) written with André Lefevere and *Postcolonial Translation* with Harish Trivedi (1999). Her latest book, a collection of poems and translations, is *Exchanging Lives* (2001).

ROY BRIDGES is Emeritus Professor of History in the University of Aberdeen and President of the Hakluyt Society. He has written extensively on explorers and missionaries and related historical matters, especially in the context of East Africa. His most recent work is a study of the 'Prelude to the Partition of East Africa' in his edited book, *Imperialism, Decolonization and Africa* (2000).

JAMES BUZARD is Associate Professor of Literature at MIT and the author of *The Beaten Track: European Tourism, Literature, and the Ways to 'Culture,' 1800–1918* (1993). His essays have appeared in *Victorian Studies, Raritan, The Yale Journal of Criticism, Modernism/Modernity, PMLA,* and other journals and essay collections. He recently co-edited a special issue of Victorian Studies on 'Victorian Ethnographies' and is currently writing the book *Anywhere's Nowhere: Fictions of Autoethnography in the United Kingdom.*

MARY BAINE CAMPBELL is Professor of English and American Literature at Brandeis University. She is the author of *The Witness and the Other World: Exotic European Travel Writing, 400–1600* (1988) and *Wonder and Science: Imagining Worlds in Early Modern Europe* (1999). Her recent academic research involves dreams and dream theory in early modern Europe and the New World. She is also a poet, currently at work on an opera based on Marie de France's *Bisclavret,* a lai about a werewolf.

HELEN CARR is Reader in English at Goldsmiths College, University of London. Her publications include *Inventing the American Primitive: Politics, Gender and the Representation of Native American Literary Traditions, 1789–1936* (1996) and *Jean Rhys* (1996). She is co-editor of *Women: a Cultural Review* and is at present working on a group biography of the imagist poets.

ROD EDMOND is Reader in Nineteenth-Century and Postcolonial Studies in the School of English at the University of Kent. His most recent book is *Representing the South Pacific: Colonial Discourse from Cook to Gauguin* (1997). Recent contributions to books include essays on imperialism and modernism, and on colonial encounter and disease. He is currently writing a book on colonialism and disease, with particular reference to leprosy.

BRUCE GREENFIELD is Associate Professor in the Department of English at Dalhousie University and the author of *Narrating Discovery: The Romantic Explorer in American Literature, 1790–1855* (1992) and of a number of essays and articles, most recently 'The Mi'kmaq Hieroglyphic Prayer Book: Writing and Christianity in Maritime Canada, 1675–1921', in *The Language Encounter in the Americas, 1492 to 1800*, ed. Edward Gray and Norman Fiering (2000).

GLENN HOOPER is a Research Fellow in the Institute of Irish and Scottish Studies, University of Aberdeen. He is editor of Harriet Martineau's *Letters from Ireland* (2001) and of the anthology *The Tourist's Gaze: Travellers to Ireland, 1800–2000* (2001), and co-editor of *Ireland in the Nineteenth Century: Regional Identity* (2000) and of the forthcoming *Ireland and the Postcolony: Writing, History, Culture*.

PETER HULME is Professor in Literature at the University of Essex. His most recent books are *Remnants of Conquest: The Island Caribs and Their Visitors, 1877–1998* (2000) and the co-edited (with William Sherman) *'The Tempest' and Its Travels* (2000). His current research relates to questions of history and fiction in the Caribbean.

BILLIE MELMAN is Professor of Modern History at Tel Aviv University. She has written extensively on colonialism and orientalism, nationalism, and gender, and on the development of women's and gender history. She is author of *Women's Orients: English Women and the Middle East, 1718–1918* (1992 and 1995) and editor of *Borderlines: Gender and Identities in War and Peace 1870–1930* (1998).

JOAN PAU RUBIÉS is Lecturer in International History at the London School of Economics. He is author of *Travel and Ethnology in the Renaissance. South India through European Eyes 1250–1625* (2000), and co-editor of *Voyages and Visions. Towards a Cultural History of Travel* (1999) and *Shifting Cultures. Interaction and Discourse in the Expansion of Europe* (1995). He is currently working on a book on the impact of travel and travel writing in the transformation of European culture from the Renaissance to the Enlightenment.

WILLIAM H. SHERMAN is Associate Professor of English at the University of Maryland. He is the author of *John Dee: The Politics of Reading and Writing in the English Renaissance* (1995) and co-editor (with Peter Hulme) of *'The Tempest' and Its Travels* (2000). He is currently finishing a book on Renaissance marginalia and editions of Ben Jonson's *The Alchemist* (with Peter Holland) and Shakespeare's *The Tempest* (with Peter Hulme).

KATE TELTSCHER is Senior Lecturer in the School of English and Modern Languages at the University of Surrey, Roehampton, and the author of *India Inscribed: European and British Writing on India, 1600–1800* (1995). She is currently working on a biography of George Bogle, the first British envoy to Bhutan and Tibet.

NEIL L. WHITEHEAD is Professor of Anthropology at the University of Wisconsin-Madison. He is the co-editor of *Wild Majesty: Encounters with Caribs from Columbus to the Present Day. An Anthology* (1992), and editor of *The Discoverie of the Large, Rich and Bewtiful Empire of Guiana by Sir Walter Ralegh* (1997). Forthcoming editions include *Travels, Explorations and Empires, 1835–1910. Volume 8 – South America* and (with Michael Harbsmeier) Hans Staden's *True History and Description of a Land belonging to the wild, naked, savage, Man-munching People, situated in the New World, America (1557)*.

TIM YOUNGS, founding editor of the journal *Studies in Travel Writing*, is Reader in English and US Studies at The Nottingham Trent University. He is the author of *Travellers in Africa: British Travelogues 1850–1900* (1994) and editor of *Writing and Race* (1997). His current projects include a volume co-edited with Glenn Hooper called *International Perspectives on Travel Writing* and an edited, critical anthology of nineteenth-century travel writing of Africa.

PETER HULME AND TIM YOUNGS

INTRODUCTION

'There is no foreign land; it is only the traveller that is foreign'
(Robert Louis Stevenson)[1]

Travel has recently emerged as a key theme for the humanities and social
sciences, and the amount of scholarly work on travel writing has reached
unprecedented levels. The academic disciplines of literature, history, geography, and anthropology have all overcome their previous reluctance to take
travel writing seriously and have begun to produce a body of interdisciplinary criticism which will allow the full historical complexity of the genre
to be appreciated.

The absence within the academy of a tradition of critical attention to travel
writing means that this Companion, unlike most others in the series, whose
areas of study are well-defined, has to bring its subject into focus in order
to 'accompany' it. As a result, our volume offers only a tentative map of a
vast, little-explored area. As far as practicable, we have opted for a broad
definition of travel writing, with the huge range of potential texts leading
us to focus on major shifts, on kinds and forms, on places written about,
and on exemplary instances, rather than on particular travel writers. The
two major limitations we have worked within are concentrations on the
period since 1500 and on travel writing in English and published in Britain.
The Anglocentric concentration is by no means exclusive: non-English travel
writing has often been influential in Britain, with translations appearing soon
after original publication, and travel writing has played an important rôle
in recent years in the creation of an international literary field, so it would
not make sense to operate rigid principles of exclusion.

The Companion's structure is tri-partite. The *Surveys* section offers broad
coverage on historical lines, the aim being to map the principal shifts in
travel writing in English over the last 500 years in five overlapping chapters.
Sites offers more specific studies, focusing on seven significant places that
have been visited by a variety of travel writers. These seven sites – spread

throughout the world – have been chosen partly because they can be seen as representative of the larger areas with which they are associated and through which they are here approached. *Topics* then returns to some of the larger themes briefly raised in this Introduction, the focus here being the broader issues on which consideration of travel writing has a significant bearing. Finally, the Chronology lists a lengthy selection of travel writing, correlated to relevant historical events, and the Further Reading offers a substantial listing of secondary texts. Our overarching aim is to provide a broad introduction to travel writing in English published in Britain between 1500 and 2000.

Early forms

Writing and travel have always been intimately connected. The traveller's tale is as old as fiction itself: one of the very earliest extant stories, composed in Egypt during the Twelfth Dynasty, a thousand years before the *Odyssey*, tells of a shipwrecked sailor alone on a marvellous island.[2] The biblical and classical traditions are both rich in examples of travel writing, literal and symbolic – Exodus, the punishment of Cain, the Argonauts, the *Aeneid* – which provide a corpus of reference and intertext for modern writers. In particular, Homer's Odysseus gave his name to the word we still use to describe an epic journey, and his episodic adventures offer a blueprint for the romance, indirection, and danger of travel as well as the joy (and danger) of homecoming. Societal attitudes to travel have always been ambivalent. Travel broadens the mind, and knowledge of distant places and people often confers status, but travellers sometimes return as different people or do not come back at all. Pilgrimages are necessary for Christian salvation, but must be carefully controlled. The Grand Tour (James Buzard's subject in Chapter 2) can lead to education or to dissolution – just like, more recently, backpacking in the 'gap' year between school and university.[3] So the ambiguous figure of Odysseus – adventurous, powerful, unreliable – is perhaps the appropriate archetype for the traveller, and by extension for the travel writer.

Within the Christian tradition, life itself has often been symbolised as a journey, perhaps most famously in John Bunyan's allegory, *The Pilgrim's Progress* (1678); and the centrality of the pilgrimage to Christianity produces much medieval travel writing as well as the framing device for Chaucer's *Canterbury Tales*. In many respects pilgrims were ancestors of modern tourists: a catering industry grew up to look after them, they followed set routes, and the sites they visited were packaged for them. Although today's travel writers will typically seek out the pre-modern, the simple, the authentic, or the unspoilt, precisely *off* the beaten track, pilgrimage and its associated writings continue to be influential, in part because their source-directed narratives fit so well with a number of the literary genres, such as romance, which travel writers still adopt.[4]

Many of the themes and problems associated with modern travel writing can be found in two medieval texts which still provoke fascination and controversy. The narratives of both Marco Polo and John Mandeville mark the beginnings of a new impulse in the late Middle Ages which would transform the traditional paradigms of pilgrimage and crusade into new forms attentive to observed experience and curiosity towards other lifeways.[5] Marco Polo travelled to Cathay (China) in the second half of the thirteenth century. On his return to Venice his story was written down by a writer of romances called Rustichello. By contrast nothing is known for sure about Mandeville – even his nationality – but his *Travels* was widely read for several centuries. Although Christopher Columbus's first voyage to America in 1492 is usually seen as a new beginning for travel writing, Columbus was, as a writer, deeply influenced by both Mandeville and Marco Polo: echoes of their words drift through early descriptions of the Caribbean islands.[6]

Writing and travel in the modern era

During the sixteenth century, writing became an essential part of travelling; documentation an integral aspect of the activity.[7] Political or commercial sponsors wanted reports and maps, often kept secret, but the public interest aroused by stories of faraway places was an important way of attracting investment and – once colonies started – settlers. Rivalry between European nation-states meant that publication of travel accounts was often a semi-official business in which the beginnings of imperial histories were constructed, a process William Sherman discusses in Chapter 1. The greatest impact of the new world of America on English writing in the early sixteenth century is seen in Thomas More's *Utopia* (1516), in which the fictional traveller, Raphael Hythloday, is said to have journeyed with Amerigo Vespucci to the New World. Like a handful of later fictional texts (particularly Joseph Conrad's *Heart of Darkness*), *Utopia* then became a foundation for subsequent travel writing, influencing the form of both expectations and reports.

Against this background, the English editor of early travellers, Richard Hakluyt, argued for a history of travel which relied on the testimony of travellers themselves: in other words he looked mostly to eyewitness accounts – even though his practice was inconsistent since in the second edition of his *Principal Navigations* (1598–1600) Mandeville was excluded as false but the Arthurian legends remained. So distinguishing fact from fiction was important for at least some sixteenth-century readers, even if the process was made much more difficult by the *topos* of the claim to empirical truthfulness so crucial to travel stories of all kinds, both factual and fictional.

Even within the construction of national epics such as Hakluyt's, however, it was recognised that the real power of travel writing lay in its independence of perspective. The claim to have been there and to have seen with one's own eyes could defeat speculation. Samuel Purchas, the second of the English collectors of travel texts and an enthusiastic proponent of a national ideology, emphasised the power of this individuality in the 1625 introduction to his *Purchas His Pilgrimes*:

> What a World of Travellers have by their owne eyes observed...is here... delivered, not by one preferring Methodically to deliver the Historie of Nature according to rules of Art, nor Philosophically to discusse and dispute; but as in way of Discourse, by each Traveller relating what is the kind he hath seen.[8]

For Purchas's contemporary, Francis Bacon, the travellers of the Renaissance had discovered a 'new continent' of truth, based on experience and observation rather than the authority of the ancients; and it was in effect travel writing which provided the vehicle for the conveyance of the new information which laid the foundations for the scientific and philosophical revolutions of the seventeenth century.[9] John Locke, a representative figure in these revolutions, owned a vast collection of travel writing on which his philosophical texts regularly drew.

Locke in fact features as a character in Richard Hurd's 1763 dialogue essay, 'On the Uses of Foreign Travel'. Locke is made to be critical of the limited value of 'sauntering within the circle of the grand Tour', generally preferring what can be learned at home, although he ends with a sudden vision of the world beyond Europe: 'to study HUMAN NATURE to purpose, a traveller must enlarge his circuit beyond the bounds of Europe. He must go, and catch her undressed, nay quite naked, in *North America*, and at the Cape of *Good Hope*.'[10] At the same moment, Jean-Jacques Rousseau – another enthusiastic reader of travel writing – was calling in his *Discourse on the Origins of Inequality* for observers of the calibre of Montesquieu, Buffon, and Diderot to travel to the far-flung parts of the earth in order to enrich our knowledge of human societies.[11] Despite this enthusiasm, neither Locke nor Rousseau travelled very widely, which meant that they had to rely on information provided by others, usually less well-educated than themselves.

As a result, all kinds of interested parties – including scientists, philosophers, and sponsors – issued instructions to travellers about how to observe and how to write down their observations, and the history of such instructions runs unbroken into the early twentieth century and the foundations of anthropology: Joan Pau Rubiés's essay (Chapter 14) explores these connections. Alexander von Humboldt's travels to the Americas right at the beginning of the nineteenth century marked a turning point in travel writing, setting an example that would be followed by major figures such as Charles Darwin and Alfred Russel Wallace, also scientists whose travels were fundamental to their research.[12] Neil Whitehead's essay (Chapter 7) touches on Humboldt and Wallace in the Amazon, which was one of the great scientific laboratories of the nineteenth century.

Instructions issued by those who stay at home have not always been followed by travellers and travel writers. One of the Royal Society's directions for seamen actually instructed them 'to study *Nature* rather than *Books*', an instruction they doubtless applied to the book containing this instruction.[13] Travellers will usually follow their instincts and opportunities, rather than directions from home, and it is travellers' eccentricities and extravagances – in the literal sense of wanderings off – which have attracted many readers to the genre of travel writing.

The idiosyncrasy that marks much modern travel writing has its early modern precedents in books such as John Taylor's *The Pennyles Pilgrimage* (1618) and Thomas Coryate's *Crudities* (1611). Taylor describes his walk to Edinburgh, dependent on his guiles and the generosity of strangers for support. Waterways and stagecoaches were at this time increasing the ease and reliability of travel within the kingdom, just as improvements in ship technology and navigation had – more partially – increased those to other shores. Coryate's gastronomic title – prefiguring a long history of relating travel to food – is made clear in the full version, which continues: *Hastily gobled up in five Monethes travels in France, Savoy, Italy, Rhetia commonly called the Grisons country, Helvetia alias Switzerland, some parts of high Germany and the Netherlands; Newly digested in the hungry aire of Somerset, and now dispersed to the nourishment of the travelling Members of this Kingdome,* a title which hints at the combination of extravagance, self-parody, and adventure still prevalent in much popular travel writing. Coryate's journey – discussed in Chapter 1 – was also a precursor of the Grand Tour.

Two particular modes of writing – forgery and its respectable cousin, parody – have specially close, even parasitic, relationships with travel writing, since the lone traveller bearing far-fetched facts from remote climes offers the perfect alibi for the forger and a tempting target for the parodist. Lucian's *True History*, written in the first century AD, was so supremely wrought that most subsequent travel parodies are mere variations on its themes: *Gulliver's Travels* (1726) is perhaps the most significant modern version. Forgery's associations with fiction continue to pose pointed questions. Some texts, such as *Madagascar: or Robert Drury's Journal, during Fifteen Years Captivity on that Island* (1729), still cause scholars problems about their authenticity; others – even accepted as 'forgeries' – continue to exert fascination and to cast light on their legitimate brethren.[14]

Prose fiction in its modern forms built its house on this disputed territory, trafficking in travel and its tales. Early modern European novels are full of traveller-protagonists such as Jack of Newberry, Lazarillo de Tormes, Don Quixote, and Robinson Crusoe; and many of their authors – pre-eminent among them Daniel Defoe – were skilled at exploiting the uncertain boundary between travel writing and the fiction which copied its form. Travel writing and the novel, especially in its first-person form, have often shared a focus on the centrality of the self, a concern with empirical detail, and a movement through time and place which is simply sequential. Interestingly, though, while Defoe was happy to exploit the ambiguities attendant upon writing about faraway places, his own travel writing was cast in more conventional mode: *A Tour through the Whole Island of Great Britain* (1726) offers a picture of the kingdom, a form of descriptive statistics which relates back to the Elizabethan surveys and chorographies and forward to modern tours such as Jonathan Raban's *Coasting* (1987) and Paul Theroux's *The Kingdom By the Sea* (1983). The relationship between the genres remains close and often troubling. Many readers still hope for a literal truthfulness from travel writing that they would not expect to find in the novel, though each form has long drawn on the conventions of the other, an often cited example being Laurence Sterne's difficult-to-categorise *A Sentimental Journey* (1768).

Defoe was interested in commerce and civility, but by the end of the eighteenth century many travellers, under the sway of Rousseau and Romanticism, were in search of various forms of 'the primitive' which, it had been realised, could also be located within Britain and its neighbouring islands – a development which forms the subject of Glenn Hooper's essay (Chapter 10). Samuel Johnson accompanied Boswell on a trip to the Scottish Highlands and Islands in the 1770s, within living memory of the final defeat of the Stuart rebellion at the Battle of Culloden. But, like many other travellers, Johnson and Boswell concluded that they had arrived too late, that change and decline were already advanced: 'A longer journey than to the Highlands must be taken by him whose curiosity pants for savage virtues and barbarous grandeur.'[15] Other travellers, led by William Gilpin, journeyed to these kinds of places – Scotland, South Wales, the Lake District – in search of types of scenery that became known as 'picturesque' or 'romantic' or 'sublime'. Modern tourist sites were being defined at this time, but travel was still for the rich and the hardy: it took ten days by coach from London to Edinburgh and a further week to get into the Highlands.

Increasingly, too, travellers were defined, or defined themselves, against the figure of the tourist. Modernity is a deeply contested term, but its original form – as Baudelaire's *modernité*, dating from an 1863 essay – ties it closely to notions of movement and individuality which, in the aristocratic figure of the *flâneur*, or stroller, stand out against the democratisation of travel marked by the appearance of Thomas Cook's first tour in 1841.[16] By this time the literature of travel and exploration was in full flow. Travel writing in English had started much later than its Spanish counterpart but had soon produced all kinds of accounts – scientific travel, voyages of exploration and discovery, descriptions of foreign manners – about almost all parts of the world. Roy Bridges (Chapter 3) here provides the general context for the eighteenth and nineteenth centuries, with Billie Melman, Neil Whitehead, Rod Edmond, Tim Youngs, and Kate Teltscher (Chapters 6, 7, 8, 9, and 11) focusing on some of the key locations: the Middle East, South America, the Pacific, Central Africa, and India. By this time, also, the USA had become an independent country and had realised the national imperative to extend its continental boundaries, including the resonant journey westwards, studied here by Bruce Greenfield (Chapter 12).

The twentieth century began with the race to the poles, and subsequent journeys across the Arctic and, especially, the Antarctic caught the public imagination with their stories of danger and endurance, of heroism and tragedy. Many participants wrote about their experiences, but one book, Apsley Cherry-Garrard's *The Worst Journey in the World* (1922) is often seen as consolidating the qualities of them all in his remarkable elegy to a world-view that had been blown to pieces in the trenches of the Great War.[17]

Polar writing reinforced travel writing's growth in popularity, already evident in the late nineteenth century. But whereas scientists and explorers would inevitably – to use an old shorthand – put content before form, literary writers were also beginning to travel and to write about their travels: Dickens, Trollope, Stendhal, and Flaubert had done so earlier in the nineteenth century; but now writers such as Robert Louis Stevenson, Henry James, Edith Wharton, and D. H. Lawrence began to commit large amounts of time to travelling and travel writing. Travel writing was becoming travel *literature* and was therefore taken with a new seriousness – as discussed in Chapter 4 by Helen Carr.

Travel writing gained new prestige from the standing of its authors, and was still immensely popular – Peter Fleming's *Brazilian Adventure* (1933) was reprinted nine times in twelve months following its publication; but critical attention was lacking, perhaps because literary modernism valued fictional complexity over mimetic claims, however mediated. The culture of the 1930s, looking both outward to the world of politics and inward to the world of the unconscious, was a rich decade for literary travel writing with works by Evelyn Waugh, Graham Greene, and W. H. Auden and Louis MacNeice; but the travel books were still seen as adjuncts to and illuminations of the authors' main craft of prose or poetry, while political travel writing, such as George Orwell's, was valued and discussed but not considered appropriate for critical analysis as travel writing. This state of affairs did not change until well after the Second World War.

Contemporary issues

In Chapter 5 Peter Hulme suggests that the last significant shift in travel writing can be dated to the late 1970s and associated with a trio of books, the best-known of which is Bruce Chatwin's *In Patagonia* (1977). *In Patagonia* appeared just a year before Edward Said's *Orientalism*, usually seen as the beginning text for postcolonial studies: Chatwin interestingly contributes an early postcolonial speculation about the origin of Shakespeare's character Caliban, from *The Tempest*. *Orientalism* was the first work of contemporary criticism to take travel writing as a major part of its corpus, seeing it as a body of work which offered particular insight into the operation of colonial discourses.[18] Scholars working in the wake of *Orientalism* have begun to scrutinise relationships of culture and power found in the settings, encounters, and representations of travel texts. Mary Baine Campbell's essay (Chapter 15) discusses this development and its consequences in detail.

Another impulse behind recent work in travel studies has been provided by feminism. Applying to travel writing principles developed in women's literary studies more generally, scholars have both rescued some women travel writers from obscurity and investigated the reasons for the popularity of others. The relationship between women as observers and as observed has come under a scrutiny that is informed by critiques of ethnographic narratives, and the position of women travellers vis-à-vis colonialism is vigorously debated. Both within and outside the colonial context, the question of whether and how women travellers write differently from men remains central. Sara Mills's *Discourses of Difference* (1991) took this as its major theme, helping to generate a dialogue about the relative weight of textual and historical determinants and approaches.[19] Some of these developments are discussed by Susan Bassnett in Chapter 13. The huge number of publications in the past few years on Mary Kingsley's late nineteenth-century travels in West Africa exemplifies the directions and energy of this scholarship. Biographies, and critical studies produced by geographers and historians of science, have turned Kingsley, with her confidently self-deprecating humour, into a symbolic figure, but have also led to a genuine revision of male (travellers' and academics') views of African exploration.[20]

The subjects of 'race', colonialism, and gender cut across any single discipline, and within the academy evidence of the centrality of travel is the spread of its study across several fields. Interest in the rôle of travel and exploration literature in contributing to and reflecting the colonial past has been joined by a growing sophistication of textual readings based on an understanding of the operation of narrative conventions and by an acceptance that claims to truth and objectivity are not always reliable. Outside literary studies and women's studies, the three disciplines that have engaged most with travel writing are anthropology, history, and geography, while sociologists have extended these concerns to the study of tourism and of other travel practices and metaphors.[21] Translation studies has brought another dimension to travel, giving thought not only to translation between languages but also to translation between cultures.[22]

Perhaps because of its surface resemblances to travel writing, for most of the twentieth century anthropology kept its distance, emphasising its seriousness of purpose, its professional ethos, and its scientific method; although many of the key sites for anthropology duplicated those for travel writing – sometimes for the same reasons of cultural isolation and distance from the centres of modernity. However, anthropology's theoretical turn in the 1980s opened it towards other disciplines, with the idea of travel central to that dialogue, especially in the work of James Clifford, whose tellingly entitled *Routes* takes a short travel account by Amitav Ghosh as its iconic text.[23] At the same time, anthropology discovered a more reflective and personal mode, which brought it closer to travel writing: Hugh Brody's *Maps and Dreams* (1981) is emblematic of this move.

But it is not only new critical approaches that have been responsible for the recent and increasing interest in travel writing. Since the late 1970s travel texts have often reflected on contemporary issues while sometimes experimenting with the conventions of the genre, drawing inspiration from the restless example of Bruce Chatwin. Chatwin's work was, for example, a prime exhibit in the first *Granta* magazine special issue on travel writing in 1984, which did much to bring the 'new travel writing' to a wider readership. Bill Buford, in his Introduction, celebrated what he called travel writing's 'wonderful ambiguity, somewhere between fact and fiction'.[24] It is telling that Ian Jack, introducing a reprint of the same volume in 1998, could suggest that none of the writers in the anthology would be very happy with Buford's description. '[W]hen I first read writers such as Chatwin and Theroux', Jack says, 'I needed to believe that the account was as honest a description of what had happened to the writer, of what he or she had seen and heard, as the writer could manage'. And he still does. He says that we need to believe that the travel writer '*did not make it up*' (p. xi). Much contemporary travel writing has been written by journalists who have a deep investment in maintaining their credibility: Colin Thubron admits the travel book to be 'postmodern collage', but the mosaic of different pieces is still 'prescribed by the traveller's experience on the ground';[25] Robyn Davidson complains in her Introduction to *The Picador Book of Journeys* about the fibbing that goes on in travel writing – though she excuses Chatwin as a consummate fibber who did not want to be labelled a travel writer.[26]

But the experiences and impressions of travel are never easy to capture, and contemporary travellers sometimes make the phenomenology of travel an aspect of their work. Davidson's Rajasthan travel book, *Desert Places*, begins with the disconcerting words: 'Memory is a capricious thing. The India I visited in 1978 consists of images of doubtful authenticity held together in a ground of forgetfulness'.[27] Stephen Muecke's *No Road (bitumen all the way)* (1997) reflects on cultural theories as well as the experience of travel, its short chapters and jumps in subject making it a relatively rare example of experimentation in the form and structure of travel writing. And Stefan Hertmans's *Intercities* (2001) interweaves philosophical meditations on modern identity with fragmented stories of his travel through cities of Australia and Europe.

If formal experimentalism is still unusual in travel writing, there can be no doubt that the range and ethos of the genre are growing in exciting and vital ways. Like the post-colonial novel, travel texts are demonstrating a 'writing back', from the example of Ham Mukasa's account of his travels with Ugandan Prime Minister Sir Apolo Kagwa to England in 1902, through Caryl Phillips's travels in white Europe, to Gary Younge's journey to the American South the better to understand, via the scenes and participants of the civil rights movement, his identity as a young black man in Britain.[28] Involuntary movement from Africa to the New World through the slave trade, as well as more recent journeys around the Black Atlantic, are the subject of Alasdair Pettinger's substantial collection *Always Elsewhere: Travels of the Black Atlantic* (1999). Travels neither from nor to the imperial 'centre' include Pankaj Mishra's *Butter Chicken in Ludhiana: Travels in Small Town India* (1995) and Rehman Rashid's *A Malaysian Journey* (1993).

In putting together this Companion we have strengthened our sense that travel writing is best considered as a broad and ever-shifting genre, with a complex history which has yet to be properly studied. Our final paragraphs convey some sense of recent developments, but just as the ways and means of travel are constantly changing, so travel writing will continue to change in their wake: stories emerging from space travel, from virtual travel, and from the 'travails' of the world's refugees and migrants will doubtless continue to extend the genre in the years to come.

We would like to thank our editor at Cambridge University Press, Ray Ryan, for his unflagging commitment to this volume; Sara Adhikari, for her meticulous copy-editing; and Susan Forsyth, for making the index.

NOTES

1 Robert Louis Stevenson, *The Silverado Squatters*, in *The Amateur Emigrant, etc.*, vol. XVIII of *The Works of Robert Louis Stevenson*, Tusitala Edition (London: William Heinemann, 1924), p. 190.

2 See Neil Rennie, *Far-Fetched Facts: The Literature of Travel and the Idea of The South Seas* (Oxford: Clarendon Press, 1995), p. 3.

3 On these aspects of travel see Mary Helms, *Ulysses' Sail: An Ethnographic Odyssey of Power, Knowledge, and Geographical Distance* (Princeton University Press, 1988); Michael Harbsmeier, 'Spontaneous Ethnographies: Towards a Social History of Travellers' Tales', *Studies in Travel Writing*, 1 (1997): 216–38; Jaś Elsner and Joan Pau Rubiés, 'Introduction', to *Voyages and Visions: Towards a Cultural History of Travel*, ed. Jaś Elsner and Joan Pau Rubiés (London: Reaktion Books, 1999), pp. 1–56. The continued importance of the pilgrimage model is discussed below in Chapters 1 and 6.

4 See Donald R. Howard, *Writers and Pilgrims: Medieval Pilgrimage Narratives and Their Posterity* (Berkeley: University of California Press, 1980), and James Buzard, *The Beaten Track: European Tourism, Literature, and the Ways to 'Culture,' 1800–1918* (Oxford: Clarendon Press, 1993).

5 See Christian K. Zacher, *Curiosity and Pilgrimage: The Literature of Discovery in Fourteenth-Century England* (Baltimore: Johns Hopkins University Press, 1976).

6 See Mary B. Campbell, *The Witness and the Other World: Exotic European Travel Writing, 400–1600* (Ithaca: Cornell University Press, 1988); Stephen Greenblatt, *Marvelous Possessions: The Wonder of the New World* (Oxford: Clarendon Press, 1991); John Larner, *Marco Polo and the Discovery of the World* (New Haven: Yale University Press, 1999); Iain Macleod Higgins, *Writing East: The 'Travels' of Sir John Mandeville* (Philadelphia: University of Pennsylvania Press, 1997).

7 See Mary C. Fuller, *Voyages in Print: English Travel to America, 1576–1624* (Cambridge University Press, 1995), p. 2.

8 Samuel Purchas, *Purchas His Pilgrimes* [1625] (Glasgow: MacLehose, 1905–7), vol. I, p. xl.

9 See Anthony Grafton, *New Worlds, Ancient Texts: The Power of Tradition and the Shock of Discovery* (Cambridge, Mass.: Harvard University Press, 1992); and Joan Pau Rubiés, 'Travel Writing as a Genre: Facts, Fictions and the Invention of a Scientific Discourse in Early Modern Europe', *Journeys*, 1:1/2 (2000): 5–31.

10 Quoted in Dennis Porter, *Haunted Journeys: Desire and Transgression in European Travel Writing* (Princeton University Press, 1991), p. 27.

11 Jean-Jacques Rousseau, *Discours sur l'origine et les fondements de l'inégalité parmi les hommes* [1755] (Paris: Gallimard, 1965), p. 175.

12 Alexander von Humboldt, *Personal Narrative of Travels to the Equinoctial Regions of the New Continent* (1815); Charles Darwin, *Journal of Researches into the Natural History and Geology of the Countries Visited during the Voyage round the World of H.M.S. 'Beagle'* (1845); Alfred Russel Wallace, *A Narrative of Travels on the Amazon and Rio Negro* (1853).

13 Quoted in Rennie, *Far-Fetched Facts*, p. 49.

14 For example, George Psalmanazar (his pseudonym because nobody knows his real name), whose *An Historical and Geographical Description of Formosa* (1704) was a popular success before, in a later memoir, he revealed that he was a European (probably French) who had never even been in Formosa (modern Taiwan). See Susan Stewart, 'Psalmanazar's Others', in her *Crimes of Writing: Problems in the Containment of Representation* (New York: Oxford University Press, 1991), pp. 31–65; and Justin Stagl, *The History of Curiosity: A Theory of Travel* (Chur, Switzerland: Harwood Academic Publishers, 1995), pp. 171–207.

15 Samuel Johnson, *A Journey to the Western Islands of Scotland*, ed. Mary Lascelles (New Haven: Yale University Press, 1971), p. 58.

16 See Marshall Berman's emphasis on the emblematic status of macadam for modernity: *All That is Solid Melts into Air: The Experience of Modernity* (London: Verso, 1982), pp. 58–61; Charles Baudelaire, 'The Painter of Modern Life', in *Selected Writings on Art and Artists*, trans. P. E. Charver (Cambridge University Press, 1972), pp. 390–436. Buzard, *The Beaten Track*, contextualises the development of guide books.

17 See Francis Spufford, *I May Be Some Time: Ice and the English Imagination* (London: Faber and Faber, 1996) and Robert G. David, *The Arctic in the British Imagination 1818–1914* (Manchester University Press, 2000).

18 Early critical work on travel writing included Paul Fussell, *Abroad: British Literary Traveling Between the Wars* (Oxford University Press, 1980) and Philip Dodd, ed., *The Art of Travel: Essays on Travel Writing* (London: Frank Cass, 1982), but they tended to look back at the great 'literary' travellers: Robert Byron, also a favourite of Chatwin's, became tl e exemplar.

19 Sara Mills, *Discourses of Difference: An Analysis of Women's Travel Writing and Colonialism* (London: Routledge, 1991).

20 See Alison Blunt, *Travel, Gender, and Imperialism. Mary Kingsley and West Africa* (New York: The Guilford Press, 1994); Cheryl McEwan, *Gender, Geography and Empire: Victorian Women Travellers in West Africa* (Aldershot: Ashgate, 2000).

21 See Dean MacCannell, *The Tourist: A New Theory of the Leisure Class* (New York: Schocken Books, 1976); John Urry, *The Tourist Gaze: Leisure and Travel in Contemporary Societies* (London: Sage, 1990); and Chris Rojek and John Urry, eds., *Touring Cultures: Transformations of Travel and Theory* (London: Routledge, 1997).

22 See Michael Cronin, *Across the Lines: Travel, Language, Translation* (Cork University Press, 2000).

23 James Clifford, *Routes: Travel and Translation in the Late Twentieth Century* (Cambridge, Mass.: Harvard University Press, 1997), pp. 1–6.

24 Quoted in Ian Jack, 'Introduction', to *The Granta Book of Travel* (London: Granta Books, 1998), p. x.

25 Colin Thubron, 'Both Seer and Seen: The Travel Writer as Leftover Amateur', *TLS*, 30 July 1999, no. 5026, p. 12.
26 Robyn Davidson, *The Picador Book of Journeys* (London: Picador, 2001), pp. 4–5.
27 Robyn Davidson, *Desert Places* (London: Penguin, 1997), p. 1.
28 Ham Mukasa, *Uganda's Katakiro in England*, ed. Simon Gikandi (Manchester University Press, 1999); Caryl Phillips, *The European Tribe* (1987); Gary Younge, *No Place Like Home* (2000). An even longer alternative tradition of travel writing is explored in an issue of the journal *Wasafiri*, 34 (2001).

I
SURVEYS

I

WILLIAM H. SHERMAN

Stirrings and searchings (1500–1720)

A good book is at once the best companion,
and guide, and way, and end of our journey.
(Bishop Joseph Hall, *Quo Vadis?* [1617])

Putting the world on paper

Among the many texts produced before, during, and after Sir Humphrey
Gilbert's expedition to Newfoundland in 1583 – from patents and provision
lists to narrative accounts and celebratory poems – was a detailed set of
instructions for a surveyor named Thomas Bavin. Bavin was charged with
compiling a cartographic, pictorial, and textual record of the east coast of
America, and with acquiring the books, instruments, and drawing materials
he would need for the task. His employers suggested that he pack an almanac,
a pair of notebooks, several large sheets of paper, various inks and leads, and
'all sorts of colours to draw all things to life'.[1]

Documentation had always played an important rôle in travel, particularly in overseas ventures. English merchants and mariners had long been
instructed to keep careful records of their movements, to direct the travellers
who would follow in their footsteps and fill in the gaps of geographical
knowledge. But Bavin's instructions – and the texts they were designed to
generate – outline a more ambitious project. Bavin and his men were to move
along the coast, mapping each successive region and writing accounts of any
features that might be 'strange to us in England'. The maps were to use a key
of symbols for rocks, rivers, hills, and trees (which were to be copied onto
a parchment card and kept handy at all times), and the notes were to pay
special attention to any commodities the country had to offer. Finally, Bavin
was instructed to 'draw the figures and shapes of men and women in their
apparel as also their manner ... in every place as you shall find them differ-
ing [from us]'. This would require him to get close enough to the natives
to study their social structure, religious customs, and relations with friends

and enemies, and to record their language in an English dictionary brought along for the purpose.

Bavin's party and any notes they may have produced were lost at sea on the return voyage. It may seem perverse to begin a survey of early modern travel writing with a work that does not survive – and may never have been written – but the figure of Thomas Bavin provides two useful reminders. First, that the written record of travel is haunted by missing texts and persons. And second, that English participation in the Age of Discovery got off to a late and rocky start: Bavin's instructions for the first English survey of America were issued exactly ninety years after Columbus's landfall in the New World.

Indeed, the English did not have a figure to set alongside Columbus in the national imagination until 1580, when Francis Drake returned from his three-year voyage around the world. As the first English circumnavigation of the globe, Drake's venture provided a significant boost to the Elizabethans' confidence in opening new markets in remote locations, and to their demand for accounts of global travel. In the wake of Drake's voyage a wide range of texts and images were produced to celebrate his achievements: they display a new sense that the English could play a rôle in the apprehension of the wider world – and of the globe itself. Perhaps the simplest and most potent image of Drake's global mastery was published by Geoffrey Whitney in 1586. Whitney's emblem illustrating 'divine assistance' shows Drake's ship sitting, literally, on top of the world: a bridle attached at one end to the bow of the ship and held at the other by the hand of God completely circles the globe. The accompanying text asks 'you that live at home' to 'give praise to them that pass the waves' – above all to Drake who, like Jason, had braved the stormy seas to bring back the Golden Fleece.[2] What Whitney does not acknowledge is the fact that it had been well over fifty years since Magellan's discovery of the strait that made Drake's passage possible, and that the gold Drake brought back came almost entirely from fleecing Spanish ships of their American treasure.

English travellers had made sporadic voyages to Brazil, the Caribbean, Newfoundland, and Northern Russia from the 1480s to the 1550s, but few of their forays had any lasting impact and as late as the 1550s they had not yet made a concerted effort to travel to, write about, or take possession of other parts of the globe. This belatedness accounts for several features in the pattern of early English expansionism. The fact that Spain and Portugal had already secured the safest and most profitable trade routes meant, first, that English accounts would be marked by a patriotic rhetoric fired by political and commercial competition. In more practical terms, it accounts for the tendency of English explorers to search for a northern rather than southern passage to the East, and it goes some way toward explaining why piracy occupied such a prominent position (alongside plantation and trade) in English overseas enterprise.

Not surprisingly, the first English travel publications were translations of foreign works, and in more than half of the regions covered by the period's travellers translations preceded works by English writers (see Table 1). The earliest collection of voyages in English was Richard Eden's *The Decades of the New World* (1555), which was based on the history of Columbus and his successors by Pietro Martire d'Anghiera (or Peter Martyr). Eden's collection was reprinted by Richard Willes in 1577, featuring new translations of travels to India, China, and Japan, along with preliminary accounts of English exploration in Persia and the Arctic. In the coming decades, as English travellers came into their own, English accounts would be translated into Latin, French, German, and Dutch. But in the 1580s English bookshops were still dominated by foreign accounts.[3]

Richard Hakluyt would soon usher in the first great age of English travel writing, but he too began his project by translating foreign texts. The first book Hakluyt had a hand in was John Florio's translation of Jacques Cartier's *Short and Brief Narration of... New France* (1580), and his first collection of travel accounts, *Divers Voyages Concerning the Discovery of America* (1582), consisted mostly of non-English sources. By 1609, he would play a rôle in eighteen other translations of travel books.[4]

Hakluyt intended his collection *Principal Navigations, Voyages, Traffics, and Discoveries of the English Nation* (1589) to challenge European perceptions of English inaction and to promote new initiatives by showing that the English had been 'men full of activity, stirrers abroad, and searchers of the remote parts of the world'.[5] As evidence of this stirring and searching, Hakluyt was able to gather from his countrymen accounts of ninety-three voyages spanning 1,500 years – enough material to fill 834 folio pages. In his second edition, published in three volumes between 1598 and 1600, he more than doubled the number of voyages and pages.

As travellers made contact with new regions and peoples, authors and editors put the world on paper for the new print marketplace at home: the number of new titles published (and old titles reprinted) during the early modern period suggests that there was a significant audience for travel writing, eager to hear news of the wider world and to reflect on England's place in it.[6] Literacy rates were still relatively low, and many of the texts spoke to very limited audiences with very specific purposes. Nonetheless, travel books became a reliable commodity for a growing number of printers, and they came to occupy a central place on the period's bookshelves.[7] Travel writing emerged as one of the early modern period's most popular and flexible genres, and in a wide range of forms it educated and entertained readers, inspired national pride and commercial investment, and contributed to a public record of the world's 'markets, trade routes, personalities, and cultures'.[8] While the genre never settled into a single paradigm, most of the geographical locations, rhetorical forms, and political issues that we now associate with travel writing had appeared at least once by the end of the seventeenth century. As English travel hit its stride, authors and their audiences learned to write and read the world in books – with surprising speed and sophistication.

Early trajectories

When the Swiss physician Thomas Platter visited London in 1599, he observed in his journal that 'the English for the most part do not travel much, but prefer to learn foreign matters and take their pleasures at home'.[9] To the extent that this was true, it was not entirely a matter of choice: throughout the early modern period travel was limited by both physical constraints and governmental regulations. Long-distance journeys within England were slow and dangerous (as well as subject to statutes against vagrancy), and a trip to any country except Scotland or Wales required a voyage by ship (and the patronage of powerful institutions or individuals). Nonetheless, at the precise moment of Platter's visit, Hakluyt's *Principal Navigations* testified to the dramatic expansion of England's geographical horizons. Table 1 suggests that by 1600 the only major regions for which readers could not yet turn to English accounts were Australia and Antarctica.

Table 1 also provides a clear measure of the impact of the nascent colonies in the Americas on the focus and pace of English travel writing: from 1580 to 1650 a staggering number of new texts were published about Virginia alone. While scholars have tended to trace English expansionism along a westward trajectory, however, the earliest English travellers looked eastward to the Holy Land – and beyond, to the marvels of John Mandeville and the legendary riches of Marco Polo. The first Englishman who travelled for the sake of travel writing was Thomas Coryate, the 'Topographical Typographical Thomas'[10] who walked through western Europe and later travelled to India. The most important of Coryate's peers included William Lithgow (whose *Most Delectable and True Discourse* [1614] described his travels from Scotland 'to the most famous kingdoms in Europe, Asia, and Africa'), George Sandys (whose *Relation* [1615] of his journey to the Holy Land formed an encyclopaedic guide to the East, past and present), and Fynes Moryson (whose massive *An Itinerary* [1617] through Europe and the British Isles

Table 1: *English travel books by region 1500–1700 (with date of earliest publication)*

Primary region of travel	Written in English	Translated into English
Collections	9 (1582)	4 (1553)
Circumnavigations	5 (1598)	2 (1555)
Western Europe	59 (1522)	19 (1549)
Northern Europe	1 (1694)	8 (1561)
Eastern Europe	9 (1591)	4 (1672)
East Indies	25 (1603)	19 (1576)
West Indies	24 (1569)	7 (1577)
Central Asia	4 (1601)	5 (1590)
Far East	2 (c.1500)	23 (1503)
Near East	33 (1511)	20 (1529)
Africa	30 (1538)	15 (1554)
Northwest Passage/Greenland	13 (1576)	1 (1694)
North America	139 (1581)	7 (1563)
South America	18 (1596)	15 (1568)
South Seas/Australia	0	1 (1617)
Fictitious Travels	12 (1516)	10 (1581)
Directions for Travellers	27 (c.1500)	4 (1575)

Note: Cox's listing is neither comprehensive nor entirely accurate: his coverage of "Fictitious Travels" (particularly in plays and poems) is especially incomplete, and some of the authors, titles, and dates of pulication have been corrected by more recent reference materials. Furthermore, Cox's numbers are lower than other lists because he does not include reprints and only rarely lists individual works within larger collections.
Source: Edward Godfrey Cox, *A Reference Guide to the Literature of Travel*

has never been published in full).[11] Moreover, the first major trading companies chartered to open new markets for English goods were the Muscovy Company (1555, for Russia and Persia), the Cathay Company (1576, for Asia via Canada), and the Levant Company (1592, for Turkey and Italy); and the Virginia Company and East India Company were created within a few months of each other in 1599–1600.[12] An oriental frame remained in place throughout the sixteenth and seventeenth centuries. The last decade has seen a renewed appreciation of early modern interest in the East – and of the differences between cultural encounters in the Orient, in sub-Saharan Africa, and in the Americas.[13]

A typology of travel writers

The two centuries of travel writing covered in this chapter have sometimes been characterised as a period in which the pilgrim gave way to the merchant, the explorer, and the philosopher. The story is not quite so neat, and to do justice to the full range of travel writing produced in early modern England we need a larger cast of characters (as well as a less linear narrative): when Sir Thomas Palmer published his chart of the various kinds of traveller in 1606 he included preachers, postmen, soldiers, and spies.[14] This section will attempt to identify the most important figures involved in travel writing, and to describe some of the changing rôles played by each between 1500 and 1720.[15]

Editors

Some of the greatest names in early modern travel writing are neither travellers nor writers but editors. During the nineteenth century, Richard Hakluyt would be credited with compiling the 'great prose epic' of England's maritime expansion.[16] Hakluyt owed his inspiration to travel in libraries and archives rather than on the high seas, and his epiphany came during a visit (while still a schoolboy) to his cousin's chambers in the Middle Temple. When he showed an interest in some books and maps lying open on a table, his cousin gave him a geography lesson before moving on to the Bible:

> Turning to the 107 Psalm, [he] directed me to the 23 & 24 verse, where I read, that they which go down to the sea in ships, and occupy by the great waters, they see the works of the Lord, and his wonders in the deep, &c...I constantly resolved...I would by God's assistance prosecute that knowledge and kind of literature, the doors whereof (after a sort) were so happily opened before me.   (sig. *2r)

When he came to assemble his massive anthologies, Hakluyt could draw not only on the earlier English collections of Eden and Willes but also on that of the Venetian civil servant Giovanni Battista Ramusio. Ramusio's *Navigationi et viaggi* was published between 1550 and 1559, and offered readers of Italian a compendium of new European discoveries in the light of classical geography.[17] Three features distinguish Hakluyt's collections from those of his predecessors. As we have already seen, he was the first to bring English achievements to the fore: in the 1589 *Principal Navigations* he set out to 'meddle...with the Navigations only of our own nation' – though he would introduce some foreign sources in the later and larger edition. Second, he insisted on the value of raw documents like itineraries and logs and included them alongside more polished narratives – keeping his editorial intervention, in both cases, to a minimum. And third, he tackled the challenge of organising a wide-ranging body of material by breaking it down into three sections according to what he called 'the double order of time and place' – which involved a general movement from the regions first explored to those

1. Title page from Samuel Purchas, *Purchas His Pilgrimes* (1625). By permission of the Syndics of the Cambridge University Library.

discovered more recently and, within each section, a chronological order from earliest to latest.

Many of Hakluyt's working papers passed to Samuel Purchas, a fact reflected in the very title of the four-volume collection he published in 1625 (more than doubling the length of Hakluyt's final collection): *Hakluytus Posthumus or Purchas his Pilgrimes*.[18] While Purchas has often been taken to task for exercising a heavier editorial hand than Hakluyt, his reputation has recently been reassessed.[19] When *Purchas his Pilgrimes* is set alongside his other, more explicitly religious writings, he looks less like a pompous and careless Hakluyt and more like a learned preacher eager to accommodate human and religious diversity within a Christian framework.

Later collections would not match the scope and length of Hakluyt and Purchas, but editorial ambitions picked up again at the end of the seventeenth century: between 1694 and 1732 at least seven major new anthologies of travel writing appeared. Awnsham and John Churchill's *Collection of Voyages and Travels* (1704) included a preface (often attributed to John Locke) entitled 'The Whole History of Navigation from its Original to This Time' as well as a bibliographical survey 'of most books of voyages and travels': travel writing had reached the point where it could not only be collected but catalogued.[20]

Pilgrims

The pilgrimage was the dominant medieval framework for long-distance, non-utilitarian travel. In England, Sir Richard Torkyngton's expedition to Jerusalem in 1517 is traditionally identified as the last of the proper pilgrimages; but Henry Timberlake's *True and Strange Discourse of the Travels of Two English Pilgrims* was first printed in 1603 and went through nine more editions before 1700. Furthermore, as the title of Purchas's work suggests, the language of the pilgrimage persisted long after the practice began to wane: in the early modern period it not only provided a model for religious travellers but helped to accommodate the worldly goals of secular travellers. Even when their travels did not involve a spiritual journey to Jerusalem (or, as in the case of the Puritans at Plymouth, to New Jerusalem), seventeenth-century travellers often drew on the pilgrimage to describe their wanderings and sufferings. When William Lithgow published the account of his *Admired and Painful Peregrination* (through Italy and Greece to the Holy Land), prefatory poems celebrated the 'adventured Pilgrimage' of 'William of the Wilderness,' and Lithgow's own text opened with a poem entitled 'The Pilgrim's Mourning Ditty'.

Errant knights

The chivalric quest was the other major paradigm inherited from medieval travel writers, and it sometimes overlapped with the spiritual quest of the pilgrims. Chivalric literature would prove more influential in the Spanish colonial imagination than in the English, and remains more visible in accounts of imaginative than of actual travels – providing important models for epic poetry such as Spenser's *Faerie Queene*, plays like Beaumont's *The Knight of the Burning Pestle*, and picaresque novels from Cervantes to Defoe. But Elizabethan travel writing – like court culture more generally – was permeated by chivalric language and ideals. William Goodyear's translation of Jean de Cartigny's allegorical *Voyage of the Wandering Knight* (1581) was turned into a tribute to Sir Francis Drake, and Sir Walter Ralegh's travels in Virginia and Guiana cast him as a secular knight on a golden quest for the sake of his Queen – and if these transformations seem fanciful, it is worth remembering that both men earned their knighthoods with their voyages.[21]

Merchants

Most early English travel was carried out (explicitly or implicitly) in the name of trade, and the profit motive marks most of the period's published accounts – whether in the author's and printer's desire to make money or in the sponsorship of specific ventures. The earliest travel publications on the Continent had been collections of letters and relations written by merchants, and in the *Principal Navigations* Hakluyt placed a heavy emphasis on mercantile travel. His foregrounding of accounts from Muscovy Company merchants reflects what Michael Nerlich has described as a shift in the early modern period from chivalric adventure to venture capitalism. In classical travel writing, adventures were fates to be passively endured, and in the Middle Ages they began to be sought out through quests. During the course of the fifteenth and sixteenth centuries, and particularly in England (where the name 'adventurer' was first applied to merchants), they became risks to be undertaken in the name of business.[22]

Explorers

The great explorers were not always interested in writing, and alongside the famous names we associate with early travels are the often obscure names of those who described them. Humphrey Gilbert initiated several decades of exploration by arguing for the existence of a Northwest Passage in his *Discourse of a Discoverie...to Cataia* (1576), but his own expedition to Newfoundland was written up by Edward Hayes, George Peckham, Thomas Churchyard, and Stephen Parmenius. Likewise, Martin Frobisher's three voyages to the Canadian Arctic (the first to act on Gilbert's argument) were described by Dionyse Settle, George Best, and Michael Lok. England's two earliest circumnavigators also relied on others to publicise their work: by contrast, Coryate was praised at the beginning of his *Crudities* by Hugo

Holland for having seen 'manners and...men outlandish;/ And writ the same: so did not Drake nor Ca[ve]ndish' (sig. d8v).

Walter Ralegh was perhaps the first great explorer to play a significant rôle in creating his own persona in print. What distinguishes his *Discovery of the Large, Rich, and Beautiful Empire of Guiana* (1595) is both its unprecedented attention to geographic and ethnographic detail and its autobiographical strategies (which projected a sense of heroism onto an otherwise unsuccessful venture).[23] Travel narratives like Ralegh's allowed early modern writers and readers to explore not only exotic others but the English selves that came into contact with them.

Colonisers

When the scientist Thomas Harriot and the artist John White went to America in 1585, as part of Ralegh's attempted settlement of Virginia, they were issued with instructions that must have been virtually identical to Thomas Bavin's. The result was what would become (along with Ralegh's own *Discovery*) Elizabethan England's most sophisticated and influential travel book, *A Brief and True Report of the New Found Land of Virginia*. In 1588 Harriot published his account in a modest pamphlet, dividing the text into three sections. The first was a list of the 'merchantable commodities'; the second a summary of the commodities that could be planted, harvested, or hunted for food; and the final section described the commodities available for building materials before moving on to 'the nature and manners' of the natives. Harriot is often praised – in spite of the colonial project he served – for his attempt to understand and describe the Virginian natives in their own terms. He not only expressed admiration for some of their characteristics but was also able to provide (with surprising accuracy) Algonkian names for many commodities – thanks largely to the two Roanoke Indians who had visited England after an earlier voyage in 1584 and who served as interpreters during Harriot's visit.[24] When Harriot's account was printed again by Theodor de Bry in 1590, as a grand folio with a monumental title-page, it was supplemented with two maps of the region and more than twenty vivid engravings – based on White's watercolours – of native costumes, settlements, and customs.[25]

Most of the texts that described and debated England's colonial ambitions in the early modern period would remain focused on Virginia. As hopes of a golden windfall faded (after the failures of Gilbert in Newfoundland, Frobisher in Canada, and Ralegh in Roanoke and Guiana), English colonisers had to concentrate on the laborious cultivation of the land and the fraught relationship with the natives they would displace. No figure better captures these concerns than Captain John Smith, who followed his two-and-a-half years in Jamestown (1607–9) and subsequent voyage to New England (1614) with a string of original and editorial publications – several of which offer versions of what has become the archetypal colonial scene, his capture by Powhatan's brother and putative rescue by Powhatan's daughter Pocahontas.[26]

Captives and castaways

Thomas Palmer began his chart of travellers by distinguishing between 'voluntary' and 'involuntary' travellers and, while he was thinking primarily of exiles, the history of travel writing is full of people who were forced to travel to places – and in circumstances – that were not of their choosing.[27] Captives and castaways produced some of the period's most popular, and harrowing, narratives. These could be vehicles for the crudest of patriotic diatribes. *Strange and Wonderful Things Happened to Richard Hasleton* (1595) is a typical celebration of English endurance in the face of foreign cruelty: Hasleton is tortured by the Spanish Inquisition and forced to fight in Turkish galleys, but proudly resists conversion to both Catholicism and Islam. While the extremity of their experiences often led to charges of fabrication, it was also their primary appeal to contemporary readers and to later writers looking for material to imitate or parody. Edward Webbe's perpetuation of the Prester John myth would lead Samuel Purchas to dismiss him as 'a mere fabler' (despite Webbe's claim that he included only 'that which is of truth, and what mine own eyes have perfectly seen'); nonetheless, at least three publishers issued editions of his vivid and patriotic narrative in 1590 alone.[28] Job Hortop, too, would pepper his *The Travails of an English Man* (1591) with wondrous monsters; but there are naturalistic observations along the way, and his twenty-three years of captivity are recounted in remarkably matter-of-fact terms.

Ambassadors

Toward the end of the early modern period, Paul Rycaut would claim that no community was in a better position to report on foreign lands than ambassadors: their longer residence and closer contact meant they were able 'to penetrate farther into the Mysteries...than hasty Travellers could do, who are forced to content themselves with a superficial knowledge'.[29] Some eighty years earlier, Giles Fletcher's account of his embassy to Moscow in 1588–9 had set the standard for what a summary of a foreign country should include: there are chapters on Russia's topography, climate, commodities, government, religion, social classes, and local customs.[30]

Many of these accounts circulated as manuscript letters or journals. Sir Thomas Roe wrote enough during his residence in India (between 1615 and 1619) to fill a two-volume modern edition, but did not publish anything during his lifetime.[31] And Dr John Covel – who served as chaplain to the embassy in Constantinople during the 1670s – produced a learned private diary of his travels through Europe, Greece, and Asia Minor, complete with sketches of harbours, towns, and monuments, and notes on foreign languages and customs.[32] But Rycaut's account of the Ottoman Empire would become one of Restoration England's bestsellers, and in Rycaut's dedication to Lord Darlington we can see something of the Enlightenment's new approach to comparative ethnography:

> [The Ottomans] may be termed barbarous, as all things are, which are differenced from us by diversity of Manners and Custom, and are not dressed in the mode and fashion of our times and Countries ... But your Lordship ... will conclude, that a People, as the Turks are, men of the same composition with us, cannot be so savage and rude as they are generally described.   (sig. A3r)

Pirates

The two circumnavigators who frame this survey, Drake and Dampier, spent much of their maritime life in piratical pursuits, and Captain John Smith began his associations with Virginia only after a stint as a pirate in the Mediterranean. Demonised as 'renegadoes', euphemised as 'privateers', and glorified as 'buccaneers', pirates had a significant presence in the early literature of travel and played a central – and ambiguous – rôle in the creation of the British Empire.[33] While their expeditions could increase both personal and national wealth, they also posed a challenge to the government and trading companies.

The seventeenth century saw an ever more successful attempt to bring the pirate into the fold of England's imperial aspirations – and the textual strategies that supported them. As in other spheres of activity, English faults could be mitigated by invoking the alleged excesses of the Spanish: the preface to Esquemeling's *The History of the Bucaniers* suggests that 'how ... real soever may be the Accusations of our Bucaniers' Inhumanity and Barbarism ... they are but meer Infants, meer Novices in Cruelty, in comparison of the Spaniards'.[34] This text, which would be continued by Basil Ringrose the following year and become better known as *The Buccaneers of America*, did more than any other to recuperate the English pirate – and particularly the reputation of its dedicatee, Sir Henry Morgan (the West Indian buccaneer who would become Lieutenant-Governor of Jamaica).

Scientists

R. W. Frantz argued that English travellers owed their new mission (and status) to the New Science more than to any other factor. Instead of presenting readers with a hodgepodge of marvels, travel accounts sponsored by and presented to the Royal Society began the systematic collection of natural knowledge in the name of reason and public utility.[35] The same motivations and methods can be found (albeit more explicitly in the service of financial gain) in the generation of Thomas Harriot. After all, the first English laboratories in the New World were created for Frobisher's installation off Baffin Island, and Ralegh's at Roanoke. But a wider range of travellers played a more influential rôle in Restoration science following the Royal Society's public calls for contributions to a comprehensive natural history.[36] Samuel Smith and Benjamin Walford's publications in the 1690s regularly advertised their position as printers to the Royal Society, and its influence is felt not only in the quality of their illustrations but in their decision to supplement an anthology of travels into the Near East with 'three catalogues of such trees, shrubs, and herbs as grow in the Levant', compiled by 'John Ray, Fellow of the Royal Society'.[37]

These two final categories fused, in the closing decade of the seventeenth century, in the figure of the buccaneer-scientist William Dampier. The most celebrated seaman between Drake and Cook, Dampier eventually circumnavigated the world three times. Born into a farming family, he made trips to Newfoundland and Java while still in his teens, served in the Dutch War, managed a plantation in Jamaica, worked with log-cutters in Mexico, and travelled with pirates through the Caribbean and East Indies. He returned to England in 1691 and six years later published *A New Voyage Round the World*. Despite Dampier's swashbuckling past and lack of formal education, the text combined a lively narrative with careful descriptions of people, plants, and animals, and in subsequent editions he would add groundbreaking accounts of hydrography and meteorology. Dampier's clear prose and keen ethnographic eye placed him squarely among those Restoration scientists who valued direct experience over book-learning, and his dedication to the Royal Society's president revealed a thorough command of its rhetoric:

> I avow . . . a hearty Zeal for the promoting of useful knowledge . . . And I must own an Ambition to transmitting to the Public through your hands, these Essays I have made toward those great ends . . . being desirous to bring in my Gleanings here and there in Remote Regions, to that general Magazine, of the knowledge of Foreign Parts.[38]

The Royal Society rewarded Dampier with the command of an ambitious expedition to the South Seas: the voyage was a failure by every measure except one – it produced his final (and equally esteemed) travel account, *A Voyage to New Holland* (1703–9).

The genre takes shape

It should be clear by now that early modern travel writing was so varied that it may not even be appropriate to describe it as a single genre. The style and tone of texts could vary widely and their organisation always seemed prone to reproduce the haphazard nature of the travels they described: when Thomas Herbert asked his readers for their help 'to call home my Itinerant Notions', he pointed out that 'If my thoughts have wandered, I must intreat the well-bred Reader to remember, I have wandered through many deserts'.[39] But Herbert and his contemporaries did start to channel their accounts into some recognisable patterns.

Most texts began – after the requisite tribute to a patron and address to the reader – with some sort of justification for both travel and travel writing, in which lists of classical precedents were commonly invoked and biblical passages commonly cited. The travellers' experiences could then be described in letters, essays, sketches, plays, and poems. By the end of the sixteenth century, however, the most characteristic form was the 'report' or 'relation', which combined a chronological narrative of movements and events with geographic and ethnographic observations. The narrative voice in these texts could be either strongly first-person (as with Coryate) or strongly third-person (as with Harriot), depending on whether the author wanted to emphasise the travellers or what they encountered. The pattern of analysis represented by the instructions for Bavin and the 'report' of Harriot and White was determined by the colonial project they served, but other models for the observation and assessment of foreign countries emerged in the work of political envoys and in the directions produced for educational tourists: Palmer's text was part of a burgeoning genre teaching noble travellers what to look for in foreign countries, how to record their observations in writing, and how to communicate their knowledge upon their return.[40]

Maps were an obvious adjunct to travel narratives, but they are less common than we might expect. This is partly because they were expensive to produce and partly because (in an age of intense national and commercial rivalry) they would be handled as state or trade secrets. By the end of the period, however, readers would have expected to see illustrations (of increasingly high quality), not just of harbours and important cities but of native costumes and exotic flora and fauna.

Even the earliest English travel writing was marked by complex rhetorical strategies. Its authors had to balance the known and the unknown, the traditional imperatives of persuasion and entertainment, and their individual interests with those of their patrons, employers, and monarchs. Given such diverse purposes, early modern travel writers were often torn between giving pleasure and providing practical guidance, between logging and narrating, between describing what happened and suggesting what could have happened. These rhetorical challenges, along with the novelty of their experiences, left travel writers with acute problems of authenticity and credibility. The myths and stereotypes which could be reproduced in otherwise sober and scholarly accounts led to associations between travel and lying, which accounts for the assurances of writers like John Cartwright (whose title page advertised a 'true journal . . . of the East Indies') that they would only report 'what mine eyes have seen in more remote parts of the world . . . contenting myself with the conscience of truth'[41] – claims that would, in turn, be mimicked in the fantastic voyages and faked travelogues that began to proliferate in the eighteenth century.[42] Baptist Goodall accordingly urged travel writers to reject 'the least of lying wonders told/ . . . of foothigh pygmies, dog-eared men/ Blue black and yellow': there was no need for such 'fables', he suggested, when the world offered natural wonders like cloves, elephants, and armadillos and architectural marvels like the Great Wall of China and the Egyptian pyramids.[43]

Modern attempts to define travel writing have often sought to limit the genre to true accounts of actual travels. As Philip Edwards has suggested, our purchase on the rhetorical work done by these texts depends, in part, on our ability to gauge the difference between their accounts of what happened and what actually happened.[44] But if travel books gave travellers licence to write they also gave writers licence to travel: authors played with the boundaries between eyewitness testimony, second-hand information, and outright invention, and readers were often unsure whether they were reading truth or fiction. Indeed, for the expectations and desires of many readers, it may not have mattered much. Authors and readers were both aware of the fact that travels were transmitted, and shaped, by textual accounts – the reading and writing of which required (in effect) a secondary journey, with its own rules and realities. Lithgow asked his readers to accompany him in 'my . . . two-fold Pilgrimage; first, in my personal progress, to these famous places, and next a second peregrination of mind, in renewing the same in the Map of my own Memory' (*Most Delectable*, sig. A3v). And Herbert expressed what many travel writers must have felt, that the second journey could be every bit as perilous as the first: 'And though I am on shore, yet I fear, the Sea is not yet calm; for each Book, sent into the World, is like a Bark put to Sea, and as liable to censures as the Bark is to foul weather' (*Some Years' Travel*, sig. B1r).

Science and satire

The fact that there were features that instantly identified a text as 'travel writing' made it available not only as a form for new knowledge but as a vehicle for satire, and from a surprisingly early date, actual and imaginative voyages were used to criticise foreign habits, domestic conditions, and even travel itself. The pattern was set by Thomas More's *Utopia* (1516), which (to those not in the know) looked exactly like the period's genuine travel books – complete with a map and an alphabet of the Utopian tongue. More uses the fiction of a perfect culture, newly discovered in the New World, to critique the economic and political conditions of Renaissance Europe.

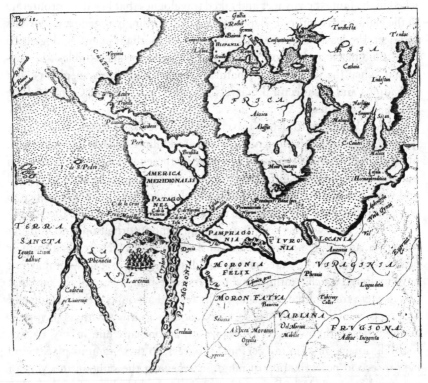

2. Satirical map of the world from Joseph Hall, *Mundus Alter et Idem* (1605). Reproduced by permission of the Folger Shakespeare Library.

More's text would inspire both sincere and satirical utopias from the sixteenth century onward. The exploits of explorers like Ralegh and the fortunes of captives like Webbe would be lampooned in texts like David Lloyd's mock-epic poem *The Legend of Captain Jones* (1631). John Taylor ('The Water Poet') was one of several seventeenth-century poets to borrow the conventions of travel writing in exercising his wit and venting his spleen. The period's most inventive mocker of travel, however, was Joseph Hall, whose *Mundus Alter et Idem [Another World and Yet the Same]* (1605) was the period's most elaborate parody. It mimics the entire apparatus of the travel book – including maps, pictures of foreign inscriptions and coins, and lists of foreign words.[45] Hall himself saw travel as both dangerous (since the only things travellers picked up abroad were foreign fashions and vices) and unnecessary (since everything essential could be learned from books and maps); and his intrepid explorer travels all the way to 'Terra Australis Incognita' to discover countries with national traits that were all too familiar – Gluttonia, Letcheritania, Fooliana, and Hungerland.

The legacy of early modern travel writing is to be found in both the scientific Harriot and the satirical Hall. The transition to the new age of travel writing in the eighteenth century was heralded not just by the appearance of Dampier's *A New Voyage Round the World* but by John Dunton's *A Voyage Round the World*, published six years earlier: both books helped to create the conventions that Defoe would draw on in his own *New Voyage Round the World* of 1725. Before Dunton began his more famous career as a bookseller and newspaper publisher, he travelled to America as part of a projected 'Ramble through Ten Kingdoms'. The letters that described his travels around Massachusetts in 1685–6 would not be published until 1867, and the *Ramble through Six Kingdoms* that he advertised in 1705 never made it through the press.[46] But he drew extensively upon his actual journeys in *A Voyage Round the World*, a satirical novel that would later inspire Sterne's *Tristram Shandy*.[47] The text begins with poems in praise of the author (probably written by the author himself), and no section of Dunton's text better captures the spirit of English travel, looking back to the commercial outreach of the sixteenth century and ahead to imperial rambles of the eighteenth:

> *Terra Incognita* shall fly before us,
> And all the Savages behind adore us.
> On *Hills* of *Ice*, as *high* as *Tenariff*,
> *Wintering*, we'll moor our *Weather-beaten Skiff* ...
> There find the *Passages*, and through 'em trade ...
> And Ramble round, and round, and round, & then,
> Ramble like Drake, 'till we come home again.   (sig. B4r)

NOTES

1 British Library, MS Additional 38823, item 1: cf. D. B. Quinn, *The Roanoke Voyages, 1584–1590* (London: The Hakluyt Society, 1955), vol. 1, pp. 51–4.

2 Geoffrey Whitney, *A Choice of Emblems* (Leiden: Christopher Plantin, 1586), p. 203.

3 G. B. Parks, 'Tudor Travel Literature: A Brief History', in *The Hakluyt Handbook*, ed. D. B. Quinn (London: The Hakluyt Society, 1974), vol. 1, pp. 97–132.

4 F. M. Rogers, 'Hakluyt as Translator', in *Hakluyt Handbook*, ed. Quinn, vol. 1, pp. 37–47.

5 Richard Hakluyt, *The Principal Navigations, Voyages, Traffics, and Discoveries of the English Nation* (London: George Bishop and Ralph Newbery, 1589), ff. *2r–v.

6 The most detailed bibliographies are Edward Godfrey Cox, *A Reference Guide to the Literature of Travel* (Seattle: University of Washington, 1935–49); John Parker, *Books to Build an Empire: A Bibliographical History of English Overseas Interests to 1620* (Amsterdam: Israel, 1965); and *European Americana: A Chronological Guide to Works Printed in Europe Relating to the Americas, 1493–1776* (New York: Readex Books, 1980–8).

7 Robin Myers and Michael Harris, eds., *Journeys Through the Market: Travel, Travellers, and the Book Trade* (Folkestone: St. Paul's Bibliographies, 1999).

8 Mary C. Fuller, *Voyages in Print: English Travel to America, 1576–1624* (Cambridge University Press, 1995), p. 7.

9 Quoted in Anthony Parr, ed., *Three Renaissance Travel Plays* (Manchester University Press, 1995), p. 1.

10 Thomas Coryate, *Crudities* (London: William Stansby, 1611), sig. d7r.

11 William Lithgow, *A Most Delectable and True Discourse of His Admired and Painful Peregrination* (London: Nicholas Okes, 1614); Jonathan Haynes, *The Humanist as Traveler: George Sandys's Relation of a Journey begun An. Dom. 1610* (London: Associated University Presses, 1986). Sandys went on to serve as Treasurer to the Virginia Colony, where he finished his famous translation of Ovid. *An Itinerary written by Fynes Moryson, Gent. First in the Latine Tongue, and then translated by him into English*, 3 pt. (London: J. Beale, 1617); and see also *Shakespeare's Europe. Unpublished chapters of Fynes Moryson's Itinerary. Being a Survey of the condition of Europe at the end of the 16th century* (London: Sherratt & Hughes, 1903).

12 Sir Percival Griffiths, *A License to Trade: The History of English Chartered Companies* (London: Ernest Benn, 1974).

13 William Sherman, 'Travel and Trade', in *A Companion to Renaissance Drama* ed. Arthur Kinney (Oxford: Blackwell, forthcoming 2002).

14 Sir Thomas Palmer, *An Essay of the Means how to Make Our Travels into Foreign Countries the More Profitable and Honourable* (London: Humphrey Lownes, 1606), sig. IA.

15 As with all taxonomies, the categories are ideal types and individual travellers will often fulfil more than one rôle. For other typologies of early modern travel writers see Robert Munter and Clyde L. Grose, eds., *Englishmen Abroad* (Lewiston: Edwin Mellen, 1986); Jean Ceard and Jean-Claude Margolin, eds., *Voyager à la*

Renaissance (Paris: Éditions Maisonneuve et Larose, 1987); and Loukia Droulia, ed., *On Travel Literature and Related Subjects* (Athens: Institute of Neohellenic Research, 1993), pp. 451–503.

16 This phrase was James A. Froude's: it is cited and discussed in Fuller, *Voyages in Print*, p. 158.

17 George Bruner Parks, 'The Contents and Sources of Ramusio's *Navigationi*', in G. B. Ramusio, *Navigationi et viaggi* (Amsterdam: Theatrum Orbis Terrarum, 1970); D. B. Quinn, 'Richard Hakluyt, Editor', in Richard Hakluyt, *Divers Voyages* (Amsterdam: Theatrum Orbis Terrarum, 1967).

18 Samuel Purchas, *Hakluytus Posthumus or Purchas his Pilgrimes* (London: Henry Fetherstone, 1625).

19 L. E. Pennington, ed., *The Purchas Handbook* (London: The Hakluyt Society, 1997).

20 Munter and Grose, *Englishmen Abroad*, p. 30.

21 See Jennifer R. Goodman, *Chivalry and Exploration, 1298–1630* (Woodbridge: Boydell, 1998), ch. 7; Gesa Mackenthun, *Metaphors of Dispossession: American Beginnings and the Translation of Empire, 1492–1637* (Norman: University of Oklahoma Press, 1997), pp. 162–85.

22 Michael Nerlich, *The Ideology of Adventure: Studies in Modern Consciousness, 1100–1750* (Minneapolis: University of Minnesota Press, 1987), vol. 1, pp. 3–5, 58.

23 See Neil L. Whitehead's edition of the text (Manchester University Press, 1997) and Fuller, *Voyages in Print*, ch. 2.

24 Alden T. Vaughan, 'Trinculo's Indian: American Natives in Shakespeare's England', in *'The Tempest' and its Travels*, ed. Peter Hulme and William H. Sherman (London: Reaktion Books, 2000), pp. 51–2.

25 Thomas Harriot, *A Brief and True Report* (London: Robert Robinson, 1588; rpt. Frankfurt: Theodor de Bry, 1590).

26 Philip L. Barbour, ed., *The Complete Works of Captain John Smith* (Chapel Hill: University of North Carolina Press, 1986).

27 Palmer only includes travellers *from* England, but the period's largest group of involuntary travellers were the slaves traded from the 1560s onwards.

28 Edward Webbe, *The Rare and Most Wonderful Things* (London: William Wright, 1590), sig. A3r; Robert Silverberg, *The Realm of Prester John* (Athens, Ga.: Ohio University Press, 1996), p. 316.

29 Paul Rycaut, *The Present State of the Ottoman Empire* (London: for John Starkey and Henry Brome, 1668), sig. A4r.

30 Giles Fletcher, *Of the Rus Commonwealth*, ed. Albert J. Schmidt (Ithaca: Cornell University Press, 1966).

31 William Foster, ed., *The Embassy of Sir Thomas Roe to the Court of the Great Mogul* (London: Hakluyt Society, 1899).

32 British Library MS Additional 22914; partly published in *Early Voyages and Travels to the Levant*, ed. J. Theodore Bent (London: Hakluyt Society, 1893).

33 Barbara Fuchs, 'Faithless Empires: Pirates, Renegadoes, and the English Nation', *ELH*, 67 (2000): 45–69.

34 John Esquemeling, *The History of the Bucaniers* (London: for Thomas Malthus, 1684), sig. A5.

35 R. W. Frantz, *The English Traveller and the Movement of Ideas, 1660–1732* (Lincoln: University of Nebraska, 1934).

36 Daniel Carey, 'Compiling Nature's History: Travellers and Travel Narratives in the Early Royal Society', *Annals of Science*, 54 (1997): 269–92.

37 Sir John Narborough *et. al.*, *A Collection of Curious Travels & Voyages* (London: Samuel Smith and Benjamin Walford, 1693).

38 William Dampier, *A New Voyage Round the World* (London: James Knapton, 1697), A2v.

39 Thomas Herbert, *A Relation of Some Years' Travel... Into Afrique and the Greater Asia* (London: William Stansby and Jacob Bloome, 1634), sig. B1v.

40 Justin Stagl, *A History of Curiosity: The Theory of Travel, 1550–1800* (Chur, Switzerland: Harwood Academic Publishers, 1995), ch. 1.

41 John Cartwright, *The Preacher's Travels* (London: Thomas Thorpe, 1611), sig. B2r.

42 Percy G. Adams, *Travelers and Travel-Liars, 1660–1800* (Berkeley: University of California Press, 1962).

43 Baptist Goodall, *The Trial of Travel* (London: John Norton, 1630), sig. C1v–C2v.

44 Philip Edwards, *Last Voyages: Cavendish, Hudson, Ralegh* (Oxford: Clarendon Press, 1988), pp. 8–11, and *The Story of the Voyage: Sea-Narratives in Eighteenth-Century England* (Cambridge University Press, 1994), p. 10.

45 John Millar Wands, ed. and trans., *Another World and Yet the Same: Bishop Joseph Hall's 'Mundus Alter et Idem'* (New Haven: Yale University Press, 1981).

46 John Dunton, *Letters Written from New-England, A. D. 1686*, ed. W. H. Whitmore (Boston: The Prince Society, 1867); *The Life and Errors of John Dunton* (London: for John Dunton, 1705).

47 John Dunton, *A Voyage Round the World: Or, a Pocket-Library Divided into Several Volumes* (London: for Richard Newcome, 1691).

2

JAMES BUZARD

The Grand Tour and after (1660–1840)

Itineraries and expectations

Travel is everywhere in eighteenth-century British literature. The fictional literature of the age 'is full of travelling heroes enmeshed in journey-plots', and 'almost every author of consequence' – among them Daniel Defoe, Joseph Addison, Henry Fielding, Tobias Smollett, Samuel Johnson, James Boswell, Laurence Sterne, Mary Wollstonecraft – 'produced one overt travel book'. To these must be added the 'numerous essayistic and philosophic performances' that were cast in the form of imaginary travelogues, such as Jonathan Swift's *Gulliver's Travels* (1726), Johnson's *Rasselas* (1759), and Oliver Goldsmith's *Citizen of the World* (1762). Writers seemed to be travelling, in reality or in their imaginations, just about everywhere. Paul Fussell speculates that travel's pervasive appeal may have owed something to the high degree of acceptance which philosophical empiricism had gained in Britain by the end of the seventeenth century. John Locke's *Essay Concerning Human Understanding* (1690) became a sort of bible for those who espoused a 'blank slate' conception of human consciousness and held that all knowledge is produced from the 'impressions' drawn in through our five senses. If knowledge is rooted in experience and nowhere else, travel instantly gains in importance and desirability. Following the great Renaissance age of colonial exploration and expansion, an articulated, systematic empiricism made travelling about the world and seeing the new and different 'something like an obligation for the person conscientious about developing the mind and accumulating knowledge'.[1] Merely reading about conditions elsewhere was not enough. Those who *could* travel, should – though of course precious few actually could.

These intriguing reflections treat travel in a very abstract way, as if one destination were neither more nor less valuable than another for stoking the knowledge engine inside us with the coal of 'experience'. During the same period, though, a whole new paradigm for travelling came into existence within Europe itself that was a good deal more forceful in specifying which were the desirable or even quasi-mandatory destinations where the proper *kind* of experience was to be garnered. The history of travelling in Europe in the period that runs, roughly, from the Restoration of the British monarchy in 1660 to the accession of Queen Victoria in 1837 is marked by the emergence of this new paradigm for travelling – that of the 'Grand Tour' – and concludes with the first glimmerings of another paradigm that absorbed and superseded it: that of mass tourism. The last sixty years or so of the period covered in this essay (1780–1840) witnessed the development of a new vocabulary for travel experience – that of 'the picturesque' – that profoundly affected the way travelling got done and written about, especially within Britain itself. The placing of the Continent effectively out of bounds to British travellers during the Napoleonic Wars from the early 1790s to 1815 gave a great fillip to inland travel and to the vogue of the picturesque. With the last fifteen years of this period (1825–40) came the rise of the railways and of a number of new businesses devoted to popularising leisure travel, at first within Britain but soon, inevitably, abroad as well.

Before embarking on a survey of this long era, it seems necessary to make two qualifications. First, we need to acknowledge that, although plenty of published books recount the experiences of travelling in Europe between 1660 and 1840, much of the relevant literature, especially on the Grand Tour, exists in private manuscript correspondence (some of it published posthumously), or in the form of arguments about the *value* of travelling, rather than that of travelogue.[2] Second, one must recognise that many other kinds of journeys, undertaken by many sorts of people for many purposes, were going on; for the purposes of the present essay, these must be consigned to the margins of the still central tale of the Grand Tour and its aftermath. This essay will emphasise the framework of expectations and assumptions within which travel writing about Europe was produced between 1660 and 1840. In telling this story, one guiding question must be: what happened to the ideals and purposes associated with travel in Europe when they became (as it seemed) scandalously accessible to wider and wider swathes of the British population? How could the *ideology* of the Grand Tour survive in, or be altered to suit, the age of Thomas Cook and Son?

The Grand Tour was, from start to finish, an ideological exercise. Its leading purpose was to round out the education of young men of the ruling classes by exposing them to the treasured artifacts and ennobling society of the Continent. Usually occurring just after completion of studies at Oxford or Cambridge University and running anywhere from one to five years in length, the Tour was a social ritual intended to prepare these young men to assume the leadership positions preordained for them at home. 'Grand Tour' began as a French phrase – *le grand tour* – but it was appropriated by Britons of the late seventeenth and early eighteenth centuries whose wealthy nation had created 'a substantial upper class with enough money and leisure to travel'.[3] In his *An Italian Voyage* (1670), Richard Lassels appears to have introduced the term into English, recommending that young gentlemen undertake a 'Grand Tour of France and the Giro of Italy'.[4] By the time it was in full swing, the Tour had a more or less common itinerary that, allowing for minor divergences, may be summarised as follows. After crossing the Channel, the Tourist, having acquired a coach in Calais, would often proceed to the Loire Valley, where the purest French accent was supposed to have its home, and where the young Briton could spend some time preparing his tongue and his manner for the rigours of Paris society. A lengthy stay in the French capital might be followed by a visit to Geneva (and even, if one had the right connections, to Voltaire at his villa in the outskirts). One would then cross the Alps, as expeditiously as possible, proceeding via Turin or Milan down to Florence, to stay probably for some months. Venice might be next, then Rome, or vice versa. The Tourist might go as far as Naples. The return journey northward might include stays in Austria, the German university towns, Berlin, and Amsterdam. Sometimes the trip went the other way around, this latter arrangement having the advantage of saving what were seen as the more challenging parts of the travelling education – Italy and socially brilliant Paris – until later in the process. Proceeding in this direction, the rough-diamond young Tourist might be 'rubbed at three of the considerable courts of Europe – Berlin, Dresden, and Vienna', before arriving in Italy 'tolerably smooth and fit for the last polish'.[5] The most important destinations, without which the entire enterprise would lose its purpose, were Paris and Italy (especially Rome, Florence, and Venice). The former was thought the natural habitat of the refined manners and gracious behaviour necessary to civilised men: as Lord Chesterfield put it in his famous letters of advice to his travelling teenage son, 'It must be owned that the Graces do not seem to be natives of Great Britain . . . Since barbarism drove them out of Greece and Rome, they seem to have taken refuge in France' (vol. 1, p. 171). The latter was not only 'Nature's Darling' to the visitor from colder northern lands, as Lassels called it (vol. 1, p. 1), but the home of classical civilisation, both in its original (ancient Roman) and its recreated (Renaissance) manifestations.

Several corollaries of the intended educative or preparatory function of the Grand Tour may be distinguished.

The first has to do with this classical tradition, by which eighteenth-century British travellers meant Rome, not Greece. As their overseas empire expanded, well-off Britons drew parallels between their nation's current position and that of the ancient Roman Empire. They styled their age an

'Augustan' one and expected men of taste to admire and imitate Roman models. In his preface Lassels urged the tour upon the young nobleman in part because 'no man understands Livy and Caesar' so well as the one who has touched the ground they trod (vol. 1, n. p.). Personal experience of the places made famous by the Latin texts which the traveller had read in school would seal the bond between ancient and modern empires. Since '[a]ll our religion, almost all our law, almost all our arts, almost all that sets us above the savages, has come to us from the shores of the Mediterranean', said Samuel Johnson in 1776, '[a] man who has not been to Italy, is always conscious of an inferiority, from his not having seen what it is expected a man should see'.[6] Joseph Addison's *Remarks on Several Parts of Italy* (1705) was for many years a nearly indispensable handbook for those who went to visit the sites and monuments associated with the ancient Romans: indeed, so focused was it upon traces of classical times that the 'Italy' of its title can sometimes appear to be a land entirely lacking in living inhabitants or post-classical edifices. What Addison and later British Augustans wanted to avoid, of course, was the colossal obstacle of the Roman Catholic Church: to Protestants it was the 'Whore of Babylon' whose corruptions had led Christians astray and under whose authority modern Rome had withered to a squalid, impoverished town. As the eighteenth century progressed and the dangers of the Reformation period receded farther into the past, the fear and suspicion once felt by British Protestant visitors in Italy gave way to a rather satisfying savouring of the 'pitiful contrast' between current conditions and 'the former greatness of Rome . . . to which they felt themselves . . . the rightful and magnificent heirs'.[7] Goldsmith's poem *The Traveller* (1764), for instance, directs the traveller-reader's attention to

> those domes, where Caesars once bore sway,
> Defac'd by time and tottering in decay,
> There in the ruin, heedless of the dead,
> The shelter-seeking peasant builds his shed . . . [8]

The British visitor would not be so heedless, but would take up the imperial banner from his fallen forerunner.

Touring might also prepare the young Englishman for his future rôle by offering him the opportunity not only to cultivate his historical consciousness and artistic tastes but actually to acquire works of art and antiquities that, displayed at home, would testify to the quality of his taste and surround him with objective confirmations of his self-worth. Travelling throughout Italy in 1613 with the artist Inigo Jones, the second Earl of Arundel more or less single-handedly initiated the large-scale acquisition of Italian antiquities for British collections: Arundel's treasures gave English viewers their first exposure to artworks made in classical times and in the Italian Renaissance; Jones came home to design the first Palladian or neoclassical buildings in England. In the early eighteenth century, figures like Richard Boyle (third Earl of Burlington), William Windham, and Thomas Coke (later first Earl of Leicester) followed Arundel's example. Along with the education in art history and in the principles of 'correct taste', Grand Tourists could amass 'a good deal of cultural booty' and build galleries where their accumulations might be shown more or less selectively to the rising number of 'connoisseurs'.[9] Furthermore, because the Grand Tourist was expected to mingle with the social and political élite wherever he went, we must include among the aims of the Grand Tour the cultivation of a certain transEuropean class consciousness, a 'horizontal' identification that linked the superior classes of Britain with their counterparts on the Continent and imposed upon the traveller a sense that he shared with these counterparts a common responsibility for the welfare of Europe as a whole. The tour of Europe, its proponents held, could usher the unformed, insular young Englishman into that domain of good manners and educated tastes which transcended single nations. As Thomas Nugent put it, the Grand Tour tended 'to enrich the mind with knowledge, to rectify the judgment, to remove the prejudices of education, to compose the outward manners, and in a word form the complete gentleman'.[10]

Finally, the training on offer in the Grand Tour could also involve some sowing of wild oats: removing its practitioner from the sphere of direct parental oversight between the ages of, say, sixteen and twenty, the tour provided a limited period of release before an adulthood in which the young man might be expected to set an example of responsibility and sobriety. While abroad, the privileged young voyager might hope to indulge in a series of 'educative', non-binding liaisons with foreign women of one social station or another. James Boswell's diaries of his youthful travels in the early 1760s, for example, recount numerous episodes of such sexual opportunism.[11]

None of these aims was invented for the Grand Tour ex nihilo, and the young man making the journey was by no means expected to undertake all its obligations alone. Depending on the size of his purse, he might be accompanied by a considerable number of servants, attendants, instructors, artists (to copy landscapes or ruins), and assorted hangers-on. At the very least he was expected to travel in company with a 'governor' or 'bear-leader'. In his essay 'Of Travel' (1625), Francis Bacon had counselled that 'young men [ought to] travel under some tutor or grave servant' who 'hath the language and hath been in the country before'. Without this vital assistance, the traveller would 'go [about his journey] hooded, and look abroad little'.[12] The 'governor' was typically a clergyman of the Church of England, classically educated and prepared both to open his young charge's eyes to the glories of antiquity and, when occasion demanded it, to act *in loco parentis*, insofar as his dependent status permitted him to do so. Such luminaries of post-Renaissance culture as Thomas Hobbes, Ben Jonson, Joseph Addison, and Adam Smith served as tutors early in their careers.

The Seven Years War (1756–63) interrupted British touring on the Continent, but the practice resumed with a vengeance after its conclusion. Perhaps because Grand Tour ideology like that stated by Richard Lassels or Thomas Nugent set impossibly high standards; perhaps because tutors failed to keep their charges in line; or perhaps because drinking, gaming, and whoring always held more attraction for the young traveller than did the other, more exalted objectives of the tour: for some combination of these reasons, the behaviour of Grand Tourists soon attracted sufficient criticism to call into question the aims of the entire enterprise. Lady Mary Wortley Montagu complained in 1758 that 'the folly of British boys and [the] stupidity and knavery of [their] governors [had] gained us the glorious title of Golden Asses all over Italy'.[13] Tobias Smollett echoed this opinion a few years later when he remarked upon the 'number of raw boys, whom Britain seemed to have poured forth on purpose to bring her national character into contempt'.[14] In his epoch-making work of political economy, *The Wealth of Nations* (1776), Adam Smith found the space to argue that the typical travelling young man 'commonly comes home more conceited, more unprincipled, more dissipated, and more incapable of any serious application...than he could well have become in so short a time had he lived at home'.[15]

Picturesqueness and sublimity

By the last third of the eighteenth century, the variety as well as the numbers of Grand Tourists had steadily increased. No longer the preserve of 'aristocratic male heirs', the tour had started to come within the grasp of 'less socially elevated and less well-educated people' (Brewer, *Pleasures*, p. 632), including women and children travelling with their families. This gradual and very partial opening up of European travelling was disrupted by the French Revolution and by the twenty-odd years of nearly ceaseless conflict between France and Britain that followed it (c.1790–1815). A new vogue of domestic travel arose to fill this gap, impelled by several cultural currents that had been decades in the making.

At the battle of Culloden in 1746, the last significant Jacobite rebellion against the Hanoverian monarchs was decisively defeated, putting an end to any realistic threat that the Catholic, Scottish Stuarts might reimpose themselves upon Britain. Looking back over the cultural developments of the subsequent half-century or so, it seems as if the demise of Jacobitism as a viable political force and the dissolution of many Celtic communities in the Highlands of Scotland made safe, and ushered in, new fascinations with the Celtic fringe of Great Britain and, a bit later, new 'Gothic' fantasies about the countries where the dark mysteries of Catholicism held sway. In 1760, James Macpherson published *Fragments of Ancient Poetry, Collected in the Highlands of Scotland...*, the first of several volumes purporting to present the lost works of Ossian and his father Fingal, bards of olden times. Controversy about the works' authenticity raged for decades, but this only lent notoriety to Macpherson's books and whetted the appetite of southern Scots and Englishmen to explore, in actual or in imaginary travels, the once-shunned landscapes of the Highlands. Even the inveterate Londoner Samuel Johnson, who denounced Macpherson's works as frauds, was eager to visit the Scottish Highlands and Islands to see the 'simplicity and wildness' of 'a system of life almost totally different' from that of the civilised south.[16] The famous man recorded his own alternately philosophic and irritated reactions to the 1773 tour in *A Journey to the Western Islands of Scotland*; James Boswell added his own more genial account in *The Journal of a Tour to the Hebrides*. Dr Johnson's verdict on Mull may stand for many similar judgments rendered throughout his text: Mull appeared to the Sage of London as a place without culture, 'where the climate is unkind, and the ground penurious, ... where life unimproved, and unadorned, fades into something little more than naked existence'.[17] For many others, though, the barren, forbidding, and ominous character of the region, newly 'permeated by the spirits of Fingal and Ossian', became part of the attraction.[18]

Whereas the Continental Grand Tourist before this period had favoured fertile, gentle landscapes, the Ossianic pilgrims were drawn to mist, mountains, and waterfalls, and their new enthusiasm was beginning to be shared by travellers to other Celtic fringe regions of Britain, such as North Wales, as well as by travellers through Switzerland. Traversing the Alps had been a necessary tribulation for the privileged young man en route to Italy: he would hire a team of *voiturins* to transport his carriage and luggage and have himself carried across in a chair called an 'Alps machine' – perhaps even shutting his eyes until the process was completed. As early as the 1760s, however, there began to be organised 'day-trips out of Geneva for the express purpose of looking at glaciers and waterfalls', and 'the first tourist inn was opened at Chamonix' in 1765.[19]

The Ossianic appeal of Scottish landscapes was increased by the deliberate efforts of some landlords who exploited the new aesthetic to attract and impress visitors. The Duke of Atholl's estate near Dunkeld featured a summer house that came to be called 'Ossian's Hall', in which a portrait of the bard could be hoisted away to reveal a large bay window giving onto the waterfall over which the house was perched. In 1803, Dorothy Wordsworth recorded the surprise of being confronted by this 'splendid room, which was almost dizzy and alive with waterfalls[,]... the great cascade... being reflected in innumerable mirrors upon the ceiling and against the walls'.[20] Her brother William later wrote a 'condemnatory effusion' in verse about this 'distressingly puerile' exhibition of 'illusive cataracts'.[21] Something of the showmanship practised by the Duke was also a feature of the enormously popular writings of Walter Scott. A Lowlander himself, Scott began his literary career at the start of the nineteenth century by collecting ballads and songs from the border region between England and Scotland; but his fame was both magnified and secured when he shifted his focus northward in *The Lady of the Lake* – set in the Trossachs – which appeared to noisy acclaim in 1810 and which almost instantly sent scores of tourists up to visit the scenes it depicted. A few years later came Scott's first (anonymously published) novel, *Waverley, or, 'Tis Sixty Years Since* (1814), which conducted both a kind of imaginary tourism in time back to the days of the Jacobite uprising of 1745–6 and a highly self-conscious series of reflections on the intimate relationship of fiction, tourism, and power – the power unevenly divided among the nations and regions of the new United Kingdom, and the power of authorship and artifice to endow places with cultural identity and value. Scott was highly ambivalent about his rôle in 'packaging' Scotland for touristic consumption by the dominant English, but this did not prevent him from playing master of ceremonies when his friend King George IV visited Scotland in 1822, the first Hanoverian monarch to venture north of the Tweed. For the King's two-week stay in Edinburgh, Scott orchestrated an elaborate Tartan fantasy, making Highland cultural accoutrements of sometimes dubious historical authenticity stand for the diverse cultures of Scotland as a whole, and capping his fiction's own contributions to the touristic stereotypes of his country.

While Macpherson's volumes and Scott's writings materially affected the attitudes and itineraries of actual travellers, Gothic fiction initially functioned to supply imaginary *substitutes* for travel to southern European places inaccessible to the English during the Napoleonic era. Horace Walpole is usually credited with beginning the vogue of the Gothic with *The Castle of Otranto* (1764), but it was not until the 1790s that the mode really flourished. Ann Radcliffe's thrilling tales of English women (and some men) imperilled by fiendish foreigners – *The Romance of the Forest* (1791), *The Mysteries of Udolpho* (1794), *The Italian* (1797) and others – made Italy's mediaeval ruined castles and murky abbeys attractively exciting to readers who would not be visiting them in the foreseeable future; the popularity of the Gothic lasted long enough to alter the tastes of those who *might* visit such places, once the wars with France had finished. By that time, Celticism and the Gothic had become almost inextricably bound up with a third strand of cultural and aesthetic attitudes that, like these, opposed Grand-Tour neo-classicism and became underpinnings of the Romantic Movement. This was the *picturesque*, which needs to be explained in terms of its relationship to two other aesthetic ideas, those of the *beautiful* and the *sublime*. Edmund Burke's *Philosophical Enquiry into the Origin of Our Ideas of the Sublime and the Beautiful* (1757) had challenged rationalist ideas about aesthetic experience by characterising the two opposed experiences of beauty and sublimity as complementary forms of sub-rational sensation. Aesthetic experience was not about making intellectual judgements (of proportion or symmetry, for example), but a matter of basic human instincts: the gentle curves, the soft and unthreatening contours Burke found in beauty appealed, he thought, to the male sexual desire that drove the species to reproduce itself; the 'agreeable horror' of the sublime addressed our impulse toward self-preservation and afforded us the *frisson* of contemplating terrifying things from a position of safety. The picturesque arose in the last third of the eighteenth century as a kind of mediator between these opposed ideas, capable of running the gamut from relatively mild English landscapes to the breathtaking cataracts and chasms of the Alps in stormy weather. The names of two seventeenth-century landscape painters, Claude Lorrain and Salvator Rosa, became shorthand for the 'placid' and 'wild' extremities of the picturesque continuum.

The picturesque was introduced into English cultural debate by the Reverend William Gilpin, who in *Observations on the River Wye, and Several Parts of South Wales, etc., Relative Chiefly to Picturesque Beauty; made in the Summer of the Year 1770* (1782) announced as a 'new object of pursuit' for travellers the examination of 'the face of a country by the rules of picturesque beauty'.[22] As the combination 'picturesque beauty' may indicate, Gilpin was not much interested in fine theoretical distinctions; as the title of his book should suggest (as contrasted with Burke's *Philosophical Enquiry into the Origin of our Ideas of the Sublime and the Beautiful*), he treated the picturesque as a practical matter for increasing the enjoyment of travellers, not as a topic for abstract philosophising. It was another decade before Gilpin tried his hand at theoretical definition in the essay 'On Picturesque Beauty': the general thrust of his idea emerges in such passages as the following, which dwells upon what it takes to make an object fit for inclusion in the picturesque category. Not accidentally, the object in question is a Palladian, neoclassically regular and orderly, piece of architecture. In such a work, Gilpin writes,

> [t]he proportion of its parts – the propriety of its ornaments – and the symmetry of the whole, may be highly pleasing. But . . . [s]hould we wish to give it picturesque beauty, . . . we must beat down one half of it, deface the other, and throw the mutilated members around in heaps. In short, from a *smooth* building we must turn it into a *rough* ruin.[23]

Following Gilpin's implicit advice, many landowners began designing gardens containing irregular sight lines and prefabricated ruins of 'classical' structures. Sir Uvedale Price attempted to subject Gilpin's concept to some theoretical rigour in his 1794 *Essay on the Picturesque*, which developed and even exaggerated Gilpin's tendency to isolate visual considerations from any historical, political, or moral ones that may arise from looking at irregular, anti-classical landscapes, ruins, or even ruined people – the ragged poor, viewed from a discreet distance.

This *aestheticised* approach caught on with travellers who were more or less confined to exploring their own island during the years of war with France: among them were William and Dorothy Wordsworth, whose Wye Valley tour gave rise to one of the most famous of all Romantic poems, 'Tintern Abbey' (1798). Picturesque-hunters began crowding into Wordsworth's own Lake District, using their 'Claude glasses' – tinted portable mirrors – to frame and darken the scenes they visited, making innumerable sketches and giving vent to effusions on the picturesque glories of the region. They quickly became the targets for satire and were most memorably skewered in William Combe and Thomas Rowlandson's 1809 poem-with-pictures *The Tour of Doctor Syntax in Search of the Picturesque*. Wordsworth himself, in many poems as well as in his *Guide to the Lakes* (1810; reprinted and revised several times up to 1842), confronted picturesque conventions of sightseeing, attempting to replace them with a morally engaged, more compassionate stance. The rage for the picturesque was also contested and opposed by a number of women travel writers – among them Helen Maria Williams, Mary Wollstonecraft, Dorothy Wordsworth, and Mary Shelley – whose travel books, diaries, and fiction explored in various ways the possibilities of reversing the anti-political, disengaged tendency of many authoritative men's texts. In her *Letters Written During a Short Residence in Sweden, Norway, and Denmark* (1796), for example, Mary Wollstonecraft repeatedly 'mobilizes the standard vocabulary of the picturesque travelogue' only to 'wickedly undercut' it by homing in upon the unaesthetic material details of the life going on about her.[24] None of these satires, criticisms, or alternatives could suffice to stamp out the picturesque, however: the very imprecision of the term seems to have aided its dissemination, and the cessation of hostilities on the Continent in 1815 opened up a host of fresh fields, especially Italian ones, for its deployment. Thus we find, for example, Anna Jameson writing in the 1820s, 'Had I never visited Italy, I think I should never have understood the word *picturesque*'; Frances Trollope remarking in the 1840s on the 'air of *historique* picturesque perfection' she detected in some Tuscan peasant women; and Henry James exclaiming at Albano in the 1870s, 'I have talked of the picturesque all my life; now at last...I see it'.[25]

The dawn of mass tourism

In surveying the post-1815 atmosphere of travel in Europe, it is important not to lose sight of continuities that carry across the Napoleonic divide: not only did the idea of the picturesque live on – stretched and applied to new purposes, to be sure – but even the classical interests of the ideal Grand Tourist did not entirely disappear. Nevertheless, most contemporary commentators thought that even if some of the aims of Continental travelling remained the same as they were in the eighteenth century, the victory at Waterloo had ushered in a new era in which opportunity and entrepreneurship were suddenly rendering the attractions of Europe open to (what they exaggeratedly characterised as) 'everybody'. 'When peace came', wrote the *Westminster Review*, 'when our island prison was opened...it was the paramount wish of every English heart...to hasten to the Continent'; the whole of a new generation 'poured, in one vast stream, across the Pas de Calais into France'.[26] In such representations, a cultural practice once identified with privileged individuals and devoted to the securing of their privilege appears transformed at once into an activity scandalously accessible to a de-individualised, metaphorically liquid mass. It is hardly too much to say that hyperbolic reactions like this one invented the idea of mass tourism before the phenomenon really existed.

The technological and institutional developments that brought it into existence began in the final years of the period covered by this essay. On the one hand, steam power, on the rails and on the water, greatly increased the speed and decreased the cost of travelling; on the other, new institutions and facilities appeared in the marketplace, offering to ease the financial and other burdens of travel's new wider clientele. Steam vessels began crossing the English Channel in 1821: estimates suggest that as many as 100,000 people a year were availing themselves of the service by 1840. The spread of railways across Europe was a highly uneven process, liable, even where quickest (as in Britain), to the chaos of a competitive free-for-all. Anything like a seamless trans-Continental rail system remained the haziest of utopian dreams for much of the nineteenth century; yet here again, observers at the very start of this long evolution seemed ready to treat it as a *revolution* already well underway. Late in his life, Wordsworth submitted several letters to the *Morning Post* protesting against the construction of a railway line reaching into the heart of the Lake District. As he saw it, the enthusiasts of the picturesque were engaged in a dangerously self-contradictory effort: the 'unavoidable consequence' of their taking tickets on the new trains would be 'a disturbance of the retirement, and in many places a destruction of the beauty of the country, which the parties are come in search of'.[27] Disruption of the pristine regions of prelapsarian travel would result not simply from the new railway lines, with all their attendant noise and smoke, but from the unwitting collective action of the ticket-holders themselves who, in their very numbers, would kill the things they loved. 'The merits of the railroad and the steamboat have been prodigiously vaunted', *Blackwood's Magazine* commented in 1848, 'and we have no desire to depreciate the advantages of either ... But they have afflicted our generation with one desperate evil; they have covered Europe with Tourists'.[28] The biblical metaphor of the plague of locusts was never very far from such accounts of tourism and its spread.

The same period (roughly 1825–40) that witnessed the rise and initial effects of steam transport also saw other developments that greased the wheels on which travel was heading into the domain of mass tourism. Such developments included the authoritative portable railway timetable, first compiled by George Bradshaw, as well as improvements in the instruments of finance that enabled travellers to change currency with comparative ease abroad. Chief among the post-1815 scene's new features, however, must be the emergence of the 'travel agent', especially in the corporate person of Thomas Cook and Son, and of the modern tourist's guidebook, as it was separately invented by Karl and Fritz Baedeker in Germany and by John Murray III in England (in 1835 and 1836, respectively). The travellers of the nineteenth century, moving more swiftly than the Grand Tourist of old and unaccompanied by any well-informed 'governor', needed the aid and counsel these new authorities provided if they were to maximise the utility of their shortened itineraries and concentrate the greatest touristic value into the least time at the lowest cost. Beginning as an organiser of cheap local excursions, Thomas Cook built and personally became an institution by offering the magical combination of 'the easiest, simplest, and cheapest method' of travelling with the 'most perfect freedom compatible' with group tours or standardised travel 'packages'.[29] Baedeker and Murray are largely responsible for the generic distinction we still observe, according to which the impersonal, objective 'guidebook' stands apart from the highly personal, impressionistic book of 'travel writing'; earlier books of travel had combined many functions in what now seems a cacophonous blend. In a work like Mariana Starke's *Travels in Italy* (1802), the guidebook-like recommendations of routes, inns, and attractions now seem out of place because they appear in a text written in the epistolary style, as if addressed to one particular recipient, and because they jostle against all manner of other material, including political commentary, observations on manners and customs, and the recounting of Starke's own concluded tour. Producing authoritative, regularly updated texts of standard appearance and format that were exclusively devoted to the 'guidebook' function, Baedeker and Murray had the collateral effect of sharpening the definition and purpose of their texts' opposites, the personal travelogues which, freed from the guidebook burden, could now specialise in recording an individual traveller's distinctive reactions to the stimuli of the tour. This new, highly individualistic purpose for travel and travel writing arrived just when these activities were widely felt to need one.

Post-Napoleonic visitors to Europe, whether or not they intended to write texts based on their journeys, were subjected to the twin pressures of feeling both one of a crowd and late on the scene, surrounded by 'hordes' of fellow-visitors and at pains to find anything new to say about the hallowed sites now opened to them. The class-specific ideals of the Grand Tour were refunctioned to suit that atmosphere in which 'everybody' seemed to be abroad: the desiderata of travelling turned inward and created the honorific sense of 'traveller', which means essentially 'the one who is not a *tourist*'. Through varieties of what the sociologist Erving Goffman has called 'rôle distance', modern travellers and travel writers identified themselves as anti-touristic beings whose unhappy lot it was to move amidst and in the wake of tourists, *for one of whom they might even be mistaken*; on the increasingly beaten path of Continental travelling, self-differentiation, not imitation, became a guiding purpose.[30] Romantic authors such as Germaine de Staël, Lord Byron, William Hazlitt, and Samuel Rogers provided prototypes and models for these efforts. Hazlitt and Rogers, among others, wrote post-Grand Tour defences of travel that characterised it as answering a universal hunger for change and freedom from social responsibilities. More than any others, though, it was de Staël and Byron, in literary sensations like de Staël's novel *Corinne, or Italy* (1807) and Byron's four-canto travelogue poem *Childe Harold's Pilgrimage* (published in parts between 1811 and 1817), who established a new paradigm suitable for the dawning age of mass tourism. Proposing that 'there are only two distinct classes of men on earth: those who feel enthusiasm and those who scorn it', de Staël's

Corinne appeared to supply readers with a way of conceiving of a traveller's superiority to tourists without appealing to the 'outward' or accidental features of wealth or social class.[31] With the captivating appeal of his verse and his travelling personae, Byron seemed capable of revivifying even the most hackneyed of sites – and he had visited and written about so many of them that volumes of his poems became almost a necessary counterpart to the Murray or Baedeker guidebook. 'Every Englishman abroad', noted the American William Wetmore Story in the 1860s, 'carries a Murray for information, and a Byron for sentiment, and finds out by them what he is to know and feel at every step'.[32] In a manner characteristic of many modern cultural practices, the devices of rebellion or rôle-distancing – in this case, anti-tourism – were themselves becoming the distinguishing features of a new type of conformity, a new rôle. Story's witticism invites us to imagine a host of Murray- and Byron-clutching 'travellers', each solitary one of whom is silently, passionately recalling the words of Childe Harold:

> in the crowd
> They could not deem me one of such; I stood
> Among them, but not of them; in a shroud
> Of thoughts which were not their thoughts . . . [33]

The image points forward to our own commodity culture, in which individuals are invited to define their individuality by means of purchases that vouch for their putatively distinctive 'lifestyle choices'. It would not be long before the institutions of the tourist industry began to market their tourist services by appealing to their customers' anti-touristic impulses.

NOTES

1 Paul Fussell, ed., *The Norton Anthology of Travel* (New York: Norton, 1987), p. 129.
2 Jeremy Black, *The British Abroad: The Grand Tour in the Eighteenth Century* (London: Macmillan, 1992), pp. xi–xiii.
3 Lynne Withey, *Grand Tours and Cook's Tours: A History of Leisure Travel, 1750 to 1915* (New York: Morrow, 1997), p. 7.
4 Richard Lassels, 'A Preface to the Reader Concerning Travelling', in *An Italian Voyage, Or, a Compleat Journey through Italy*, 2nd edn (London: Richard Wellington, 1698), vol. I, n. p.
5 Earl of Chesterfield, *The Letters of Philip Dormer Stanhope, Earl of Chesterfield, with the Characters*, ed. John Bradshaw (London: George Allen & Unwin, 1926), vol. I, p. 197.
6 James Boswell, *Life of Johnson* (Oxford University Press, 1970), p. 742.
7 Kenneth Churchill, *Italy and English Literature, 1764–1930* (Cambridge University Press, 1980), p. 1.

8 *The Traveller; or, a Prospect of Society*, in *The Collected Works of Oliver Goldsmith*, ed. Arthur Friedman (Oxford: Clarendon Press, 1966), vol. IV, p. 255, lines 159–62.

9 John Brewer, *The Pleasures of the Imagination: English Culture in the Eighteenth Century* (New York: Farrar, Straus, Giroux, 1997), p. 207.

10 Thomas Nugent, *The Grand Tour*, 3rd edn (London: 1778), p. xi.

11 Frederick A. Pottle, ed., *Boswell on the Grand Tour: Germany and Switzerland* (New York: McGraw-Hill, 1953), p. 91.

12 Francis Bacon, *The Essays* (London: Penguin, 1985), p. 113.

13 Robert Halsband, ed., *The Complete Letters of Lady Mary Wortley Montagu* (Oxford: Clarendon Press, 1967), vol. III, p. 148.

14 Tobias Smollett, *Travels Through France and Italy* [1766] (Oxford University Press, 1981), p. 241.

15 Adam Smith, *An Inquiry into the Nature and Causes of the Wealth of Nations*, ed. Edwin Cannan (University of Chicago Press, 1970), vol. II, p. 295.

16 James Boswell, *The Journal of a Tour to the Hebrides*, in Samuel Johnson and James Boswell, *A Journey to the Western Islands of Scotland* and *The Journal of a Tour to the Hebrides* [1775 and 1786] (London: Penguin, 1984), p. 161.

17 Johnson, *A Journey to the Western Islands of Scotland*, in Johnson and Boswell, p. 133.

18 Malcolm Andrews, *In Search of the Picturesque: Landscape Aesthetics and Tourism in Britain, 1760–1800* (Stanford University Press, 1989), p. 204.

19 Maxine Feifer, *Going Places: The Ways of the Tourist from Imperial Rome to the Present Day* (London: Macmillan, 1985), p. 107.

20 Dorothy Wordsworth, *Recollections of a Tour Made in Scotland* (New Haven: Yale University Press, 1997), p. 174.

21 William Wordsworth, 'Effusion in the Pleasure-Ground on the Banks of the Bran, Near Dunkeld' and note accompanying this poem, in *The Poems*, ed. John O. Hayden (New Haven: Yale University Press, 1981), vol. II, pp. 295–9, 969.

22 Quoted in Andrews, *In Search of the Picturesque*, p. 56.

23 William Gilpin, *Three Essays: On Picturesque Beauty; On Picturesque Travel; and On Sketching Landscape* . . . (London: printed for R. Blamire, 1792), pp. 7–8.

24 See Elizabeth A. Bohls, *Women Travel Writers and the Language of Aesthetics, 1716–1818* (Cambridge University Press, 1995), p. 151 and *passim*. I have changed 'undercuts' to 'undercut' here.

25 Anna Jameson, *Diary of an Ennuyée* (1826; Boston: Ticknor & Fields, 1857), p. 321; Frances Trollope, *A Visit to Italy* (London: Richard Bentley, 1842), vol. I, pp. 245–6; Henry James, *Letters*, ed. Leon Edel (Cambridge, Mass.: The Belknap Press of Harvard University Press, 1974–84), vol. I, p. 173. See the discussion in James Buzard, *The Beaten Track: European Tourism, Literature, and the Ways to 'Culture,' 1800–1918* (Oxford: Clarendon Press, 1993), pp. 172–216.

26 'English in Italy', *Westminster Review*, 4 (October 1826): 325.

27 Reprinted in Wordsworth, *The Illustrated Wordsworth's Guide to the Lakes*, ed. Peter Bicknell (New York: Congdon & Weed, 1984), p. 192.

28 'Modern Tourism', *Blackwood's Magazine*, 63/394 (August 1848): 185.

29 *Cook's Excursionist* (18 June 1863), p. 4.

30 Erving Goffman, 'Role Distance', in his *Encounters: Two Studies in the Sociology of Interaction* (Indianapolis: Bobbs-Merrill, 1961), pp. 85–152.

31 Germaine de Staël, *Corinne, or Italy*, trans. Avriel H. Goldberger (New Brunswick, N. J.: Rutgers University Press, 1987), p. 183.
32 William Wetmore Story, *Roba di Roma*, 2nd edn (London: Chapman & Hall, 1863), vol. I, p. 7.
33 Byron, *Childe Harold's Pilgrimage*, canto III, stanza CXIII, in *Poetical Works*, ed. Frederick Page (Oxford University Press, 1970), p. 225.

3

ROY BRIDGES

Exploration and travel outside Europe (1720–1914)

During the period which is the subject of this essay, travel writing became increasingly identified with the interests and preoccupations of those in European societies who wished to bring the non-European world into a position where it could be influenced, exploited or, in some cases, directly controlled. In the case of Britain, the identification was particularly close. There was some political control but more significant were various kinds of relationships stopping short of direct administration which historians have struggled to characterise by terms such as 'informal empire' or 'unofficial imperialism'. Trade, diplomacy, missionary endeavour, and scientific exploration might all contribute to the British expansion and each produced its own travel writing. Increasing European technological expertise provided advantages which made it easier to influence or dominate non-Europeans. With technological superiority came presumed intellectual superiority: Europeans could claim to be able to understand and interpret not only the terrain they entered but the inhabitants as well.

Travel writing, then, has a complex relationship with the situations in which it arose. In this essay it is taken to mean a discourse designed to describe and interpret for its readers a geographical area together with its natural attributes and its human society and culture. Travel writing may embrace approaches ranging from an exposition of the results of scientific exploration claiming (but rarely managing) to be objective and value-free to the frankly subjective description of the impact of an area and its people on the writer's own sensibilities. There was, in fact, a tension between supposedly scientific discourses on discoveries and travel writing of wider sympathies. 'Exploration' and 'travel' may indeed be distinguished even if there is a large grey area between them.

As the relationship between Britain and the wider world changed during this long period, there were many pressures tending to make travel writing not only more precise and scientific but also more obviously utilitarian, more explicitly concerned with issues of trade, diplomacy, and prestige. Three broad phases may be distinguished. In the middle and later eighteenth century, the beginning of the end of the old mercantilist empire of plantations, slavery and Atlantic trade is apparent. A 'swing to the East' and to Africa may be detected. The era from about 1830 to 1880 is the period of Victorian non-annexationist global expansion characterised by considerable confidence about Britain and its place in the world. From 1880 to 1914 is a period of severe international competition and territorial annexations accompanied by considerable anxiety. Subjects of concern ranged from Britain's military and naval capabilities and the health and fitness of its young men to the signs of the breakdown of the certainties of the Victorian 'bourgeois synthesis' in intellectual and cultural matters.

Eighteenth-century developments

By 1720, among the European powers struggling for primacy in the wider world, Spain and Portugal had been eclipsed by France, Britain, and the Netherlands. These three societies now competed to control what was assumed in the current 'mercantilist' theory to be a limited supply of wealth. All three were successful because they had linked state and capitalist mercantile interests. Britain was to forge ahead of the Dutch and even the French by 1815, probably because the interests of the landowning élite who dominated politics and those of the mercantile bourgeoisie overlapped to a much greater extent than elsewhere. The most visible signs of Britain's growing supremacy were the victories in wars: territories were gained in 1744–8 and again on a massive scale in 1763 after the Seven Years War which, leaving aside the European dimensions involving Prussia, Austria, and Russia, was a global struggle between Britain and France that meant large gains for Britain, especially in India and Canada. Even defeat in the War of the American Revolution and the loss of the thirteen colonies was less of a disaster than it seemed with the infant USA effectively remaining in a British sphere of trade and influence. By 1783 it was becoming apparent that the old Navigation Acts, which allowed colonies to trade only with the home country and restricted all transport to British ships, together with other mercantilist restrictions no longer suited Britain's economic interests.

The French Revolutionary and Napoleonic Wars further undermined the old empire of regulations and of plantation production in the West Indies with its attendant slave trade. The Caribbean islands were less worth fighting for because, important as their products like sugar and coffee might be, they offered a very poor market for the industrial exports which were now becoming so vital for Britain. Naval victory at Trafalgar in 1805 was more important than Wellington's triumph on mainland Europe at Waterloo ten years later; Britain emerged as a truly global power. Vast areas in Canada and Australasia with considerable bodies of settlers as well as the West Indian islands were under direct rule, while large parts of India had come under the control of a handful of East India Company officials. Just as significant was the opportunity Britain's merchants and investors now had to operate in former Spanish and Portuguese territories of the New World and that they were poised to gain access to 500 million possible consumers in China. In addition, West Africa had come to be seen as offering a potentially valuable market; the British government and other agencies were beginning to decide for Africans with whom they should trade and whether they should be permitted to sell slaves.[1]

Britain's ever closer engagement with the wider world meant that larger and larger numbers of travellers and explorers made journeys to report upon it. The three voyages of James Cook set the pattern of government demanding scientific investigation as part of a search for precise and accurate information whether or not this pointed to economic opportunities. By 1815, the government was organising landward as well as maritime exploration, notably in western Africa. In India, the Company encouraged land travellers while Admiral Malcolm sent his Indian Navy officers to explore all around the Indian Ocean and founded the Bombay Geographical Society to publish the results. Such technically private organisations in India or Britain itself tended to have close links with government because their leaders were aristocrats and the travellers they sponsored, officials or servicemen. Sir Joseph Banks (1743–1820), President of the Royal Society and effectively Director of the Royal Botanic Gardens at Kew from about 1773, sent plant collectors to all parts of the world. Under Banks's encouragement, the 'Saturday's Dining Club' meeting on 9 June 1788 transformed itself into the 'Association for Promoting the Discovery of the Inland Parts of Africa'. The association was composed entirely of aristocrats, including a few women.[2] Of course, many aristocrats themselves travelled, if only on the Grand Tour to Italy or France, and presumably returned with some interest in other cultures. A few, most notably Banks, were themselves significant travellers and explorers. Others might go on important embassies abroad and take with them a corps of secretaries and assistants capable of writing accounts of the travels, as did Sir John Barrow while serving as secretary to Lord Macartney in both China and South Africa.

The official and semi-official organisations were joined in the 1790s by the missionary societies. The impulse of north European Protestants to spread the Gospel became especially strong in Britain and was closely linked to the slave trade abolition cause. Abolitionists had founded the freed slave settlement of Sierra Leone in 1787 and were to bring about the end of the British slave trade in 1807. High-minded evangelical aristocrats associated with abolition campaigns, some of whom had links with those promoting scientific travel, founded the Church Missionary Society in 1799. Although far more effective than existing Anglican societies, it was initially unable to find many recruits from the clergy; like the government, it recruited Germans for service in West Africa. The possibility of missionary travel writing produced by those outside the normal limits of polite society began to increase. The tendency was encouraged by the non-denominational London Missionary Society, founded in 1795. Drawing on Congregationalists, other non-conformists and Scottish Presbyterians, it began to have a powerful impact upon South Africa and islands in the Pacific.

Missionary societies and the other organisations published literature which supplemented the travel books for which commercial publishers found a rapidly growing market during the eighteenth century. Early on, the characteristic outlet looked back to the Hakluyt tradition – a multi-volume collection of travels from a variety of sources, periods, or regions. Thomas Astley's four-volume *A Collection of Voyages and Travels* (1704–5) and A. and J. Churchill's *A New General Collection of Voyages and Travels* (1745–7) are the best-known edited collections. Even the initial published account of Cook's first voyage was a rather unsatisfactory version of his journal in a collection of travels.[3] Such compilations were rather costly works designed for gentlemen's libraries but John Knox's *A New Collection of Voyages and Travels* (1773) was issued in seven deliberately inexpensive volumes. The popularity of travel writing in the lending libraries which sprang up during the later eighteenth century confirms the widening interest as does the emergence of periodicals in which travels became a frequent subject. The *Gentleman's Magazine* is an early example but the early nineteenth century saw periodicals aimed at a wider readership. The Tory *Quarterly Review* was matched by the Whig *Edinburgh Review*, while aiming at a more popular market than either was *Blackwood's Magazine*. A specialised form of periodical was the transactions of a scientific body; by the 1770s, travellers and explorers would be expected to contribute papers as Cook himself did to the Royal Society's *Philosophical Transactions*. The most important change by the early 1800s, however, was the arrival of books in which travellers described their own exploits. In this, as in so many other respects, Cook's explorations were a landmark: volumes emerged written by himself and by numerous of his associates.[4]

Early in the eighteenth century, a traveller's discourse might not be very carefully structured or systematic but, by 1800, a typical pattern had emerged. Proceeding from a base in civilisation to an unknown region, the traveller must describe experiences and observations day to day on the basis of a log or journal. This format left some scope for the depiction of the picturesque or the exotic but the emphasis was more and more on science and precision. Certainly, admixtures of fact and fiction such as Defoe's *Robinson Crusoe* (1719) and *The Life, Adventures and Piracies of the Famous Captain Singleton* (1720) were becoming unacceptable by the end of the eighteenth century. One reason that James Bruce did not receive the admiring reception he expected (and deserved) on his return from Africa in 1774 was that he was assumed to be inventing the stories, later repeated in his five-volume *Travels to Discover the Source of the Nile*...(1790), such as the Ethiopian practice of cutting steaks from living cattle. The tendency was for literary success (if not necessarily literary merit) to be guaranteed by the presumed 'scientific' and utilitarian importance of the information garnered.

Mary Louise Pratt sees scientific exploration as part of a process of 'territorial surveillance, appropriation of resources and administrative control' and Roxanne Wheeler makes a similar claim in respect even of Defoe's novel, *Captain Singleton*.[5] The latter judgement is certainly anachronistic, and it seems to be rarely understood how reluctant governments always were to take 'administrative control' of large areas. Nevertheless, as the century proceeded, there was a growing army of authentic travellers who strove to write with precision about the wider world and with some concern for perceived British interests. Certainly, preoccupations in travel writing became more and more secular. Travellers' information made it possible for Adam Smith to include Chinese and Indian examples in his *Wealth of Nations* (1776). As far as political society was concerned, some travellers reported 'stagnant despotisms', others cruelty and barbarism. Ideas that China represented anything superior to Europe soon disappeared. At best, non-Europeans were 'innocent primitives'; even the idea of the 'noble savage' was a construct to which few practical travellers gave much credence.[6]

Superiority seemed most manifest in science. Europeans claimed to understand the earth and its physical processes, knew how to plot their positions, and could classify plants and animals. By 1830 science had made possible an 'intellectual conquest' of most of the rest of the world which implied that 'those who understood nature's laws' could bring about an 'imperialism of improvement'.[7] There was often arrogance and insensitivity but science could produce at least the attempt to observe dispassionately, characteristic of travellers like Captain Cook, Mungo Park, or William Burchell. Burchell collected over 63,000 botanical and zoological specimens while travelling in South Africa. He tells us he had 'a mind free from prejudice'. He thought his observations were objective because he recorded everything as he saw it and had allowed no editor to interfere. Hence, he tells us, all his information about a country 'still in a state of nature' and 'man in an uncivilized state of society' is 'on a basis never to be shaken'.[8] Burchell's naivety is touching if unwittingly arrogant.

Travels to 1830

Maritime discoveries proceeded apace in the eighteenth century. In about 1700, the semi-pirate Dampier had said that it could not be expected 'that a seaman should affect Politeness'.[9] By 1748, Anson's *A Voyage Round the World*, written at his direction if not by him, aspires to sober scientific description although its general popularity owed much still to the 'Robinson Crusoe' element – catastrophe, suffering, and adversity bravely borne.[10] Adventure made Cook popular, too, although it was he who really set the pattern of supposedly 'scientific' observation. Cook's second voyage on the *Resolution* of 1772–5 has been called 'arguably the greatest and most perfect of seaborne voyages of exploration' (Marshall and Williams, *Great Map*, p. 276). The idea of a great southern continent was disposed of and the reality of Australia, New Zealand, and many islands revealed to Europeans. Some have seen this as the end of significant maritime exploration, but Cook himself and navigators like Wallis, Cartaret, and Vancouver did further work in the Pacific and described it in their books, although probably the best-known book involving seafaring was William Bligh's *Narrative of the Mutiny of the Bounty* (1790). Flinders was yet to circumnavigate Australia and Owen to survey in detail the coasts of Africa and Arabia.

In North America, the most notable British traveller was Alexander Mackenzie, who not only walked from Hudson's Bay to the Great Slave Lake and then followed the river which bears his name to the Arctic in 1789 but also crossed the Rockies to the Pacific in 1793 – the first known European to achieve the crossing of the continent. His *Voyages from Montreal . . . to the Frozen and Pacific Oceans* was published in 1801. The continuing British obsession with a navigable route to the Pacific Ocean by the Northwest Passage led to voyages by Knight, Middleton, and then, under Barrow's influence, a new series by Ross, Parry, and Franklin in the early part of the nineteenth century. In this latter period, first moves towards serious Antarctic discovery began with Weddell's voyages.

Increasing numbers of British travellers visited Latin America as trade overcame Spanish exclusionism and the dependencies became independent. Yet the outstanding traveller was Humboldt. His travels from the Orinoco to the Amazon produced thirty volumes of data which seemed to be the epitome of European science and inspired many scientists in Britain, including Charles Darwin. Humboldt's science was actually far from neutral: he 're-invented' South America as an 'exploitable wilderness' which the Creoles, not their Spanish rulers, could develop with the aid of northern European capitalists.[11]

By 1800, northern European capitalists were also hoping to enter China. Macartney's famous embassy found the Chinese and their Emperor regrettably insensible to the blessings of British manufactures but a mass of information which Macartney's associates, Barrow, Staunton, and others gathered was duly published.[12] The extension of Company rule in India made possible the gathering of immense quantities of data by James Rennell, whose *Memoir of a Map of Hindoostan* was published in 1788. The work of the Indian Navy has been noted. Information was needed at the Cape, too, where direct rule was taken over from the Dutch in 1806. Travellers like Burchell and several London Missionary Society men, not infrequently accompanied by intrepid wives, now pushed beyond the colony limits into the South African interior.

In West Africa, the travels sponsored by the African Association, of which Mungo Park's was the most important, gave way to government-organised expeditions having also economic and diplomatic objects. These included, after 1807, ending the slave trade. The purely geographical puzzle concerned the direction and termination of the Niger. Park saw it in 1796 'glittering to the morning sun and flowing slowly *to the eastward*'[13] but lost his life trying to follow it further on a second expedition. The travels of Denham, Clapperton, and the Lander brothers meant not only the solution of the Niger problem but also the forging of ever-closer British links to the region – a region which, not least because of the slave trade, was normally portrayed in the travel writing as badly in need of such links.[14] Elsewhere in Africa, the only outstanding travel activity was James Bruce's visit to Ethiopia and the source of the Blue Nile in 1768–73. Bruce was a philanderer and a bombast but much less mendacious than Dr Johnson alleged. The more sober Henry Salt, whose *A Voyage to Abyssinia* appeared in 1814, learned much of Egypt and the Red Sea region.

From 1830 to 1880: the triumph of capitalist expansionism

From about 1830, industrial and commercial capitalism triumphed in Europe and this made possible its equal triumph around the world. The European bourgeoisie threw off any remaining revolutionary inclinations and became the establishment, moulding institutions to its own ends, including those concerned with travel. In Britain, the close alliance of the middle classes with the landed class gave added security. There was optimism that the creation of wealth, progressive science-based change, and religious redemption might all be promoted to the mutual advantage of Britain and overseas areas.

No-one better expressed the spirit of the age in this respect than the country's most admired explorer and missionary, David Livingstone. Writing in 1857, he saw himself part of a large company:

> Each man in his sphere, either knowingly or unwittingly, is performing the will of our Father in heaven. Men of science searching after hidden truths, which, when discovered will, like the electric telegraph, bind men more closely together – soldiers battling for the right against tyranny – sailors rescuing the victims of oppression from heartless man-stealers – merchants teaching the nations lessons of mutual dependence – and many others as well as missionaries, all work in the same direction, and all efforts are overruled for one glorious end.[15]

Capitalist influence spread in three main ways. Emigration created markets. It continued on a large scale in this period although mainly in the form of the reinforcement of existing European communities overseas. Secondly, world trade vastly increased in volume because European industries required both raw materials and markets. Britain's need for markets was especially acute; the country could not feed itself from its own agriculture after about 1850. Thirdly, there was investment in the wider world, principally in railways, telegraphs, and shipping services. All this activity took large numbers of Europeans overseas to manage the various activities. Just occasionally, management might take the form of political control but setting up new colonies was regarded as highly undesirable. Free trade and access to all markets, not just colonial ones, most suited Britain's interests. Even India, which saw tremendous expansion of British overrule, was regarded as best controlled indirectly through its own princes where possible.

The promotion of travel reflected this non-annexationist approach. There were some official expeditions, but it was generally felt better to extend modest subsidies to scientific societies. The Royal Geographical Society (hereafter RGS) emerged in this period as the greatest promoter of travel and exploration and the key institution in what Felix Driver calls the 'culture of exploration'. Driver emphasises the heterogeneous nature of this culture and the many ambiguities and uncertainties which can be detected in the RGS and its work, such as reconciling information 'from the field' with that 'from the cabinet'. There were also difficulties over the nature and purpose of geographical knowledge and sometimes doubts about the testimony of particular travellers.[16] The RGS tendency under Sir Roderick Murchison to promote an explorer as the 'lion of the season' for publicity purposes was frowned upon and the Society's intellectual credibility questioned by some purists. Even so, the RGS was an incredibly successful institution precisely because it linked the tradition of travel writing associated with the Grand

Tour and the search for the exotic or picturesque with hard-nosed science and even harder-nosed diplomatic and economic concerns. It is significant that, at its foundation in 1830, the RGS actually developed out of the Ralegh Travellers' Club and shortly afterwards absorbed the African Association, so embracing aristocrats and their travel interests. Yet most of the support soon came from naval and army officers, surveyors, administrators, and practical scientists, especially those who managed Britain's multifarious interests around the world. It was an institution which reconciled the interests of upper and middle classes to which the government would have little hesitation in according a quasi-official status.

Whatever reservations scientists might have had intellectually, the RGS was one of the institutions which helped to make them 'gentlemen of science' and give public recognition to their vital rôle in Britain's overseas affairs; they became members of a 'service class'.[17] A vital feature of the period is, indeed, the capture of science for the purposes of overseas expansion. Travel writing had a crucial part in the process. Plant collecting as a spur to travel continued with the work of Sir Joseph Hooker of Kew. His *Himalayan Journals* were published in two volumes in 1854. Hooker was a champion of Darwin, whose theory of natural selection resulted from a world tour recorded in a travel journal, the second edition of which he rendered 'more fitting for popular reading'.[18] Scientist-travellers advanced into the non-European world ever more enthusiastically and in greater numbers. However, something yet more fundamental was happening: science itself was becoming 'imperialistic'. This has been brilliantly demonstrated by James Secord in relation to Murchison.[19] As a former military man who became a geologist, Murchison expanded his 'empire of Siluria' – that is, his formulation of the stratigraphy of the older rocks of Britain – to cover vast areas of the rest of the world. The 'conquest' began with what was essentially a travel work on Russia.[20] As Murchison became increasingly dominant in the RGS, he was, it has been powerfully argued, capturing the world for Britain in a much wider sense through geography and exploration.[21] Murchison's easy relations with government made it possible for him to obtain favours for scientists in general and the RGS in particular. He died in 1871 having dominated the RGS for the previous twenty years. His mantle fell on Clements Markham who was fully willing that the RGS continue to provide a service of 'national value and importance'.[22]

How far commerce was associated with the 'culture of exploration' is a complex question. The RGS always insisted on its devotion to pure science and refused to allow itself to become a commercial geography institution in the 1870s and 1880s. For their part, chambers of commerce were reluctant to become involved in schemes suggested by geographers and explorers. Yet there is a connection. The 'service class' identified here was drawn from or integrated with the class which produced the 'gentlemanly capitalists' associated with the City of London and its management of financial affairs around the world.[23] Missionary societies were drawn into the 'culture of exploration' in more obvious ways. Their leading officers were laymen, usually successful in business, who did not find it too difficult to engage with gentlemanly capitalists or gentlemanly scientists, while many of the missionaries themselves could reconcile their interests with those of the service class as did David Livingstone. Conversely, Sir Bartle Frere, later RGS President, is an example of a major official figure enthusiastic to co-operate with missionaries.[24] Missionary publications often became travel writing: Livingstone showed the way with his best-selling *Missionary Travels* of 1857.

The writing associated with the 'culture of exploration' took a number of forms. While the RGS enthusiastically promoted new travels, its 1846 offshoot, the Hakluyt Society, printed travel texts from the past so perhaps validating current travel activities by reference to history.[25] Since 1800, scientific periodicals had vastly increased in number. The RGS produced not only its *Journal* but, from 1858, *Proceedings* as well so that the discussions following a traveller's report were recorded. Returned explorers were expected to present their results to their sponsor society in proper scientific form and then write a more popular book. If someone it sponsored gave material to a commercial publisher first, the RGS would object. The discoverer of the source of the Nile, Speke, offended in this way in 1863. No doubt the temptation to cater immediately to the public interest was very great in such a case because the large travel volume could bring fame and, in a few cases, a handsome financial return, especially if there were cheaper reprints.

Among the publishers who fed the enormous public interest in popular travel works, John Murray was probably the leader. His links with Murchison and the RGS were close. Stanford was also important in this field. Edinburgh, with Blackwood and two specialist geographical and educational publishers, Johnston and Bartholomew, was able to rival London. Periodicals like *Macmillan's Magazine* or the *Westminster Review* noticed travel books or commissioned articles by explorers. The *Athenaeum* occupied a special position as providing a forum for the literary and scientific élite where, for example, the more abstruse questions such as how much the Ancients had known of the source of the Nile would be debated. The *Illustrated London News* reported on receptions for explorers and tried to show some scenes from their travels. Illustrations became more important in the travel books themselves with skilled and not so skilled engravers interpreting – or misinterpreting – travellers' sketches or, towards the end of the period, photographs. All in all, then, there were many ways by which knowledge of the wider world might impinge on the consciousness of the reading public in Britain.

Major British travel, 1830–1880

The peoples and regions which, by whatever medium, impinged on Victorians' minds and the kinds of travel, exploration, and science writing they produced may be placed in five broad categories. First, there was the work of sailors, especially in the polar regions. The Royal Navy continued its unprofitable attempts to break through ice with big ships. No doubt science benefited in various ways but one suspects that the RGS under both Murchison and Markham was more interested in promoting the ideal of the heroic sailors battling with a harsh environment and triumphing because of their bravery: twelve years and forty expeditions in a continuing search for Sir John Franklin after he had died in the Arctic now looks absurd. Interest shifted to what was really a question of national prestige – reaching the North Pole. Nares got within 400 miles of it, but perhaps practised more science when he commanded the *Challenger* expedition which made the first deep ocean studies in 1873–6. Also notable was the pioneering Antarctic expedition by James Clark Ross in 1839–43.[26]

Major non-European polities which maintained political independence from Europe are the second category. The Turkish Empire, Siam, Japan, and, most important, China, were all investigated by travellers. Much of the resulting writing concerned the remains of antiquity but even more dealt with current diplomatic and political problems. The encounter with Islam was very important to Britain because of its Middle Eastern strategic interests. Attitudes to Arabia have been brilliantly analysed by Kathryn Tidrick.[27] Biblical and historical interests produced a vast literature on this and other parts of the Turkish Empire. W. J. Hamilton, Burton (in several works), Palgrave, and Doughty are the names which stand out.[28] Beyond Turkey, in Persia and other frontier regions of India, strategic considerations vie with antiquities as in the many works of a future RGS President, Sir Henry Rawlinson.[29] In this whole region, perhaps, can be found the classic examples of what Edward Said calls 'Orientalism' – interpreting the East in order to dominate it.[30] Literature on China and Japan is not dissimilar though there is more emphasis on prospects for missionary work and trade. Another future RGS President, Sir Rutherford Alcock, wrote extensively on Japan.[31]

A third category is the Americas. Former European colonies in North America inspired little British pioneer exploration in this period although there was some travel writing of note, for example by Burton on Utah. Some important scientific ventures took place in South America, for example by

WAGANDA MUSICAL INSTRUMENTS.—FROM A SKETCH BY CAPTAIN GRANT.

3. The explorer J. A. Grant produced over 100 sketches and watercolours during his trek
through East Africa in 1860–3. He had some skill as an artist and the depiction of the
musicians of the kingdom of Buganda (NLS Ms 17919/32) aimed to show the nature of the
instruments and the way they were held and played. The engraver for the version in the
Illustrated London News of 4 July 1863, however, gave the players Indian rather
than African features and made them hold the instruments as he thought fit rather
than as Grant had observed. Visual messages from the heart of Africa were as likely
to be distorted as the verbal ones. (The original watercolour by Grant is reproduced by
permission of the Trustees of the National Library of Scotland.)

Darwin himself, his rival, Wallace, and a noted naturalist, H. W. Bates, later
to become the Assistant Secretary of the RGS.[32]

The fourth category is British settler colonies, with the most significant
pioneer travellers those like Eyre, Leichardt, and Sturt who penetrated the
Australian interior, and J. McDouall Stuart who achieved the first north to
south crossing in 1858–62, recounted in his *Journals of Exploits in Australia,
1858–1862* (1864).

The fifth region, Equatorial Africa, had substantial populations who made a much greater impact on travellers than did Australian aborigines. Exploration involved a series of encounters with its inhabitants; most of the information contained in African travel works is not so much from direct observation as from edited interview material. Generally, the African informants themselves were portrayed as open to religious conversion, needing to be saved from slave traders and awaiting the aid of European ingenuity which alone could unlock the vast resources of the continent. Just a few peoples were not totally 'backward' and might become suitable allies. It was accepted in the travel writing of this period, which provided the guide to African affairs, that European governments were not likely to create colonial dependencies. Hence the way was open for various private schemes to redeem Africa, many of them drawn up in Britain by members of the service class and their missionary allies in the 1870s; here was a case where exploration and the associated travel writing led directly to 'unofficial empire'.[33] Unfortunately, King Leopold II of Belgium also wanted a large unofficial empire for himself. This and a changing world situation meant a different solution to Africa's perceived problems in the subsequent period.

The exploration of Africa attracted enormous attention during the middle decades of the century and was in many ways the spur to the most classic forms of Victorian travel writing. Exploration was guided by the attempt to discover and describe the physical setting. The travel-reading public were fascinated with snow-covered mountains on the Equator, large inland lakes (on which surely one could use steamboats) and, above all, speculations on the source of the Nile. The search for the source was important because the Nile nourished Egypt, because one could speculate on whether the ancients had known the source, and because the traveller who found it would have lasting fame. Hence the series of disputes between 1858 and 1875, the alleged suicide of Speke, and the certain death of Livingstone in 1873 still seeking the source among 'fountains' reported by Herodotus 2,330 years before. All the disputes continue to fascinate modern writers, which unfortunately tends to distract attention from the rôle the travellers were playing in the ultimately more important questions of African and imperial development. However, there is now a corpus of studies which tackles some of these questions.[34] The travel writing itself exists in very large quantities. Livingstone's work meant three books. Burton's massive article in the RGS *Journal* was followed by a two-volume work in 1860 while his companion and rival Speke let Blackwood edit and rush out a large volume on the Nile. Stanley wrote voluminously for his newspapers and produced avidly read books on his highly efficient, if often ruthless, exploratory work. Joseph Thomson was admired for his attractive personality as well as for the adventures he described.[35]

Late nineteenth-century imperialism

By 1885, Joseph Thomson felt himself to be at odds with what was happening in Africa. Stanley and men like him were not only erroneously depicting Africa as a cornucopia waiting to be opened by Europe but also taking the romance out of African travel. Certainly, Stanley easily made the transition from geographical explorer to land grabber and exploiter. In fact, during the 1880s and 1890s, the situation changed in many overseas theatres of European activity – often very abruptly. Crises arose from the arrival of the ambitious new powers Germany and Italy in Africa and from the demands Russia and Japan now made upon China. Local reactions against the increasing interference by incomers took the form of what Europeans called 'rebellions' and 'risings'. As such events became more common, European governments became less reluctant to give chartered company status to their traders, force concessions for them, create 'protectorates', or even directly annex territories. Fear of other Europeans was matched by fear of the 'natives': the Zulus, without firearms, had defeated the British army in 1879, white Africans – the Boers – frequently did the same in 1899–1901, Ethiopians overcame the Italians in 1896, the 'Boxers' rose in rebellion against Europeans in China in 1900, and then the non-European power, Japan, humiliated Russia in 1904–5.

Travel writing reflected all these developments. It became at once more strident in asserting Europe's technological and racial superiority over non-Europeans and full of fears about 'falling behind' rival powers. Perhaps there was a subliminal realisation that all the annexations of territory in Africa and the wresting of concessions from China were signs of weakness rather than strength. The movement to bring about a defensive federation of Britain and its settler colonies began with Sir Charles Dilke's *Greater Britain* (1867–8), essentially a travel work describing Canada, Australia, and New Zealand. In Africa, the admirable Mary Kingsley, author of *Travels in West Africa* (1897), dared to question Europe's purposes in Africa, but much more influential was Stanley's *In Darkest Africa* (1890), which recorded his attempts to capture large swathes of territory for imperial exploitation. In *Heart of Darkness* Joseph Conrad saw such activities as a metaphor for humanity's attempts to face up to its psychic ills but the transition to imperialism is illustrated in a more straightforward way by Harry Johnston. Sent by the Royal Society, no less, to examine the flora and fauna of Kilimanjaro in 1886, he tried to annex the mountain.[36] Similar transitions may be found in travel writing to the other main theatre of great-power rivalries, the Chinese Empire, W. S. Percival's *The Land of the Dragon* (1889) being one example.

Of course, some of the older traditions of travel writing remained. Markham insisted that polar exploration should preserve the model of supposedly disinterested science plus brave endeavour but even here international rivalry much affected the races to reach the poles. This made Scott's heroic failure to be first to the South Pole tragic in British eyes and only to be compensated for by the even more heroic failure to return. All this and the equally indomitable work of Shackleton produced an extensive and highly popular literature.[37] Yet these Antarctic adventures were anachronistic in an age of great power rivalries.

Europe dominated the world in 1914 but its internal rivalries were about to produce a war which would end that dominance. Moreover, the non-European subjects of either formal colonial rule or economic and cultural dominance would now begin to question or throw off European control. However, the end of Europe's and Britain's period of world power is another story. The key point is rather that the developments of the previous 200 years had effectively created one world. An understanding of this momentous historical development needs to embrace the study of the travel writing of the period. At the very least, travellers illustrate for us the thinking of some key actors and opinion formers in the historical process. In fact, the nineteenth century had seen travel writing reach a position of influence greater than had ever previously been the case and certainly greater than was to be the case after 1914. Yet the achievement of European global power is not the whole story: albeit through a distorting mirror, travel writing can also give us information about the non-Europeans who were the recipients of imperial visitors and conquerors and, rather too often, their victims.

NOTES

I am grateful to Professor John Hargreaves who was kind enough to offer valuable comments on the first draft of this chapter. Responsibility for the views expressed and the remaining mistakes is entirely mine.

1 Peter J. Marshall, 'Introduction', *Oxford History of the British Empire. Vol. II: The Eighteenth Century*, ed. P. J. Marshall (Oxford University Press, 1998), pp. 1–27. This work provides a brilliant short overview of the eighteenth-century period.

2 R. Hallett, *The Records of the African Association* (London: Nelson, 1964), p. 46 and *passim*.

3 John Hawkesworth, *An Account of the Voyages... Undertaken for Making Discoveries in the Southern Hemisphere*, 3 vols. (1773).

4 For example, James Cook, *A Voyage towards the South Pole and Round the World*..., 2 vols. (1777); Johann Forster, *A Voyage round the World*...(1777); James King, *A Voyage to the Pacific Ocean*..., 3 vols. (1784).

5 Mary Louise Pratt, *Imperial Eyes. Travel Writing and Transculturation* (London: Routledge, 1992), p. 38; Roxanne Wheeler, 'Limited Visions of Africa. Geographies of Savagery and Civility in Early Eighteenth-Century Narratives', in *Writes of Passage. Reading Travel Writing*, ed. James Duncan and Derek Gregory (London: Routledge, 1999), p. 37.

6 P. J. Marshall and Glyndwr Williams, *The Great Map of Mankind: British Perceptions of the World in the Age of Enlightenment* (London: Dent, 1982), pp. 150, 201, 212–19.

7 Richard Drayton, *Nature's Government: Science, British Imperialism and the 'Improvement' of the World* (New Haven: Yale University Press, 2000).

8 William J. Burchell, *Travels in the Interior of Southern Africa*, 2 vols. (London: Longman, 1822–4), vol. I, pp. vi–viii.

9 William Dampier, *A New Voyage Round the World* [1697] (London: hummingbird, 1998), p. 2.

10 See also Glyndwr Williams, *The Great South Sea* (New Haven: Yale University Press, 1997), pp. 254–6.

11 See Pratt, *Imperial Eyes*, pp. III–52.

12 A. Anderson, *Narrative of the British Embassy to China*...(1796); G. Staunton, *An Authentic Account of an Embassy to the Emperor of China*..., 2 vols. (1797); J. Barrow, *Travels in China*...(1804).

13 Mungo Park, *Travels in the Interior Districts of Africa*...(London: Bulmer, 1799), p. 194.

14 See Philip D. Curtin, *The Image of Africa. British Ideas and Action, 1780–1850* (London: Macmillan, 1965).

15 David Livingstone, *Missionary Travels and Researches in South Africa*... (London: Murray, 1857), p. 674.

16 Felix Driver, *Geography Militant. Cultures of Exploration and Empire* (Oxford: Blackwell, 2001), pp. 21–2, 24–48.

17 Roy Bridges, 'Towards the Prelude to the Partition of East Africa', in *Imperialism, Decolonization and Africa*..., ed. Roy Bridges (Basingstoke: Macmillan, 2000), p. 90.

18 Charles Darwin, *Journal of Researches...during the Voyage of HMS* Beagle (London: Colburn, 1839; 2nd edn, 1845), preface.

19 James Secord, 'King of Siluria: Roderick Murchison and the Imperial Theme in Nineteenth-Century British Geology', *Victorian Studies*, 25 (1982): 413–42.

20 R. I. Murchison, A. de Vermeuil and A. von Keyserling, *The Geology of Russia in Europe*..., 2 vols. (1845).

21 See Robert A. Stafford, *Scientist of Empire. Sir Roderick Murchison, Scientific Exploration and Victorian Imperialism* (Cambridge University Press, 1989).

22 Clements R. Markham, *The Fifty Years' Work of the Royal Geographical Society* (London: Murray, 1881), p. 126.

23 Peter J. Cain and Antony G. Hopkins, *British Imperialism: Innovation and Expansion, 1688–1914* (Harlow: Longman, 1993), pp. 124–5 and *passim*.

24 Bridges, 'Towards the Prelude', pp. 91–6.

25 Roy C. Bridges and Paul E. H. Hair, eds., *Compassing the Vaste Globe of the Earth* (London: Hakluyt Society, 1996), pp. 67–72, 230–2.

26 George S. Nares, *Narrative of a Voyage to the Polar Sea during 1875–6*, 2 vols. (London: Sampson Low, 1878); James C. Ross, *Voyage of Discovery and Research in the Southern and Antarctic Regions*, 2 vols. (London: Murray, 1847).

27 See Kathryn Tidrick, *Heart-beguiling Araby* (London: Tauris, 1981).

28 William J. Hamilton, *Researches in Asia Minor*, 2 vols. (1842) and Charles M. Doughty, *Travels in Arabia Deserta*, 2 vols. (1880) are examples. George Adam Smith, *Historical Geography of the Holy Land* (1895) is a late and impressive development of this genre of travel works.

29 Henry C. Rawlinson, *England and Russia in the East*, 2nd edn. (1875).

30 Edward Said, *Orientalism* (London: Routledge & Kegan Paul, 1978).

31 For example, Laurence Oliphant, *Narrative of the Earl of Elgin's Mission to China and Japan in 1857–9* (1859); Rutherford Alcock, *The Capital of the Tycoon...*, 2 vols. (1863).

32 Charles Darwin, *Geological Observations in South America* (1846); Alfred R. Wallace, *Narrative of Travels on the Amazon and Rio Negri* (1853); Henry W. Bates, *The Naturalist on the River Amazons...*, 2 vols. (1863). See Neil Whitehead's essay (Chapter 7).

33 Bridges, 'Towards the Prelude', p. 105.

34 For example, Roy C. Bridges, 'John Hanning Speke: Negotiating a Way to the Nile', in *Africa and Its Explorers*, ed. Robert Rotberg (Cambridge, Mass.: Harvard University Press, 1971), pp. 95–137; Roy C. Bridges, 'Nineteenth-Century East African Travel Records', *Paideuma*, 33 (1987): 179–196; Driver, *Geography Militant*, chs. 4, 6; Tim Youngs, *Travellers in Africa* (Manchester University Press, 1994).

35 David Livingstone, *Missionary Travels* (1857); *The Zambezi and its Tributaries* (1865); *The Last Journals of David Livingstone*, ed. Horace Waller, 2 vols. (1874); Richard F. Burton, 'Lake Regions', *Journal of the RGS*, 29 (1859), *passim.*; Richard F. Burton, *The Lake Regions of Central Africa*, 2 vols. (1860); John H. Speke, *Journal of the Discovery of the Source of the Nile* (1863); Henry M. Stanley, *How I Found Livingstone* (1872), *Through the Dark Continent*, 2 vols. (1878); Joseph Thomson, *Through Masai Land* (1885).

36 Harry H. Johnston, *The Kilimanjaro Expedition* (1886).

37 Ernest H. Shackleton, *The Heart of the Antarctic* (1909); Ernest H. Shackleton, *South* (1919); Robert F. Scott, *The Voyage of the Discovery* (1905); Leonard Huxley, *Scott's Last Expedition* (1913).

4

HELEN CARR

Modernism and travel (1880–1940)

In his book, *The English Novel*, Ford Madox Ford comments that over the preceding hundred years a growing 'ease of locomotion' had profoundly changed the English-speaking world. 'The habit of flux', he says, had been born; people moved around in an unprecedented way.[1] Ford, a romantic Tory, was in theory ambivalent about this change, but in practice he embodied it. A prefatory note to the book underlines his point. It was written, he tells us, 'in New York, on the S. S. Patria, and in the port and neighbourhood of Marseilles during July and August, 1927', though he 'made certain alterations' in Paris over the new year of 1930; appropriate creative circumstances for the editor of an avant-garde magazine called the *transatlantic review*, whose contributors were chiefly highly mobile cosmopolitan expatriates based in Paris, London, and New York.

The English Novel appeared in 1930, towards the end of the period covered by this chapter. Ford dated the beginnings of this increased mobility to the 1840s, a decade in which railway trains were already reaching thirty-five miles per hour, the first propeller-driven iron steamship, Brunel's *Great Britain*, crossed the Atlantic (it cautiously carried a full quota of sails), Thomas Cook was already in business, and Karl Baedeker's famous guidebooks for travellers had been in circulation for over a decade. Stephen Kern reminds us that by 1880 the American Transcontinental Railway and the Trans-Indian Peninsular Railroad had been built, the Suez Canal opened, and that if Jules Verne's *Around the World in 80 Days* was a fantasy when published in 1873, by 1890 an American woman journalist, Nellie Bly, had been round the globe in a mere seventy-two.[2] Railroads criss-crossed Europe and beyond and, as liners grew faster and more luxurious, steamship companies produced a crop of shipping millionaires. Increasing 'ease of locomotion' was not, however, simply the product of disinterested technological advance, and those on the move not only bands of tourists. Improvements in transport were fanned by, and helped to fan, the empire building, trade expansion and mass migrations of the late nineteenth century. As Eric Hobsbawm points out, in the four decades between 1876 and 1915 a quarter of the world's land mass was acquired as additional colonies by the main imperial powers, Britain itself adding about four million square miles to its territory.[3] Much of British travel writing in these decades emerged, in one way or another, out of the possibilities opened up by such colonial and trade development. Hilaire Belloc's 1898 poem, *The Modern Traveller*, is not about a tourist setting off with Thomas Cook, but a returned colonial adventurer reporting on his exploits to the *Daily Menace*. Along with a fiery mercenary, Commander Sin, and the rapacious Captain Blood, he pursues the quest for gain, en route looking out in case 'there was by chance a native tribe/ To cheat, cajole, corrupt, or bribe'. The native porters, thoroughly ill-treated, become restless, but

> Blood understood the Native mind.
> He said 'We must be firm but kind.'
> A mutiny resulted.

Blood grimly mutters, 'Whatever happens we have got/ The Maxim Gun, and they have not', and the mutiny is put down. 'We shot and hanged a few, and then/ The rest became devoted men.'[4] The expedition is a complete disaster but reported as a great heroic achievement. The anti-imperialist Belloc clearly has in mind one of the most successful travel books of the period, Henry Morton Stanley's *In Darkest Africa* (1890), which sold 150,000 copies within a few weeks of publication and was immediately translated into five languages. Stanley's book could not have been more directly a product of that colonialist expansion, for it recorded an expedition funded by King Leopold II of Belgium, who hoped thereby to acquire the Sudan, with additional money raised by Sir William Mackinnon, a man who had made his money in ships and now wanted to build up a trading company in East Africa. Belloc, it should be noted, represents an important strand of anti-colonialism of the period, one which was conservative and anti-modern, and which associated imperialism with vulgar middle-class commerce, Jewish bankers, and the mass press. Commerce and a jingoistic popular press were certainly central factors in late nineteenth-century imperialism, but opposition to them could be snobbish rather than idealistic. The complex imbrications of issues of race and class in this period need to be borne in mind in reading its travel writing.

The period from 1880 to 1940 was the heyday of the British Empire, and much travel writing shows the complicity with imperialism – if not its outright support – that Mary Louise Pratt identifies in her study *Imperial Eyes*.[5] Yet, as Nicholas Thomas has argued, contrasting a colonialist past with a liberal present disguises many continuities. Colonialism, he suggests, needs undoing as a 'coherent object'; we must recognise that 'colonial ideologies may

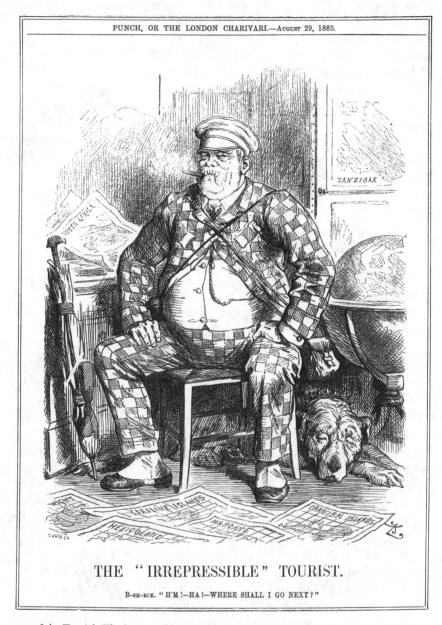

THE "IRREPRESSIBLE" TOURIST.

B-sm-rck. "H'M!—HA!—WHERE SHALL I GO NEXT?"

4. John Tenniel, 'The Irrepressible Tourist' (*Punch*, 5 August 1882, p. 141). Photograph courtesy of The Punch Library.

have been more variable, complex, and ambivalent than has been generally acknowledged'.[6] One needs to account for the anxieties, uncertainties, and increasing dissent of those years, the fragmented, haphazard, contentious nature of imperialism, the profound doubts about the continuation of Western progress, indeed doubts about the possibility of progress at all. There is no simple homogeneity of attitudes within these texts. The years between 1880 and 1940 are perhaps best seen as the beginning of the era of globalisation in which we live today, a process set in motion by that vast expansion of territorial colonialism in the late nineteenth century, and one that continues today through neo-colonial economic imperialism. There are those who see globalisation simply as a deceptive synonym for Westernisation, but growth of worldwide trade and communications has transformed the West as well. Dependent though colonial expansion was on technological advance, also fundamental to it was the belief in the moral and intellectual superiority of the white races. The later eighteenth and the nineteenth century had seen the invention of distinct national identities, the establishment of firm racial hierarchies, the consolidation of narratives of progress, development, scientific advance, and white supremacy; those were the ideologies that made imperialism possible. Yet the very process of colonisation meant that these clear distinctions began to dissolve: transculturation, miscegenation, the barbarism necessary to impose rule – all conspired to make the question of which was the savage and which the civilised a disturbing one to answer. Meanwhile, J. G. Frazer's influential *Golden Bough* identified savagery close beneath the surface of British society, and put Christianity on a par with pagan or primitive myth. Psychoanalysis demonstrated the fragility of civilised rationality. Suspicion of the 'masses' undermined nationalist ideologies. Identities, either of self or other, were no longer stable. Homi Bhabha has influentially written of the colonists' anxieties provoked by their colonial servants, so white in their ways, and yet not quite; these mimic men were, I would argue, just one of the disturbingly uncategorisable products of colonialism. Travel writing in this period becomes increasingly aware of globalisation – not a word used but a condition that was widely recognised – and the resulting mixtures of cultures and people it brought with it. At the same time, many writers became increasingly anxious about the condition and value of modern Western civilisation: was it and the white race degenerating? Might there be an alternative elsewhere?

Such questions were, of course, also central to imaginative literature. Any account of travel writing in this period must take note of the fact that in these years a remarkable number of novelists and poets were *travelling* writers, whether or not they were in addition actually *travel* writers, as indeed a number were. Many of the contributors to Ford's *transatlantic review* – Hemingway, Pound, Jean Rhys, H. D., Djuna Barnes, Stein, Eliot and Joyce, for example – had also acquired what he had dubbed 'the habit of flux'. Many lived much of their lives as expatriates, and most of them moved their place of abode with some frequency. From Henry James onwards, central to modernism is what Peter Nicholls has described as 'the shock of "exile" and cultural contrast'.[7] Modernism, it is widely agreed, was predominantly an urban and metropolitan movement but, significantly, many writers and artists of the period worked in someone else's metropolis; the modern metropolis was as much a contact zone, in Pratt's phrase, as were the colonies. Other writers went further afield: in the period of that late nineteenth-century and early twentieth-century imperial expansion, for example, Joseph Conrad, Rider Haggard, Rudyard Kipling, R. L. Stevenson, Jack London, and Somerset Maugham, and in the interwar years, D. H. Lawrence, E. M. Forster, Graham Greene, and Evelyn Waugh. Many incorporated their travels in parallel in fiction and travel writing, as did, for example, Stevenson, London, Lawrence, Waugh, and Greene. Modernist texts register a new consciousness of cultural heterogeneity, the condition and mark of the modern world; in both imaginative and travel writing, modernity, the meeting of other cultures, and change are inseparable.[8]

The shared concerns of imaginative literature and travel writing at this time, as well as the mobility of so many novelists and poets, perhaps account for the emergence of travel writing in the latter part of this period as the more literary and autonomous genre that we understand it to be today. Earlier travel writing often came out of travel undertaken for reasons of work, as soldier, trader, scientist, or whatever, or perhaps for education or health; increasingly in the twentieth century it has come out of travel undertaken specifically for the sake of writing about it. As Michel Butor put it, 'they travel in order to write, they travel while writing, because for them, travel *is* writing'.[9] If in the nineteenth century, travel writing might often be produced by missionaries, explorers, scientists, or Orientalists (Livingstone, Darwin, and Burton, for example) in texts in which the purveying of privileged knowledge was a central concern, increasingly in the twentieth century it has become a more subjective form, more memoir than manual, and often an alternative form of writing for novelists. The period from 1880 to 1940 saw this change take place. There was a move – as in imaginative literature – from the detailed, realist text, often with an overtly didactic or at any rate moral purpose, to a more impressionistic style with the interest focused as much on the travellers' responses or consciousness as their travels. In the twentieth century, the scientific or scholarly text is usually written for academic fellow experts and, perhaps particularly in the case of ethnography, has striven to distance itself from what it sees as the 'amateurism' of travel writing – even though travel writing can now be a profession in itself. Yet if the formal characteristics of travel writing changed over the period, many of the themes did not. Tim Youngs has argued of Victorian travelogues about Africa that their perception of that unknown land is suffused with 'their growing, if sometimes subliminal, unease with the changes in the Britain they knew so well'.[10] That double sphere of reference becomes increasingly apparent in travel writing in this period. Though doubts about the efficacy and morality of European civilisation took on a deeper resonance following the horrors of the First World War, they were already emerging in the late nineteenth century, and even the most jingoist of travellers' tales could not always gloss over the conflicts at the heart of the white civilising mission.

It is possible to see three stages of travel writing within this period. From 1880 to 1900, the long, 'realist' (not of course synonymous with reliable), instructive tale of heroic adventure remained dominant. In the years from 1900 to the First World War, the 'realist' texts have not disappeared, but much travel writing becomes less didactic, more subjective, more literary. By the inter-war years, which saw a surge in the popularity of travel and travel writing, the literary travel book had become the dominant form: many of the best known examples of the genre were written by writers equally or better known for their fiction or poetry. I shall look at some of the well-known or significant travel books from each of these periods, identifying the central trends. By the time the first of these stages had begun, the era of 'discovery' by white explorers was growing to a close, at least in already peopled areas like Africa or the Far East. Richard Burton, in the last decade of his life, now confined himself to translations of erotic Arabic works. Stanley produced one more travelogue, *In Darkest Africa*, mentioned earlier, a long and defensive book, part geographical textbook, part pious jingoism, part adventure story. Like Belloc's *Modern Traveller*, Stanley was attempting to tell as triumph what was near disaster, the story of a futile barbarous venture that had failed in almost every way except as the source for another bestseller. Stanley was an intriguing precursor of the modern professional travel writer, a journalist who went exploring specifically to produce copy, but he also represented the uglier face of nineteenth-century colonialism. His brutal racism and the readiness with which he flogged or hanged his troops or massacred villagers – always, he insisted, with justice on his side – was shocking to many even at the time. The controversies that followed the publication of his book contributed to the growing unease with the conduct of imperialists. The tales that circulated, encouraged by Stanley to conceal his own incompetence, of the excesses and abominations practised by the white leaders of his rear column were one of the likely sources for Conrad's *Heart of Darkness*.

Mary Kingsley, whose *Travels in West Africa* (1897) was also a bestseller, appears enlightened by comparison with Stanley, with her frequent warm comments on the native West Africans. She is, however, in no doubt of African inferiority to the whites, though she believes they have their own virtues, especially if missionaries' hands can be kept off them. Her lively, unorthodox, and self-mocking persona is very different from Stanley's self-presentation as a dauntless, stern, and upright hero, but her book aims to instruct just as much as his, with an array of ethnographic information about West African groups and, in particular, about their beliefs in magic and fetishes. Another woman traveller was Isabella Bird, who published one of the earliest travel books about Japan, only opened to the West in the 1850s, and a source of fascination to many Westerners. Bird herself did not take at all to Japan, and in *Unbeaten Tracks in Japan* (1880), a long and detailed account of her journey to the north of the country, she expresses deeply ambivalent feelings about 'this heathen land' which she found 'sunk in immorality', though she does make the interesting comment that the Japanese treat the aboriginal people, the Ainos, whom she met on the northern island of Yezo, rather better than the Americans treat the 'Red Indians'.[11] Bird, unlike Kingsley, was a strong supporter of missionaries and their attempts to save these heathen others, but she combined piety with prodigious energy, and had earlier written of the American West and Hawaii, and would later write of Tibet, Korea, China, Persia, and Kurdistan. Bird was one of a number of Victorian women, including Florence Nightingale and the anthropologist Mathilda Stevenson, who at home suffered ill health that immediately vanished when they got away. In the confines of Victorian domesticity they sunk despondently in invalidism; escaping to freedom and activity they flourished. One of the most eccentric travel books of the late nineteenth century was Charles Doughty's *Travels in Arabia Deserta* (1888), with its strange mixture of archaic English and Arabisms, whose language appears designed to distance the Arabs in time as much as space, as nineteenth-century thought so often did. The book was not a success at the time, and lost money for its publishers (Cambridge University Press), but it later became something of a cult book for certain modernists. Ezra Pound read it with enthusiasm to W. B. Yeats, and James Longenbach argues that it significantly influenced Yeats's writing of *A Vision*.[12] It was re-published in 1921, with a glowing introduction by T. E. Lawrence.

Two travel writers of the period point significantly forward in different ways to twentieth-century modernism. One was the trenchant critic of imperialism, the aristocratic Wilfrid Scawen Blunt, married to the granddaughter of Lord Byron, on whom he based his energetic life as supporter of liberation movements, womaniser, and poet. Blunt's aims are polemic, but he on several occasions used the device of a travel narrative, drawing on his own extensive diaries to give the authority of first-hand knowledge to his arguments. Like the younger writers whom he was to influence, Blunt rejects the ideology of Western civilised superiority, already crumbling in the new globalising world of imperialism; he constructs an alternative to the hegemonic racial hierarchy of the West against the rest, in his case by a return to a feudal model. The modern British abroad, he believes, are destroying ordered and admirable societies, just as they have done at home. Blunt, like Ford, was a romantic Tory; he had a warm if condescending regard for the peasantry and a belief in aristocracy; the new middle classes at home or abroad are what he distrusts. He wrote of his visit to Algeria:

> I found my sympathies in Algeria going out wholly to the Arabs . . . The contrast between their noble pastoral life on the one hand, with their camel herds and horses, a life of high tradition filled with the memory of heroic deeds, and on the other hand the ignoble squalor of the Frank settlers, with their wineshops and their swine, was one which could not escape us, or fail to rouse in us an angry sense of the incongruity which has made of these last the lords of the land and of those their servants.[13]

For Blunt, imposing Western modernity only brings degradation and misery. He argues that the policy of 'developing' India (his inverted commas) with money raised from taxation on the peasants means that 'the inhabitants will have, sooner or later, to resort to cannibalism, for there will be nothing but each other left to eat'.[14] That Western civilisation will produce cannibalism rather than stamp it out is a neat rhetorical turn in an era in which supposed cannibalism in the Congo was used as an excuse for imperialist plunder, but his sympathy for the peasantry goes along with his admiration of Indian intellectuals and leaders, who he insists are perfectly capable of self-government. In his account of these Indians, as in his attitude to Arabi Pasha, who led the fight for Egyptian liberation, or to the Bedouin sheiks, there is a remarkable sense of his acceptance of them as equals. (Westernised Jewish financiers were another matter.) In India he was shocked by the way the British lived their social lives segregated from the Indians, but disturbingly puts forward the idea that relations have deteriorated in India since the civil service examinations made it possible for the middle classes to become colonial servants. Blunt's admirable resistance to most contemporary racial stereotypes is inextricably bound up with his reactionary class attitudes.

Blunt's friends Lady Gregory and W. B. Yeats were among those who followed him in his admiration of the peasantry and aristocracy, rejecting the 'filthy modern tide' of English commerce,[15] and Blunt's other admirer, Pound, developed the idea of the artist as a kind of aristocrat, who despises the bourgeoisie but not the artists of other cultures. Another travel writer whose work presages that of the modernist period was the Irish-Greek Lafcadio Hearn, something of a nomad himself, who wrote principally about Japan, unlike Isabella Bird finding it entrancing. Hearn was another of the intellectuals increasingly pessimistic about Western modernity, and he created a picture of a Japan that was wise, calm, beauty-loving, and mysterious, a 'fictive nation' that *became* Japan for a generation in the West, though Hearn himself soon began to despair of the Japanese desire to modernise.[16] Influenced by the French writer, Pierre Loti, his work is impressionist rather than realist, as the title of his first book on the country, *Glimpses of Unfamiliar Japan* (1894) indicates, marking something of a modest retreat from the claims of the Western omniscient gaze. Although Hearn failed to learn Japanese, his evocative descriptions of the role of poetry in Japanese life and his aestheticising vision of Japanese culture helped to raise the interest of modernist poets like Pound in forms such as the haiku, as significant in the evolution of modernist poetry as the discovery of Japanese art had been earlier for impressionist and post-impressionist artists.[17]

The period between 1900 and the First World War, seen in retrospect as a golden calm before the cataclysmic storm, was in fact a deeply unsettled period outside Europe. Russia was defeated in the East by Japan in 1905, an event that shocked the West, which had not credited that a non-European power would be able to defeat a European one. (Russia then suffered a revolution which, though unsuccessful, presaged yet more profound shocks to come in 1917.) The Ottoman Empire collapsed in 1908, and the Chinese Empire in 1911, whilst there were pre-war revolutions in Mexico, Persia, and Morocco. In the wake of these upheavals, rivalries between the European powers for spheres of influence were to play their part in bringing about the European conflict. However, if the consequences of this distant turmoil were as yet unsuspected, no doubt its existence is one reason that many of the better-known travel works of this period stay nearer home. Europe, and particularly southern Europe, continued to fascinate both British and American writers. Belloc moved from parody to actual travel writing with his 1902 book, *The Path to Rome*, which he illustrated with sketches he made on his travels. It is a rambling, meditative, anecdotal book, interspersed with conversations between the 'Lector' and 'Auctor'; nineteenth-century didacticism is already evaporating. Evelyn Waugh protested later that Belloc had invented a new and most uncongenial kind of modern traveller, one who insists on avoiding modern comfort precisely because it is there. 'All the world is my oyster', Waugh quotes Belloc as saying, 'since men made railways and gave me leave to keep off them'.[18] But travelling in ostentatious discomfort was not new – Robert Louis Stevenson had, one could argue, invented that kind of European traveller much earlier, and certainly Victorian African travelogues describe with relish, and one suspects embellishment, the hardships endured, though admittedly the possibility of modern travel was not for them on offer.

Yet there are two features of Belloc's book which, if not new, were to become increasingly pervasive. Firstly, there is his desire to put a distance between himself as traveller and the burgeoning droves of tourists. Belloc's book is an account of a pilgrimage on foot through Germany, France, and Italy to Rome, and he is dismissive of the tourists that he sees on a passing train, who 'seemed to [him] common and worthless people, and sad into the bargain'.[19] Such dismay at the democratisation of travel was widely shared among travel writers, many of whom showed the same suspicion of popular travel that modernists exhibited towards popular culture in general. Secondly, Belloc's book describes by-ways, not the famous sights, again an example of a wider shift, for it was no longer easy for books about European travel to present the traditional Grand Tour style homage to its cultural heritage. As Edith Wharton shrewdly realised, now that Baedeker was there to describe authoritatively every famous church and statue, travel writers had to find other approaches. She negotiates this in her 1905 travel book, *Italian Backgrounds*, by insisting that Italy is 'a foreground and a background. The foreground is the property of the guide-book and of its product, the mechanical sight-seer; the background, that of the dawdler, the dreamer and the serious student of Italy', such, of course, as herself.[20] Wharton always travelled in comfort, but she too was turning to the by-ways and, like Belloc, she is keen to make clear that 'sight-seers' or tourists are quite different from travellers like herself. Travel writers, if at all possible, wanted to write of areas for which guide-books could not be purchased – Wharton achieved that, or so she thought, with her 1920 book *In Morocco*[21] – and preferably to which Thomas Cook did not run tours. Wharton's *Italian Backgrounds* contrasts tellingly with Henry James's 1884 travel book, *A Little Tour in France*, an account of a journey around provincial French cities; James covers all their major sights, and quite happily describes himself as a tourist.

Although James also published collections of essays about Italy and England, mainly written in his first years in Europe, his finest travel writing is not about Europe, but came out of his visit, in 1904–5, to the United States, after twenty-five years' absence. *The American Scene* (1907) describes a journey from New England to Florida, covering explorations around city streets and views from behind the plate glass of Pullman cars. All travel writing is a form of autobiography, and this book is sometimes considered as the first in the series of James's late autobiographical writings. It has all the complexity of response of his novels; James describes how his visit brings back his childhood, and yet offers him a country disturbingly changed, so that interpreting it is 'like the spelling out of foreign sentences of which one knows but half the words'.[22] James attempts to be scrupulously honest, not so much about the American scene as about his own response to it, and he writes in his preface that 'I would take my stand on my gathered impressions, since it was all for them, for them only, that I returned; I would in fact go to the stake for them' (p. 3). The book was criticised for what was seen as James's snobbish distaste for American modernity, and more recently for his ambivalent responses to the numbers of immigrants that had entered the States since his departure. Yet his reactions are never simple, and he is fascinated with the cultural changes that a new environment brings – not that he thinks them necessarily for the best, particularly in the case of the Italians. In addition, he is well aware of the irony of American suspicion of immigrants. 'Which', he asks, 'is the American...which is *not* the alien?' (p. 95) This is in the chapter called paradoxically 'Aliens at Home', an apt term for much of the migratory modern world. The international theme is as present in this travel memoir as in any of his novels.

Pound, who described *The American Scene* as the 'triumph of the author's long practice',[23] also wrote an account of his own return visit, after a mere two years, to the States. Like James, Pound has ambivalent feelings about American modernity, though unlike James, who describes New York as a 'huge jagged city' with a skyline like a 'broken hair-comb turned up' (p. 106), he admires its architecture, and is bewitched by the city at night: 'Squares after squares of flame, set and cut into the aether. Here is our poetry, for we have pulled down the stars to our will.'[24] Like James, however, he decides that it is a country inimical to creative activity, quoting James's own comment: 'It is strange how all taint of art or letters seems to shun that continent' (p. 20). Ironically, just three months after the last instalment of *Patria Mia* appeared in *The New Age*, the Armory Show, the famous exhibition of modernist art that marked the beginning of a new era, took place in New York, and American modernist art and writing exploded.

One traveller who went beyond Europe in those years – apart that is from the bold Polar explorers – was Gertrude Bell, one of a number of travel writers in the Middle East, including T. E. Lawrence and Freya Stark, who became intimately involved with the British political interests in the area. She came to know the region first through family connections in the diplomatic services, and her works are, like the earlier travelogues, detailed and informative. Although she admits she is not travelling on 'ground virgin to the traveller', she wants to expand and correct previous accounts.[25] Her opening to her first book, *The Desert and the Sown* (1907), though it does not address the question of gender, suggests powerfully the particular joys for women at that period in escaping home ties through travel:

> To those bred under an elaborate social order few such moments of exhilaration can come as that which stands at the threshold of wild travel. The gates of the enclosed garden are thrown open, the chain at the entrance to the sanctuary is lowered, with a wary glance to right and left you step forth and behold! the immeasurable world.   (p. 1)

Yet Bell, like Kingsley, was fiercely anti-feminist; perhaps subverting women's rôles in practice made it too alarming to subvert them in theory as well.

During the First World War military mobilisation meant that leisure travel had to cease. D. H. Lawrence's first travel book, *Twilight in Italy* (1916), appeared during the war, though it recorded his pre-war visit, whilst the other Lawrence (T. E.) put his wartime experiences, or his version of them, into one of the most famous and controversial of travel books on the Middle East, *The Seven Pillars of Wisdom* (1926). Ironically, one of the most pervasive moods in travel writing of the inter-war years is a certain world-weariness, springing from disillusionment with European civilisation and dismay at its impact on the rest of the world. T. S. Eliot – for whom journeying and displacement are constant motifs, although he was not a travel writer himself – encapsulates many of the themes of inter-war travel writing in *The Waste Land*: sordid metropolis, fragmentation, tawdry present, jumbled cultures, the flotsam and jetsam of a decayed civilisation, nostalgia for an earlier, lovelier world, fear of past and future horrors. The word 'seedy' that Graham Greene uses to sum up Liberia in *Journey Without Maps* (1936) could apply to many of the depictions of travellers' destinations – and departure points – at this time.

This sense of an older, more aesthetic world in the throes of decay was not entirely new. Mary Louise Pratt has argued that travel writing in the eighteenth and nineteenth centuries '*produced* "the rest of the world" for Europeans' (*Imperial Eyes*, p. 5), but creeping into the travel writing of the late nineteenth century and beyond is the fear that 'the rest of the world' is losing its distinctive otherness, and the perturbing recognition that the lines of demarcation between Europe and the other are becoming disturbingly blurred. Most travel writers now wrote of areas whose repertoire of characteristics had been well established; what becomes increasingly evident is that the repertoire is no longer what it was. Rod Edmond has pointed out that travellers to the South Pacific in the nineteenth century already found it hard to avoid acknowledging the destruction of a world earlier depicted as an innocent paradise; indeed, as he says, the 'legible evidence of Western diseases on blemished native bodies haunted Western writing about the Pacific from the early moments of contact'.[26] This only too literal contact zone had become a zone of sexual disease, contamination, and death, as R. L. Stevenson makes clear in his melancholy account of the region, *In the South Seas* (1896). Travel writers became increasingly aware that they were describing fragmented, hybridised cultures, the shabby remnants of the tapestry of otherness their predecessors had woven. If this was the era of 'salvage anthropology' for ethnographers who felt their subjects were rapidly disappearing from the globe, it was also, for some, the era of 'salvage travel writing'. Stevenson believes he is depicting a dying race, soon to be no more. For others, modernity, in the shape of tourists if not colonialists, is about to sweep away the picturesque customs they have come to seek. Edith Wharton, a warm admirer of French colonialism, writes regretfully in *In Morocco*: 'In spite of the incessant efforts of the present French administration to preserve the old monuments of Morocco from injury, and her native arts and industries from the corruption of European bad taste, the impression of mystery and remoteness which the country now produces must inevitably vanish with the approach of the "Circular Ticket"'.[27] For Wharton, one might note, as for many intellectuals of her day, there is no simple hierarchy between the West and the rest. The native arts are superior to Western vulgarity, even if the best of the West is superior to both.

Change came more slowly to the Middle East, which, thanks largely to the power of the Ottoman Empire, while it lasted, and to its Islamic beliefs, remained amenable for longer to familiar and reassuring exoticisation, perhaps one reason for its popularity as subject matter. Yet, even there, modernity began to enter in the inter-war years. Freya Stark begins her 1932 *Baghdad Sketches*, the first of some twenty travel books she wrote about the region:

> In a very short time a railway will link Baghdad with Europe.
>
> Even now the crossing of the desert is an every day affair, and although the Nairn Motor Transport do what they can, and cook your breakfast-sausage romantically for you in the open desert over a fire of camelthorn, with an paraffin box ready to help in case of need, they do not quite succeed, one must admit, in giving the true nomadic feeling to any except most innocent travellers.[28]

Freya Stark, like others in the twenties and thirties, mocks those who continue to dream of exotic otherness. Yet if travel writing had become deliberately anti-romantic, it was in addition anti-heroic. Peter Fleming – the brother of Ian – says insouciantly in his 'Foreword' to *Brazilian Adventure*, that although 'in treating of the Great Unknown one has a free hand, and my few predecessors in this particular field had made great play with the Terrors of the Jungle', he himself had found that 'the hardships and privations were of a very minor order, the dangers which we ran were considerably less than those to be encountered on any arterial road during a heat wave'.[29] In *Labels: A Mediterranean Journey*, Waugh cheerfully informs his readers that he has gone on his travels as a device to keep his name in the public eye. He refuses to emulate the professional travel writer who finds 'a peculiar relish in discomfort. Bed bugs, frightful food, inefficient ships and trains, hostile customs, police and passport officers, consuls who will not cash cheques, excesses of heat and cold, night club champagne and even imprisonment are his peculiar delights'. Nor however, does he wish to be like 'those pitiable droves of Middle West schoolteachers whom one encounters suddenly at street corners and in public buildings, baffled, breathless, their heads singing with unfamiliar names ... How their eyes haunt us long after they have passed on to the next phase of their itinerary – haggard and uncomprehending eyes, mildly resentful, like those of animals in pain, eloquent of that world-weariness we all feel at the dead weight of European culture' (p. 36). Animal imagery, used by earlier travellers to describe savage others, is now applied to the hapless American tourists. Refusal of a heroic posture does not make Waugh's judgments any less confident; Waugh's travel writing is ruthless satire, like his novels, and is as much about his fellow-travellers as about indigenous inhabitants. European culture, middle-class tourists, and foreign lands have neither worth nor glamour. Yet if Waugh implies his own superiority, it is not a superiority that he feels his compatriots or even his class necessarily share. Tellingly, one of the few groups that he admires are the Kenyan colonials, with 'their wish to transplant and perpetuate a habit of life traditional to them, which England has ceased to accommodate – the traditional life of the English squirearchy'.[30] Like Blunt and indeed Eliot, he turned to a myth of a previous ordered, hierarchical, spiritual age, and embraced religion the year he published *Labels*, though he became a Catholic, like Blunt, while Eliot had taken the much more English line, perhaps necessary for an unhappy anglophile American, of becoming a High Churchman.

Paul Fussell suggests in his study of travel writers of this period that travel in the inter-war years often appeared to be more about escaping from England than anything else.[31] Travellers might not think much of what they found elsewhere, but at least it was not home; hence Evelyn Waugh's gloomy conclusion on his return in *Remote Places*: 'Just watch London knock spots off the Dark Continent' (p. 240). Yet some travellers still went in hope: Lawrence, for all his bitterness against post-war England, was not just escaping. His travels were energised by a passionate quasi-primitivist quest; he longed for a truer, simpler, more intense way of being, and was endlessly disappointed. Lawrence loathed modern hybridity; he wanted to seek out the pure essence of the people he visited. Rebecca West describes how he would go 'straight from the railway station to his hotel and immediately sit down and hammer out articles about the place, vehemently and exhaustively describing the temperament of the people'.[32] Lawrence writes with extraordinary lyricism and vitality, but he writes, even more than most travel writers, about imaginary others. Ironically, there is often more description and evocation of place in his fiction than his travel writing, in which it is the nature of these others that he obsessively pursues. In *Mornings in Mexico* (1927) he creates his own intoxicated version of the Indian soul. He despises the Indians with whom he has contact, his servant and the local villagers, who live a mongrel half-European, half-Indian existence, but when he comes to describe their dances he insists that 'so long as he is pure' the Indian is in touch with the vital universe, unlike the modern European or American, trapped in their mechanical existence.[33] For the Indians, he says, 'Creation is a great flood, for ever flowing, in lovely and terrible waves. In everything, the shimmer of creation, and never the finality of the created' (p. 61). Yet Indians are 'mindless', their religion is 'animistic... dark and impersonal' (p. 89). They have their limitations, as does the modern world, and neither can satisfy him. Only in his loving reconstruction of the long lost Etruscan civilisation did he find solace, and even then *Etruscan Places* (1932) ends with Lawrence's raging against the Florentine museum's attempt to systemise Etruscan culture.

Other novelists in this period turned to travel writing. Orwell wrote some essays about his experiences in colonial Burma, but as a travel writer he is most famous for books like *Down and Out in Paris and London* (1933) and *The Road to Wigan Pier* (1937), written in the long tradition of the middle-class ethnographer – Mayhew, Booth or London – uncovering the dark underside of civilisation, in which the lower classes are discovered to be, metaphorically speaking, a race apart. Graham Greene wrote a couple of bleak and troubled travel books, which were spiritual as well as geographical journeys, expeditions into an inner 'heart of darkness', as he says of his visit to Liberia.[34] Robert Byron, who wrote one of the most famous travel books of this period, *The Road to Oxiana* (1937), confined himself to travel writing. Like Fleming and Orwell, he was an old Etonian – Fleming, when he applied to join the expedition to Brazil, mentioned his school, knowing the selectors would consider that 'an Old Boy is worth two young men' (*Brazilian Adventure*, p. 16). Certainly Byron had a web of influential connections, untroubled self-confidence, the command of several languages, and a rich range of cultural reference, all useful characteristics in a traveller, and some of which might be attributable to his schooling. His book is passionate and urbane, witty and politically acute. Byron is sharply aware of the Nazi threat, Britain's dubious scheming in its Middle Eastern intrigues, and the corruption of the puppet regimes the West maintains there in power. His book has a modernist timbre – it is composed of brief, sometimes quite imagistic, sporadic diary jottings, surprising juxtapositions, letters, reported conversations, historical facts, and anecdotes. Much is not explained, with the reader left to fill in: only near the end does one discover why this journey has been undertaken. Like his fellow writers, Byron has little time for the motley present, although he warmly acknowledges kindness when he meets it, and thinks longingly of good food and wine and comfortable beds; but his passion is early Islamic architecture, which he journeys to find in Afghanistan, and which gives him enormous pleasure and satisfaction, emotions rarely in evidence in other travel writing at the time. Yet all through the book the political menace is there as a dark undercurrent. By the time Byron's book was published many were fleeing out of Europe, in search not of adventure but of safety; Byron himself died in 1941, still on the move, on a boat torpedoed in the Mediterranean, in the words of Lawrence's late poem, his own travelling 'Ship of Death'.

NOTES

1 Ford Madox Ford, *The English Novel* [1930] (Manchester: Carcanet, 1983), p. 9.
2 Stephen Kern, *The Culture of Time and Space, 1880–1918* (Cambridge, Mass.: Harvard University Press, 1983), p. 213.
3 Eric Hobsbawm, *The Age of Empire 1875–1914* (London: Cardinal, 1987), p. 59.
4 Hilaire Belloc, *The Modern Traveller* (London: Edward Arnold, 1898), pp. 25, 41.
5 Mary Louise Pratt, *Imperial Eyes: Travel Writing and Transculturation* (London: Routledge, 1992).
6 Nicholas Thomas, *Colonialism's Culture: Anthropology, Travel and Government* (Cambridge: Polity, 1994), p. 17.
7 Peter Nicholls, *Modernisms: A Literary Guide* (London: Macmillan, 1995), p. 165.
8 See Helen Carr, 'Imagism and Empire', in *Modernism and Empire*, ed. Howard Booth and Nigel Rigby (Manchester University Press, 2000), pp. 64–92.
9 Michel Butor, 'Travel and Writing', in *Temperamental Journeys: Essays on the Modern Literature of Travel*, ed. Michael Kowalewski (Athens: University of Georgia Press, 1992), p. 67.
10 Tim Youngs, *Travellers in Africa: British Travelogues 1850–1900* (Manchester University Press, 1994), p. 1.
11 Isabella Bird, *Unbeaten Tracks in Japan* (London: John Murray, 1880), vol. I, p. 390; vol. II, pp. 347, 8.
12 James Longenbach, *Stone Cottage: Pound, Yeats and Modernism* (Oxford University Press, 1988), p. 145.
13 Wilfrid Scawen Blunt, *The Secret History of the English Occupation of Egypt* (London: Fisher Unwin, 1907), p. 5.
14 Wilfrid Scawen Blunt, *Ideas about India* (London: Kegan, Paul, Trench & Co, 1885), pp. xvi–xvii.
15 W. B. Yeats, *The Poems: A New Edition*, ed. Richard J. Finneran (London: Macmillan, 1983), p. 337.

16 Carl Dawson uses Roland Barthes's phrase to describe Hearn's picture of Japan in his book, *Lafcadio Hearn and the Vision of Japan* (Baltimore: Johns Hopkins Press, 1992), p. 157.

17 See Carr, 'Imagism and Empire', especially pp. 69–72, for a discussion of the influence of the haiku.

18 Evelyn Waugh, *Labels: A Mediterranean Journey* (London: Duckworth, 1930), p. 35.

19 Hilaire Belloc, *The Path to Rome* [1902] (London: Nelson, 1917), p. 168.

20 Edith Wharton, *Italian Backgrounds* (London: Macmillan, 1905), p. 177.

21 Gareth Stanton points out her mistake in 'The Oriental City: a North African Itinerary', *Third Text*, 3, 4 (1988): 22.

22 Henry James, *The American Scene* [1907] (Harmondsworth: Penguin, 1994), p. 5.

23 *Literary Essays of Ezra Pound* (London: Faber, 1954), p. 327.

24 *Patria Mia* was first published in *The New Age* in 1912, then in revised form as a book in 1950: Ezra Pound, *Patria Mia and Treatise on Harmony* (London: Peter Owen, 1962), p. 19.

25 Gertrude Bell, *The Desert and the Sown* (London: Heinemann, 1907), p. x.

26 Rod Edmond, *Representing the South Pacific: Colonial Discourse from Cook to Gauguin* (Cambridge University Press, 1997), p. 194.

27 Edith Wharton, *In Morocco* (London: Macmillan, 1920), p. ix; Gareth Stanton in 'The Oriental City' notes her laments for the spoliation of North African cities.

28 Freya Stark, *Baghdad Sketches* (Baghdad: The Times Press, 1932), p. 1.

29 Peter Fleming, *Brazilian Adventure* (London: Jonathan Cape, 1933), p. 9.

30 Evelyn Waugh, *Remote People* (London: Duckworth, 1931), pp. 182–3.

31 Paul Fussell, *Abroad: British Literary Traveling Between the Wars* (Oxford University Press, 1980).

32 Edward Nehls, *D. H. Lawrence: A Composite Biography* (Madison: University of Wisconsin Press, 1957), vol. II, p. 62.

33 D. H. Lawrence, *Mornings in Mexico; Etruscan Places* (Harmondsworth: Penguin, 1950), p. 63.

34 Graham Greene, *Journey Without Maps* (London: William Heinemann, 1936), p. 294.

5

PETER HULME

Travelling to write (1940–2000)

In December 1933 Patrick Leigh Fermor set out to walk from Rotterdam to Constantinople, a journey across many of the parts of Europe which would soon be devastated by fascism and war. After distinguished military service in Crete, Fermor made his career as a travel writer, finally narrating his account of that epic pre-war walk in *A Time of Gifts* and *Between the Woods and the Waters*. His compendious learning and literary style link Fermor to the 1930s tradition of Robert Byron and Peter Fleming discussed in the previous chapter. But *A Time of Gifts* was not published until 1977, coinciding with a raft of books by younger writers – notably Paul Theroux, Peter Matthiessen, Bruce Chatwin, and Robyn Davidson – which in different ways announced a decisive shift in modern travel writing and which will provide the pivot for this chapter's survey.

Post-war voices

Fermor's first travel book, written after an extensive post-war tour of the West Indies, was *The Traveller's Tree* (1950). Winner of the Heinemann Foundation Prize for Literature, *The Traveller's Tree* signalled – in the continuity of its voice with pre-war writers – that a bridge had been successfully thrown over the turbulent decade of the 1940s, and that English gentlemen were still able to travel the world and to write with witty nonchalance about what they encountered. Wilfred Thesiger, Eric Newby, and Norman Lewis are other members of Fermor's generation whose work spans the entire second half of the twentieth century and has proved enduringly popular.[1]

Of these writers it is Thesiger who seems most firmly positioned within earlier traditions of travel and exploration. His two major books, *Arabian Sands* (1959) and *The Marsh Arabs* (1964), demonstrate his prolonged immersion in forms of desert life in Arabia and marsh culture in Iraq which have now virtually vanished, giving his work substantial ethnographic value (as discussed by Billie Melman in Chapter 6). His celebration of the Arabs' ancient spirit and his own flight from the materialism that will eventually change the Arabs' world tint his work with a nostalgia reinforced by the romance of a strongly masculine asceticism. Yet, although Thesiger's themes may look old-fashioned (even for their time), interest in the nomadic life has remained a constant theme in subsequent travel writing, as witnessed by Geoffrey Moorhouse's *The Fearful Void* (1974), Bruce Chatwin's *The Songlines* (1988), and Robyn Davidson's *Desert Places* (1996).

Thesiger makes a brief appearance at the end of Eric Newby's *A Short Walk in the Hindu Kush* (1958), when their two parties meet. Newby calls Thesiger 'a remarkable throwback to the Victorian era, a fluent speaker of Arabic, a very brave man, who has twice crossed the Empty Quarter and, apart from a few weeks every year has passed his entire life among primitive peoples'.[2] Thesiger offers a brief rant – 'England's going to pot' (p. 283) – before he is allowed to speak the book's final words when he sees Newby and his travelling companion, Hugh Carless, blowing up a pair of airbeds: 'God, you must be a couple of pansies' (p. 284). Thesiger is the real thing, a genuine explorer, committed to the 'primitive' peoples among whom he spends his life, while Newby – on his own presentation – is the bumbling newcomer wedded to Western comforts. Both are amateurs, but their contrasting images at the end of Newby's book marks the change in the significance of that word over the course of the twentieth century; and it was Newby's blend of amateurism which largely set the tone for popular travel writing in the second half of the century. In his preface to *A Short Walk*, Evelyn Waugh pinpointed the book's qualities:

> It exemplifies the essential traditional (some, not I, will say deplorable) amateurism of the English. For more than two hundred years now Englishmen have been wandering about the world for their amusement, suspect everywhere as government agents, to the great embarrassment of our officials . . . And in his writing [Newby] has all the marks of his not entirely absurd antecedents. The understatement, the self-ridicule, the delight in the foreignness of foreigners, the complete denial of any attempt to enlist the sympathies of his readers in the hardships he has capriciously invited.   (viii–ix)

In retrospect, though, particularly as travel writing rediscovers its connections with journalism and cultural history, Norman Lewis's career is the one which seems best to define the mainstream: a broad range of political interests, a lack of affectation, a robust sense of the value of the independent travelling voice, an ability to take minor hardships in its stride in order to report on what is happening in parts of the world which do not necessarily feature on the global news. Lewis made his reputation with his travels in

Asia, recounted in *A Dragon Apparent: Travels in Indo-China* (1951) and *Golden Earth: Travels in Burma* (1952); but he has travelled through and reported on most parts of the world in later books such as *Cuban Passage* (1982), *A Goddess in the Stones: Travels in India* (1991), and *An Empire of the East: Travels in Indonesia* (1993).

Travel and mobility and international relations were all crucial dimensions of modernism. As the previous chapter demonstrates, travel writing was not usually seen as the basis of a literary career before the Second World War. Only Robert Byron and Alec Waugh (Evelyn's brother) provide significant exceptions: Byron was killed in 1941, but Alec Waugh's career as travel writer continued into the 1960s.[3] For the post-war generation, travel writing could become the basis of a writing career – perhaps because those who had just fought a war felt the need for the kind of direct engagement with social and political issues that journalism and travel writing seemed to offer.[4]

When a major writer again combined fiction with travel writing, a decisively new voice and new trajectory were involved, since V. S. Naipaul – already acclaimed for his novel *A House for Mr Biswas* (1961) – was returning to the islands of his West Indian 'home' from Britain in order to write the travel book, *The Middle Passage* (1962). The complexities of this move are worth spelling out. Naipaul was writing during the height of decolonisation, with the West Indian islands deeply engaged in discussions about the nature and form of post-colonial independence. Britain, meanwhile, was involved in heated debates about the impact of post-war immigration, especially from the West Indies. Naipaul's ideological self-location was clearly metropolitan and his evident impatience with the West Indian islands made his book controversial, as did the use, by a writer of Indian ancestry whose family had arrived in the Caribbean by a different, if only marginally less traumatic route from that of slaves, of a title indelibly associated with the slave trade. Subsequently, in no fewer than three travel books, of increasing complexity, Naipaul has written about India, a country he returns to at least in part for complex reasons of personal heritage.[5] Naipaul's later fiction, such as *The Enigma of Arrival* (1987) and *A Way in the World* (1994) perhaps belongs to a still emergent genre: allusive and literary meditations, with elements of autobiography and travel writing.

Although there had been plenty of women travel writers in the first part of the century, and although one of the few important travel books published during the Second World War was Rebecca West's *Black Lamb and Grey Falcon* (1942), the post-war tradition was male-dominated well into the 1970s.[6] Only one woman travel writer, Dervla Murphy, has a long career during this period. Indeed, given that she conceived her first journey, from

Ireland to India on a bicycle, in 1941, that career is almost as long as Fermor's and Lewis's; but she was only ten at the time, and did not make the journey until 1962.[7] Like her male counterparts, Murphy has travelled widely and written about many parts of the world, though she has a particular association with south Asia. Her *Muddling Through in Madagascar* (1985) takes its epigraph from the *OED* definition of her title phrase: 'to attain one's ends in spite of blunder after blunder' – which serves to place her within the mainstream tradition of travel writers' self-deprecation. But she also takes her young daughter with her, which introduces a rather different set of concerns.

New forms (or, the leopard, the giant sloth, and four camels)

V. S. Naipaul acted as a mentor for the US writer, Paul Theroux, one of the quartet whose work in the late 1970s marks the beginnings of the most recent upsurge of interest in travel writing.[8] Theroux's innovation was the invention of an American persona which combined the rough edges of the hard-bitten traveller with the learning and literariness of his European counterparts. His first two books, *The Great Railway Bazaar: By Train Through Asia* (1975) and *The Old Patagonian Express* (1979) cleverly used the older but ordinary mode of travel by train to places (Siberia, Patagonia) remote from his readership. Planning his routes with timetable in hand, Theroux established the respectability of a mode of travel accessible to his readers but long since associated with the regimentation of tourism. His example proved infectious, and his boundless enthusiasm for travel and for writing about it has kept his work at the forefront of the genre.[9] However, although a forceful writer, Theroux reinvigorated rather than reformulated the genre; and, in retrospect, three books contemporary with his railway journeys mark more significant turning points.

Peter Matthiessen had been a traveller and a writer since the mid-1950s, with numerous scientific expeditions under his belt and a solid reputation established for his fiction and non-fiction, but *The Snow Leopard*, first published in 1978, was acclaimed as a book of a quite different order. Organised as a quest, undertaken with the renowned zoologist George Schaller (who went to study the blue sheep of the region), in search of the rare Himalayan snow leopard, *The Snow Leopard* reintroduced spirituality and earnestness to travel writing, with Matthiessen producing a pilgrimage into the unknown where the physical travel doubles as, and intensifies, an inner journey. This was not just a memoir, but a powerfully confessional book in which the author struggles for spiritual renewal while mourning and reflecting on the death of his wife:

I feel great gratitude for being here, for *being*, rather, for there is no need to tie oneself to the snow mountains in order to feel free. I am not here to seek the 'crazy wisdom'; if I am, I shall never find it. I am here to be here, like these rocks and sky and snow, like this hail that is falling out of the sun.[10]

The Snow Leopard's urgent and immediate tone is partly a product of its journal format and insistent use of the present tense, giving the impression that one is reading lines written on the move and in response to shifts of weather and consciousness.[11] As Matthiessen comes to terms with his failure to see a snow leopard, he learns lessons about himself and his desires, and turns back towards the world of humanity, guided by the example of the Sherpa, Tutken, whom he comes to regard as his teacher.

Whereas Matthiessen was an experienced traveller and writer breaking through to wider recognition, Bruce Chatwin's *In Patagonia* (1977) and Robyn Davidson's *Tracks* (1980) were first books by young and unknown authors, English and Australian respectively. *In Patagonia* tells the story of the narrator's quest for a piece of mylodon skin to replace the example he had admired in his grandmother's house as a child in Birmingham, but which was later lost. The skin proves almost as elusive as Matthiessen's snow leopard, but whereas the quest for the living animal is an ever-present factor which supplies constant metaphorical subtexts for Matthiessen's journey, Chatwin's quest is constantly ironised, frequently forgotten, and only finally fulfilled in a distinctly unheroic and almost surreal fashion. But the book's laconic and elliptical style, its ninety-seven short sections averaging little more than a couple of pages each, seemed finally to bring a modernist aesthetics to a fundamentally nineteenth-century genre. In print, Chatwin was as offhand about his actual travelling as Matthiessen was earnest, yet both were committed writers, shaping their respective books into twin landmarks of contemporary travel writing.

Tracks may be less formally innovative than the other two books, but made its mark through the sheer difficulty of the expedition to walk across 1,700 miles of Australian desert and bush with four camels and a dog, and the freshness of its narrative persona. Davidson's feminism and anti-racism articulated the views of a new generation and showed how a genre long associated with colonial and imperial attitudes could be freed from some of that heritage. Though both are concerned with inner as well as physical journeys, the contrast between Matthiessen and Davidson can be gauged from their respective epigraphs: Rilke on visions and the spirit world, Doris Lessing on crossing a desert and shedding burdens.

The comparison and contrast between all three writers can be extended. Nepal, Central Australia, and Patagonia all provide difficult, occasionally arduous conditions, betokening a seriousness of purpose. Matthiessen takes this further, pushing beyond the snow line, and largely beyond the line of social relationships, except for those involving his travelling companions, most of whom are Sherpas. Freezing temperatures and deep snow have a particular symbolic resonance, connecting *The Snow Leopard* with the long history of both polar and mountain exploration and travel writing. Davidson's journey across the deserts of western Australia brings her into contact with aboriginal communities, but she also writes with unusual openness about her relationship with her sponsors, *National Geographic*, turning the financing of travel writing into part of its subject matter.[12] Chatwin remains a more obviously social writer, largely dependent on the anecdotes he can collect from the eccentric characters he meets – or perhaps one should say from the people he meets whom his writing turns into eccentric characters. *The Snow Leopard* and *Tracks* are personal books, openly embracing the journey as a form of therapy. In contrast, Chatwin has little directly to say about himself, standing firmly in the modernist tradition of authorial self-effacement.

Two contrasts are particularly telling. At the front of *The Snow Leopard* and *Tracks* are maps tracing Matthiessen's and Davidson's routes, which are singular and precise: there is no backtracking, no deviation – just single-mindedness and originality. The map in *In Patagonia* has no route line, nor does the text allow the reader to piece together Chatwin's actual movements since the chronology is discontinuous. *The Snow Leopard* is traditionally and masculinely heroic in its defiant originality, *In Patagonia* anti-heroic in its cheerful willingness to acknowledge earlier writers, such as E. Lucas Bridges's (heroic) *Uttermost Part of the Earth* (1948).[13] *Tracks* acknowledges technical difficulties and set-backs in a very non-masculine way, but is also defiantly heroic, in a feminist register, about its author's ability to learn about and control the camels on which she relies.

The three works also share an ethnographic dimension in their concern for the fate of indigenous cultures and their appreciation of indigenous lifeways and thinking. In this sense all three operate in the shadow of Claude Lévi-Strauss's seminal autobiography-cum-travel-book-cum-ethnography, *Tristes Tropiques* (1955), which famously raised the problem of the relationship between anthropology and travel writing in its opening sentences:

> I hate travelling and explorers. Yet here I am proposing to tell the story of my expeditions . . . Adventure has no place in the anthropologist's profession; it is merely one of those unavoidable drawbacks, which detract from his effective work through the incidental loss of weeks or months . . . The fact that so much effort and expenditure has to be wasted on reaching the object of our studies bestows no value on that aspect of our profession, and should be seen rather as its negative side.[14]

Lévi-Strauss's pointed remarks are reflected in Matthiessen's own Amazonian travel book *The Cloud Forest* (1961) and the related novel *At Play in the Fields of the Lord* (1965) – contextualised in Neil Whitehead's essay (Chapter 7); as well as in Matthiessen's later engagement with American Indian life in the USA in the travel book, *Indian Country* (1984), and the huge and powerful investigative volume about the miscarriage of justice which sent Leonard Peltier to gaol, *In the Spirit of Crazy Horse* (1983). Lévi-Strauss's leitmotif of ethnographic mourning, emblematised in the *tristesse* of his title, is equally, if more obliquely, applicable to *In Patagonia*, whose epigraph offers its own sadness in the French poet, Blaise Cendrars' famous line, 'Il n'y a plus que la Patagonie, la Patagonie, qui convienne mon immense tristesse...' [Only Patagonia, Patagonia, can match my immense sadness]. The genocide of the Indians of Patagonia and Tierra del Fuego slowly emerges as a significant theme for Chatwin,[15] though his subsequent engagement with a surviving indigenous population – in Australia in *The Songlines* (1987) – would prove more controversial.[16]

Chatwin's work was taken up by the literary magazine *Granta*, whose first special issue on travel writing, which came out in 1984 and was reprinted thirteen times, did much to rekindle popular interest in the genre.[17] *Granta* has sometimes been seen as peddling a form of gentlemanly English arrogance, but it also helped British travel writing become more international in scope and more culturally self-aware, and was responsible for reconnecting travel writing with investigative journalism and contemporary political issues, publishing Salman Rushdie on Nicaragua, Ryszard Kapuściński on Angola, James Fenton on Cambodia, Timothy Garton Ash on Prague, and Hanif Kureishi on Bradford. This same decade also saw the beginnings of what Patrick Holland and Graham Huggan call 'countertravel writing': the jeremiads of Jamaica Kincaid (*A Small Place*, 1988) and Caryl Phillips (*The European Tribe*, 1987) directed respectively at the tourist industry in Antigua and at the kind of European racism that the idea of a black traveller brings to the surface.[18]

The state of play

This final section surveys five broad and overlapping strands that can be detected within travel writing of the last twenty-five years – the comic, the analytical, the wilderness, the spiritual, and the experimental.

Granta's second collection of travel writing was called *In Trouble Again*, which might have referred to travel writers' renewed engagement with the world's political hotspots, but in fact proved to be the title of Redmond O'Hanlon's Amazon adventure (1988), in which the well-read and scientifically trained author deliberately creates trouble for himself by his choice of a spectacularly inappropriate travelling companion, thereby proving that the comic tradition of travel writing could flourish alongside its more serious counterparts. That comic tradition in fact has many facets and has usually provided travel writing with its most popular works, from Thomas Coryate's *Crudities* (1611) to Bill Bryson's *Notes from a Small Island* (1995). Parody has recently tended to dominate, especially in the working of the narrow and bizarre seams exemplified in Tony Hawks's *Round Ireland with a Fridge* (1998) and Coryate's follower (in his Rolls Royce), Tim Moore's *Continental Drifter* (2000).

Given that the world is constantly in flux, there is still a prominent place for the mixture of personal reportage and socio-political analysis which has been a component of travel writing since its earliest days. The collapse of communism opened up opportunities for travel in Eastern Europe and Central Asia which many writers have been keen to take; and Central Africa and Central and South America continue to offer intriguing mixes of ancient cultures and changing political landscapes. Norman Lewis's *The Missionaries* (1988) set an important example here, proving that travel writing still could – as earlier with Roger Casement and others – report with an urgency that demanded action.[19] Scott Malcolmson's *Tuturani: A Political Journey in the Pacific Islands* (1990) and Rebecca Solnit's *Savage Dreams: A Journey to the Landscape Wars of the American West* (1994) offer further examples of the genre at its most trenchant and observant.

The few remaining wildernesses in the post-modern world are sought as avidly as ever. The jungles of the Amazon and New Guinea prove surprisingly capable of throwing up a never-ending stream of 'lost tribes' for the intrepid travel writer to find – the latest being the Liawep located and visited by Edward Marriott in *The Lost Tribe: A Search through the Jungles of Papua New Guinea* (1996). But the 'wildernesses' are now as often ecological as indigenous: places such as Siberia, Alaska, and the poles feature heavily in contemporary travel writing, although even stories about climbing Everest are likely to concentrate as much on internecine rivalry as on physical hardship and spiritual enlightenment.[20]

As the earth's wildernesses get paved over, travel writing increasingly emphasises the inner journey, often merging imperceptibly into memoir. Matthiessen and Davidson have been powerful influences here in reasserting the spiritual dimension of travel and its capacity for renewal. But the inner journey can take many forms, variously demonstrated by Rob Nixon's journeys back to South Africa and to childhood memories, moulded into a cultural history of ostrich farming (*Dreambirds: The Natural History of a Fantasy*, 1999), and by Amitav Ghosh's story of his own swerve away from a social anthropology project in Egypt into a more historical analysis still based on an intimate engagement not only with place, but also with movement (*In An Antique Land*, 1993).

A more experimental final strand pushes the genre in a variety of new directions, actively continuing the generic hybridisation which has periodically reinvigorated travel writing throughout its history, but by definition difficult to categorise or even recognise. Some recent travel books will exemplify the cross-cutting of these five strands and serve to suggest the genre's current range.

Colin Thubron is probably the most distinguished of the generation of travel writers whose work confronts the political upheavals of the last thirty years, continuing – and overlapping with – the tradition of Norman Lewis. After earlier books on the Middle East, Thubron produced the acclaimed *Among the Russians* (1983) at a time when travel there was restricted and difficult. His recent books have explored the vast areas of Asia opened up to Western travel since the collapse of the Soviet Union: *Behind the Wall: A Journey through China* (1987) and *The Lost Heart of Asia* (1994).[21] *In Siberia* (1999) is the story of a 17,000-mile trip through an area that had become synonymous in the West with the freezing terror of Stalin's death-camps, which indeed provide Thubron's ultimate destination: another trip into a heart of darkness. For all that Siberia has been marked by 'the violences of geography and time', it has also been seen 'as a haven of primitive innocence and salvation', so Thubron's journey combines a quest to discover what has 'replaced [Siberia's] shattered Communist faith' with a pilgrimage to one of the world's last true wildernesses.[22] Although not without self-deprecating humour, Thubron's narrative persona radiates an unfussy authority: he knows the history, he speaks the language, he gets around without difficulty – but he flaunts nothing. His spare literary style, combined with modest hints of shyness and sensitivity, exude integrity. Above all, although he shares his impressions and opinions, he speaks to Siberian people of all sorts and lets their words appear in his book, in extensive quotation. Siberia begins in the book as 'less a country than a region in people's minds' (p. 2), but takes form and shape through Thubron's narrative of his journey and his encounters.

As Thubron journeys from the Urals to the Sea of Okhotsk, so Jonathan Raban, in his *Passage to Juneau: A Sea and its Meanings* (1999), is moving from Seattle up the inside passage to Alaska, a parallel move from 'civilisation' to 'wilderness', the two equally chilly wildernesses located at roughly the same latitude (just below 60°) but separated by the Bering Sea. The contrasts between the two writers are, though, more striking than the similarities. If Thubron is determinedly unliterary, seeking his own unmediated view,

Raban's work manages to be both deeply personal and brimming with other people's writing. Baudelaire and Conrad provide his epigraphs; Vancouver and Cook are constant companions along with a host of lesser-known travellers and writers who have had something to say about the inside passage. He cheerfully admits to buying his boat because of its extensive bookshelves. Whereas Thubron's actual journey is subordinate to what the journey provides – access to communities which could only recently be visited by Westerners – Raban's journey has no goals other than to provide the opportunity to relive earlier passages along the same route, to meditate on the sea and its meanings, and to read and write. As usual, though, the journey itself proves metaphorically rich, even in ways which Raban does not expect. Thubron has relatively little to say about the mechanics of his travel, but Raban is in a small boat, perhaps the one mode – apart from Shanks's pony – which genuinely recreates the dangers and divagations of earlier travel. Whereas Thubron shows modest signs of sensitivity beneath his bluff exterior, Raban is like a cat on a hot tin roof, always alert to the nuances of slight, easily tipped into guilt and anxiety – but usually able to turn his social misadventures into comedy and satire, although *Passage to Juneau* does not offer quite the same opportunities as his earlier American works, where his Englishness is used to good effect.[23]

The sea itself is the finest symbol of the uncertainties of travel, and Raban's 'passage' turns into more than he had bargained for when his father dies in the course of it, and his wife makes her own journey to Juneau to announce that their marriage is over. The ironies here are deep. Previously a relatively rootless traveller, Raban makes a point in *Passage to Juneau* of stressing his heartache at leaving his wife and daughter, even for three weeks. His boat is called *Penelope*, a name he dislikes and uses as little as possible, perhaps in unconscious anticipation that his own Penelope will refuse to stay quietly weaving in Seattle and will fly out to confront her Odysseus. Raban here moves closer than previously to the combination of travel account and personal memoir pioneered in *The Snow Leopard*; and the book's emotional heart comes in the long passages recalling his relationship with his father, and describing the old man's death and funeral, beautifully set alongside Raban's evocation of Shelley's death by water.

Although 'extreme travel' has become a significant sub-genre, most writers, even the adventurous ones such as Thubron and Raban, wave at danger rather than embracing it. Siberia and southern Alaska are in any case further north than most readers will have travelled, just as Patagonia was further south and Nepal higher up, but to go even further usually means that the journey has priority over the writing about it, as with the fatal travels of Chris McCandless, which themselves produced only fragments of writing but were turned into the exceptional *Into the Wild* (1996) by Jon Krakauer. The polar regions have been – from most perspectives apart from the indigenous – traditionally a man's world, 'a testing-ground for men with frozen beards to see how dead they could get', in Sara Wheeler's words at the beginning of her *Terra Incognita* (1996).[24] In many respects Wheeler's journey is truly epic – it takes two years' planning, involves prior contact with several countries' scientific Antarctic programmes, and her trip from one side of the Antarctic to the other necessitates a journey via New Zealand, England, and the Falkland Islands. Her interests are partly social and partly in the extraordinary landscape. The different national communities – US, New Zealand, Italian, British – are represented largely by how they respond to the presence of a woman writer, the all-male British section coming off considerably the worst: 'Here were British men doing what they did best – reverting to childhood and behaving like gits' (p. 196). The landscape, finely described, induces the confessional mode of a book like *Tracks*, although in its evocation of a polar world *Terra Incognita* most closely resembles Barry Lopez's *Arctic Dreams*. In many ways, however, the book's most interesting encounter is with the writers of the Heroic Age of polar travel, pre-eminently Scott, Amundsen, Mawson, and Shackleton. While their belated followers (like Ranulph Fiennes) are given short shrift, Wheeler shows increasing empathy with the early heroes, for all that they occupied a world antagonistic to the presence – or even the thought – of women. The book's most poignant sentence is perhaps the one she quotes from an early biography of Scott: 'In some ways, Scott's sensibility was more like a woman's than a man's' (p. 225), and she ends her polar odyssey asleep in Scott's bunk.

The parameters of travel are almost impossible to set. Xavier de Maistre wrote about a voyage around his bedroom,[25] and there is no minimum length of stay laid down in the travel writer's handbook. However, most travel writing involves the experience of foreign cultures and languages, and some travel writers practice a kind of deep immersion in the cultures they are visiting, acquiring the sort of intimate knowledge which gives them access to people and places unknown to short-stay travellers, let alone tourists.[26] Peter Robb's richly textured *Midnight in Sicily* (1996) is based on many years of living in and visiting southern Italy and Sicily, building up contacts, visiting libraries, galleries, and restaurants. That investment of time is, of course, not inducive to a career as a specialist travel writer: in general, the latter will inevitably either be more dependent on local interpreters, who will have *their* own particular position within and take on the culture, or will rely on a more subjective account of what they see and experience, actively seeking 'exile from language as a means of communicative rebirth', as Michael Cronin puts it.[27] Robb stretches the genre in certain respects: rather than the traditional single journey, his book is made up of innumerable shorter journeys so that he has to look elsewhere, to the trial of ex-Prime Minister Andreotti, for his narrative impetus. But *Midnight in Sicily*, evoking the sense of a place and its depths with extraordinary skill, offers a fine example of travel writing as cultural history.

Despite the huge volume of travel writing produced over the last five centuries, travellers' routes and traces are often tenuous and difficult to decipher, and later travellers and travel writers have been keen to find their footsteps and to follow them. Sometimes, of course, as with Franklin and Fawcett (discussed in Chapters 3 and 7), the earlier traveller has not returned and is being physically sought; more often the routes are being retraced in order to mark the historical gap between the two moments and perhaps to throw light on the earlier work, though the connection with earlier and usually better-known travellers can also serve as an attractive marketing device. *Passage to Juneau* and *Terra Incognita* are both intensely aware of earlier travellers and writers to Alaska and the Antarctic, and *Midnight in Sicily* follows the traces of Italian writers Lampedusa and Sciascia, but the outstanding exponent of the footsteps genre is Charles Nicholl, who has recently followed his work on Walter Ralegh in South America (*The Creature in the Map*, 1995) with a study of Arthur Rimbaud in Africa. As with *Midnight in Sicily*, *Somebody Else: Arthur Rimbaud in Africa, 1880–1891* (1997) is based on considerable research, which gives the book academic credibility as a study of Rimbaud's life (and to an extent his work), but Nicholl's strong presence as a traveller and investigator, and his interest in the contemporary Ethiopia he visits, marks his book as travel writing, though as with Nicholl's earlier work, there is often the sense of also reading a detective story.[28]

The travel writer often doubles as a journalist: a good deal of contemporary travel writing seems to be written by journalists looking for a larger canvas, and Robb certainly makes good use of a press card. *Midnight in Sicily* addresses some large and serious issues – thousands of people were murdered by the Mafia in Sicily and southern Italy during the period covered by Robb's book – yet his approach, with its careful attention to gastronomy and to painting, looks at a larger cultural picture: the bodies are mostly out of sight. That travel writing can confront the major events of our age is proved by Philip Gourevitch's *We Wish to Inform You That Tomorrow We Will Be Killed With Our Families: Stories from Rwanda* (1998), a harrowing account of his visits to Rwanda in an attempt to understand the genocide that took place in 1994. Carefully balancing personal response, extensive interviews, historical research, and vivid descriptions, Gourevitch manages – against all odds – to produce a life-affirming book out of the late twentieth century's most depressing episode. Gourevitch's book is written with a degree of detachment, but it also tells the story of his deepening awareness of Western complicity in the Rwandan genocide. Travel writing's concern with witness and event make it an attractive vehicle for the engagement with contemporary politics (in the larger sense of that word).

The forensic nature of Gourevitch's writing demands an absolute attention to factual detail. Here travel writing meets – and is perhaps indistinguishable from – investigative reporting. Even where the stakes are not as high, most travel writers will expect to be taken at their word: the conventions of the genre with respect to embellishment and minor invention are well-understood by readers. In another margin of the genre, however, different rules apply, as W. G. Sebald's *The Rings of Saturn* (1995) demonstrates. Although German, its author lived in England and the book opens in deceptively simple fashion with the statement: 'In August 1992, when the dog days were drawing to an end, I set off to walk the county of Suffolk, in the hope of dispelling the emptiness that takes hold of me whenever I have completed a long stint of work.'[29] When, by the end of the first chapter, readers have followed an intricate path through the Norwich hospital, Kafka's 'Metamorphosis', a colleague's work on Flaubert, and Thomas Browne's skull, it is apparent that this allusive and enigmatic book is no ordinary piece of travel writing – although Sebald does complete his walk, by recognisable roads, and does offer, in the most indirect fashion imaginable, a portrait of post-imperial England. In such ways is the genre of travel writing subverted and renewed.

NOTES

I would like to acknowledge the unpublished work of Jan Borm on contemporary British writing and the considerable assistance received from Tim Youngs. The chapter also draws on the best and most extensive analysis of its area: Patrick Holland and Graham Huggan, *Tourists with Typewriters: Critical Reflections on Contemporary Travel Writing* (Ann Arbor: University of Michigan Press, 1998).

1 All four were born between 1910 and 1919.
2 Eric Newby, *A Short Walk in the Hindu Kush* (London: Secker and Warburg, 1958), p. 281. Newby's first book was *The Last Grain Race* (1956), in the tradition of Dana and Melville. His later books include *Slowly Down the Ganges* (1966) and *The Big Red Train Ride* (1978).
3 Byron is discussed by Helen Carr in Chapter 4. Alec Waugh, *The Coloured Countries* (1930); *The Sugar Islands* (1958).
4 Fermor has written one novel and Lewis several, but they are not as well-regarded as their travel books. Both Lewis and Newby have written about their war-time experiences, a form of memoir which places a premium on accuracy of recall:

Norman Lewis, *Naples '44: An Intelligence Officer in the Italian Labyrinth* (1978); Eric Newby, *Love and War in the Apennines* (1971).

5 Naipaul's books on India are briefly discussed by Kate Teltscher in Chapter 11. The best assessment of Naipaul's travel writing is Rob Nixon, *London Calling: V.S. Naipaul, Postcolonial Mandarin* (Oxford University Press, 1992).

6 On women travel writers earlier in the century, see Chapters 4 and 13. Jan Morris (previously James) is a special case, also discussed in Chapter 13.

7 Dervla Murphy, *Full Tilt: Dunkirk to Delhi* (1965). Her other books include *In Ethiopia with a Mule* (1968), *Eight Feet in the Andes* (1983), and *Tales from Two Cities: Travel of Another Sort* (1987), which is about Bradford and Birmingham.

8 See Paul Theroux, *Sir Vidia's Shadow: A Friendship across Five Continents* (London: Hamish Hamilton, 1998).

9 Among Theroux's many travel books are *Riding the Iron Rooster: By Train through China* (1988) and *The Pillars of Hercules: A Grand Tour of the Mediterranean* (1995). His *The Happy Isles of Oceania* (1992) is discussed by Rod Edmond in Chapter 8. See also Theroux's collections of essays and journalism, *Sunrise with Seamonsters* (1985) and *Fresh-Air Fiend: Travel Writing 1975–2000* (2000).

10 Peter Matthiessen, *The Snow Leopard* (London: Picador, 1980), p. 110.

11 Most travel writers keep some form of journal, but the journal format for published work is now relatively rare. One exception is Dervla Murphy, *Full Tilt and South from the Limpopo: Travels through South Africa* (1997).

12 Davidson's second book, *Desert Places* (New York: Viking, 1996), about some months spent with the Rabari nomads of Rajasthan, 'was packaged according to the exigencies of the market – exotic travel: subsection, female' (Robyn Davidson, 'Introduction', in *The Picador Book of Journeys* ed. Robyn Davidson (London: Picador, 2001), p. 2.

13 Although he was born in Patagonia and an Argentine citizen, Bridges's book was read in Britain as if it were a travel account of a place remote to and from the author.

14 Claude Lévi-Strauss, *Tristes Tropiques*, trans. John and Doreen Weightman (Harmondsworth: Penguin, 1976), p. 15.

15 See Peter Hulme, 'Patagonian Cases: Travel Writing, Fiction, History', in *Seuils et Traverses*, ed. Jean-Yves Le Disez and Jan Borm (Brest: Centre de Recherches Bretonne et Celtique de l'Université de Bretagne Occidentale, 2002) vol. II, pp. 223–38.

16 See the discussion in Nicholas Shakespeare, *Bruce Chatwin* (London: The Harvill Press, 1999), pp. 486–92.

17 Others followed in 1986 and 1989: a selection of these pieces was published as *The Granta Book of Travel* in 1991, and republished with a new introduction by Ian Jack in 1998. On *Granta* and travel, see Jim Philip, 'Journeywork', *Studies in Travel Writing*, 1 (1997): 199–215, and Charles Sugnet, 'Vile Bodies, Vile Places: Traveling with *Granta*', *Transition*, 51 (1991): 70–85.

18 See Patrick Holland and Graham Huggan, *Tourists with Typewriters: Critical Reflections on Contemporary Travel Writing* (Ann Arbor: University of Michigan Press, 1998), pp. 48–53.

19 Further Central and South American examples include Ronald Wright, *Time Among the Maya: Travels in Belize, Guatemala, and Mexico* (1989) and *Cut*

Stones and Crossroads: A Journey in the Two Worlds of Peru (1984); and Richard Gott, *Land Without Evil: Utopian Journeys Across the South American Watershed* (1993); for Central Africa, see Chapter 9.

20 Classic texts here would include Barry Lopez, *Arctic Dreams: Imagination and Desire in a Northern Landscape* (1986); and Jon Krakauer, *Into Thin Air: A Personal Account of the Mount Everest Disaster* (1997).

21 Thubron is also an intelligent commentator on the genre: 'Travel Writing Today: Its Rise and Dilemma', in *Essays By Divers Hands: Being the Transactions of the Royal Society of Literature, New Series: Volume XLIV*, ed. A. N. Wilson (Woodbridge: Boydell Press, 1986), pp. 167–81; 'Both Seer and Seen: The Travel Writer as Leftover Amateur', *TLS*, 30 July 1999, no. 5026, pp. 12–13; and Susan Bassnett, 'Interview with Colin Thubron', *Studies in Travel Writing*, 3 (1999): 148–71.

22 Colin Thubron, *In Siberia* (London: Chatto & Windus, 1999), pp. 2–3.

23 Raban, *Bad Land: An American Romance* (1996); *Old Glory: An American Voyage* (1981); *Hunting Mr Heartbreak* (1990).

24 Sara Wheeler, *Terra Incognita: Travels in Antarctica* (London: Jonathan Cape, 1996), p. 1.

25 Xavier de Maistre, *A Nocturnal Expedition Round My Room* (1794), trans. Edmund Goldsmid (Edinburgh: [s.n.], 1886).

26 Other examples here would be William Dalrymple, *City of Djinns: A Year in Delhi* (1993); and Ian Buruma's writing about Japan in *A Japanese Mirror* (1984) and *The Missionary and the Libertine* (1996). William Least Heat-Moon practices extreme deep immersion in *PrairyErth (A Deep Map)* (1991), where he writes 624 pages about a few square miles of Kansas.

27 Michael Cronin, *Across the Lines: Travel, Language, Translation* (Cork University Press, 2000), p. 3. Others, like Thubron or Buruma, may build up knowledge (including linguistic expertise) over a number of extended journeys.

28 Other examples of this genre are William Dalrymple, *In Xanadu: A Quest* (1989); Nicholas Rankin, *Dead Man's Chest: Travels After Robert Louis Stevenson* (1987); Gavin Young, *In Search of Conrad* (1992); Gavin Bell, *In Search of Tusitala: Travels in the Pacific after Stevenson* (1994); and Stephen Minta, *Aguirre: The Re-Creation of a Sixteenth-Century Journey Across South America* (1993).

29 W. G. Sebald, *The Rings of Saturn*, trans. Michael Hulse (New York: New Directions, 1998), p. 3.

II
SITES

6

BILLIE MELMAN

The Middle East/Arabia: 'the cradle of Islam'

It is noteworthy that Westerners' oldest destination of travel, seasonal migration, and colonisation should have received its name only in recent times. The term 'Middle East' is a neologism, invented in 1902 by US naval historian Alfred Thayer Mahan to designate the sea and land stretching between a farther East – India – and a nearer one, extending towards the westernmost territories of Asia and the eastern Mediterranean. The centre of Mahan's idiosyncratic map was the Persian Gulf – anticipating later US interest in the area. The new epithet was immediately taken up by *The Times*, put into circulation by officialdom, and gradually extended to include the mass of land under Ottoman rule – stretching from the Black Sea to equatorial Africa and from India to the heart of the Mediterranean.[1]

'Middle East' did not supplant the considerably older term 'Orient', but was used interchangeably with it, replicating images of the West's 'other' which characterised European discourses on the East. Both terms embody the ambiguous position of this area in these discourses and reflect an ethnocentric and hierarchical view of the world with the West at its centre and as its standard but, at the same time, indicating the relational positions of Europe and the Middle East and of the latter and the Far East. Raymond Schwab captures this relationality in his classical distinction between the Indian Orient discovered by European Orientalists in the eighteenth century and that older Orient, part of the 'European room', the *locus* of Graeco-Roman and Judeo-Christian civilisations which had shaped Europe itself.[2] Thus its midway position and very proximity to Europe, as well as the longevity of religious, cultural, and political exchanges with the West, defined the Middle East as a border zone. It was *of* the West, yet *outside* it, familiar, yet alien. It was the birthplace of Christianity and the two other revealed religions – Judaism and Islam – accorded by Westerners with the powers of pernicious apostasies. And it particularly threatened Christian Europe because Islam, which in the eighth century emerged as the area's dominant religion, evolved as the basis of a succession of organised and militarised state systems. From the second half of the fifteenth century until the late seventeenth century the Ottoman Empire literally encroached on Europe's borders, claiming a supremacy in the Mediterranean, and challenging the very existence of a fragile and divided Christian West. The Ottoman challenge was not merely military. As Albert Hourani has pointed out, Westerners deemed the Muslim East so pernicious precisely because it presented an alternative culture dangerously close to home.[3] Hence, on the one hand, the attraction to that culture and its site and, on the other, a repulsion perpetuated in the cultural stereotypes which remained such a staple of travel writing even after the reversal of power relationships. Historians usually date this reversal from the naval battle of Lepanto in 1572, which arguably eliminated the Ottoman Empire as a Mediterranean power. Thereafter, Europe's relatively peaceful coexistence with this empire was intermittently broken in Ottoman forays into central Europe's hinterland (culminating in the siege of Vienna in 1683). Yet for Europeans the sense of the Ottoman peril was real enough. Later, and until the outbreak of the First World War, the power of the vast supra-national empire was increasingly contested within the Middle East and in its European territories. The gradual disintegration of the Ottoman Empire notwithstanding, its domains still presented the power of a highly organised polity with a complex societal system – both relating to a unifying and powerful Islam. Though a British Middle-Eastern policy seeking influence in the area may be traced back to the Mediterranean campaign against post-revolutionary Napoleonic France, before the First World War this policy remained consistently Ottomanist and supported the territorial integrity of the weakening empire. With the exception of Cyprus and Egypt, occupied in 1878 and 1882 respectively, military occupation and direct intervention evolved only during the Great War and in relation to the collapse of the Ottoman Empire. Characteristically, intrusion took on multiple indirect forms: finance imperialism based on investments, intense missionary activity, and last, but most relevant here, the enormous collective effort known as 'Orientalism', defined and addressed throughout this chapter, of which travel writing was such a quintessential part.

One of the truisms of the scholarship on travel to, and travel writing on, the Middle East is that both were indices to Western and especially British political and military superiority. British curiosity about the Orient and distinct Anglo-American travel cultures are taken as the ultimate sign of an asymmetry of power between Britain and the Middle East; and the Western traveller's eye is identified as an 'imperial eye', performing a colonial act of appropriation.[4] There never has developed, it is argued, a comparable Middle-Eastern interest in Britain. However, neither the British experience of travel nor the diverse representations of this experience were homogeneous.

They may not be understood solely as configurations of an insidious and all-powerful imperialism, nor simply as manifestations of a systematic discourse of power and knowledge. Elaborated by Edward Said in his epochal 1978 book, the term 'Orientalism' has become the single most influential paradigm in studies of travel writing and indeed of colonial cross-cultural exchanges. Although this paradigm is now habitually applied to exchanges between the West and non-Western cultures generally, it was within the Middle-Eastern context that Said developed it. Briefly, he defines 'Orientalism' as an academic tradition, a style and, most importantly, a way of 'making sense' of the Middle East that draws on a binary epistemology and an imaginary geography that divides the world into two unequal and hierarchically positioned parts: the West and the East, the Occident and the Orient, Christianity and Islam, rationalism and its absence, progress and stagnation.[5] 'Orientalism' denotes a discourse of power that is always and inescapably systematic, repetitive, and unchanging. It perpetuates stereotypes of the Middle East and Middle-Eastern people that, Said and others have argued, hardly changed over a millennium. These include the image of the oriental despot, the corrupt prophet Muhammad, the religiously fanatic Muslim, the lascivious oriental female, and the somewhat different image of the noble Arab nomad studied in this chapter. Real orientals are denied humanity, history, and the authority to speak about and represent themselves, an authority which Orientalist travel writing reserves for occidentals.[6]

Over recent years students of British travel writing have contested the Saidian paradigm and modified it considerably. Ali Behdad, Charles Issawi, Billie Melman, and Lisa Lowe among others have pointed out that travellers' representations were not homogeneous but were inflected by gender, class, and nationality. They have also indicated changes over time: early explorers were quite different from 'belated travellers' (Behdad's expression). Most importantly, some of the critics have doubted the utility of the binary model as the key to our understanding of British or other exchanges with the Middle East. They have also argued that the definition of the association between travel writing, the Orientalist traveller's authority, the politics of colonialism, and colonial institutions needs to be rethought.[7] This chapter outlines the development of this kind of heterogeneous and diverse body of work. To highlight this diversity and the coexistence of distinct travel cultures and traditions of writing, it begins with a brief survey of two dominant models which were first formulated and conventionalised within the discourse on the Middle East, the pilgrimage and the domestic ethnography focused on Muslim everyday life. The field then narrows to discuss travel experience and its representations in writings on 'Arabia', the term used in the twentieth century to designate the Arabian peninsula. It is to this particular site that the term 'belated travel' is most easily applicable. Arabia emerged late as a destination of exploration, but quickly became both an object of political and economic interests and an iconic place. Its protracted and incomplete discovery spanned the century between the 1850s and 1950s, thus covering the late phase of imperialism. From about the 1950s, decolonisation, Britain's decline as a world power and empire, and, later, globalisation seem to have reversed Anglo-American relationships with the oil-supplying states of the peninsula. While these combined changes have impinged upon British Arabian travel writing, here too some features of older forms and strategies of representation have persisted.

Sacred and domestic geographies: an overview

From the fourth century and for well over a millennium, the pilgrimage was the dominant mode of travel through the Middle East and the most available paradigm for travel writing. Significantly, this mode survived longest and retained its central place in the British discourse on the Orient even after the Reformation and secularisation. Religious travel to the sites of the stages of Christ's life and suffering had an extraordinary revival during the nineteenth century. Moreover, the pilgrimage survived not only as a practice but also as a central organising metaphor of travel, drawn on and utilised by travellers, notably travellers in Arabia. Initially, pilgrimage had presented the very reverse of travel and had been perceived and represented as 'anti-travel'. In Christian dogma and culture, *curiositas*, that is curiosity about the world, is a sin, related to the Original Sin and the Transgression, hence identified with humanity's Fall. Yet even the earliest, fourth-century pilgrims to Palestine were not immune to ethnographi: curiosity.[8] In addition to the tension between the pilgrim's spiritual experience and his or her curiosity, Christian pilgrimage to the Holy Land retained another, between the praxis of a this-worldly experience and the notion of a wholly spiritual and allegorical journey. The *peregrinatio por christo* became an allegory of the Christian life and was increasingly regarded not as an actual voyage but as an experience which Christian men and women could undergo everywhere: Jerusalem the Heavenly could be reached without travelling.[9] That allegorical interpretation and the notion of the voyage to the Holy Land persisted long after the decline of the pilgrimage movement in the West is best exemplified in constitutive texts such as John Bunyan's *The Pilgrim's Progress* (1678).

The revival of the actual practice of pilgrimage during the first half of the nineteenth century coincides with the rise of British interest in the Middle East and was facilitated by the transport revolution, including the introduction of steamships in the Mediterranean and of carriages and, later, railways to connect Ottoman coastal cities and ports. Towards the end of the century Jerusalem was connected to Damascus and the latter to the Muslim holy cities of Mecca and Medinah by the *Hijazi* railway. Organised pilgrimages, inaugurated by Thomas Cook in 1869 and catering for British and American clienteles, considerably popularised and commercialised the spiritual journey, making it accessible to the middle classes. A Cook's pilgrim's package averaged 31 shillings a day inclusive of accommodation, a *dragoman* or translator, a military escort, and imported British food. The tourists, disdainfully referred to by those travelling individually as 'Cookites', could choose between a shorter route – including sacred places in Syria and the Lebanon and Palestine, and a longer one which also included Transjordan.[10]

Changes in the technology and infrastructure of travel do not account for the revival and predominance, recorded by a number of contemporary sources, of the pilgrimage, nor for the radical change in its form. This change has to do with the shift in the status of the journey to Palestine in evangelical faith and discourse, a discourse so vital to the making of the British and US middle classes. Evangelical reading of the Scriptures was literal rather than allegorical: hence evangelical travel in the Middle East was a practice meant to corroborate God's revealed text. Literal biblism easily led to a millenarianism which elevated the text, and especially the prophesies on a universal regeneration and the Second Coming, to literally realisable truths. Thus evangelicals perceive the Middle East as the actual *locus* of sacred events in the past, as well as of prophesied occurrences, and 'read' the terrain, Palestine's flora and fauna and its inhabitants, as illustrations to 'the book'.[11] Exactly such an illustrative approach is the most salient feature of key texts such as Edward Robinson, *Biblical Researches in Palestine* (1838), William Maclure Thompson, *The Land and the Bible* (1859), and Henry Tristram Baker, *A Natural History of the Bible* and *Flora and Fauna of Palestine* (1867 and 1884), the last a survey of western Palestine sponsored by the London-based Palestine Exploration Fund. Robinson, a product of the Theological Seminary in New York and the century's most influential biblical geographer and archaeologist, argued that all tradition and knowledge respecting Middle-Eastern places was 'of no value except so far as it is supported by circumstances known to us from the Scriptures'. Equipped with a 100-foot tape to measure the walls of Jerusalem, Bibles, early pilgrims' accounts, and a compass, he toured the Sinai peninsula and Palestine in the 1830s and 1840s, soliciting data and place names from local peasants, whose Arabic (which he did not quite understand) he believed to have preserved biblical nomenclature. His *Researches*, a seemingly unedited log, records Robinson's every move to the exact hour. What most characterises his biblical science is a de-historicisation of the places he seeks to authenticate and the subsequent collapse of place into text. Take for example his report on the Arab village of Dura, in the district of Hebron, which his party entered on 6 June 1838, at four o'clock in the afternoon and left at four-forty, after 'a delay of forty minutes'. In this span, Robinson condenses a report on the place, noting that it has 'no traces of antiquity' and skimping over its present, then identifies it with the biblical Adoraim. The countryside, which he starts touring at precisely six-forty that same afternoon, interests him for the flocks and crops of wheat it abounds with, attended by 'reapers and gleaners'.[12] Contemporary Arab agricultural methods are but an illustration to a supposedly biblical one, referred from a text in the Psalms, which Robinson reads literally. Such de-historicisation is emblematic of myriad texts which construct a timeless and changeless Middle East, outside secular history. As Frances Power Cobbe, evangelical turned agnostic, a reformer and well-known feminist, notes in 1862: travellers were 'Walking where they [the patriarchs and early Christians] walked, living in the same kind of houses, with the same kind of flowers and trees and animals around us, the same food and wine'.[13] Writers trace connections between scriptural occurrences and contemporary ones, with each of the sets seen as equally concrete. The modern Arab who, being a Muslim, had no place in evangelical cosmogony, but also the modern Middle-Eastern Jew, are described as scriptural types, unchanged from the times of the Patriarchs, or that of Christ. A storm like the one experienced by the missionary to Syria, Augusta Mentor Mott on Lake Galilee, is the very same as the one that rocked the Saviour's boat on that lake.[14] The interchangeability of past and present and of text and land made it possible for travellers to locate themselves in Christian eschatology as active agents and at the same time strengthened their sense of identity as 'true Christians'. As proponents of the biblical sciences of scriptural archaeology, topography, and even natural sciences, these travellers also utilised the pilgrimage as a weapon against positivism, modern biblical criticism and, from the 1860s, Darwinism. Significantly, a considerable number of topographical Holy Land surveys and ethnographies were sponsored by evangelical bodies in Britain.[15]

Alongside the modernised pilgrimage, there evolved another distinct field of interest and writing which may be conveniently described as an ethnography of modern everyday life. Whereas the evangelical travelogue and the description or survey of antiquities (mainly Egyptian ones) largely ignored Muslim culture and society, the ethnography focused on Muslim customs and manners. Here again, the experience of travel was textual even as travellers claimed, and in many cases drew on, actual experience and sometimes participant observation.[16] Travellers' reports responded to and engaged with an expanding corpus of Orientalist texts, as much as they were renditions of impressions acquired on the spot. The single most influential such text is the ensemble of Arabic tales transmitted orally and collectively known as *Alf Laila wa- laila* (*Thousand and One Nights*) first transcribed by Antoine Galland as *Mille et Une Nuits* between 1704–14, thus becoming a Western oriental text over a century before ever appearing in Arabic. Galland's version was followed by editions for every taste and audience, from the traveller and Orientalist Edward William Lane's savagely bowdlerised family edition (1838–41) to the lucrative edition for collectors of erotica by Richard Burton (1882–4). Additionally, travellers had access to a plethora of translations from Turkish and Persian, as well as to pseudo-oriental tales fabricated in Britain and France, such as William Beckford's *Vathek* (1795). Significantly, these largely Western works of fiction drawing on collective fantasy and considerable prejudice regarding Muslim practices acquired the status of ethnographic sources on the contemporary Middle East.

Already during the early Augustan Enlightenment, Orientalist authority was effectively contested, especially with regard to subjects like private life, sexuality, and the segregation of women and polygamy: subjects about which Western travellers knew very little, as Muslim law and custom practically excluded males from the segregated Middle-Eastern house. Domestic ethnography thus evolved largely as a female genre, initially aristocratic, then from the early nineteenth century distinctly middle class. The genre's earliest and most influential exemplar is Lady Mary Wortley Montagu's so-called *Turkish Embassy Letters*, compiled during her journey to Istanbul in 1717–18 as the wife of Edward Wortley, Ambassador Extraordinary to the Sublime Porte (Sultan Ahmet III). Written to fifty-two female and male correspondents, widely circulated during Lady Montagu's lifetime, and published posthumously in 1763, the *Letters* became a blueprint for the travel writing which integrated movement across open spaces with detailed accounts of domestic and largely feminine spaces. This formula was emulated by travellers throughout the Middle East as well as India and South America.[17] Montagu's entire project of addressing cultural difference between Christianity and Islam, Britain and the Ottoman Empire, revolves around presentations of Muslim women's veiling and the system of segregation within the Ottoman *Haremlik* or women's and children's separate quarter. She famously argues that:

> 'Tis very easy to see they have more Liberty than we have, no woman of what rank so ever permitted to go in the streets without 2 Muslins, one that covers the face all but her Eyes and another that hides the whole dress of her head...This perpetual masquerade gives them more Liberty of following their inclinations.[18]

In Montagu's rhetoric, liberty signifies a complex of juridical, customary, and economic freedoms and above all sexual freedom, which Enlightenment concepts did not extend to women. This rhetoric is buttressed in minutely detailed descriptions of houses of the Turkish-Circassian élite in Istanbul, Edirne (Adrianopolis), Belgrade, and Sophia, in which Montagu rejects clear-cut distinctions between private spaces, identified with women and taken to signify powerlessness, and public ones, between customs that are deemed Western and those regarded as quintessentially Eastern. Montagu's evidently Turcophile writing suggests a cultural relativism that challenges Orientalist essentialism.

Her numerous Victorian emulators extended their interest to other urban classes outside the élites. Some writers like Julia Sophia Pardoe in the 1830s, Mary Eliza Rogers in the 1850s, and Mary Lucy Garnett in the 1900s and 1910s, inherited Montagu's Turcophile attitudes. The Victorians, though, de-sexualised oriental female spaces and the oriental woman herself and constructed a middle-class harem, not unlike the Victorian household, a harem which they imagined as an autonomous feminotopia.[19] Not all writers were capable of tolerance towards the culturally different. Edward William Lane's encyclopaedic *Manners and Customs of the Modern Egyptians* (1836), probably the first description of modern Egypt, is one salient example of the condemnation of a non-Western family system as corrupt, depraving, and even demographically disastrous. Lane's vast knowledge, acquired over years of travel and residence in Egypt, did not sustain him while writing on private life. *Manners* demonstrates the power of textual authority even in the new ethnography based on direct participant observation.

Arabia

In travellers' 'real' and imaginary geographies of the Middle East the Arabian peninsula has held a singular place, ridden with ambiguities and contradictions. Its geography and climate have made its hinterland almost inaccessible to non-mechanised travel. Until late in the nineteenth century this, combined with a lack of direct Western military and strategic interest, left the peninsula peripheral from both touristic and imperial viewpoints. British interest focused on the peninsula's coastal fringes, along the Red Sea, at the south-eastern tip in the port of Aden, and along the coast of the Gulf, practically ruled by the British from the middle of the nineteenth century. This limited expansion was the reflection of a lack of a British Arab policy before the Great War: the attraction of Arabia's fringes lay in their significance for the Indian empire, especially after the opening of the Suez Canal in 1869, which considerably shortened the route from Europe to India, making civil and military travel cheaper and easier. Separate policies with regard to the hinterland would emerge only during the First World War, when Britain played a central rôle in the shaping of modern Arabia – a term sometimes used inclusively to cover Transjordan and a part of Mesopotamia.[20]

Notwithstanding its peripheral status, Arabia came to be imagined as an iconic place, the *locus* of a pristine and authentic Arab way of life, a land of utopian dreams and, for some of its most renowned explorers, an asylum from an ailing and degenerate modern Western civilisation. Idealisation of the Arabs as noble and free may be traced back to early travellers like Laurent d'Arvieux, G. A. Wallin, and Jean Louis Burckhardt, author of *Travels in Arabia* (1819). However their experiences of the peninsula differed widely and were too dispersed to have formed a distinct tradition and a body of authority.[21] Later authorities like Richard Burton, whose *Personal Narrative of a Pilgrimage to Al-Madinah and Meccah* appeared in 1856, were knowledgeable about the Hijaz in the west of the peninsula but had limited interest in and access to hinterland tribal society and polity. A tradition, a distinct body of travel writing, and indeed a genealogy of Arabists emerged in the 1870s, with the epic voyage of Anne Noel King Blunt and Wilfrid Scawen Blunt to the plateau of Nadj in central Arabia, which coincided with that of Charles Montagu Doughty. The last desert adventure was Wilfred Thesiger's crossing of the Rub' al Khali, or 'Empty Quarter' in the south, one of the world's largest sand areas, uncharted until 1931.

What is so distinctive about these belated travellers is that they were not just travelling Orientalists, or Orientalists who happened to experience Arabia – but Arabists. Put slightly differently, they were travellers who, individually and collectively, allied themselves to the belief that an Arab nationalism based in the peninsula would regenerate the entire Middle East under British tutelage, drawing on novel concepts of imperialism as 'indirect' and integrative: the Great War was these Arabists' 'moment in the Middle East'.[22] As T. E. Lawrence characteristically overstated the case, the Arabists sought to 'build a new People in the East'.[23] Allegiance to the new notion of the Middle East was not merely sentimental or ideological, but took on institutional form. With the exception of the Blunts, all the major explorers of the peninsula were affiliated to British political and military agencies. Lawrence and David Hogarth were in the Arab Bureau in Cairo, which masterminded and backed the anti-Ottoman revolt led by the Sharifian house of Hussein (protectors of the holy places in the Hijaz) and supported the establishing of Arab kingdoms headed by his sons throughout a larger Arabia. Gertrude Lowthian Bell, traveller to Mesopotamia and Nadj, diplomat and archaeologist, was political secretary to the agency in Basra and a staunch supporter of the Sharifian policy. Freya Stark, who travelled to the Hadramawt area (in Yemen), was affiliated to intelligence. However, to interpret the Arabists' experience and its representations solely in terms of institutional imperial affiliation and politics would be to reduce desert travel to an epiphenomenon of late colonial diplomacy. It was travellers' individual quests and their particular searches for personal redemption in the desert (quite often rendered in the religious or quasi-religious terms of the pilgrimage) that shaped their political vision of the peninsula, as well as building their own identities as Orientalists.

The desert narratives may be superficially described as stories of the conquest of the void, or wilderness, as well as tales of risk which position the individual explorer in front of a hostile nature. They draw on the late Victorian penchant for barren and wild landscapes as well as on earlier Romantic concepts of the 'Great' in nature.[24] The great desert is sometimes associated with emptiness and stands for the infinity of the universe and the human condition within it. C. M. Doughty's *Travels in Arabia Deserta*, a 600,000-word account published in 1888 and considered among Arabists as the authority on northern Arabia, is one characteristic example of the rendition of the wilderness. Doughty's deliberately archaic prose swarms with references to emptiness, waste, and death. 'Commonly the Arabian desert is an extreme desolation where the herb is not sufficient for the sufficiency of any creature', he writes. A barrier cliff is 'an horrid sandstone desolation, a death' and the landscape 'a desolation of the land that is desolate'. This vast emptiness impinges on the life of the Bedouins and on the traveller himself: 'The Arabs are barren-minded in the emptiness of the desert life'.[25] Some of the originality of the co-produced and co-written travelogues of the Blunts lies in Anne Blunt's domestication of the wilderness. Her *Pilgrimage to Nadj* (1879), drawn on the fifth of the couple's seven Middle-Eastern voyages taken between 1873 and 1882, was based entirely on Anne Blunt's detailed logs and pocket diaries but edited and prefaced by Wilfrid Blunt. Travelling at the same time as Doughty, their land journey covered over 2,000 miles from Aleppo to the Persian Gulf. They were the first Europeans to have travelled by land from the Mediterranean to the Indian Ocean and the first to have travelled in Arabia undisguised. The couple observed a variety of landscapes culminating in the Nafud, or great red sand desert, separating the oases of northern Arabia from Nadj. Anne Blunt not only 'tames' the Nafud but paints it with an abundance of colour, resorting to metaphors of maritime travel, a device used by a number of travellers in the desert:

> At half past three o'clock we saw a red streak on the horizon before us, which rose as we approached it, stretching out east and west in an unbroken line...[O]n coming nearer we found it broken into billows, and but for

its colour not unlike the storming sea from shore to shore, for it rose up as
the sea seems to rise, when the waters were high, above the level of the land.
Somebody called out 'the Nefud' [sic] and though for a while we were incred-
ulous were soon convinced. What surprised us was its colour, that of rhubarb
and magnesia, nothing at all like the sand we had hitherto seen, and nothing
at all like what we had expected.[26]

In contrast to earlier travellers like Gifford Palgrave, whose *Narrative of
A Year's Journey through Central and Eastern Arabia* (1865) Anne Blunt
trashes, her *Pilgrimage* endows the desert with order, proportion, and harmony. Her attempt to domesticate the chaos of the wilderness (note the
reference to rhubarb and magnesia used in domestic medicine) and to make
it meaningful, is characteristic of the belated explorers. They represent their
journeys as spiritual, often structuring them in accordance with the pilgrimage, while reversing this model as well as transforming that of the traveller-
pilgrim. The *Hajj* (every Muslim's obligatory pilgrimage to the holy shrines
in Mecca, and the fifth of Islam's seven pillars) marks the believer's identity and her or his membership of the community of Muslims. Travellers
like the Blunts and Doughty locate the Christian and universalist quest in
the quintessential Muslim and anti-Christian site. They apply the notion of
the *Hajj* to the whole of Arabia, which they regard as the *locus genii* of an
authentic Islam. The Blunts focus on Nadj, the centre of the religious revival known as Wahhabism, originating in the mid eighteenth century and
becoming a unifying force in the twentieth century mobilised by the Sau'di
dynasty to build up Saudi Arabia. But their journey is explicitly modelled on
Bunyan's *The Pilgrim's Progress*. Moreover, after the journey Anne Blunt underwent a religious experience which resulted in her subsequent conversion
to Roman Catholicism.[27]

Travellers endow the desert with redemptive and purifying powers which
'cleanse' the suffering individual, as both Lawrence and Thesiger have noted.
Lawrence's interpretation of redemption is unique in that he resorts to a
particular version of the pilgrimage paradigm: the Crusade. An expert on the
Crusades' military architecture (the basis for the entire design of the *Seven
Pillars of Wisdom*), Lawrence medievalised Arabia and applied chivalric
ideas to the Arab Revolt of 1916–18 which he helped organise.[28] *Seven
Pillars* is structured as a Crusade story, progressing towards the moment of
the liberation of Damascus, a reversal of the ethos of Saladin's victory over
the Christians in the twelfth century. It was precisely the epic and chivalric
dimension of the 'war in the desert' that instantaneously made the book a
myth and Lawrence an international cult figure, for during the 1920s and
1930s it represented an opposite kind of war to the great upheaval which had

just devastated Europe. The moving front of the Arabian campaign, and the tribesmen who carried it forth, formed a desirable contrast to the Western Front and static and impersonal artillery trench warfare. Though bloody, as a number of episodes in Lawrence's account make clear, the violence in the revolt was depicted by him and seen by readers averse to the industrial carnage in Europe as 'clean'.[29]

The new travelogue and the emerging Arabist vision of the Middle East involved not only the relocation of Arabia, but also that of the Arabs themselves. Late travellers' treatment of nomad life and culture departs, albeit not entirely, from the ethnocentric idiom and epistemology of Orientalist discourse. More specifically, they differ from earlier writers like Burton and Palgrave who had had little first-hand knowledge of Bedouin life. One important such departure is the ethnographic search for an understanding of nomad culture on its own terms, stressing the need to make the authentic Arab voice audible. The word 'authentic' has different meanings: historical (denoting the descendants of the inhabitants of the peninsula before Islamisation), biological and even racial (indicating Arab racial purity), or socio-cultural (defining a nomadic and pastoral life and economy). The Bedouin was deemed superior to the Ottoman, the Levantine, and even to the Arab city dweller of the Hijaz who had been exposed to outside influences, including Western material culture and ideas. Such influences were condemned as contaminating. Even writers who had only passed through the peninsula picked up this juxtaposition of the town and the desert and made it the pivot of their writing. The purity of the Bedouin, they argued, was the result of the hardship of his life and his isolation from the outside world. Views concerning authenticity influenced Arabist policy. Thus Mark Sykes, known less as a traveller than as one of the architects of the 1916 Anglo-French Sykes-Picot agreement which divided the Middle East into areas of direct British and French rule, spheres of influence, and independent Arab states, transposes the notion onto Arabist policy. As he notes: 'Arabs cannot be run on the lines of the "White Man's burden"...they have physique, fire and nimbleness of mind and a sense of breed which makes it impossible to adopt the white versus coloured attitude'.[30] Though Sykes's cultural and racial arrogance comes through clearly, it is not amply evident in the writing of other Arabists. But what is common to writers as different as Sykes, the Blunts, Henry St John Philby, and Wilfred Thesiger is their notion that the traveller/ethnographer should be the preserver and keeper of the pristine Arab way of life and of the true and pure Arabia. Hence the insistence not only on documentation but on what may be described as dialogical writing that would 'present the case on the seldom heard voice from within before it shall have been stifled by the growing pressure from without, as might well happen even as a more or less immediate consequence of the appalling upheaval of 1914'.[31]

Of course, the dialogue as both a literary device and a world-view allowing for cross-cultural exchanges is by no means peculiar to writing on Arabia.[32] However, the rôle allocated to the tribesmen in the Arabian travelogue involves more than their speaking up or back to the Western observer: they become co-travellers. During the long and arduous journeys, all travellers, regardless of their religion and nationality, but Westerners especially, depended entirely on the tribes' protection of life and limb, and protection of caravans became an important source of living throughout the Nafud and Empty Quarter. Under such circumstances conventional colonial hierarchies broke down. With a few exceptions, travellers describe their guides and, by extension the guides' tribes, as companions, in familial terms which do not necessarily denote a parental-filial bond (this would be entirely within the paternalist Orientalist framework), but rather a bond between siblings. This is a distinctly masculine bond and indeed the travel epic purports to be a masculine genre. Male travellers celebrate a physical prowess and admire the Bedouin for his manliness. They also appreciate his being an *asil*, that is of pure Arab blood and therefore apparently the upper-class Englishman's equal. Occasionally the male bond has a homoerotic streak to it (Lawrence is a case in point). Although at least three of the major explorers of the greater Arabia, Anne Blunt, Bell, and Stark, were women and one of them, Anne Blunt, practically defined the terms of the discussion on nomad Arabs, they were marginalised by contemporary and following travellers and excluded from the Arabist succession. Such an omission in a genre that is excessively citationary is revealing.[33]

The travellers' project of humanising the Arab, documenting his life and making him audible is marked by a paradox. What they describe as 'authentic' is itself about to disappear. Put slightly differently, the discovery of the Arab means his loss to the traveller and, one may add, to a nostalgic Western reading public. This is so because the related processes of imperialism, Westernisation, and modernisation were irreversible. Moreover, some of the most enthusiastic Arabists were directly involved in the very processes they scathingly criticised: suffice it to mention Lawrence's part in introducing mechanised warfare into the Hijaz during the Revolt and St John Philby's interest (in both senses of this term) as agent of the US car and oil industries during the early 1930s. The sense of loss is most apparent in Thesiger's *Arabian Sands* (1959), which revolves around his crossings of the Empty Quarter in 1946, from south to north then back and from south-west (Manwwaki in Yemen) to north-east (the Trucial Coast on the Gulf). Thesiger's is a collective conquest of the desert, achieved with the Bait Kathir and Rashid Bedouins he lives and travels with and whose company he values as the most significant bond of his life. It is to them that the book is dedicated. Throughout he avoids 'criticizing their standards and ways of life different from my own', and adopts these ways. He thinks them doomed by the political and economic impact of global and local changes such as US oil imperialism and the centralisation carried out by the Saudi state. His tone is elegiac: 'I realized that the Bedu with whom I had lived and travelled, and in whose company I had found contentment, were doomed...I shall always remember how often I was humbled by those illiterate herdsmen who possessed, in so much greater measure than I, generosity and courage, endurance, patience and light-hearted gallantry. Among no other people I have felt the same sense of personal inferiority.'[34]

The elegiac tone and indeed the overall criticism of modernity are entirely in line with the Arabists' anti- or counter-modernity. However, the lament for the transformation of the peninsula denies the Arabs the ability to take an active part in processes of change. Thesiger predicted that the nomad would become a passive lumpenproletariat in shanty towns (p. 310). It is precisely on the complexities of modernisation that more recent travellers have focused. During the last four decades of the twentieth century travel to and inside the peninsula changed radically. Jet travel, supplanting exploration and giving discovery new meanings, has combined with overall economic prosperity in Saudi Arabia and the Gulf states (from the establishment of the organisation of the oil-importing states (OPEC) around 1960) to redirect interest towards the peninsula's new or renewed urban centres. The desert, the *locus idealis* of the Arabist utopia, has become peripheral in the recent narratives. Jonathan Raban's *Arabia: A Labyrinth*, first published in 1979 as *Arabia Through the Looking Glass*, is arguably the best exemplar of the changed modes of travel and their representations. Raban's itinerary is from Earls Court, London, to the Gulf states of Bahrain, Qatar, Abu Dhabi, and Dubai, then (after a stay in Yemen, Egypt, and Jordan) back to Earls Court. In literary and cultural terms this itinerary signifies a journey away from the great explorers' construct of Arabia, as well as being a commentary on the anti-Arab discourse in the West during the world oil crisis of 1978. Modernity and rapid change excite Raban. Indeed the peninsula's 'headlong plunge into modernity', its dynamism, constant expansion, and optimism seem to him 'like stumbling through a time-lock into the heyday of the Industrial Revolution' in the West. Raban is quite aware that modernisation, rather than controlling the Arabs of the Gulf states and ruining them, was controlled by them through acculturation.[35] The signposts in the distinctly urban landscapes he describes include skyscrapers and highways, oil drums and refineries, airports and fast cars, and mammoth constructions of concrete and glass. In this urban mock-utopia built with oil money, the nomads' poverty may not be idealised, and the Bedouins seem to have become part of an archive. In one central scene Raban describes Qatar's folk museum, where Qataris view their own Bedouin heritage (pp. 81–2). Thus definitions of the Western gaze and of 'Westernisation' are relativised. The traveller and travel, too, are redefined. In the Gulf states there are very few permanent residents – the former nomads – but hoards of travellers/workers, British, Palestinians, and Indians, the latter forming a cheap labour force. These reversals and re-definitions reflect the swing of power in the post-colonial world. Yet Arabia is represented as a labyrinthine text, still awaiting to be 'made sense of' by a traveller relying on previous texts (recall the subtitle 'Through the Looking Glass'). This, like the comparisons between Arabia's present and Europe's past (the First Industrial Revolution) effectively de-historicises the changes observed. The tension between the sensitivity to change, on the one hand, and the resort to texts that would serve as 'key' to the Orient, on the other, exemplifies that coexistence of older and newer authorities, models of narrative, and travel cultures.

NOTES

1 Alfred Thayer Mahan, 'The Persian Gulf and International Relations', in *National Review* (September 1902), cited in B. Lewis, *The Middle East and the West* (New York: Harper and Row, 1964), p. 9; Valentine Chirol, *The Middle Eastern Question* (London: John Murray, 1903).

2 Raymond Schwab, *The Oriental Renaissance: Europe's Discovery of India and the East 1680–1880*, trans. G. Patterson-Black and V. Reiking (New York: Columbia University Press, 1984).

3 Albert Hourani, *Islam and the West* (London: Macmillan, 1980).

4 Mary Louise Pratt's term in *Imperial Eyes: Travel Writing and Transculturation* (New York: Routledge, 1992); Edward Said, *Orientalism* (New York: Routledge and Kegan Paul, 1978).

5 Apart from Said's own work, see Rana Kabbani, *Europe's Myths of Orient: Devise and Rule* (London: Macmillan, 1986).

6 See Norman Daniel, *Islam and the West: The Making of an Image* (Edinburgh University Press, 1960); R. W. Southern, *Western Views of Islam in the Middle Ages* (Cambridge, Mass.: Harvard University Press, 1980).

7 James Clifford, 'On *Orientalism*', in his *The Predicament of Culture: Twentieth Century Ethnography, Literature and Art* (Cambridge, Mass.: Harvard University Press, 1988), pp. 155–77; Billie Melman, *Women's Orients: English Women and the Middle East, 1718–1918: Sexuality, Religion and Work*, 2nd edn (London: Macmillan, 1995); Ali Behdad, *Belated Travelers: Orientalism in the Age of Colonial Dissolution* (Durham: Duke University Press, 1994); Charles Issawi, *Cross-Cultural Encounters and Conflicts* (Oxford University Press, 1999); Lisa Lowe, *Critical Terrains: British and French Orientalisms* (Ithaca: Cornell University Press, 1991).

8 Jaś Elsner and Joan Pau Rubiés, 'Introduction', *Voyages and Visions: Toward a Cultural History of Travel* (London: Reaktion Books, 1999), pp. 1–57.

9 P. W. L. Walker, *Holy City, Holy Places: Christian Attitudes to Jerusalem and the Holy Land in the Fourth Century* (Oxford: Clarendon Press, 1990); R. J. Zvi Werblowsky 'The Meaning of Jerusalem to Jews, Christians and Muslims', in *Jerusalem in the Mind of the Western World, 1800–1948. With the Eyes to Zion-V*, ed., Y. Ben-Arieh and M. Davis (Westport, Conn.: Praeger, 1997), pp. 7–25.

10 On the transformation of Mediterranean travel see John Pemble, *The Mediterranean Passion: Victorians and Edwardians in the South* (Oxford: Clarendon Press, 1988). For Cook and contemporary estimates see Ruth Kark, 'From Pilgrimage to Budding Tourism: The Role of Thomas Cook in the Rediscovery of the Holy Land in the Nineteenth Century', in *Travellers to the Near East*, ed. S. Searight and M. Wagstaff (Durham: Astene Publications, 2001), pp. 155–74.

11 Sarah Kochav, ' "Beginning in Jerusalem": The Mission to the Jews and English Evangelical Eschatology', in *Jerusalem in the Mind*, ed. Ben-Arieh and Davis, pp. 91–109; Melman, *Women's Orients*, pp. 165–75.

12 Edward Robinson, *Biblical Researches in Palestine, Mount Sinai and Arabia Patraea: a Journal of Travels in the Year 1838* (Boston: Crocker and Brewster, 1841), pp. iii, 4, 6, cited in Naomi Sheppard, *The Zealous Intruders, The Western Discovery of Palestine* (London: Collins, 1987), p. 80.

13 Frances Power Cobbe, *Cities of the Past* (London: Trübner & Co., 1864), p. 175.

14 Augusta Mentor Mott, *Stones of Palestine. Notes of a Ramble Through the Holy Land* [1865] (London: Seeley, Jackson and Halliday, 1891), preface.

15 J. J. Moscrop, *Measuring Jerusalem: The Palestine Exploration Fund and British Interests in the Holy Land* (London: Leicester University Press, 2000).

16 On the latter term, see Clifford's 'Preface' to *The Predicament of Culture*.

17 See Pratt, *Imperial Eyes*, pp. 167–71; Melman, *Women's Orients*, pp. 77–99.

18 Lady Mary to Lady Mar, 1 April 1717, in *The Complete Letters of Lady Mary Wortley Montagu*, ed. R. Halsband (Oxford: Clarendon Press, 1967), vol. 1, p. 328.

19 See Melman, *Women's Orients*, pp. 137–59.

20 On Britain's Arab policies, see Clive Leatherdale, *Britain and Saudi Arabia 1925–39: The Imperial Oasis* (London: Frank Cass, 1983).

21 See Kathryn Tidrick, *Heart Beguiling Araby* (Cambridge University Press, 1981).

22 See Elizabeth Monroe, *Britain's Moment in the Middle East 1914–56* (London: Methuen, 1963).

23 T. E. Lawrence, *Seven Pillars of Wisdom* (Ware: Wordsworth Classics, 1997), p. 41.

24 See Elizabeth Freedgood, *Victorian Writing about Risk: Imagining a Safe England in a Dangerous World* (Cambridge University Press, 2000).

25 C. M. Doughty, *Arabia Deserta* (New York: Dover, 1979), vol. 1, pp. 95, 172, 538; vol. 11, pp. 302–3.

26 Anne Blunt, *A Pilgrimage to Nedj, the Cradle of the Arab Race. A Visit to the Court of the Emir and 'Our Persian Campaign'* (London: Murray, 1879), pp. 155–6.

27 See Anne Blunt's letter to Wilfrid Blunt, quoted in Noel S. A. Lytton, *Wilfrid Scawen Blunt: A Memoir* (London: Macdonald, 1967), pp. 301–2.

28 See Malcolm D. Allen, *The Medievalism of Lawrence of Arabia* (University Park: Pennsylvania University Press, 1991).

29 On the Lawrence cult see John E. Mack, *A Prince of Our Disorder: The Life of T. E. Lawrence* (Cambridge, Mass.: Harvard University Press, 1998), pp. 274–8.

30 Quoted in Tidrick, *Heart Beguiling Araby*, p. 169.

31 Anne Blunt, *The Authentic Arabian Horse and his Descendants* (London: G. Allen & Unwin, 1945), pp. 311–12.

32 It is, for example, also a feature of the domestic ethnographies: see Melman, *Women's Orients*; and Reina Lewis, *Gendering Orientalism: Race, Femininity and Representation* (London: Routledge, 1996).

33 See Behdad, *Belated Travelers*, pp. 92–7.

34 Wilfred Thesiger, *Arabian Sands* (London: Longman, 1959), pp. 48–50, 310.

35 Jonathan Raban, *Arabia Through the Looking Glass* (London: Picador, 1979), p. 35.

7

NEIL L. WHITEHEAD

South America / Amazonia: the forest of marvels

The very first documents to emerge from the New World were travel accounts. Although this was not the earliest travel writing in Europe the encounter with the Americas certainly stimulated a vast production of such literature and arguably made textual experience of the exotic a much more mundane occurrence. At the time of the discovery of the New World, the horizons of colonial Europe were also being expanded by travel to the east and south, but the unanticipated discoveries of Columbus provided a frisson of mystery and a need for explanation. This was the basis not just for recurrent attempts to detail, catalogue, and locate the peoples, creatures, and geographies of the continents, but also for a particular sense of the possibility of encountering the marvellous, the novel, and the extreme. The cross-cutting of these themes and ideas has produced a travel writing in South America that is filled with the discovery of the fantastic, the survival of the anachronistic, and the promise of marvellous monstrosity.[1]

In this way, South America – more than its northern counterpart – and particularly the Amazon region, has been largely imagined through such travel writing. This becomes very evident in attempts to define and locate the region. The 'Amazon' might be restrictively identified with the main river channel or the river basin, but the Amazon river basin actually has a watershed connection with that of the Orinoco, so that hydrology defies neat boundaries and definitions. Likewise, although western Amazonia has an intensity of rainfall that is unrivalled elsewhere in the river basin, the actual extent of the 'tropical rainforest' in South America exceeds the limits of the Amazon basin itself, stretching into Peru, Ecuador, Colombia, Venezuela, Guyana, Surinam, and French Guiana. The Amazon could therefore be seen to comprise not only the contiguous forests that spread beyond the river-system, but also savanna and scrub forest environments. Writers of travel literature and of other kinds of account conflate these differences and distinctions into an idea of 'Amazonia' that is migratory and dislocated from specific physical spaces, allowing it to become an intense object of the imagination.

As a result, the notion of a heart to this forest darkness, an essence that lies deeper and ever deeper under the arboreal canopy, repeatedly drives the narrative forms of description, from the El Dorado of Walter Ralegh to Col. Percy Fawcett's pursuit of the Seven Cities of the Matto Grosso. In this sense nothing could more clearly mark the region east of the Andes and north of the River Plate as a field of dreams for the external imagination than their identification, in the first traveller's account of the river, by Gaspar de Carvajal, as the land of Amazon women. This imaginary geography excludes both the grasslands of the southern cone and, more significantly, the Andes and its Incan Empire, which have otherwise loomed large in the literature of the Americas. However, from the perspective of travel the literary production of those locales, being relatively devoid of surviving savages or uncharted spaces, has taken second place to the descent into the 'green hell' of jungle Amazonia.

Thus, as with any 'place', the Amazon is constituted through the cultural imagination but, unlike even 'Africa' or the 'Orient', the Amazon has been produced especially through the 'imperial eyes' of the colonial traveller.[2] The relatively swift (in some places) and deeply destructive (in all places) European occupation of the South American shoreline and major riverways allowed the effective social and cultural domination of the indigenous population, but left the larger continental geography untamed. No railways or roads came to criss-cross the forests, no pioneers sustained the sense of occupation, and the enigmas of forest ecology challenged even the most brutal efforts of extractive industries to make the jungle profitable. These socio-political realities have defined the place of the Amazon in the colonial imagination, from Columbus to the present day, and have interacted with the imagining of the Americas more generally to produce a particular aesthetic in the writing of the Amazon. This aesthetic reflects a deeply historical sense of the epistemological disjuncture involved in encountering a 'new world', coupled with the persistent experience of an intractable ecology – be that the intemperate nature of the climate, fauna, flora, or 'natives'.

This chapter will try to reflect that deep history, the purpose being to suggest a significant continuity in the aesthetics of travel writing from the sixteenth century to the twentieth. Given the vast diversity of travel accounts only a few can receive attention, and writing in languages other than English can only be alluded to in passing, even though much of the framework for imagining Amazonia originates in Spanish and Portuguese texts. Nonetheless, some Iberian, as well as Dutch, French, and German accounts were rapidly translated and issued in English and knowledge of such texts among readers is often presumed by subsequent authors. Later travel texts were also regularly translated or redacted into various compilations of voyages or 'histories' and so became part of English-language travel writing, especially with the foundation of the Hakluyt Society in the nineteenth century.

Given this borrowing from and translating of early travel texts, it is evident that certain key metaphors and representations dominate this diverse body of writings which have their origins in the earliest encounters between Europeans and Americans. As the purposes of travel and exploration became increasingly disengaged from the direct business of colonial occupation and exploitation so the cultural space emerged where accounts of travel and discovery could use the genre to explore inner jungles, as much as vegetal ones. In this more restricted sense travel writing only really exists from the late nineteenth century on, whereas previously travellers' writings were conceived and understood as instructive primarily in virtue of authors' encounters with unaccounted for human difference and unfamiliar natural phenomena.

The chapter will also examine the relationship between travel writing and the emergence of academic genres such as ethnography, geography, and zoology in which scientific description is often as important as the tale of travel itself. Also considered will be the way in which the literature of travel in Amazonia is echoed in the production of scientific knowledge. By the same token travelling as a professional exercise has become the occasion for ethnological speculation and such works illustrate the current state of Amazon travelogues.

Imaginary origins: locating the civilised and the wild, 1500–1700

In the European exploration of South America, the Caribbean Islands, coastal Guiana, and the Brazilian littoral south of the Amazon were the easterly starting points for journeys into the hinterland. However, Spanish occupation of the Incan Empire in the 1530s meant that the first journeys down the Amazon channel were made from the west, following the headwaters to the mouth. It is from these four regions that the first travel accounts began to emerge, all projecting different kinds of imagery of the interior, but – since simultaneously concerned with how that interior might be better known – also emphasising the character of indigenous peoples, the ramification of their social and political systems, and the opportunities for trade and plunder that existed among them. Equally significant for these early writers were the hydrology, topography, and agricultural potential of the land, for both writing about one's travels and getting them published required financial investment, and publication had to have demonstrable political utility.

The first accounts of travel along the Amazon were neither in English nor ever published by their authors. Gaspar de Carvajal's account of the journey made in 1541 by Francisco de Orellana from the Amazon headwaters in Peru to its mouth is nonetheless one of the most important documents of New World exploration for its description of societies of the Amazon before significant European occupation of the river in the 1630s.[3] Carvajal also set a tone for the way in which the river would be described in most subsequent accounts – vast, incomprehensible, filled with wonder, and rich in life and culture. Such marvels also implied connections both with the Inca and the walled city of El Dorado, and these connections are repeatedly evidenced in the journey through references to the presence of llamas, copper axes, clothing, and so forth. Carvajal also announces the presence of the Amazons who came to fight against the Spanish expedition and informs us of a probable location of their principal city that was the seat of their ruler, Coñori. Later writers would also adopt this location, on the north bank of the Amazon along the Trombetas river, as the focal point for tales of the Amazons. Carvajal initiated an ethnological framework for understanding the great diversity of peoples whereby those upstream subtly approximate the 'civilised' Indians of Peru, while those downstream, noted for their use of poison arrows and display of severed heads, appear more wild and distant. The Amazons thus occupy an ambiguous mid-point, both culturally and fluvially, as eminent women capable of brutal ferocity.

These themes of ethnological marvel and wondrous promise are all fully present in the idea of 'El Dorado', a persistent concern in English travel writing about the Amazon of this period. This concern definitively originates with Walter Ralegh's *Discoverie*... [1596] where he describes his encounters in 1595 with various native leaders on the lower Orinoco river and how he garners intelligence on the establishment of a golden empire in the Pakaraima mountains by Incan refugees from the Spanish conquest in Peru. He also alludes to the Amazons encountered by Carvajal and unites a whole series of ethnological materials, taken from Spanish accounts, to describe the trade in golden objects, the wars and conflicts between the peoples of the Orinoco and the uplands, and to document such marvels as men with heads in their chests and the presence of cannibals.[4]

Overall, Ralegh's constant iteration of place names, ethnic designations, and the names of native leaders serves to authenticate his broader claims, giving the reader the sense of someone who has (paradoxically) more than just a passing acquaintance. However, in Ralegh's as in Carvajal's account, the vastness of the landscape defies accurate mapping. Ralegh writes of the mouth of the Orinoco: 'if God has not sent us another helpe, we might have wandered a whole yeer that laborinth of rivers, ... for I know all the earth doth not yeeld the like confluence of streames and branches' (p. 156). Such riverine entanglements also prompted the use of the name *Marañón* (from the

Spanish *marañas*, meaning thicket) for the Amazon, and hence the notion of a 'River of Entanglements' poetically alludes to the many ways in which Amazonia threatened a dissolution of moral, cultural, and geographical norms.

In the writings from the Brazil coast the experience of cultural difference is marked by the rumour and surmise of cannibalism, a topic only passingly mentioned in the materials reviewed so far. Despite the fact that the European encounter with the Tupi peoples of the Brazilian coast was geographically beyond even the most expansive definition of the Amazon region, the intensity and detail of the writings that describe those encounters have exercised a profound influence on subsequent attitudes to native South American peoples. The Tupi came to be seen as 'cannibals' par excellence. Early images of their rituals and descriptions of their cultural practices were often transposed to new settings, especially within French writings, since they became an exemplary case of the ethnologically pristine. Key amongst the various travel accounts that establish the Tupi in this cultural rôle is that written by Hans Staden.[5]

Little is known of Staden aside from the story of his nine-month captivity among the Tupi in Brazil. While in Portuguese service as a gunner in the early 1550s, Staden was surprised by a party of Tupinambá warriors, stripped naked and beaten, and immediately carried off. It was apparent that he was destined for sacrifice as a prisoner of war. He was duly prepared to be ritually killed but a timely attack of toothache led him to refuse food and he grew thin. Questioned about the disposition of the Portuguese, Staden instead suggested that it was the Tupinikin who were planning to attack his captors. When this prediction came true, Staden went on to suggest that the moon, a source of evil and sickness in native cosmology, was angry with the Tupinambá. When his captors subsequently fell sick this became a further proof, and gave Staden an opportunity to perform as a prophet-healer and to suggest that he had interceded with his 'all-powerful' god to relieve them of their afflictions. His success gave him an untouchable status, but the Tupinambá did not want to give up their strange and potent new prophet-healer and his captivity continued. Staden recounts his observation of the cannibal demise of other captives, including Portuguese, and the frustrated attempts he made to escape with various visiting ships. He also joined his captors on raids against enemy villages and observed and commented upon the practice of war. Finally, however, Staden was able to parlay his way aboard a French ship, reaching Honfleur, France, on 20 February 1555.

Staden's text is also important because it is as much a homily of redemption and faith as it is a travel text, Tupi cannibalism being but one of the many tests and redemptive proofs of Christian faith his experience offers. The etymology of 'travel' as 'travail' becomes fully realised. Amazonia certainly offers, as Carvajal first indicated, many such travails for the traveller. Moreover, as a repeated eyewitness to ritual anthropophagy, Staden's account stands apart from other French materials of this period which intellectualised Tupi rituals by analogy with Catholic and Protestant doctrinal disputes. Jean de Léry's far more extensive account of his travels to Brazil in 1556–8, likewise intricately described Tupi culture;[6] but it is his position as captive that invests Staden's account with particular significance. Given the highly sympathetic portrait of the Tupi which emerges, despite their cannibal practices, Staden's book alerts us – like other American captivity narratives – to a dimension of 'captivity' beyond those of physical restraint and personal erasure: the threat of cultural dissolution offered by a captivity of the senses, an enchantment, a bewitching of the imagination by the freedoms, lack of constraint, and force of exotic cultural practice: 'going native' or 'going bush' as it was expressed in the colonial lexicon. Staden remarks that, at the time of this physical capture, 'I knew less of their customs than I knew later' (p. 71), and that encounter with extreme exoticism was the key aspect of his experience that required explanation. This possibility of a moral capture recurs most strongly in twentieth-century writing, but is ever present in travel writing about the Amazon, first as imminent possibility, later as an aspect of colonial nostalgia for what had been destroyed.

These early narratives of travel thus set a framework for the European imagination that most subsequent writers employed: the vast and intricate nature of the land and riverscapes, the elusive presence of native peoples, enigmatic if not hostile, who threaten death and dismemberment by poison arrow or cannibal feast, and always the lure of marvellous discovery, whether of native empires of women, unsuspected fluvial connections, cities of gold, or wonders of nature. In short Amazonia provoked and inspired an aesthetic of extremes.

Colonial glimpses into the interior, 1650–1850

As the colonial regimes in South America moved permanently to occupy and expand their initial coastal enclaves, so the place of travel accounts in the cultural work of conquest changed. Although travellers coming directly from Europe are still represented, a new kind of traveller emerges – one who negotiates not so much geographical distance as cultural difference. The codification of that difference, its repeated proof and extension through journeys into the hinterlands beyond administrative control – the tribal zone of anthropology or the contact zone of literary scholarship – now becomes the site for the production of exemplary experience and useful knowledge.[7] The fact of encounter is itself no longer remarkable, rather specific kinds of encounter with moral and natural phenomena provide the evidence of authentic travel. As a result, seventeenth- and eighteenth-century accounts move from more general evocations to the minutiae of particular landscapes, plants, and animals, or to the investigation of specific cultural proclivities and practices. Occasionally, unknown and wild peoples are seen at the terminal points of such journeying, sustaining a sense of boundless possibility in a limitless environment, and so the definitive searches for the elusive river highways of the continent, or even the great and golden city of El Dorado itself, begin in hope and end in expectation. Amazon women flit through the forest, while cannibals with poison arrows emerge unannounced from the apparently peaceful dispositions of more familiar natives. Nonetheless, it is the defeat of such possibilities by the continuing textual delineation of place, culture, and nature, which together with the success and profitability of the colonial project itself, underwrites and makes plausible these notices from the interior. Much of this literature was produced by travel writers with more sustained colonial (as opposed to metropolitan) identities, such as missionaries and administrators, signalling that the authenticating features of travel accounts now required evidence of more sustained journeying undertaken on the basis of already existing experiences of distance and difference.

The missionary narratives of Padre Acuña and Padre Fritz return us to the sites first visited by Carvajal, but tell of the loss and destruction of native culture in the intervening 130 years. This apparent gap in writing about the Amazon was not absolute: there exist manuscript accounts of individual reconnoitering and even of a journey to the palace of Coñori, Queen of the Amazons. The hiatus in published accounts was due to the fact that after Carvajal the only European presence in the river basin itself was provided by scattered trading posts manned by small companies of French, English, Irish, and Dutch adventurers. Only in 1639 did the Portuguese make their first attempt at settlement of the river, and Father Acuña was part of that armed ingress. He is therefore overwhelmingly concerned with the economic and political prospects for the river and its peoples. He also explicitly revisits many of the sites of Carvajal's narrative as if to exorcise the shadow of that Spanish emissary in favour of his Portuguese King. In emulating the track of Carvajal, Acuña's narrative harks back to the initial metaphors of vastness and mystery, even resurrecting by allusion the conjecture of Columbus that the hydrology of the southern continent was consistent with it being the site of the biblical Eden:

...if the Ganges irrigates all India...if the Nile irrigates and fertilizes a great part of Africa: the river of the Amazons waters more extensive regions, fertilizes more plains, supports more people, and augments by its floods a mightier ocean: it only wants, in order to surpass them in felicity, that its source should be in Paradise.[8]

The theme of an Amazonian dystopia thus becomes firmly embedded in subsequent writings, both anthropological and literary.

However, it is Fritz's account, covering the years 1689–91, 1697–1703, and 1707–23 that gives the more intimate picture of the Amazon, since he was a stationary traveller, moving in cultural rather than geographical space in the upper reaches of the river. He gives himself this kind of identity as a 'traveller', not just an evangelical functionary, through his partial intellectual detachment from the immediate missionary project. This is signalled through a nostalgia for the native past, a sense of the destruction of native people through disease and slavery, and an ambivalence towards the eradication of their superstitions.[9]

In similar vein the French Jesuit missionaries Pierre Barrère, Antoine Biet, Jean Grillet, and Pierre Pelleprat supply accounts of their evangelical jour-neying in the interior of French Guiana that anticipate the rigorous de-scriptive forms of later science writing;[10] just as missionary writing from British Guiana a century later anticipates the establishment of a 'scientific' anthropology.[11] Conventionally these accounts begin with a description of the colony, in this case Cayenne, which rather than the continent as a whole has become the orbit of journeying. To this is then added, in proof of cultural and not just geographical journeying, extensive ethnological descriptions of native peoples and their customs. Indeed this native element becomes the defining characteristic of the traveller over the colonial observer, for no jour-ney can be said to have been at all remarkable unless some tale of a previously unknown 'nation', or unrecorded ritual, can be advanced to show the pen-etrating nature of both geographical exploration and intellectual inquiry. In this way such travel accounts begin to appear quite uniform in their content and choice of subject matter, so that the social and intellectual positioning of the traveller himself begins to intrude as a means of signalling the relative uniqueness of an experience of the familiarly exotic.

In the sphere of non-missionary writing we find many of the same features occurring, but with apparently greater cultural space for the play of the indi-vidual characteristics of the writer. Nonetheless, the authenticating forms of travel accounts, particularly encounters with exotic peoples or biota, remain an important element in suggesting authenticity and authority. Increasingly, though, it is journeying within the confines of the colony rather than the grand voyages of exploration that come to dominate travel writing, often as a result of the kinds of social connection that individuals had to the colonial scene. It is striking that all the following authors of travel accounts were either in the employ of the colonial government or had their own financial interests in the colonial economy. As a result, the colonial orbit itself, rather than the hinterland which lay beyond it, became the main object of description. This is particularly true of the works by Adriaan van Berkel, Edward Bancroft, Henry Bolingbroke, or Philippe Fermin, where the overall shape and character of the colony, its statistical features, its resources and local fauna and flora are the dominant matters discussed.[12] One no longer travels to a new world, merely to a portion of it under the reforming hand of the local colonial administration. Accordingly, the sense of unlimited possibility, golden cities, Amazon women, and monstrous humanoids is replaced by the infinite wonder of a complex natural world, and the variety of social being is offered no longer just by a native presence, but by the exotic and threatening world of black slavery and rebellion.

John Gabriel Stedman's 1790 account of his five-year expedition against 'the revolted Negroes of Surinam' perfectly exemplifies all these trends.[13] Stedman gives a full account of his romantic entanglements with a black slave woman and the nature of slave society itself, descriptions of exotic plants and animals, an analysis of the relations between master and slaves, and a narrative of military actions in the interior. Here also the individual positioning of Stedman becomes critical to the way the text is understood for, though he was no abolitionist, the empathy with which he treats the slave population transcends any stated political views.

The creation of Amazonia, 1750–1900

Subsequent travel accounts offer a counterpoint to these kinds of narratives and indicate a new phase in writing on Amazonia, since they describe a determined seeking of wonders beyond the orbit of the colonial world so thoroughly travelled in the preceding era. A sense of nostalgia for the eclipse of a native Amazon now really begins to take hold. This nostalgia developed during the eighteenth century as the European colonies throughout Amazonia became less dependent on their relationships with the native population, and the problems of managing burgeoning slave-based societies preoccupied many writers and thinkers. In this context the 'vanished Indians' could become a safe and comforting object of moral reflection on the passing of sylvan simplicity.

Among the best known travel writings about the Amazon are those of the explorer-scientists, such as Baron von Humboldt, La Condamine, Karl

Martius, and Johann Spix, or Henry Bates, Richard Spruce, and Alfred Russel Wallace.[14] However, a body of lesser-known writing, by such authors as William Hilhouse, Charles Barrington Brown, and Robert and Richard Schomburgk, extends and imitates these more familiar works:[15] extends in the sense that they developed a style of travel writing that strongly emphasises the correct cataloguing and the rational ordering of both natural and moral phenomena; imitates in the sense that they were aware of the larger frameworks of knowledge which these 'master works' laid down. These master works gain their authority partly through direct funding by government bodies and the consequent ease of access to the interior that implied – scientific exploration being a logistically complex operation; partly through the wide dissemination of the publications themselves; and partly through the intellectual break they make with the Amazon of earlier times. In this way they created a field of knowledge, a scientific construct – 'Amazonia' – and then proceeded to expound its innate logic and form. For Humboldt this explicitly involved a contrast with earlier writers who barely wandered from the shoreline of their arrival, but it also produced an Amazonia shorn by rational investigation of its mysterious empires and Amazons, exotic poisons and cannibal headhunters. This now becomes a mythically pristine Amazonia, de-historicised and recreated as a field for the play of new kinds of knowledge. The pristine myth erases both the native population and the evidence of its past. It is also blind to the processes and consequences of conquest: the empty rivers and silent forests, the vast gloom and trackless glades are not in fact the pristine indications of an undisturbed domain of nature but rather the consequence of the violent and catastrophic actions of colonial culture on the ecology of the Amazon itself and on the native peoples who once lived there. Native peoples are relegated to the status of an evanescent curiosity, among whom a few final determinations as to the riddles of local culture might be made, but whose destiny is now extinction. As such they may require ethical commentary but have become irrelevant to the potential of Amazonia for scientific enlightenment.

Henry Bates, Richard Spruce, and Alfred Russel Wallace (Spruce's editor), who all travelled for a time together, are at the core of the production of Amazonia as a scientific object for British audiences of this period. As such the facts produced were truly voluminous and to be admired as much for their commercial utility as for their scientific significance. This was also the moment when British agribusiness interests were able to 'collect' both chincona and rubber plant materials in order to establish rival plantation businesses in Asia. The contrast between the vast economic potential of Amazonia and its feeble development by the Portuguese and Spanish much exercises the imagination of these authors. As Bates puts it: 'The incorrigible nonchalance

5. Quindiu Pass, from Humboldt and Bonpland, *Atlas pittoresque – Vue des Cordillères et monuments des peuples indigènes de l'Amérique* (1810).

and laziness of the people alone prevent them from surrounding themselves with all the luxuries of a tropical country.'[16] This sets up a key theme in the subsequent writing of Amazonia, that of the unfulfilled or chimerical paradise of ecological potential, which is reflected in the scholarly production of

6. Humboldt in his study in Oranienburger Strasse, Berlin. Watercolour by Eduard Hildebrandt (1856). Courtesy of Stiftung Stadtmuseum Berlin.

anthropologists as much as in the political rhetoric of the Brazilian military that waged a campaign of colonisation in the 1960s and 1970s. Amazonia had become an internationally known site for the literary production of science and, as that scientific literature attempted to order and control what it understood as wild and natural, so the 'Science of Paradise' was born.

The Science of Paradise, 1940–2000

The 'Science of Paradise' is clearly announced in the influential anthropological writings of Julian Steward and Betty Meggers.[17] Their work set the tone for the details of any number of anthropological and archaeological research programmes from the 1940s onwards, and firmly entrenched the notion that Amazonia is a place inimical to the development of human culture, despite its appearances as ecologically productive. Accordingly, indigenous human cultures are viewed as basically small-scale, necessarily mobile and therefore unable to produce the higher forms of cultural endeavour such as cities, temples, roadways, and so forth.

At the same time, ethnographic writing was influenced by European as well as American anthropologists, none more so than Claude Lévi-Strauss, whose *Tristes Tropiques* (1955) stands out as a key work for defining the ethnographic enterprise and how it might be written. For Lévi-Strauss, Brazil offers a last chance to recapture the moments of first encounter among the remnants of the colonial conquest. His journeys into the interior are narrated as an ever-deepening path into the past, as if distance from Rio de Janeiro was also a form of time travel. This sets up the native population as exemplars of a humanity frozen in time, with the ethnographer travelling through the space of the forest to reach a moment in the past. So influential is this notion of ethnography as a kind of salvage of the pristine that it also subtly inflects even the most materialist American ethnographies, otherwise only interested in the determination of indigenous culture by the rigours of forest survival.

For example, Napoleon Chagnon's notorious work on the Yanomami of Venezuela, *Yanomamö, The Fierce People* (1968), presents itself as a scientific investigation into the environmental limits of social-cultural capacity, but also as a tale of derring-do among the last untouched savages, our 'contemporary ancestors' as the phrase became. There is therefore a sense of domination and control which emerges from these narrations of last encounters, for although we may marvel at the persistence of such antiquity, its imminent destruction and evidently anachronistic nature is obvious to the scientist but not to the natives. They become creatures at one with the forest, but therefore unreflective as to the nature of that relationship, merely acting out their material destinies according to the newly uncovered laws of science – ecology and development. The natives are unable to grasp the complexities of the modern world just beyond the horizon of the forest clearing and, though their arcane philosophies are intriguing, they are insufficient for the challenges of modernity. Here the anthropologist appears both as culture bearer and protector. Ken Good's narration of his fieldwork, *Into the Heart: One Man's Pursuit of Love and Knowledge Among the Yanomama* (1991), along with the tale of his seduction of / by an underage Yanomami girl whom he eventually marries and brings to the United States, nicely illustrates these themes. The ethnobotanist Mark Plotkin likewise offers *Tales of a Shaman's Apprentice* (1993), which relies on the strong contrast between the all-knowing scientist and the mystical savage. However, with this kind of writing it becomes all too easy to take every meeting as a replay of the Columbian moment, every old shaman as a last repository of traditional wisdom. This places actual people outside time, de-historicises their condition, and so justifies the author's ambiguous rôle as both bringer of the modern and preserver of the traditional. Of course this is more the fantasy of the writer than the condition of the written, but the power of this idea for Western culture is shown clearly in the less professionally orientated accounts of Amazonia from the twentieth century. One final work that merits special attention in this section is Phillip Descola's *The Spears of Twilight* (1996), a compelling account of the author's fieldwork with the Shuar of Ecuador. This quite overt reprise of *Tristes Tropiques* brings to the task of description an intimacy of engagement with native peoples that outdoes Lévi-Strauss's earlier work. Nonetheless, the irritating presence of the modern is effectively erased in favour of a somewhat nostalgic view of that biographical moment and of the condition of the Shuar themselves. Significantly this genre of writing is itself now under fierce attack by journalistic accounts of anthropologists which try to suggest more sinister colonial impulses at play in their research, as in Patrick Tierney's *Darkness in El Dorado* (2000) or Joe Kane's *Savages* (1995). The ethnographic eye is represented as erratic if not misleading, and somewhat baleful.

The forest of marvels, 1900–2000

Paralleling this production of Amazonia as a field of scientific and humanistic investigation increasingly known, delineated and so possessed, is a counter-narrative of the rediscovery of marvel that echoes the earliest travel writing on South America. In this way a sense that Amazonia has given up its mystery, or is about to, provokes a nostalgic, even atavistic, search for some last hidden tokens of its former wild savagery and exoticism.

In some cases this takes the form of an overt quest to discover some cultural feature or landscape 'lost' to scientific knowledge. For example, Colonel Fawcett's search for 'lost cities' in the Matto Grosso, Alex Shoumatoff's search for the 'lost tribe' of Amazons, Stephen Minta's attempt to re-create the journey of Lope de Aguirre, or Charles Nicholl's search for the lost El Dorado of Ralegh.[18]

Equally, the challenge of travel itself becomes a way of connecting the modern travel experience with the conquistadors of old, thereby again placing native peoples and their landscapes outside historical time, waiting patiently for the pen of the discoverer to bring them into the light of understanding and knowledge. Here works by Evelyn Waugh, Colin Henfrey, Nicholas Guppy, and Peter Matthiessen seem the most relevant.[19] All these authors share the experience of extensive and persistent travel, for travel has become an end in itself, a context for re-creation, if not recreation, even though the idle and playful aspect of recreation is part of the way such experiences are written. Although these writers make no claim to systematic presentations of scientific data they do display a knowledge of professional literatures which serves to legitimate their observations and to place them in a superior position with respect to the mere jottings of 'tourists'. The distinction between travellers and tourists marks all these works as their authors are at pains to show that theirs is a quite exceptional experience of travel – made so by the rigours, hardships, distances, and length of time spent in its pursuit. As such they imitate the ethnographic form itself with its emphasis on the quality of professional engagement with other peoples, as opposed to an automatic assumption of the integrity of the eyewitness.

The forest of marvels finally becomes a playground for the absurd as the distance between possible observations and actual experiences invites parody and then plagiarism of the ethnographic form. The recent works of Redmond O'Hanlon, Tobias Schneebaum, and Florinda Donner respectively illustrate these developments but a host of other works from earlier in the twentieth century also reflects such tendencies to varying degrees.[20] All rely on the notion that readers will be unable to gainsay experience and so are susceptible to any tale that invokes the key Amazonian tropes – exotic mystery, peculiar cultures, and hazardous wildlife – that dominate later twentieth-century literature not just on this region but on 'jungles' more generally.[21] Indeed both Schneebaum and O'Hanlon have also written travel works about Borneo and New Guinea.

Conclusions

Travel writing is really a hybrid result of the negotiations between the writers' expectations and experiences, and between the timeless presence of the native and the contingent invasion of the colonial. As a 'new world', Amazonia could not simply be assimilated to existing ideas, and so the intellectual ferment that the encounter with this vast and still unknowable region created was necessarily borne not just from the single experience of a particular colonial power but also from the interrelation of colonial desires throughout Europe, and from the ways in which they were enacted in this 'new world'.

Writing for English audiences constructed 'Guiana' as a British Amazon. From the work of Walter Ralegh onwards 'Guiana' was a metonym for the Amazon, since Ralegh had found there the full panoply of what came to be understood as the defining qualities of Amazonia – cannibals, amazons, gold, wild nature, moral and natural entanglements, paradisiacal bounty, mysterious thickets, hidden cities, evanescent feminised natives, and so forth. In this way the river and its environs was actually less travelled than other locations, since the Amazon channel offered no people, no places, only distant vistas. In native thought it is Paraná, the Great Water, that most elusive of elements.

This elusive quality marks the Amazon as a migratory concept, transposed perhaps to the confines of a peculiarly British 'Guiana', or brought within cultural comprehension by the way in which one journey is metonymic of all. Each journey recapitulates the defining experiences of tropical travel – the discomfort of the traveller, the disingenuousness of the natives, and ultimately a disgust at the weakness of the self – which can then be expressed as a nostalgia, but for something that never was. Knowledge of ourselves, not others, is therefore the real discovery that is made through travellers' tales.

NOTES

1 On the notion of the marvellous, see Stephen Greenblatt, *Marvelous Possessions: The Wonder of the New World* (New York: Clarendon Press, 1991).
2 See Mary Louise Pratt, *Imperial Eyes: Travel Writing and Transculturation* (London: Routledge, 1992).
3 *The Discovery of the Amazon According to the Account of Friar Gaspar de Carvajal*, ed. H. C. Heaton (New York: American Geographical Society, 1934).
4 *The Discoverie of the Large, Rich and Bewtiful Empire of Guiana by Sir Walter Ralegh*, ed. Neil L. Whitehead (Manchester University Press, 1997), pp. 145, 149, 178.
5 *Hans Staden: The True History of his Captivity, 1557*, trans. and ed. Malcolm Letts (New York: R. M. McBride & Company, 1929).
6 Jean de Léry, *History of a Voyage to the Land of Brazil*, trans. Janet Whatley (Berkeley: University of California Press, 1990).
7 See R. B. Ferguson and Neil L. Whitehead, eds., *War in the Tribal Zone. Expanding States and Indigenous Warfare* (Santa Fe: School of American Research Press; Oxford: James Currey, 2nd edn, 1999); and Pratt, *Imperial Eyes*.
8 Cristobal de Acuña, *Voyages and Discoveries in South-America* ... (London: Printed for S. Buckley, 1698), p. 61.
9 Samuel Fritz, *Journal of the Travels and Labours of Father Samuel Fritz*, trans. and ed. George Edmundson (London: Hakluyt Society, 1922).
10 Pierre Barrère, *Nouvelle Relation de la France equinoxiale* (1753); Antoine Biet, *Voyage de la France equinoxiale* ... (1664); *A Journal of the Travels of John Grillet and Francis Bechamel* (1698); and Pierre Pelleprat, *Relation des Missions des PP. de Compagnie de Jesus dans les isles et dans la Terre Ferme d'Amerique Meridionale* (1656).
11 See Rev. William H. Brett, *Indian Missions in Guiana* (1851); and Everard Im Thurn, *Among the Indians of Guiana* (1883).
12 Adriaan van Berkel, *Amerikaansche voyagien* (1695); Edward Bancroft, *An Essay on the Natural History of Guiana, in South America* (1769); Henry Bolingbroke, *A Voyage to the Demerary* ... (1807); Philippe Fermin, *Histoire naturelle de la Hollande équinoxiale* (1765).
13 John Gabriel Stedman, *Narrative of a Five Years Expedition Against the Revolted Negroes of Surinam*, ed. Richard Price and Sally Price (Baltimore: Johns Hopkins University Press, 1988).
14 Alexander von Humboldt, *Personal Narrative of Travels to the Equinoctial Regions* ..., trans. Helen Maria Williams (1800); Charles-Marie de La Condamine, *A Succinct Abridgment of a Voyage made within the Inland Parts of South-America* ... (1747); Johann Baptist von Spix and C. F. Phil. von Martius, *Travels in Brazil, in the years 1817–1820* (1824); Henry Walter Bates, *The Naturalist on*

the River Amazons (1863); Richard Spruce, *Notes of a Botanist on the Amazon & Andes* (1908); Alfred Russel Wallace, *A Narrative of Travels on the Amazon and Rio Negro with an Account of the Native Tribes, and Observations on the Climate, Geology, and Natural History of the Amazon Valley* (1853).

15 William Hilhouse, *Indian Notices* (1825); Charles Barrington Brown, *Canoe and Camp Life in British Guiana* (1877); Richard Moritz Schomburgk, *Travels in British Guiana*, ed. Walter Roth (1922–3); Robert Hermann Schomburgk, *A Description of British Guiana* (1840). In fact Robert Schomburgk, a tireless contributor to the *Journal of the Royal Geographical Society*, was more widely travelled in Guiana than better-known contemporaries.

16 Henry Walter Bates, *The Naturalist on the River Amazons* (London: J. Murray, 1863), p. 139.

17 Julian H. Steward, ed., *Handbook of South American Indians* (Washington: US Government Print Office, 1946–59) and Betty J. Meggers, *Amazonia: Man and Culture in a Counterfeit Paradise* (Washington: Smithsonian Institution Press, 1996).

18 Percy H. Fawcett, *Exploration Fawcett; Arranged from his Manuscripts, Letters, Log-books, and Records by Brian Fawcett* (1953); Alex Shoumatoff, *In Southern Light: Trekking through Zaire and the Amazon* (1986); Stephen Minta, *Aguirre: The Re-creation of a Sixteenth-Century Journey Across South America* (1993); Charles Nicholl, *The Creature in the Map: A Journey to El Dorado* (1995).

19 Evelyn Waugh, *Ninety-Two Days. A Journey in Guiana and Brazil* (1934); Colin Henfrey, *The Gentle People* (1964) and *Through Indian Eyes: A Journey among the Indian Tribes of Guiana* (1965); Nicholas Guppy, *A Young Man's Journey* (1973) and the 'ethnological' version of his travels: *Wai-Wai: Through the Forests North of the Amazon* (1958); and Peter Matthiessen, *The Cloud Forest: A Chronicle of the South American Wilderness* (1961) and his novel *At Play in the Fields of the Lord* (1965), also made into a film by The Saul Zaentz Company: Universal, 1992.

20 Redmond O'Hanlon, *In Trouble Again: A Journey Between the Orinoco and the Amazon* (1988); Tobias Schneebaum, *Keep the River on Your Right* (1969); and Florinda Donner, *Shabono* (1982). Donner's book was reviewed in a number of scholarly journals and was widely held by anthropologists to have substantially borrowed without acknowledgement from existing published materials on the Yanomami.

21 For example, Victor Norwood, *Jungle Life in Guiana* (1964); Arthur Friel, *The River of Seven Stars* (1924); Herbert Dickey, *My Jungle Book* (1932); Hassoldt Davis, *The Jungle and the Damned* (1954); and Henry Larsen and May Pellaton, *Behind the Lianas* (1958).

8

ROD EDMOND

The Pacific / Tahiti: queen of the South Sea isles

The earliest written accounts of Tahiti date from the 1760s and 1770s when a succession of European voyagers arrived at the island.[1] The first of these was the Englishman Samuel Wallis in 1767, followed by the Frenchman Louis de Bougainville in 1768 and then James Cook in 1769. The subsequent colonisation of Tahiti was slow and marked by co-operation between the two major European powers in the region, with French and British influence on the island alternating until the mid-nineteenth century. British missionaries arrived in 1797 and by the 1820s had established a virtual Protestant theocracy across the Tahitian archipelago. The arrival of French Catholic missionaries in the 1830s resulted in tension between the two missions and a French protectorate being established in 1842. Both missions persisted but Britain accepted French claims to the group in the 1847 Declaration of London, and French annexation of the islands was completed in the 1880s. British and French writing about Tahiti has a similar history of intersection and mutual influence. Bougainville's *Voyage Autour du Monde* (1771) was translated into English the following year by the father-and-son team of J. R. and George Forster, the German-born but English-domiciled scientists who sailed on Cook's second voyage in 1772 to 1775, and whose own subsequent accounts of the voyage are a vital source of knowledge of the Pacific at this time. This cross-Channel discourse inaugurated a tradition that has persisted so strongly that to concentrate entirely on anglophone travel writing would be to distort the picture.

Early contacts

Although Europe did not discover Tahiti until the 1760s the idea of it had been invented long before. Remote tropical islands, places of ease and plenty, prelapsarian worlds free of the guilty burdens and prohibitions of Judeo-Christian cultures, had been a glint in the eye of Europe for centuries before the arrival of Wallis at Tahiti. This dream of islands informed the terms in which Tahiti was first described, as for example by Joseph Banks, the gentleman-scientist and patron of exploration who travelled on Cook's first voyage. In his *Journal* he described going ashore at Tahiti for the first time:

> we walked for 4 or 5 miles under groves of Cocoa nut and bread fruit trees loaded with a profusion of fruit and giving the most gratefull shade I have ever experienced, under these were the habitations of the people most of them without walls: in short the scene we saw was the truest picture of an arcadia of which we were going to be kings that the imagination can form.[2]

The island was a place of bounty and gentle license. The scene described by Bougainville, when a young Tahitian woman swam out to the *Boudeuse* and, standing on the quarter-deck, 'carelessly dropt a cloth, which covered her, and appeared to the eyes of all beholders, such as Venus showed herself to the Phrygian sheperd, having indeed the celestial form of that goddess' established the dominant terms in which Tahiti has been imaged ever since.[3]

But, as voyages to the Pacific continued, and particularly as Cook returned for further visits, Tahiti took on deeper, less sensational significance. As observers became increasingly sensitive to the differences between superficially similar island cultures, Tahiti became the central point of reference for a whole ocean and its inhabitants, the gold standard against which other Pacific cultures were measured. The predictable contrasts between Europe and the Pacific – between self and other in postcolonial parlance – were, in part, replaced by a series of comparisons between different others, in which Tahiti was the fixed term.

This was partly because Tahitians were hospitable, and officers and crew alike could feel a measure of being 'at home' on the island. As John Elliott, midshipman on Cook's second voyage wrote on returning to Tahiti: 'we arrived . . . to the great joy of both ourselves, and our friends the Natives . . . here we might be said to be at home, enjoying ourselves in perfect safety, and being as happy as people could be, at such a distance from England'.[4] Apart from Queen Charlotte Sound in the South Island of New Zealand, Tahiti was the place that Cook visited most and stayed at longest. And unlike the dispersed warrior culture of New Zealand Maori, Tahitian culture appeared settled and peaceable. The difference between these two main anchorages of Cook's voyages – Tahiti and New Zealand – can be illustrated in terms of that fundamental dividing line between the civilised and the savage: cannibalism.

Tahitians were not cannibals, although it was believed they had once been so. Maori, on the other hand, were suspected of cannibalism, and in November 1773, while anchored in Queen Charlotte Sound, this seemed to be confirmed. The head of a native youth was brought on board *Resolution* where, as Cook's *Journals* record, 'a piece of the flesh had been broiled and eat by one of the Natives in the presince of most of the officers'. Cook himself had been ashore at the time, but returning on board and hearing of the matter he suppressed his 'horor and . . . indignation . . . and being desirious of being an eye wittness to a fact which many people had their doubts about . . . ordered a piece of the flesh to be broiled and brought on the quarter deck where one of these Canibals eat it with a seeming good relish before the whole ships Company'. Cook adds that this sight caused some of the company to vomit, but his account of the effects of this public display of cannibalism concentrates on 'Oediddee' (Mahine), a young native of the Society Islands who had been taken on board at Raiatea:

> [Oediddee] was [so] struck with horror at the sight that [he] wept and scolded by turns, before this happened he was very intimate with these people but now he neither would come near them or suffer them to touch him, told them to their faces that they were vile men and that he was no longer their friend, he used the same language to one of the officers who cut of the flesh and refused to . . . even touch the knife with which it was cut, such was this Islanders aversion to this vile custom.[5]

This young man is also the focus of both the Forsters' accounts of the same scene. J. R. Forster provides a more differentiated report of the European reaction than Cook: some laughed; for others 'their bowels were acted upon as by a dose of Ipecacuanha'; yet others felt sorrow for the victim and deplored this display of the 'debased brutality of human Nature':

> But among all these Europeans there was only young . . . Oi-diddy whose tender soul was so much struck with horror that he hardly could see the cruel Scene, & went immediately into the Cabbin & shed a flood of tears. A proof that all our artificial Education, our boasted civilization, our parade of humanity & Social virtues, was in this case outdone by the tender tears & feelings of the innocent, goodnatured boy, who was born under the benign influence of the sun within the Tropics, had the Education suitable to a Man of Quality in his country, where it seems cruelty & ferociousness have not so much gained ground, as to destroy the principles of humanity.[6]

This carefully constructed account arranges different kinds and levels of reaction into a hierarchy of response in which the native's horrified and soulful reaction heads all the rest. Forster has constructed an emblematic *mise en scène* in which natural man is rescued from the enormity of cannibalism by Mahine, and the humanity of Tahitian culture is used to redeem the savagery of the Pacific and provide an example to Europe.

George Forster's account of the scene follows his father's in detail, but with some different emphases. Of those described by J. R. Forster as having laughed, George adds that they 'did not seem greatly disinclined to feast' themselves.[7] This suggestion of transgressing a tabooed frontier further dignifies the Tahitian at the expense of the Europeans. Once again 'the sensibility of Mahine... shone out with superior lustre among us' (vol. I, p. 279), and this is underlined by the concern he goes on to express for the parents of the victim, a domestic sentiment that brings 'infinite pleasure' to the observers. George Forster, however, is not merely contrasting a noble savage with barbaric Europeans. Maori, he argues, will renounce cannibalism when, like the Tahitians, they become more united by the bonds of society. This evolutionary perspective has the Tahitian demonstrating that Maori will abandon the practice, and implies that Mahine's reaction is more likely to hasten this process than any European expressions of abhorrence. George Forster believes that Tahitians are better equipped than Europeans to civilise New Zealanders because of their intermediate position between the 'narrow views' of Maori and the 'extended sphere of knowledge' of the European (vol. I, pp. 127–8). Although it was customary for accounts of cannibalism to be framed with expressions of humane horror,[8] the casting of a native in this rôle is unusual and significant.

That Tahiti came to be seen as a place of virtue, 'the Queen of the So sea Isles', as one of Cook's officers put it,[9] is underlined by several of the commemorations of Cook's death. In Anna Seward's famous 'Elegy on Captain Cook' (1780), the highly popular pantomime *Omai: or a Trip round the World* (1785), and Helen Maria Williams's 'The Morai: an Ode' (1786), Tahiti is exonerated from the region's responsibility for Cook's death. Cook was killed on Hawaii but each of these works has him being mourned on Tahiti. Once again two island cultures are sharply distinguished from each other, allowing something to be salvaged from the killing of the great explorer. As with the cannibal scene, Tahiti functions as the Pacific's mitigation.

The most developed version of Tahiti's superiority to emerge from the Cook voyages was in J. R. Forster's *Observations Made During a Voyage Round the World* (1778). According to Forster, Tahiti is just the right size of island to prevent nomadism and promote civilisation, compact enough for a well-regulated society but not so small as to render that organisation vulnerable.[10] It is in every way the golden mean between undesirable extremes. In its political and social structure, for example, it avoids both the lack of deference that vitiates life on the Marquesan islands, and the undue subservience demanded by the chiefs in Tonga (pp. 229–30). Furthermore, the position of women in their society is much better than that of other island cultures and this in itself allows Forster to declare that they 'have emerged from the state of savages, and ought to be ranked one remove above barbarians' (p. 260).

Tahiti also represents a golden mean between European over-refinement and South Seas savagery. Its people are 'capable of the warmest attachment, of the most generous friendship, and of the most tender connexions, of which, in our mixed and degenerating societies, we have very few instances' (p. 222). Their taste for ornaments is a further sign of their 'polished manners', but this is threatened with debasement by the trifling European baubles used in exchange between ship and shore. This is not, as it might seem, an early version of the 'fatal impact' narrative which was to dominate later writing about Tahiti and other Pacific island groups. As Nicholas Thomas has pointed out, Forster places Tahitian culture within a general theory of the emergence of civility.[11] Europeans and Pacific islanders alike were susceptible to the same processes, in this case the moral ambiguities of commercial society and the dangers of opulence. The Tahitian desire for trifles and baubles is intrinsic to the stage of development they have reached, and derives from those very features that mark their culture as the most developed of all Pacific societies. The advancement of Tahitian culture is therefore as double-edged as that of its more polished European counterparts. In this way Tahiti became assimilated to contemporary eighteenth-century theories of the history of civil society, and was used to express unease about the universal social and moral implications of civil advancement.

In sum, Tahiti and the Society Islands are the most developed and the happiest of all Pacific nations. They also provide Europe with an example and a warning. Unlike 'the pampered epicure in Europe ... [whose] palled appetite remains indifferent to the almost infinite variety carried to his table from every quarter of the globe ... the more happy inhabitant of Taheitee plants his own breadfruit tree, and plucks the fruit for his own use ... there is not a single article of his food, which owes not its existence to his or his fathers industry or care' (p. 345). Similarly, in dress and habitation Tahitian life is distinguished from European by its elegance and simplicity. The island has emerged from barbarism without yet being seriously threatened by the undermining effects of luxury.

In these and other ways, then, Tahiti was represented in eighteenth-century travel writing as the jewel in the crown. This view was based on Tahiti as the 'first-found' island, on a selective account of what the voyagers discovered, and on the comparisons they made with other Pacific islands. And it derived from ready-made European discourses of happy isles and civil progress. Forster's observations, for example, were based on extensive reading but limited first-hand acquaintance. Although his account of Tahitian life is of great ethnographic value, it is also a prime example of how travel writing can tell us as much about Europe as about its others. Like any traveller, Forster was always in two places at once.

Alien practices

The longest period of contact between Europeans and Tahitians before the arrival of the missionaries in 1797 was experienced by those *Bounty* mutineers who remained on Tahiti rather than going on to Pitcairn with Fletcher Christian. The *Bounty* had spent six months on Tahiti in 1788 and 1789 before the mutiny, and those who decided not to follow Christian to Pitcairn lived there for a further eighteen months before being captured and taken back to England for trial. Foremost among these was James Morrison, whose account of his experiences, begun while awaiting trial, was the most developed piece of writing on Tahiti to this date. This prolonged experience of settlement provides the basis of Morrison's claim for the authority of his text:

> the Idea formed...of the Inhabitants of this Island...by former Voyagers
> could not possibly extend much further than their own Oppinion, None having
> remained a sufficient length of time to know the Manner in which they live and
> as their whole system was overturned by the arrival of a ship, their Manners
> were then as much altered from their Common Course, as those of our own
> Country are at a Fair, which might as well be given for a specimen of the
> Method of living in England – and such was always their situation as soon as
> a ship Arrived their whole thought being turnd towards their Visitors, & all
> Method tryd to win their Friendship.[12]

Morrison's insistence that the observer is also a participant must apply in some degree to his own narrative as well, but there is no doubt that living on shore was very different from coming on shore. In his descriptions of the investiture of a chief, for example, or of the social category of the *mahu* – transvestite males who assumed female rôles and styles – he provides access to social practices that had remained invisible to the voyagers of the 1760s and 1770s.

The *Bounty* mutiny, however, confirmed existing stereotypes rather more than it added to knowledge about Tahiti. It reinforced the allure of the islands and raised in heightened form the contrast between the discontents of civilisation and the satisfactions of so-called natural life. The spectacle of young Englishmen, some of good birth, getting tattooed, wearing native dress, and fathering native children was arresting. The shocked fascination with which this was greeted in England also had a political dimension. The mutiny occurred only a few months after the French Revolution, and when news of it reached England it seemed a distant replay of events in France.[13] It therefore divided opinion along similar lines as the French Revolution. The poet Southey, for example, though uneasy about the mutineers' treatment of Bligh, sympathised with their motives as he understood them:

Otaheitia independent of its women had many inducements not only for the sailor but the philosopher. He might cultivate his own ground and trust himself and friends for his defence – he might be truly happy in himself and his happiness would be increased by communicating it to others. He might introduce the advantages and yet avoid the vices of cultivated society.[14]

Tahiti seems to have been a model for the utopian community, the so-called Pantisocracy scheme, that Southey and Coleridge were planning to establish in the new back settlements of America. Ten years later, however, when Southey's revolutionary enthusiasm had expired, he had come to decide that the Tahitians were 'the most degraded of the human species'; Coleridge too, by now, dismissed the Tahitians as 'more detestably licentious than we could have imagined'.[15]

The seeds of this re-interpretation of Tahiti had been present from first contact. Certain aspects of Tahitian life had caused unease among the early voyagers, although these were sometimes edited out of the published record. Bougainville's private journal, for example, included passages on the stratified nature of Tahitian society and the practice of human sacrifice that did not appear in the *Voyage*.[16] Some of the more scandalous aspects of Tahitian culture were assimilable. Hawkesworth's recension of Cook's account of the scene at Point Venus where a 'young fellow above 6 feet high lay with a little Girl about 10 or 12 years of age publickly before several of our people and a number of the Natives' was bound to raise eyebrows in London but was at least consistent with the heterosexual freedom that constituted the primary terms in which Tahiti was represented.[17]

Much less titillating were the accounts of the *arioi*, a privileged élite of men and women who celebrated the seasonal festivals connected with the god 'Oro. The particular scandal of the *arioi* was not so much their licensed promiscuity as the fact they were obliged to abstain from reproduction. The offspring of both male and female *arioi* were therefore killed. The Tahitian antipathy to cannibalism, as represented by Cook and Forster, was always potentially offset by their practice of human sacrifice and infanticide. Even here, however, proto-anthropological attempts were made to understand the practice. Bligh, for example, discusses it as a form of population control in *A Voyage to the South Sea* (1792), and in his *Log* suggests that the *arioi* began as a celibate society whose members were accorded honour and privilege in compensation for not having children. Infanticide, he speculates, was an unfortunate by-product of the failure of this arrangement.[18]

There were, however, even worse practices than infanticide in the exotic thicket of Tahitian culture. Morrison had referred to 'a set of Men called Mahoo':

> These Men are in some respects like the Eunuchs in India but are not Cast-erated. They never Cohabit with weoman but live as they do; they pick their Beards out & dress as a weoman, dance and sing with them & are as effem-inate in their Voice...They are esteemed Valuable friends...and it is said, tho I never saw an instance of it, that they Converse with Men as familiar as weoman do – this however I do not aver as a fact as I never found any who did not detest the thought. (p. 238)

By 'Converse' Morrison means sexual relations. Earlier journal writers and observers had been silent about the *mahu* and same-sex practices, either out of tact or ignorance. Such gaps are difficult to read, but it would seem likely that conversation across the beach was always conducted in more than one language.

The way in which Morrison introduces the subject only to disavow it inau-gurates a largely suppressed or covert discourse on Tahitian homosexuality that was to shadow Western writing well into the twentieth century. Bligh's *A Voyage to the South Sea*, for example, makes no reference to *mahu* but his *Log* gives a vivid and detailed account based on his questioning of the Tahitian chief Pomare. Mahu, he was told, are selected when boys and kept by the women for the enjoyment of the men. A *mahu* is actually present and responds to Bligh's questioning by removing his mantle and allowing himself to be examined:

> He had the appearance of a Woman, his Yard & Testicles being so drawn in under him, having the Art from custom of keeping them in position; those who are connected with him have their beastly pleasures gratified between his thighs, but are no further Sodomites as they all positively deny the Crime. On examining his privacies I found them both very small and the Testicles remarkably so, being not larger than a boys of 5 or 6 Years Old, and very soft as if in a State of decay or a total incapacity of being larger, so that in either case he appeared to me [as] effectually a Eunuch as if his stones were away...It is strange that in so prolific a country as this, Men should be led into such sensual and beastly acts of gratification, but perhaps no place in the World are they so common or so extraordinary as in this Island. Even the mouths of Women are not exempt from the polution, and many other as uncommon ways have they of gratifying their beastly inclinations. (*Log*, vol. II, p. 17)

The microscopic scrutiny of this passage makes it no surprise that Bligh provoked three mutinies during his career. In fact both Morrison's *Journal* and Bligh's *Log* remained unpublished until the 1930s, but some of this material must have been in circulation.

A Missionary Voyage to the Southern Ocean (1799), a work compiled from the journals of officers and missionaries on the ship *Duff*, simultaneously draws attention to and suppresses the subject of the *mahu*. One narrator describes an encounter with a *mahu* in Pomare's train: 'He was dressed like a woman, and mimicked the voice and every peculiarity of the sex...As I fixed my eyes upon the fellow, he hid his face: this I at first construed into shame, but found it afterwards to be a womanish trick.'[19] 'Making eyes' can easily be misunderstood, and the embarrassing confusion of mistaken appearances in this passage overwhelms the description of the lifeways of the *mahu* that follows. Eventually the account breaks down altogether, with the narrator 'obliged...to draw a veil over other practices too horrible to mention' (p. 201). Recourse to the trope of preterition – the figure by which attention is drawn to something while professing to omit it – was to become a recurring rhetorical technique when dealing with the *mahu*.

John Turnbull's *A Voyage Round the World* (1805), also reported an ocular encounter with a *mahu*: 'Whilst among them I saw too of their mahoos; the one in the train of Pomare, the other was pointed out to me as he passed my house: observing me fix my eyes on him with a look expressive of my abhorrence, he sneaked off without speaking'.[20] There is no way of reading the *mahu*'s response to the outraged gaze of the European. The visitor feels compelled to outface this embodiment of perversion, but finds it easier to eyeball his denunciation than to express it verbally in any but the most general terms. Turnbull's linguistic recourse is, again, the trope of preterition: 'There are a set of men in this country whose open profession is of such abomination, that the laudable delicacy of our language will not admit it to be mentioned' (p. 382). Whereas the *arioi* practice of infanticide is an abomination that must be spoken about, the *mahu* is unspeakable. Turnbull agrees with the missionaries in believing that the accounts of Tahiti by the early navigators were seriously incomplete, but like them he finds there is a problem in setting the record straight.

William Ellis was a missionary in the Society Islands from 1817–22, and his *Polynesian Researches* (1829) is our most important source of knowledge of early nineteenth-century Tahitian culture. On the *mahu*, however, his text is resoundingly silent. They are never mentioned as such, but Ellis ostentatiously draws 'the veil of oblivion' over that part of the Polynesian character which 'the first chapter of the epistle to the Romans, revolting and humiliating as it is, affords but too faithful a portraiture'.[21] The reference must be to Romans I, 26–7: 'The men...gave up natural relations with women and were consumed with passion for one another, men committing shameless acts with men'. How to speak the unspeakable and describe the indescribable? Ellis is by now part of a tradition of an imperfectly suppressed discourse of Tahitian sexual perversity in which missionaries, and others, highlight the need for the saving presence of Christianity but cannot be explicit about one of the main reasons for this.

This writing sometimes associates infanticide and homosexuality, *arioi* and *mahu*, as related forms of unregenerate behaviour but more frequently they are kept apart. Infanticide is never condoned but attempts are made to explain it culturally, and it remains a topic of detailed discussion among visitors and commentators. Perverse sexuality epitomised by the figure of the *mahu*, however, only enters the record with Morrison and Bligh, and thereafter is mentioned only to be hushed.

Although early accounts of Tahitian same-sex practices are horrified by the thought of sodomy, their concentration on the *mahu* as a group exhibiting patterned cross-gender behaviour is significant. Other forms of male-to-male sexual behaviour received no attention. This focus on the figure of the ef-feminate sodomite can be understood in terms of the developing European construction of homosexuality as identity- rather than act-oriented.[22] And later in the nineteenth century when European theories of the third sex were emphasising the association of homosexuality with femininity and gender disorder, the *mahu* began to figure prominently and explicitly in Western writing. Edward Carpenter's *Intermediate Types Among Primitive Folk* (1914), for example, looked back to early accounts of the *mahu*. According to Bleys, by the end of the nineteenth century there were frequent attempts to explain same-sex behaviour in Tahiti within an emerging European cognitive framework of homosexual and transsexual identity, and to use the example of the *mahu* as evidence for this identity (p. 215).

Western theories of the third sex were clearly an inadequate way of explaining same-sex practices in Tahitian and other non-Western cultures, but the interrelation of this European construction and the Tahitian practice is seen in Paul Gauguin's life and work in Tahiti. In 1891 the painter left Europe, where the binary model of sex and gender was being questioned by theories of the third sex, for Tahiti, a culture in which the binary model had never been as dominant.[23] When Gauguin arrived on the island he was dubbed *taata vahine* (man-woman), apparently because of his shoulder-length salt-and-pepper hair. The local population seems to have taken him for some kind of *mahu*.[24] Androgyny is a recurring theme in Gauguin's Pacific writing and painting. The most erotic passage in *Noa Noa*, for example, is the scene where Gauguin follows a young woodcutter on a journey into the mountains. The young man's natural grace, beauty, and 'sexlessness' (that is, genderlessness) is a perfect embodiment of the 'androgynous aspect of the savage', a vivid and highly eroticised example of the lighter accentuation of gender difference characteristic of Tahitian society.

This fascination with ambivalence is also found in Gauguin's painting, explicitly in the feminized male figure of his painting *Le sorcier d'Hiva Oa* (1902), and in muted form in the soft-masculine quality of so many of his

7. Paul Gauguin, *Le sorcier d'Hiva Oa* (1902). Courtesy of the Musée d'Art moderne et d'Art contemporain de la Ville de Liège.

female figures, with their solid arms, heavy thighs, and muscular calves. *Te nave nave fenua* (1892) is a striking example of this. Gauguin, then, can be seen as an example of how the contemporary European interest in transsexuality was read into a culture where such behaviour was normative. The *mahu* had originally roused horror and bewilderment among European observers, whether missionaries or not. Now there was a determinate place for such a figure in Western representation.

Modern views

By the mid-nineteenth century the construction of Tahiti as at a point of development between civilisation and savagery had been given a negative turn. Whereas the Forsters had seen this stage as a condition of promise, it had now come to be regarded either as an inability to develop further, or as a measure of the contaminating influence of long-term contact with Europe, the so-called fatal impact. Herman Melville saw it as a mixture of the two. In *Omoo* (1847) his persona Tommo travels from 'the primitive valley of the Marquesas', the setting of *Typee* (1846), to the 'partially civilised' culture of Tahiti.[25] Seventy years on from the Forsters, all the comparisons are now to the disadvantage of the Tahitians: 'Years ago brought to a stand, where all that is corrupt in barbarism and civilization unite, to the exclusion of the virtues of either state; like other uncivilized beings, brought into contact with Europeans, they must here remain stationary until utterly extinct' (p. 192). Although the Forsters' fears of the effects of luxury on an already leisured culture could be seen as confirmed in Melville's picture, the new emphasis on stasis and degeneration is characteristic of writing about Tahiti from this time on.

This redefinition of 'partial civilisation' as a state of debasement rather than evolution informs the decadent romanticism of Pierre Loti, progenitor of the modern tradition of Pacific Orientalism. His bestselling autobiographical fiction *Le Mariage de Loti* (1880) updated Bougainville by incorporating the powerful contemporary idea of the 'doomed race', and with it a soft-focus picture of the inevitable guilt of empire, into the dominant persisting view of Tahiti as feminine, lulling, and seductive. Loti's text derived from his stay on Tahiti in 1872 when serving in the French navy, and looks back further to the beguiling reports of Tahiti sent by his older brother who had visited the island in 1859. Loti's picture of Tahiti is a familiar one:

> In Oceania toil is a thing unknown. The forests spontaneously produce all that is needed for the support of these unforseeing races...The years glide over the Tahitians in utter idleness and perpetual dreaming, and these grown-up children could never conceive that in our grand Europe there should be so many people wearing out their lives in earning their daily bread.[26]

The prelapsarian dispensation from labour in a timeless world of play, contrasted with work- and time-bound Europe, has become standard. So too has the narrative of the cross-cultural romance which in Loti's text involves the eponymous narrator meeting and living with Rarahu, a fourteen-year-old child of nature, in a reprise of his brother's time with his Tahitian lover, Taimaha. In *Le Mariage de Loti* the narrator sails home to Europe leaving Rarahu to pine and eventually to die romantically of tuberculosis (Loti's *Madame Chrysantheme* (1887) was to be the basis of Puccini's opera *Madame Butterfly* (1904)). In life and in death Rarahu is a figure for the island itself: beautiful and innocent, but ineducable, tainted by contact with Europeans, and therefore doomed to expire. Tahiti is, by now, demonstrably unable to fulfil the Enlightenment dream that it might redeem Europe, and therefore no longer has any reason to survive. Loti's romantic fatalism defined an increasingly static tradition of 'fatal impact' accounts of Tahiti and the South Pacific, in which Europe is guiltily tantalised by a vision of beauty and otherness it can never possess but is fated to destroy. Loti also exposes the narcissism implicit in fatal impact narratives by presenting this as a European rather than a Tahitian tragedy.

In order to illustrate the appropriative nature and enduring currency of this kind of visioning, it is instructive to compare Loti's use of the lost child motif with Paul Theroux's use of the same motif in his travel narrative *The Happy Isles of Oceania* (1992). The most distinctive feature of Loti's version of the cross-cultural romance as self-serving colonial allegory is his search for the child he believes was born to his brother and Taimaha. As his time on the island and his relationship with Rarahu begins to run out, Loti's search for this child becomes the final quest of the narrative. Eventually, however, and like everything else to do with the island, this quest proves chimerical. Taimaha's sons are too young to be his brother's, Loti is forced to abandon the idea of a Tahitian family, and 'the islands on a sudden were desolate, all the witchery of Oceania was killed at one blow, nothing bound me any longer to this land' (p. 174). This failure of the island to perform as it should has haunted every episode of the novel from the disappointment of arrival at its opening when Loti realised that 'if this land of dreams was to remain the same to me I ought never to have laid my finger on it' (p. 15).

The Happy Isles of Oceania is much closer to the dominant traditions of Western representations of the Pacific than its author realises, and his use of the lost child motif is one example among many. Theroux, in Tahiti, hears of a namesake, Mimi Theroux, living on the adjacent island of Moorea. This gives him 'a powerful sense of belonging to the islands'; as he explains, it is a belief in his family that every person with that surname is a descendant of his great grandfather and his 'nine prolific sons'.[27] With patriarchal assurance, therefore, Theroux makes the same journey from Tahiti to Moorea that Loti took in search of his nephews. He tracks down his assumed kin who proves to be Chinese, and who is looking after a small, dark child. Theroux wonders if Mimi also has 'a tincture of Polynesian blood' (p. 516). It transpires that she is married to a distant cousin of the author, a man who is known throughout Oceania as a surfer, sailor, and navigator. (He sounds rather like one of the heroes of Jack London's South Sea tales.) The little girl, it turns out, is soon to become a Theroux. Her Marquesan mother has given her to Mimi and adoption will soon be legally established. Theroux writes that, 'Seeing the impish face of this little islander and hearing my own name made me glad' (p. 518); the unnamed child is about to join the clan and, unlike Loti, Theroux has found something to bind him to the island.

The narrative structure of both stories is remarkably similar, with Theroux's distant cousin guesting as Loti's brother. In this case, however, Loti's failed quest has finally been satisfied. Theroux has gone beyond the common travel-writing ploy of adopting an ancestor whose trail the writer follows, and secured himself a descendant. *The Happy Isles of Oceania* has in fact opened with the break-up of Theroux's marriage and this loss becomes a theme of the book. The discovery of Mimi and her child provides a kind of answer to that loss, just as Hawaii seems to be offering him a home of sorts by the end of the book. The deep structure of Theroux's text is familiar. The Western traveller, enchanted by the natural beauty of the islands but repelled by the colonial culture he cannot disentangle himself from, discovers and consolidates a family connection he will in future be able to contemplate with pleasure from a safe distance.

Theroux's *The Happy Isles of Oceania* is a relatively sophisticated example of the kind of travel writing that has dominated accounts of Tahiti, and more generally the Pacific, since the mid-nineteenth century. The rich multivalent discourse of early travellers to the islands stagnated, its tropes and conventions became inert, and the result has been a static debased discourse that mimes the very process it is locked into describing. Rarely has Barthes's contention that 'it is language which speaks, not the author' been better illustrated.[28] Modern reporting is also trapped within this language and structure of thought. The coup in Fiji in 2000, for example, produced repeated 'trouble-in-paradise' headlines and stories in the British and French press. Modern travel writing and journalism (the two are closely allied) are much less attentive to the specificity and complexity of Oceanian cultures than the works of Bougainville, Cook, the Forsters, or a missionary like William Ellis. Whereas this early writing was concerned to compare Tahiti with other island cultures and establish its distinctiveness, in the texts of later travellers Tahiti has become one of many interchangeable island paradises. Such writing is therefore unable to deal with Oceanian modernity, and can only represent it as a betrayal of Europe's cultural investment in a romantic myth of islands. It is not civil violence in Fiji, or the effects of a French nuclear presence in Tahiti and the surrounding ocean, that causes disquiet but rather the failure of 'South Sea islands' to live up to another culture's dream.

A partial exception to this is Mel Kernahan's *White Savages in the South Seas* (1995), a work that engages critically and energetically with many of the dominant traditions of representation I have been discussing. It opens with the humility topos that travellers to the Pacific have frequently indulged in: 'It's always the same story: the adventurer rushes forth, arms reaching out – the South Seas meets them, swaying, smiling, arms outstretched in welcome. They drift right through one another like ghosts, never really understanding, frustrated, love unrequited.'[29] These Loti-like cadences seem too familiar to be trusted, a prefatory disclaimer we are not intended to believe, or else a rhetorically self-aggrandising means of creating a mysterious allure around the exotic other.

But Kernahan proceeds differently from most. Her first chapter, 'Striptease comes to Tahiti', in which a pair of none-too-young female Australian strippers perform to an impassively resistant indigenous audience – 'no man whistled, no woman muttered, no child stirred, no foot stamped, no hands clapped' (p. 11) – ironically reverses the scene of two centuries earlier when a young Tahitian woman had stood naked on the deck of the *Boudeuse* and the crew had thronged eagerly to the hatchway. Later chapters include an account of the nuclear politics of contemporary Tahiti, and of the Californian Tahitian diaspora. Here, and elsewhere in the book, Kernahan describes Tahiti in terms of its complex interdependency with other parts of the world rather than as a marooned and decaying culture. Like some of the island's earliest voyagers, Kernahan keeps returning to Tahiti and is thereby able to perceive and describe change, avoiding the fixed snapshots of so much later writing. Stock comparisons between the Pacific and the West are replaced by more tentative comparisons between and within the different indigenous cultures she encounters, another parallel to those first voyagers. By getting much closer to her subjects she has a better sense of her distance from them; judgement and valuation accordingly become more difficult, or perhaps just less important.

As Kernahan arrives, not without difficulty and embarrassment, at a realisation of her own insignificance for the world she is visiting, she also understands there is no superior vantage point from which to regard it. She seldom forgets the ironies of her position as a Western visitor, and she denies herself the indulgence of cheap hits at missionaries or other sentimental versions of fatal impact. In this respect Kernahan is quite different from Theroux. Instead she offers a much sharper political awareness of contemporary French colonialism and New Zealand neo-colonialism in the region. Her ironising of the tropes and conventions of Pacific colonial discourse is also considerably subtler than Theroux's self-regarding superiority to it, preventing her from falling into the trap of unconsciously replicating those enduring forms of Western writing about Tahiti that are ostensibly being disparaged.

NOTES

1 The island of Tahiti is one of a group including Raiatea and Moorea. Cook named Tahiti's neighbouring islands the Society Islands. This now refers to the entire Tahitian archipelago.

2 J. C. Beaglehole, ed., *The Endeavour Journal of Joseph Banks 1768–1771*, 2 vols. (Sydney: Angus & Robertson / Public Library of New South Wales, 1962), vol. I, p. 252.

3 Louis Antoine de Bougainville, *A Voyage Round the World*, trans. J. R. Forster (London, 1772), pp. 218–19.

4 Christine Holmes, ed., *Captain Cook's Second Voyage: The Journals of Lieutenants Elliott and Pickersgill* (London: Caliban Books, 1984), pp. 29–30.

5 J. C. Beaglehole, ed., *The Journals of Captain Cook on His Voyages of Discovery*, 3 vols. (Woodbridge: The Boydell Press, rpr. 1999), vol. II, p. 293.

6 Michael E. Hoare, ed., *The Resolution Journal of Johann Reinhold Forster 1772–1775*, 4 vols. (London: Haklyut Society, 1982), vol. III, pp. 426–7.

7 George Forster, *A Voyage Round the World*, 2 vols., ed. Nicholas Thomas and Oliver Berghof (Honolulu: University of Hawaii Press, 2000), vol. I, p. 278.

8 Geoffrey Sanborn, *The Sign of the Cannibal: Melville and the Making of a Postcolonial Reader* (Durham: Duke University Press, 1998), p. 24.

9 Beaglehole, *The Journals of Captain Cook*, vol. III, p. 620.

10 Johann Reinhold Forster, *Observations Made During a Voyage Round the World*, ed. Nicholas Thomas, Harriet Guest, and Michael Dettelbach (Honolulu: University of Hawaii Press, 1996), pp. 221–2.

11 Editors' Introduction to *Observations Made*, pp. xxxv–xxxvii.

12 O. Rutter, ed., *The Journal of James Morrison, Boatswain's Mate of the 'Bounty'* (London: Golden Cockerel Press, 1935), p. 235.

13 For some of the perceived connections between these two events see Greg Dening, *Mr Bligh's Bad Language: Passion, Power and Theatre on the Bounty* (Cambridge University Press, 1992), pp. 147, 257.

14 Kenneth Curry, ed., *New Letters of Robert Southey*, 2 vols. (New York: Columbia University Press, 1965), vol. I, p. 19.

15 Southey and Coleridge quotations are cited in Neil Rennie, *Far-Fetched Facts: The Literature of Travel and the Idea of the South Seas* (Oxford: Clarendon Press, 1995), pp. 163, 180.

16 The journal was eventually published in Etienne Taillemite, ed., *Bougainville et ses compagnons autour du monde 1766–1769: Journaux de navigation*, 2 vols. (Paris: Imprimerie Nationale, 1977).

17 Beaglehole, *Journals of Captain Cook*, vol. I, pp. 93–4. The first published account of Cook's initial voyage to the Pacific appeared in John Hawkesworth, *An Account of the Voyages...for making Discoveries in the Southern Hemisphere...performed by Commodore Byron, Captain Wallis, Captain Carteret, and Captain Cook* (3 vols. 1773).

18 O. Rutter, ed., *The Log of the Bounty*, 2 vols. (London: Golden Cockerel Press, 1936), vol. II, p. 77.

19 William Wilson *et al.*, *A Missionary Voyage to the Southern Pacific Ocean, performed in the years 1796, 1797, 1798 in the Ship Duff, commanded by Captain James Wilson* (London: T. Chapman, 1799), p. 200.

20 John Turnbull, *A Voyage Round the World, in the years 1800, 1801, 1802, 1803, and 1804* [1805] (London: A. Maxwell, 1813), pp. 382–3.
21 William Ellis, *Polynesian Researches*, 2 vols. (London: Fisher, Son and Jackson, 1830), vol. II, p. 25.
22 Rudi C. Bleys, *The Geography of Perversion: Male-to-Male Sexual Behaviour Outside the West and the Ethnographic Imagination 1750–1918* (London: Cassell, 1996), pp. 64, 77–8.
23 Stephen F. Eisenman, *Gauguin's Skirt* (London: Thames and Hudson, 1997), pp. 94–5.
24 David Sweetman, *Paul Gauguin* (London: Hodder and Stoughton, 1995), pp. 274–5.
25 Herman Melville, *Omoo* (London: KPI, 1985), p. 189.
26 Pierre Loti, *Tahiti: The Marriage of Loti*, trans. Clara Bell (London: KPI, 1986), p. 40.
27 Paul Theroux, *The Happy Isles of Oceania: Paddling the Pacific* (Harmondsworth: Penguin Books, 1992), p. 507.
28 Roland Barthes, *Image-Music-Text* (Glasgow: Fontana/Collins, 1979), p. 143.
29 Mel Kernahan, *White Savages in the South Seas* (London: Verso, 1995), p. 5.

9

TIM YOUNGS

Africa/The Congo: the politics of darkness

Fact and fiction

The best-known Congo journey is a fictional one that does not name its setting. Marlow's voyage to find Kurtz, the agent who has 'gone native', in Joseph Conrad's *Heart of Darkness* (1899), operates on several levels: the story's critical engagement with colonialism is flanked by the mythical and psychological dimensions of the protagonists' experiences. All sorts of later travellers to the Congo refer to this tale. Most of the narratives discussed towards the end of this chapter (and still others that are not) cite it. Journalist Michela Wrong even turns to it for the title of her admirably self-effacing book chronicling the downfall of Zaire's President Mobutu, *In the Footsteps of Mr Kurtz* (2000).

Conrad spent six months in the Congo in 1890 working for the Belgian Société Anonyme pour le Commerce du Haut-Congo. His 'Congo Diary' records his 250-mile trek from Matadi to Kinshasa and notes the discomfort, obstacles, sickness, and the sight of murdered Africans. His 'Up-river book', written on board the steamer 'Roi des Belges', contains mainly technical information on the navigation of the river.[1] The experiences of both journals inform *Heart of Darkness* and the short story 'An Outpost of Progress' (1898) but are different in kind from them. Curiously, the travellers who later take *Heart of Darkness* as their reference point tend not to mention these documents of Conrad's actual travel. On the whole it is easy to tell such journals and fictions apart: Graham Greene's *Congo Journal*, for example, which has Greene re-reading *Heart of Darkness*, after having 'abandoned' Conrad in 'about 1932 because his influence on me was too great and too disastrous',[2] records a trip to the Belgian Congo in 1959 to research the novel *A Burnt-Out Case*. But Europe's mythologising of Africa in general and of the Congo in particular means that fact and fiction do sometimes overlap. Adam Hochschild begins his monumental history of the Congo Free State by reminding himself that:

I had read something about that time and place after all: Joseph Conrad's *Heart of Darkness*. However, with my college lecture notes on the novel filled with scribbles about Freudian overtones, mythic echoes, and inward vision, I had mentally filed away the book under fiction, not fact.[3]

Conversely, a popular history of the river begins: 'Congo: the two sudden syllables beat on the imagination like the beat of a jungle drum, calling up nightmare visions of primeval darkness, unfathomable mystery, dreadful savagery'.[4] The heavy percussion of such writing reverberates through the battered imagination of popular histories of Africa anyway, but the West's perceptions of the 'heart' of Africa encourage this monotonous rhythm.

A high degree of intertextual reference, cutting across explorers' accounts, missionaries' reports, ethnography, journalism, and literary travels, aids the accretion of a mythical Congo as the essence of Africa in a process that may occur in other parts of the world but which it is hard to imagine happening anywhere else with the same intensity. Even Edward Hooper's inquiry into whether the AIDS virus may have originated with contaminated oral polio vaccines in Central Africa has a foreword comparing him with 'Burton or Livingstone – making his halting progress toward some center of mystery'.[5]

Early writing

The comparatively recent 'discovery' of the Congo produced much speculation about the region. Difficult terrain, illness, and native resistance created an image of heroic – usually masculine – and sometimes tragic endeavour to penetrate into Africa's interior. The high mortality rate amongst missionaries created a sense of martyrdom. European enslavement of Africans had been partially enabled by, and in turn reinforced, an image of black Africans as inferior and uncivilised, while the nineteenth-century movement against Arab and Portuguese slavers fostered a paternalistic feeling that Africans required European protection. Anthropological discourse in its specialised and popularised forms classified black people as humanity in its most primitive state. Marlow's resonant phrase about the recognition of some 'remote kinship' with the 'wild and passionate uproar' of the howling men on the riverbank is a memorable expression of this feeling of connection and difference,[6] explored even more intensely as Freudian ideas about the unconscious, described in racialised and hierarchical terms, became obsessively investigated in the twentieth century.

Europe's engagement with Africa goes back many centuries: much of North Africa had been part of the Roman Empire before coming under the power of the Arabs and of the Ottoman Turks, and Egypt had been known through its connections with the classical and biblical worlds. Ancient and early modern accounts of Africa had long currency, informing travellers' views of the continent up at least to the mid-nineteenth century. 'The best preparation for a first glance at the Congo River is to do as all do, to study the quaint description which old Purchas borrowed from the "Chronica da Companhia de Jesus em Portugal"', wrote Burton.[7] In turn, nineteenth-century journeys set the scene for late twentieth-century travel writers. Caroline Alexander's *One Dry Season: In the Footsteps of Mary Kingsley* (1989) is just one example. Neither Burton nor Alexander sees or experiences exactly as their predecessor but the repetition keeps the earlier view alive.

Homer's *Odyssey* refers to two kinds of Ethiopians, a division also found in the *Histories* of Herodotus, who journeyed along the Nile in the fifth century BC, and in Diodorus Siculus, who visited Egypt 400 years later.[8] Van Wyk Smith tells us that Diodorus reports the Ethiopians as calling the Nile 'the *Astapus*, which he translates as "Water from Darkness"'. During the next hundred years or so, the imperial Romans Strabo and Pliny began the process of ethnocentrically positing the Mediterranean world as the norm against which Africa should be judged. With Pliny, in particular, the tropes of degeneration, savagery, and monstrosity gained force. The latter images especially would be found in medieval representations of Africa and underlie still later attitudes. Highly influential and durable also were myths of the ancient, wealthy Christian kingdom of Prester John and Ptolemy's description of the Nile as flowing from two great lakes fed by the Mountains of the Moon. The former helped motivate Portuguese activity in the fifteenth and sixteenth centuries, including the 'discovery' of the Congo, resurfaced in Rider Haggard's *King Solomon's Mines* (1885), and did not die until the horrors of King Leopold's Congo Free State; the latter continued to fascinate many of the nineteenth-century explorers, notably Livingstone and Stanley.

Classical texts continued to influence views of Africa up to and well beyond the Middle Ages. The most important early modern text was Leo Africanus's *Description of Africa* (1550). Leo was born a Muslim, Hasan Ibn Muhammal al-Wazzan, and travelled extensively in Africa before being captured by Christian pirates and sent to Italy where he converted to Christianity. The 'single most important figure to link North Africa and Europe between the years 1500 and 1800', he moved between many cultures.[9] His *Description*, part-travel account, part-descriptive geography, displaced many of the classical myths of Africa by presenting detailed information on the cultures of North and West Africa, a fact which does not prevent his making some contemptuous judgements, often couched in bestial imagery, of various African peoples.

In the eighteenth and early nineteenth century, narratives of slavers, anti-slavers, and of other travellers pictured the West African coast as the 'white man's grave', and the motifs of paternalism, suffering, and death would be carried inland into Central Africa. However, descriptions of other parts of Africa had different emphases. In the north, the long Roman and Islamic presences imbued the region with a deep history. In the modern age Napoleon's 1798 expedition to Egypt stimulated European fascination with that country's ancient past – as well as making Britain more aware of the strategic importance of North Africa to India – but attention to its contemporary life also followed. Edward Lane's classic Orientalist text, *An Account of The Manners and Customs of the Modern Egyptians* was published in 1836. In the south of Africa, as elsewhere, crudely racist descriptions of indigenous peoples were rife and directed in the main at the Khoi, so-called bushmen, and the 'Hottentots', and later transferred to the Bantu. But the relatively recent history of colonial settlement, the equitable climate, and agreeable scenery led generally to more positive representations of the land.

Mungo Park's expedition of 1795–7, arranged by the African Association, signals the beginning of modern scientific interest in African exploration. Park became the first European to report seeing the Niger but his death on his second trip in 1805 occurred too soon for him to prove that it was not the Congo. Recently, scholars of Romanticism have begun serious study of Park and of his *Travels into the Interior of Africa* (1799), a sign of the growing interest in and respectability of travel writing as well as an indication of how travel texts can be used to throw more light on the culture of the author than on the destination.

In the second half of the nineteenth century many anthologies, such as John Camden Hotten's *Abyssinia and Its People* (1868), N. Bell's *Heroes of North African Discovery* (1877) and *Heroes of Discovery in South Africa* (rev. edn 1899), Robert Richardson's *The Story of the Niger* (1888), and Robert Brown's four-volume *The Story of Africa and Its Explorers* (1892–5) placed recent expeditions and accounts alongside ancient descriptions of Africa. Besides these, countless missionary biographies, especially of Livingstone, Alexander Mackay, Robert Moffat, and Mary Slessor, were written for children, published by missionary societies, and handed out as prizes at Sunday School.

Of course, if Africa was known through the literature about it, it was not known *only* by that literature. Exhibitions and other kinds of visual representation, artefacts, and the culture of exploration all shaped British perceptions of Africa and Africans.[10] This was no less true of the Congo than of other regions of the continent: indeed, it may apply even more so since the late nineteenth-century focus on the Congo coincided with the rise of commodity culture. Merchandising and advertising produced images of explorers and the explored on an unprecedented scale. This essay, however, focuses on the travel writing, and will concentrate on travels in and around the former Zaire from 1850 to the present.

Discovery and exploration

Although the mouth of the Congo had been 'found' in 1482 by the Portuguese Diogo Cão, and contacts and exchanges followed (including, after the 'discovery' of Brazil in 1500, slavery to America), it was not until the second half of the nineteenth century that Europeans identified the source of the Congo. In comparison with other areas of Africa, the interior, through which the Congo coursed, was mysterious to them and came to stand for Africa itself. Captain James Tuckey's 1816 expedition to locate the Congo's origins got only 150 miles along the river and lost twenty-one of its fifty-five members (including Tuckey himself). For a while afterwards, Europe's attention stayed on the Niger rather than on the Congo.

If the Congo had been confused by Park and others with the Niger, so, too, would it become mistaken for the Nile. The explorer-missionary David Livingstone grew so obsessed with finding the Nile's sources that when he discovered the source and headwaters of the Congo, he did not realise it. The arguments between Speke and Burton over the origin of the Nile (see Chapter 3) helped stimulate Livingstone's interest, already fired by biblical and classical accounts, in locating the source. The British perception of and engagement with Africa was immensely influenced by Livingstone, who would have his stature enhanced both by Henry Morton Stanley who 'found' him in 1871 and by Horace Waller who edited his posthumously published *Last Journals* (1874).

Livingstone was the first European to have made a documented crossing of Africa from coast to coast. This he did from west to east between 1853 and 1856. His long campaign against slavery, often and ultimately without regard to his own health, endowed him with an aura of sainthood that for many was confirmed by the devotion shown by his black African followers in carrying his wrapped corpse across Africa from where it was shipped to England. But Livingstone had a worldly side, too. A proponent of the 'three Cs': commerce, Christianity, and civilisation, he viewed 'the end of the geographical feat as the beginning of the missionary enterprise', and believed that 'no permanent elevation of a people can be effected without commerce'.[11]

It is common to regard Stanley as ushering in a new era of commercial hard-headedness but Livingstone's earnings of more than £12,000 from the sales of 70,000 copies of his *Missionary Travels and Researches in South*

Africa (1857) showed the profits that could be made from travelling in and writing about Africa. His second book, *Narrative of an Expedition to the Zambesi and its Tributaries*, co-authored with his brother Charles, was published in 1865. This followed a government-backed expedition to investigate the Zambezi as a possible trading route. Returning to Africa in 1866, backed by the Royal Geographical Society and the Foreign Office, Livingstone's subsequent years of exploration were hindered by the slave-trade, illness, and his own mistakes. The Lualaba, the river he hoped was the source of the Nile, would later be proved by Stanley to be the source of the Congo.

Stanley's highly popular books are mostly patterned around their author as adventurous hero, favoured by providence, overcoming physical obstacles to reach his goal. His writing is influenced more by the Bible, classical tales of heroism, adventure stories, and the new journalism than by the narratives of other explorers. As a brilliant reporter who knew how to frame his stories for best dramatic appeal (he had been in the service of the *New York Herald* when he 'found' Livingstone), Stanley constructed his accounts of Africa accordingly. In *Through the Dark Continent* (1878) he describes handing over to superstitious 'savages' his 'volume of Shakespeare' instead of his own 'valuable notes'.[12] The 'Mowa' people burning the book offers a striking image of culture consumed by nature. According to Stanley's diary, however, what he handed over was actually worthless scribbles.[13]

In 1871–2 the Royal Geographical Society, embarrassed by Stanley's scoop, sent out three expeditions to aid Livingstone. The most important of these was led by Lt. Verney Lovett Cameron, who became the first European to cross tropical Africa from east to west and mapped much of the Congo basin. His writing and conduct were more restrained than those of the often brutal Stanley. Cameron declared that 'the merit of any geographical discovery would be irretrievably marred by shedding a drop of native blood except in self-defence', and included in his narrative a flirtatious passage in which 'the handsomest women I had seen in Africa' became so inquisitive about his white skin that 'I began to fear they would undress me altogether'. On the other hand, references to the 'primeval forest' and to the Manyuéma as 'filthy cannibals' are closer to Stanley.[14] Explorers' narratives are rarely uniform.

In 1874 Stanley set out on an expedition of 7,000 miles over three years to complete Livingstone's work. Backed by *The New York Herald* and *The Daily Telegraph*, he charted the Central African great lakes, answered the question of the Nile's sources, and showed that the Lualaba was the Congo. Stanley was the most ruthless of explorers and this expedition, recounted in *Through the Dark Continent*, saw the notorious Bumbireh Island massacre, in which he and his party killed and wounded many Africans without themselves suffering loss. However, widespread condemnation of his actions showed that on this occasion at least his excited relation of the one-sided conflict misjudged the public mood.

Proclaiming philanthropic and scientific motives Stanley and Cameron followed Livingstone in calling for communications, transport, and trade as ways of tackling slavery. Their reports of the Congo's commercial potential attracted Belgium's King Leopold II who would create his own private state. He invited Stanley to lead a five-year expedition, which began in 1879, to help set it up. Stanley's narrative of this expedition, *The Congo and the Founding of its Free State* (1885), is different from his others: less sensational and more positive, it stressed the natural riches of the country and the prospects for commerce. Stanley's activities while working for Leopold stimulated commercial interest and political competition in the Congo. From November 1884 the European powers met for three months at the Berlin Conference, in a failed attempt to prevent, rather than, as commonly believed, to precipitate the Scramble for Africa. The Berlin Act of 26 February 1885 defined the area of Leopold's Congo Free State as nearly one million square miles. The agreement obliged Leopold to keep the area open for free trade and missionary activity, but critical voices soon began to make clear that these conditions were being broken.

It was in the context of Leopold's ambition to expand his state northwards into southern Sudan and to gain the Nile that Stanley's Emin Pasha Relief Expedition of 1887–9 took place. This extraordinary venture brought the nineteenth-century exploration of Africa to an introspective and inglorious close. The expedition aimed to rescue Emin Pasha, the Governor of Equatoria, from Mahdist forces. Backed by Sir William Mackinnon, later President of the Imperial British East Africa Company, who hoped to gain from Emin's valuable store of ivory, Stanley was also secretly acting for Leopold, who wished to annex Equatoria to the Congo Free State. This disastrous expedition saw terrible loss of life, brutality, bitter disputes between the protagonists, the humiliating deaths of two white officers, and the embarrassment of finding Emin better provided for than his rescuers. The expedition's narratives often conflicted with one another, while the questioning of the officers' and gentlemen's versions of events mirrored a crisis in and doubting of authority in British society.[15]

The expedition's best-known text is Stanley's *In Darkest Africa* (1890). It is a massive work that swaggers with its rhetoric. Stanley turns to the Bible for authority. He cites classical and early modern travellers and geographers as well as more recent authorities. He quotes from Shakespeare, Browning, and Tennyson. He combines science with sensation. Most prominent of all the features is his dramatic first person narrative, which a random sentence will illustrate: 'I should have abandoned the river on this day, but the wilderness, the horrible, lonely, uninhabited wilderness, and the excessive physical prostration and weakness of the people, forbade it.'[16] In its suggestion of Stanley's leadership, the inconvenient infirmity of others, and the inhospitableness of the landscape, this is not a bad indication of the book's tone.

But the expedition's most remarkable book was James Sligo Jameson's *Story of the Rear Column* .... Rumours that Jameson had participated in the cannibal killing of a young girl put him at the centre of a national scandal. His account of the episode was published by his widow who wanted to clear his name (Jameson died in Africa in 1888) but it showed that he was at least to blame for commissioning the murder through a bet he had not thought would be accepted. Jameson's haunting and repulsive narrative charts the officers' violence, the capture of local women in exchange for food, the monotony and despair of existence in the Yambuya camp where Stanley left his 'rear guard' for over a year, and the death of scores of men through hunger and sickness. The book vibrates with the tension between discipline and dissolution. The 'cannibal' episode occurs when Jameson, who has been credulous of cannibalism throughout, responds to slaver Tippoo-Tib's stories by telling him that 'people at home generally believed that these were only "travellers' tales," ... or, in other words, lies'.[17] This is a strange statement to make, given his earlier claims to have seen evidence of cannibalism himself. Although the killing of the girl is described in horrifying detail, the act of cannibalism is not. We are left to infer it, just as Jameson must have done.

Horrors perpetrated by agents and soldiers of the Congo Free State were documented by its opponents using information gained from travels. E. D. Morel included the testimony of missionaries and others in his campaigning books.[18] Roger Casement travelled in and interviewed natives of the region for his 1904 report, ordered by Parliament, in which he also detailed atrocities – in particular the chopping off of hands – that were committed as punishments for collecting insufficient rubber. A Belgian commission of inquiry confirmed Casement's charges in 1905. In 1908 the Belgian Parliament voted an annexation treaty and the Congo Free State became the Belgian Congo.

Black African-American missionaries, notably George Washington Williams and William Henry Sheppard, also reported on the cruelties. Williams, who visited the Congo in 1890, published two remarkable documents addressed to the US president and to Leopold.[19] These denounce the fraudulent means by which land was obtained from the Congolese, condemn Stanley's deceit and brutality, and call for an international commission to investigate the crimes for which Williams holds Leopold responsible. Sheppard, who was a resident missionary, was less direct, entangled as he was in the racial discourses of white US missionaries and their backers.[20]

Of course, African voices were normally heard, if at all, only as ventriloquised by white authors. True, African missionaries wrote reports and it would be wrong to suggest they were somehow less African for it,[21] but the porters who accompanied European explorers were generally known to the outside world only through their employers' accounts and the views of those through whose countries the explorers passed usually went unheard in Britain. The labour for many of the European-led expeditions had been supplied by Zanzibar Arabs, a number of whom appear in narratives by more than one explorer. Their perspectives are never given, however, and they are depicted only for their qualities of service. Indeed, Arab competition for the wealth of Central Africa around the great lakes contributed to Europeans' negative portrayal of Arabs as slavers, which helped Leopold adopt the cloak of humanitarianism.

Yet for all their biases, the writings of explorers and travellers offer a record of Central African society that scholars (black African as well as white) have found useful. Missionaries made important studies of African languages, among them William Holman Bentley's *Dictionary and Grammar of the Kongo Language...*(1887). These were usually designed to promote Christianity through translations of the Bible, and Bentley's attitude is obvious – 'the whole country lay in the power of the evil one', he proclaims[22] – but they have proved a helpful resource to anthropologists and ethnolinguists studying the migrations and relationships of African peoples.[23]

Art, apes, and anthropology

Interest in African cultures has been long-standing but was revitalised in the late nineteenth century and in the first half of the twentieth. One of Stanley's officers on the Emin Pasha expedition, Herbert Ward, was a sculptor and had already collected African artefacts that entered the collections of the Smithsonian Institution in Washington DC. Prominent European artists including Picasso, Matisse, and Leger drew on – many would say exploited – African forms and thought. In the USA, meanwhile, encouraged by the Harlem Renaissance of the 1920s and 1930s, black African-American artists turned to Africa with new pride, though the exoticism and spontaneity with which they invested the continent were entangled with the fascination it held for whites seeking a sensuousness and vitality lacking in their own lives. Comparison of (white) Vachel Lindsay's poem 'The Congo: A Study of the Negro Race' (composed in 1913; published in 1917) with Langston Hughes's poems 'The Negro Speaks of Rivers' (1921) and 'Danse Africaine' (1922/1926) illustrates this nicely.

8. 'Seated Congolese Woman' (1942), by Irma Stern. Irma Stern Museum collection, courtesy of Irma Stern Trust.

These strains are also evident in the work of (white) South African artist Irma Stern, who published in 1943 a short illustrated journal of the first of three trips to the Congo. She tells the 'King of the Bakubas' that she wishes 'to show your people's work with my pictures, so that the white people in my country may learn what beautiful things the black man in the Congo creates'. Many of Stern's paintings challenge racist stereotypes by emphasising the humanity of the Congolese. Even for her, however, 'The Congo has always been ... the very heart of Africa. The sound "Congo" makes my blood dance, with the thrill of exotic excitement.'24 With paintings it is easier than with literature to see that representations are constructions: one can tell at a glance. Stern's beautiful paintings, influenced by expressionism and impressionism, interpose modern artistic movements between observer and observed, but the new conventions look contrived now and the gracefulness forced.

A similar mediation, though a more technological one, is evident in US film-maker Martin Johnson's *Congorilla* (1932), which narrates the journey of the author and his wife Osa, with white film and sound technicians, a large party of black Africans, and masses of film equipment, to make, they claim, the first sound films of the pygmies of the Ituri forest and of the mountain gorillas of Central Africa. Johnson's announcement that he and Osa were determined to 'find these primitive people living their natural lives, untouched by the influence of civilization and the world of modern man',[25] suggests a romantic turn away from modernity, despite their transportation of it in the form of their movie machinery.

A shift in attitudes towards those previously regarded as savage is evident in anthropologist Colin Turnbull's *The Forest People* (1961). Stanley had included some ethnographic description of the pygmies in *In Darkest Africa* but had also felt able to describe a pygmy woman as 'characteristic of the link long sought between the average modern humanity and its Darwinian progenitors' (p. 219). Drawing lessons from his fieldwork among the BaMbuti (pygmy) people of the Ituri forest, among whom he hears tales of the 'dreadful wars' and the 'trail of destruction that Stanley left behind him' (p. 159), Turnbull finds a wisdom that 'we' possess no longer. It has to do with the people's harmonious and loving relationship with their environment which they feel is threatened by the outside world. 'It is a world that will soon be gone for ever, and with it the people'.[26] These sentiments evoke the heavy nostalgia of salvage ethnography, the urge to record a way of life that seems about to disappear.

Vanishing is also a concern in primatologist Dian Fossey's *Gorillas in the Mist* (1983), the result of many years observing – and trying to protect from poachers, who would later murder her – these creatures from her base in Rwanda. More important to her than her own travels are those of the gorillas themselves which Fossey is at pains to record. The book is even dedicated to four of them. (Cameron's *Across Africa* was dedicated to Queen Victoria.) None of the other narratives discussed here comes close to entertaining Fossey's conviction that 'Any observer is an intruder in the domain of a wild animal and must remember that the rights of that animal supersede human interests'.[27]

Mobutu's Zaire

During the wave of post-war decolonisation in Africa, the Belgian government abruptly granted independence to the Congo on 30 June 1960. During the turmoil that followed Colonel Joseph Mobutu seized power in September with the approval of the UN. The democratically elected Prime Minister Patrice Lumumba was murdered in February 1961, his assassination backed by the USA as well as by the Belgians.[28] Mobutu was installed as president in 1965 and began a long reign of corruption and terror in which he was propped up by the USA and other Western powers, who saw the country (renamed Zaire in the 1970s) as a bulwark against communism and wanted the country's mineral wealth. While Zaire grew poorer after the fall in price of copper in 1973, Mobutu grew richer until his personal fortune was estimated at five billion dollars.

The civil war that followed independence produced its own travel narratives and Mobutu's rule generated others. Of the former, the most interesting and thoughtful is *Che in Africa: Che Guevara's Congo Diary*, published posthumously in 1999. Guevara, who described as 'the most sacred of duties: to fight against imperialism wherever it may be',[29] served in the Congo from April 1965 to February 1966. In contrast to Guevara's principled, selfless, and anti-racist text is *Congo Mercenary*, by the most infamous of the white mercenaries fighting on the opposing side, the South Africa-based Mike Hoare. Hoare's dull book mixes adventurism with militarism without the insight or moral justification of Guevara. His proclamation that 'the Belgian presence in the Congo from the earliest beginnings of the Congo Free State ..., was an epoch of achievement in Africa which no other country can equal' is not meant ironically.[30]

It may be stretching a point to include Hoare's war memoir here. John Roberts' book, *Congo Adventure* (1963), on the other hand, does begin as a travel narrative before heading in another direction. Roberts, a Briton who had served in the Northern Rhodesian police force, starts his narrative in 1959 planning to walk and work his way over three years from the Cape of Good Hope to Norway. The first part of his text is taken up with conventional observations of self, others, and landscape. After deciding to accept lifts, he reaches the Belgian Congo at the time of independence. Attacks on Europeans help decide the fiercely anti-Lumumbist, anti-Communist Roberts to join President Kalonji's Army of Liberation in Kasai Province. He is taken prisoner by the UN and, after a short spell in captivity, is flown out of the Congo.

In an effort to draw international attention to the achievements of his nation, and to bolster pride in it, Mobutu had his country host the World Heavyweight boxing championship between Muhammad Ali and George Foreman on 30 October 1974. Among the many reports on this famous bout is *The Fight* (1975) by US novelist Norman Mailer.[31] Mailer's marvellously written, if troubled and sometimes troubling text plants the familiar motifs of discovery and mystery on a new canvas. The book, in which the author refers to himself throughout in the third person, is part reportage, part memoir, and part travel narrative. It is impossible to separate *The Fight* from the situation of African-Americans. Ali's profile and politics made sure this was so anyway but Mailer had already in his writings shown himself to be fascinated with the cultural values of blackness and in *The Fight* he strives for further understanding. As he does so we witness something of the fraught and ambivalent relationship between whites and blacks at the time.

The novelist, essayist, and travel writer V. S. Naipaul visited Zaire shortly after the bout, from January to March 1975, publishing 'A New King for the Congo: Mobutu and the Nihilism of Africa' in the *New York Review of Books*.[32] In this journalistic piece, he examines Mobutu's rule, viewing it as a curiously African mixture of the old and the new. He compares Mobutu with Leopold II, and sees some continuities: like the former king, Mobutu treats the country as a personal fiefdom. Naipaul shows that corruption, tyranny, and absolutism in modern-day Zaire had their roots in the practices of Belgian colonialism. Bizarrely, he makes no mention of Lumumba's murder or of the US- and Belgian-backed plots that led to Mobutu's succession.

There are no such omissions in *East Along the Equator*, in which US journalist Helen Winternitz weaves around her personal account of travel in Zaire information and views on the country's economic and political situation. In a splendid revision of the symbolic construction of Africa as the dark continent, she turns our attention away from nature to humanity; from the metaphysical to the political. Detained by the secret police, she remarks:

> Zaire's darkness was not geographic. It was not a fruit of the entangling forest, but a creation of man. The dark legacy of the Portuguese slavers who betrayed the Mani Kongo has carried through the years of the tyrant Leopold, to Mobutu and his system grounded in torture, repression, and corruption. Those who put Mobutu in place and have kept him there have been foreigners, first among them the American policymakers, who can pretend, as the Belgians and the other Europeans did, that they have been bringing light to the darkness.[33]

In Peter Hudson's *A Leaf in the Wind* (1988), a third of which is taken up with Zaire, 'Conrad's "heart of darkness"',[34] the people's suffering under Mobutu and their powerless desire for change remains largely unspoken. Hudson can be criticised for his lack of attention to politics but he may feel that he is respecting the credo of the people as voiced by a man who tells him: '"But of this we should speak no more. What is the point in it? Accept for now and be merry is what I say"' (p. 156).

Keith B. Richburg's *Out of America* covers many parts of Africa but has a chapter largely devoted to Zaire.[35] The subtitle – *A Black Man Confronts Africa* – suggests a fresh perspective on its subject, but the author (formerly the African bureau chief for the *Washington Post*) merely presents a dreary manifesto for the cause of self-help. To him self-pitying complaints about the continuing effects of colonialism are an excuse for inaction which suggests to him a problem he believes to be continent-wide and perhaps innate: 'Is there something in the nature of Africans that makes them more prone to corruption?' (p. 175), he asks.

Another African-American traveller, Eddy L. Harris, writes in his *Native Stranger* (1992) of the Central African Republic and Zaire as typifying, in their corruption and greed, all that is wrong with the new Africa. But Harris recognises that 'Africa is a myriad of peoples and their ways'.[36] He is less inclined than Richburg to make crass generalisations and reminds us that Zaire alone has more than 200 ethnic groups. His narrative of a year-long journey by bus, plane, and on foot through several African countries, stresses the primacy of culture in identity-formation. Harris cannot be at home in Africa but the knowledge of his African ancestry and the force of the continent upon his imagination and emotions is such that he feels trapped between the 'blackness of my skin and the whiteness of my culture' (p. 108), and suggests that even ten years is not enough to get to know Africa.

Fish ponds, humour, the missionary, and genocide

Mike Tidwell's *The Ponds of Kalambayi: An African Sojourn* is a sensitively written record of two years spent working as a Peace Corps volunteer digging fish ponds in the mid-1980s. His lyrical and politically thoughtful book seems to portray the people of Kalambayi (whose language, Tshiluba, he learns) knowledgeably, with sincerity, and with some affection. He neither romanticises nor refrains from criticising the people and his portraits of them are almost novelistic in their depth. He examines his own motivations, conduct, and flaws, and gives information on the history of the colonial encounter from the Kalambayi perspective. Yet he still benefits from Africa, learning 'what it means to be human'.[37] When he returns to the consumer culture of the USA, he will miss the simplicity and clarity of his life in Kalambayi. His original hope – 'to travel my inner continent... and come back with a better focused picture' (pp. 12–13) – seems fulfilled.

Redmond O'Hanlon's *Congo Journey* (1996) announces itself as a record of a journey to the communist People's Republic of Congo: 'the most difficult equatorial African country to get into',[38] though the reader, in fact, learns very little about this infrequently visited nation. O'Hanlon's interest is more in the flora and fauna than in the people and the peg on which his story is hung is the search for a probably mythical dinosaur-like ceature in Lake Télé. O'Hanlon's book has been widely praised for its humour, which arises from his suitably post-colonial self-presentation as a bumbling and inefficient Englishman. But no less than the self-deprecation of Mary Kingsley in *Travels in West Africa* (1897), which is taken by many to be a necessary strategy for a woman travelling and writing in a man's world, it is highly constructed and may mask a secure self-confidence. Although O'Hanlon movingly conveys the limitations imposed on educated Africans by poverty, he employs them to carry his own fascination with the residual beliefs in superstition and magic that underlie their scientific training and exposure to rationalism.

'Even today, travellers such as Redmond O'Hanlon won't take their wives with them so that it doesn't look too easy', writes Paul Hyland in *The Black Heart* (1988), a work which sees him and his wife Noëlle following, mostly by boat, the journeys of Conrad, Casement, and Hyland's great-uncle the missionary and explorer Dan Crawford. Hyland writes that 'I wanted to look at the old white myths of the Dark Continent in today's light',[39] but his responses to the welcome he receives in Luanza, the home of Crawford's mission, from Africans who remember his great-uncle, give new meaning to his life in a way that seems distinctly colonial. The Africans' gratitude and reverence towards Crawford and his wife fill Hyland with a sense of worth through his freshly felt tie with his ancestor. When, later, he visits the Crawfords' granddaughter in Scotland, tells her of 'the elders who recalled her grandparents with such love' (p. 270), and shows her a photograph of the place where her father's birth-cord was buried, she thanks him for having 'given me back my history' (p. 271).

A more self-critical narrative than Hyland's is Jeffrey Tayler's *Facing the Congo* (2000). Tayler, from the US but resident in Moscow after a spell working for the Peace Corps in Uzbekistan, decides in 1994 at the age of thirty-three that his life lacks direction. During this period of 'musing and searching', a reading of Naipaul's *A Bend in the River* 'limn[ed] a Congo motif in my life'.[40] After further researches, he resolves to 'remake myself' by travelling alone by pirogue the 1,084 miles from Kisangani to Kinshasa. This 'would be a partial recreation of Stanley's historic journey' and, he hopes, will 'settle...all my doubts about who I was and what I could accomplish' (p. xvii). Once in the Congo, Tayler, like Tidwell and Winternitz, realises the extent to which 'It was my country that had helped create this hell' (p. 40) but he also grows to understand that 'the denouement that I had come to Africa to force upon my life' (p. 236) means that he has 'exploited Zaire as a playground on which to solve my own rich-boy existential dilemmas' (p. 249).

Not all recent travel writing on the Congo is concerned ultimately with self-discovery. Philip Gourevitch's travels in Rwanda to learn about the 1994 genocide in which up to a million Tutsis were killed may indeed have some personal motivation – his parents and grandparents fled to the US from Nazi Germany – but there can be no doubting the public nature of his harrowing *We Wish to Inform You That Tomorrow We Will be Killed with Our Families: Stories from Rwanda* (1998). He demonstrates the UN's failure to prevent the killings and in particular the culpability of the US and French governments. The self-serving view of ancient tribal or ethnic conflict that gave Western governments the excuse of inevitability for their inaction is demolished as he brilliantly exposes the inadequacy of treating crises as though they were humanitarian and not political problems.

Gourevitch's researches have taught him that the landscape and the people are not as they seem to him as a traveller. He has been criticised for being too uncritical of the Rwandan Patriotic Front, and there are more authoritative accounts of the genocide,[41] but the stories he hears and shares are a stunning revelation of the possibilities of travelling and writing.

NOTES

Preliminary drafts of this essay were given as papers at universities in France, England, and South Africa. My thanks to Jean-Yves Le Disez, Jan Borm, Steve Clark, Carl Thompson, Sarah Moss, Brenda Cooper, Liz Gunner, David Attwell, and Carlotta von Maltzan. I am also grateful to David Espey for telling me about Tidwell's book; and to Peter Hulme and Roy Bridges for suggesting ways through.

1 Both are reprinted in Joseph Conrad, *Heart of Darkness*, ed. Robert Kimbrough (New York: W. W. Norton & Company, 1988), pp. 142–94.
2 Graham Greene, *In Search of a Character. Two African Journals: Congo Journal and Convoy to West Africa* (London: Vintage, 2000), p. 48. *Congo Journal* was first published in 1961.
3 Adam Hochschild, *King Leopold's Ghost: A Story of Greed, Terror, and Heroism in Colonial Africa* (London: Macmillan, 2000), p. 3.
4 Peter Forbath, *The River Congo: The Discovery, Exploration and Exploitation of the World's Most Dramatic River* (New York: Harper Row, 1977), p. ix.
5 W. D. Hamilton, Foreword to Edward Hooper, *The River: A Journey Back to the Source of HIV and AIDS* (London: Penguin, 2000), p. xxxiii.
6 Conrad, *Heart of Darkness*, ed. Kimbrough, p. 38.
7 Richard F. Burton, *Two Trips to Gorilla Land and the Cataracts of the Congo*, 2 vols [1876] (New York: Johnson Reprint Corporation, 1967), vol. II, p. 589.
8 This paragraph draws extensively on Malvern van Wyk Smith, 'Prester John and the Anthropophagi: The Africa of Expectation' in *Journeys of Discovery*, ed. Rosalie Breitenbach (Grahamstown: 1820 Foundation, 1988), pp. 70–82. The quotation is at p. 71.
9 See Oumelbanine Zhiri, 'Leo Africanus's *Description of Africa*', in *Travel Knowledge: European 'Discoveries' in the Early Modern Period*, ed. Ivo Kamps and Jyotsna G. Singh (New York: Palgrave, 2001), pp. 258–66, quotation at p. 262.
10 Annie E. Coombes, *Reinventing Africa: Museums, Material Culture and Popular Imagination in Late Victorian and Edwardian England* (New Haven: Yale

University Press, 1994); Jan Nederveen Pieterse, *White on Black: Images of Africa and Blacks in Western Popular Culture* (New Haven: Yale University Press, 1992); Felix Driver, *Geography Militant: Cultures of Exploration and Empire* (Oxford: Blackwell, 2001).

11 David Livingstone, *Missionary Travels and Researches in South Africa...* (London: John Murray, 1857), pp. 673, 228.

12 Henry M. Stanley, *Through the Dark Continent...* [1878] (London: Sampson Low, Marston, Searle, & Rivington, 1890), p. 571.

13 See Norman R. Bennett, ed., *Stanley's Despatches to the New York Herald 1871–1872, 1874–1877* (Boston University Press, 1970), p. 387.

14 Verney Lovett Cameron, *Across Africa*, 2 vols. (London: Daldy, Isbister & Co., 1877), vol. II, p. 25; vol. I, pp. 16, 352, 357.

15 See Tim Youngs, *Travellers in Africa: British Travelogues, 1850–1900* (Manchester University Press, 1994), chs. 4, 5.

16 Henry M. Stanley, *In Darkest Africa...* [1890] (London: Sampson Low, Marston & Company, 1893), p. 131.

17 Mrs. J. S. Jameson, ed., *Story of the Rear Column of the Emin Pasha Relief Expedition by the Late James S. Jameson...* (London: R. H. Porter, 1890), p. 291.

18 See for example Edmund D. Morel, *King Leopold's Rule in Africa* (London: William Heinemann, 1904).

19 These are reprinted in Conrad, *Heart of Darkness*, ed. Kimbrough, pp. 84–97, 103–13.

20 Katja Füllberg-Stolberg, 'African Americans in Africa: Black Missionaries and the "Congo Atrocities," 1890–1910', in *Black Imagination and the Middle Passage*, ed. Maria Diedrich, Henry Louis Gates, Jr., Carl Pedersen (New York: Oxford University Press, 1999), pp. 215–27.

21 For example the Rev. Samuel Crowther and the Rev. John Christopher Taylor, *The Gospel on the Banks of the Niger: Journals and Notices of the Native Missionaries Accompanying the Niger Expedition of 1857–1859* (1859).

22 Rev. W. Holman Bentley, *Pioneering on the Congo*, 2 vols. (London: The Religious Tract Society, 1900), vol. II, p. 64.

23 For example, anthropologist Robert W. Harms, *River of Wealth, River of Sorrow: The Central Zaire Basin in the Era of the Slave and Ivory Trade, 1500–1891* (New Haven: Yale University Press, 1981), pp. 132, 140.

24 Irma Stern, *Congo* (Pretoria: J. L. Van Schaik, Ltd., 1943), pp. 24, 1.

25 Martin Johnson, *Congorilla: Adventures with Pygmies and Gorillas in Africa* (London: George G. Harrap & Co. Ltd., 1932), pp. 12–13.

26 Colin Turnbull, *The Forest People* (London: Triad/Paladin, 1984), p. vii.

27 Dian Fossey, *Gorillas in the Mist* (London: Phoenix, 1985), p. 14.

28 See Ludo de Witte, *The Assassination of Lumumba*, trans. Ann Wright and Renée Fenby (London: Verso, 2001).

29 William Gálvez, *Che in Africa: Che Guevara's Congo Diary*, trans. Mary Todd (Melbourne: Ocean Press, 1999), p. 178.

30 Mike Hoare, *Congo Mercenary* (London: Robert Hale, 1967), p. 283.

31 See also the 1996 film *When We Were Kings* (dir. Leon Gast, Polygram).

32 Reprinted in V. S. Naipaul, 'A New King for the Congo: Mobutu and the Nihilism of Africa', in *"The Return of Eva Perón" with "The Killings in Trinidad"*

(Harmondsworth: Penguin Books, 1981), pp. 165–96. See also his travelogue, *A Congo Diary* (Los Angeles: Sylvester & Orphanos, 1980), and his novels *In a Free State* (1971) and *A Bend in the River* (1979). The forty-four page *Congo Diary*, published in a limited edition of 330 copies, is in note form, making both the travel and the author's impressions seem more immediate. One feels Naipaul's disappointment when he remarks that 'no one, African, Asian, European, has heard of Conrad or *Heart of Darkness*' (p. 13).

33 Helen Winternitz, *East Along the Equator: A Journey up the Congo and into Zaire* (New York: The Atlantic Monthly Press, 1987), p. 263.

34 Peter Hudson, *A Leaf in the Wind: Travels in the Heart of Africa* (London: Flamingo, 1989), p. 171.

35 Keith B. Richburg, *Out of America: A Black Man Confronts Africa* (New York: BasicBooks, 1997), ch. 8: 'Wake-up Calls'.

36 Eddy L. Harris, *Native Stranger: A Black American's Journey into the Heart of Africa* (London: Viking, 1993), p. 18.

37 Mike Tidwell, *The Ponds of Kalambayi: An African Sojourn* (New York: The Lyons Press, 1990), p. 4.

38 Redmond O'Hanlon, *Congo Journey* (London: Penguin Books, 1997), p. 12.

39 Paul Hyland, *The Black Heart: A Voyage into Central Africa* (New York: Paragon House, 1990), pp. 11, 12.

40 Jeffrey Tayler, *Facing the Congo* (London: Little, Brown and Company, 2001), p. xv.

41 See Alison Des Forges, *Leave None to Tell the Story: Genocide in Rwanda* (New York: Human Rights Watch, 1999).

GLENN HOOPER

The Isles / Ireland: the wilder shore

While it is commonplace to associate the eighteenth-century traveller with traditional Grand Tourism, this period also witnessed the emergence of a more locally focused form of travel, sometimes described as the Home Tour.[1] Literally cut off from continental Europe at the time of the Napoleonic wars (c.1790–1815), increasing numbers of British travellers turned to their 'own' countries from the late 1760s onwards, visiting the Peak District and the Lake District within England, while the more adventurous journeyed into Wales, and eventually towards the Scottish Highlands and Islands, as well as across the sea to Ireland. In order to give some sense of the cultural background to these developments, this essay provides a brief account of several eighteenth-century travel accounts written about Britain before moving to a fuller consideration of Irish travel, which saw sustained interest during the same decades, but an even greater emphasis after 1800. Throughout the nineteenth century, discussions concerning national identity, security, and the future political relations between these islands permeate travellers' accounts, indicating that geographical distance was not the sole criterion for determining 'strangeness'.[2]

Picturesque and romantic travel

The picturesque traveller is described by Christopher Hussey as the sort 'who has a conception of an ideal form of nature, derived from landscape painting', and he attributes some of the earliest picturesque writings to Dr Thomas Herring, Archbishop of Canterbury, who travelled through Wales in 1738–9, and who described his impressions in terms of 'the magnificence of nature'.[3] This search for magnificent nature largely involved looking for rocks and precipices, 'stations' from which to appreciate a particular scene, and later for ruins, especially of abbeys, castles, and keeps. Although these elements could be found across several parts of Britain and Ireland, some of the most popular places travellers turned to were the Wye

Valley, North Wales, the Lake District, and the Scottish Highlands. While Hussey points to the publications of two notable Oxbridge academics – Dr Dalton's *A Descriptive Poem* and Dr Brown's *Letter to Lord Lyttelton*, both written in 1758 – as having stimulated interest in the picturesque, directing Arthur Young to the Lakes in particular, Hussey also attributes such 'discoveries' to new road-building measures which made travel that much easier: 'All over England the appreciation of scenery, the experiencing of romantic emotions, and the perception of the sublime in nature increased in direct ratio to the number of turnpike acts' (p. 101). The rugged and exposed areas of Britain might have sharpened the appetites of the hardier traveller, but not until those places were made more physically accessible were tourists able to travel in greater numbers to share in such delights.

Armed with a variety of accessories, usually a 'piece of tinted glass through which to view the landscape, drawing pads, memorandum books, a small watercolour set, pens and pencils, a telescope, a barometer, [and] maps', the picturesque traveller was nothing if not well prepared.[4] And as word spread about how aesthetically gratifying these trips could be, so too did the number of publications on the subject increase. Perhaps the best-known writer on picturesque travel was William Gilpin. Born in Carlisle, educated at Oxford, Gilpin's tours of the River Wye and South Wales in 1770, of the Lakes in 1772, and of the Scottish Highlands in 1776, represent the most explicit connection between a form of landscape appreciation and travel. In his *Observations on the River Wye, and Several Parts of South Wales*, he suggested that we 'travel for various purposes; to explore the culture of the soils; to view the curiosities of art; to survey the beauties of nature; to search for her productions ... [however the] following little work proposes a new object of pursuit; that of examining the face of a country *by the rules of picturesque beauty*'.[5] The first of Gilpin's picturesque handbooks, *Observations on the River Wye*, is full of painterly detail, as well as suggestions to travellers on how best to read and appreciate a scene. Gilpin therefore not only blends an interest in the picturesque with travel writing, but offers a direct challenge to the ideology of Grand Tourism, showing how an exploration of rural Britain could compete with the fascination with continental Europe. And in his *Observations of Cumberland and Westmoreland* (1772), he appears to push this connection even further, suggesting that his work is 'meant to *illustrate and explain picturesque ideas*', but also to '*characterize the countries*, through which the reader is carried'.[6]

Moreover, writers like Gilpin not only promoted the aesthetic elements of such an encounter, but presented such travels as acts of discovery, as though for a certain class of traveller an element of risk was a clear bonus.

As Malcolm Andrews remarks, there is 'something of the big-game hunter in these tourists, boasting of their encounters with savage landscapes, "capturing" wild scenes, and "fixing" them as pictorial trophies in order to sell them or hang them up in frames on their drawing-room walls', and he quotes Gilpin himself, who asked, shall 'we suppose it a greater pleasure to the sportsman to pursue a trivial animal, than it is to the man of taste to pursue the beauties of nature?' (pp. 67–8). Certainly there were many 'beauties' to be found on the south coast, and the west of England, travelled by Gilpin in 1774 and 1775 respectively. There were also, however, regional differences. One place where physical hardship was expected routinely to accompany aesthetic experience was the Scottish Highlands, of which the traveller Thomas Gray in 1765 wrote:

> The mountains are ecstatic, and ought to be visited in pilgrimage once a year. None but those monstrous creatures of God know how to join so much beauty with so much horror. A fig for your poets, painters, gardners and clergymen that have not been among them; their imaginations can be made up of nothing but bowling-greens, flowering shrubs, horse-ponds, Fleet-ditches, shell grottoes and Chinese rails.[7]

In common with parts of Cumbria, Scottish tourism received a boost during the same decades, although a number of interconnected issues and events, some of them very unlike the interest developed within England for the picturesque, may also be discerned. The Jacobite defeat at Culloden in 1746, for example, created the need to secure Scotland, addressed mainly through constructing roads into the Highlands. But if we compound this need to provide Scotland with an improved infrastructure with the publication of James Macpherson's *Fragments of Ancient Poetry* (1760), *Fingal* (1762), and the *Works of Ossian* (1765), which captured the imagination of many through their depiction of Highland scenery, we can see what lay behind Scotland's arrival as a major tourist destination within Britain. Of course, earlier travel accounts of Scotland do exist, such as Daniel Defoe's *A Tour Through the Whole Island of Great Britain*, published between 1724 and 1726, which included several Scottish chapters. But the real interest in Scottish culture, at least in terms of travel writing, developed from the 1760s onwards, with the publication of texts such as Thomas Pennant's *A Tour in Scotland, 1769* (1771). For writers like Pennant, Scotland appeared available, yet seldom travelled ('struck ... with the reflection of having never seen Scotland, I instantly ordered my baggage to be got ready'), and the extent to which he capitalised on the novelty of the place is prevalent throughout his writing ('Continued our journey over a wild, black, moory, melancholy tract').[8] Doubtless, such changing political and economic realities encouraged travellers like Pennant to promote Scotland as a tourist venue, capable of competing with North Wales and the Lakes, as well as further afield. That said, although Linda Colley cites the Treaty of Paris in 1763 ('in which Britain restored some of its winnings to France and Spain in the vain hope that they would refrain from going to war in the future to regain the rest') as a turning-point – a moment of English re-evaluation in which Scotland came to be regarded as effectively absorbed within the Kingdom – she also points to the willingness of Scots to join in this process of absorption themselves: as combatants within the British army, as emigrants to the British colonies in America, and as southward-bearing movers who would do well in the English capital, and then overseas as part of the British Empire.[9] Indeed, this change in the attitude of the English and Scots towards each other, but also towards the idea of the Union, helped reorientate the notion of centre and periphery, and culturally remapped the notion of the Celtic fringe.

In 1763, the year cited by Colley as marking a cultural and geo-political reassessment within Britain, a young James Boswell was considering a trip to Europe, and possibly also a publication of his experiences should they prove as fruitful and stimulating as he hoped. Between 1765 and 1766 he travelled throughout the continent, publishing his *Account of Corsica, The Journal of a Tour to that Island* in 1768. However in 1773, in the company of a mature Samuel Johnson, then sixty-four, Boswell struck out for more tempting terrain: the Western Islands of his native Scotland and the Hebrides. Even if Peter Levi's suggestion that Pennant's *Tour* is the more thorough is correct, the publication of Johnson's *Journey to the Western Islands of Scotland* (1775) marked an important moment in Scottish travel literature, despite the less than favourable impressions conveyed. As Andrews suggests, 'Scotland was unfortunate in having attracted Samuel Johnson as one of her first English tourists. Many later eighteenth-century tours to the Highlands were undertaken specifically for the pleasure of challenging or endorsing Johnson's censorious commentary' (p. 197). Johnson declared that, 'All travel has its advantages. If the passenger visits better countries, he may learn to improve his own, and if fortune carries him to worse, he may learn to enjoy it',[10] but found Scotland to be much worse than expected. Nevertheless, he single-handedly enhanced Scottish tourism, securing the peripheral areas of Britain as eligible destinations for travellers. Indeed, for Johnson and Boswell, no less than for the modern tourist, these remote, sometimes hostile environments were the incentives for making a Scottish trip, and the attractions of rural Scotland would long dominate over urban interests. The predominant image of Scotland even today, suggest Gold and Gold, is of lakes and landscapes, of highlands and islands, a place where only 'Edinburgh, the cultural heart of Glasgow and the Old Town of Stirling are offered as counter-attractions'.[11] A cultural re-evaluation of what had been previously disregarded, in addition to improved levels of security, roads, and maps, invited tourists to the country in significantly greater numbers. Not only that; these early travellers helped to create a version of Scotland that would endure for many years.

The rediscovery of Ireland

Throughout the eighteenth century Ireland also witnessed an increase in the number of travellers, in part a response to improved conditions, and to the relatively pacific nature of the country, but also because of a reappraisal of the Celtic fringe as a political entity and as a viable alternative to traditional Grand Tour destinations in continental Europe. As noted, tourist venues in England, such as the Lake District, the Pennines, and the Peak District, were drawing an enthusiastic response, but in the case of Scotland and Ireland travellers were responding as much to perceived political changes as to shifts in aesthetic judgement and taste. As we saw in the decades following the Jacobite rebellion of 1745, travellers to Scotland increased significantly as the country appeared contained, politically pacified and, more importantly, embraced with greater coherence than before. And not surprisingly, many travellers began to see Ireland – now also relatively stable – as a similarly inviting venue. Philip Luckombe's *A Tour Through Ireland* (1780), for example, captures something of the element of discovery expressed in a number of Scottish tours, especially where he pits the attractions of an Irish visit against those of a European one: 'I was advised not to begin with the Grand Tour of Europe...but to pass over into that country first, which, on account of its laws, religion, political dependence, &c. ought to be regarded and thoroughly known next to Great Britain.'[12] Like several other late eighteenth-century travellers to Ireland, Luckombe not only cherished the notion of abundant Irish antiquities, but regarded the long history that marked Anglo-Irish relations as an additional stimulus to travel, even if the final decade of the eighteenth century would prove more than a test for Britain. In December 1796, 15,000 French troops attempted a landing at Bantry Bay, County Cork, but were checked by storms and internal divisions. In May 1798 the first stages of rebellion, initiated by the United Irishmen, began in Leinster, and in August of the same year General Humbert and a French force of about 1,000 men landed in County Mayo. Despite these various efforts, all attempts at the overthrow of British authority in Ireland failed, and the Act of Union of 1800, which brought about the legislative Union of Great Britain and Ireland, signalled for many in Britain an end to Irish instability.

However liberated eighteenth-century travellers to Ireland had felt, the expectations raised by the Act of Union created a sense of optimism and drew travel writers to Ireland in swarms. Almost without exception all travellers who visited in the aftermath of the Union were responding to the newness of the event: the fact that Ireland was no longer the allegedly seditious neighbour, forever courting French territorial ambitions, but the 'Sister Isle', bonded in constitutional, if not ideological affiliation to the larger island. But a number of issues and problems nevertheless arose. Because Ireland was increasingly associated – at least according to the ideologues of the day – with political stability, it became imperative to stress the harmonious nature of these political developments. Ireland, in other words, had to be presented not only as the 'Sister Isle', but as an equal partner, with full rights within the Union, and with a rôle that reflected a degree of parity with her closest neighbours. And yet it was precisely this newly established relationship which presented the greatest challenge, for no sooner did travellers disembark, keen to savour the concord promoted in Britain as the corollary of Union, than they realised that Ireland was as difficult as ever. More than that, where they had previously narrated their sense of unease amidst incomprehensible otherness, they had now to reconcile these tensions, genuinely reflecting something of their experiences in the country, while at the same time holding to the new line that Ireland was the safe and happy venue the Union would have them believe it to be.

For many post-Union writers, then, Ireland was both a spectacle and a domestic arena; a place apparently not that different from Britain, yet utterly so. And although many arrived in the years following the Union to assess the country's long-term future, on how it might be made more politically amenable, and why it was still unknown, especially after centuries of involvement with Britain, what they discovered was that no simple, unified model existed. All too aware of the hollowness at the heart of the Union – and the 1798 rebellion, with its notorious cruelties and 30,000 deaths, was a considerable narrative impediment – travellers reflected these tensions, and showed that if Ireland could be associated with parity and equivalence, so too could it be associated with insurrection and sedition. The country was no longer at war, but neither was it entirely at peace, and the fact that a constitutional relationship attempted to smooth out these narrative (and in many instances material) irregularities only made matters worse. Anne Plumptre, reflecting something of this anxiety, stressed the new-found relationship during the years 1814–15:

If we are anxious to be introduced to a knowledge of the face of their country, to understand its natural advantages and disadvantages, [so] that we may be enabled to compare them with our own, and judge between them and ourselves, – a much deeper interest will surely be excited when these injuries, these comparisons, relate to an object so near to us as a SISTER.[13]

But when Plumptre later narrates an attack on a mail car outside Cashel, an act prompted by a desire for munitions by the now 'loyal' Irish, her despair is all too apparent: 'Such violence must be repelled by violence; and the consequence ensued, which was reasonably to be expected, that *martial law*, that *law* without *law*, was soon proclaimed here. Devoted Ireland! Are these things never to be otherwise?' (p. 310). Not all post-Union travellers reveal as clearly as Plumptre just how traumatic the newly established relationship with Ireland could sometimes be, but this conflictual sense of the country – as both a security threat and a constitutional ally – made for a number of sobering reflections on the prospect of an harmonious outcome.

Although post-Union enthusiasm for travel to Ireland continued to grow, a sense that not all was well with the Union, indeed that it was positively rancorous, became increasingly apparent. The country's Catholics, who believed that Union would bring Catholic Emancipation, would have to wait until 1829 for such rights to be confirmed. Moreover, since the Irish parliament no longer existed, many of the country's landowners removed themselves for most of the year to England, leaving their estates to be managed, sometimes badly, in their absence. When absenteeism, as it was generally called, was combined with the day-to-day humiliations that faced the Catholic majority, a sense of utter despair was conveyed by many of the country's peasantry. Travellers such as John Christian Curwen, MP for Carlisle, recorded their deplorable state in 1818: 'Assuredly there must be something radically wrong in this country – humanity proclaims it, and appearances justify the assumption [...] it belongs perhaps to some absentee whose utter ignorance of his property here, and complete indifference to the hapless condition of the peasantry on it, paralyzes all efforts of industry, blights the harvest of hope, and produces poverty and misery all over the domain'.[14] But only two years later, Thomas Kitson Cromwell evoked a much greater sense of Irish dissatisfaction, especially when he compared the Irish and English 'rustic' in ways that suggested a capacity for violence was not that far away in the case of the former:

Everywhere in Ireland, we meet with lengthened and pale if not darkened visages, the indexes to the minds of men employed in the common agricultural labours, which, contrasted with the ruddy open countenances of English rustics, might appear to the traveller from the latter country those of banditti, of beings detached from civilized society, and ready for the perpetration of any attack upon its legal institutions.[15]

Not all travellers, of course, note the potential instability of Ireland, although since many journeyed to Ireland with the specific intention of inquiring into the political health of the country, or to look more closely at a largely Catholic country in legislative Union with Britain, remarks on the native Irish, and on their quality of life, their relationship to their priests, and on their vocal support for the repeal of the Union, abound in many travel accounts of the 1820s and 1830s. Indeed, even after Catholic Emancipation had been granted, things looked decidedly unstable. Henry Inglis, travelling through parts of Wicklow in 1834, was told that he would find 'all so comfortable in Wicklow', but found instead that although the place is full of 'villas and gentlemen's seats [...] I found little satisfactory in the condition of the people'.[16] And the anonymous author of *Ten Days in Ireland* (1835), also travelling around Wicklow, was even blunter about how poorly governed the country had become:

> 'Where's your master?' – 'In England.' 'Where's your mistress?' – 'In England.' 'Where's everybody that has fine mansions and rich estates?' – 'In England,' may be truly answered. Struck with this remark, I made a memorandum, which I intended to hand over to Miss Laconic, for insertion in her notebook, when I returned to Dublin; it was as follows: – 'Everybody in Ireland who has got money to spare, has gone to England to spend it.'[17]

James Grant, a Scottish novelist and devout Calvinist who embarked on a three-month visit of the country, also catches something of the decline in optimism from those early years after the Union, and warns of an impending collapse. Although Grant's intention was to report on a number of Irish issues, the Repeal of the Union appeared to be the most pressing political topic of the day, in danger of threatening not only the relationship with Great Britain, but the very stability of Ireland itself:

> The political condition of Ireland has for centuries been the subject of deep anxiety to England...Ireland is in a most critical state. I am aware that there is, for the moment, a lull in the repeal agitation, by which Ireland has been violently convulsed for some years past, but that lull is only for a moment.[18]

This anxiety, which was reflected by many writers in the 1830s and early 1840s, demonstrates how fluid the Anglo-Irish relationship continued to be, even after almost half a century of Union, and throughout these decades the subject of political dissatisfaction became ever more pronounced.

Although Grant's description of Ireland as 'convulsed' is not inappropriate, the term would gain additional power only the following year as the

9. 'Derrynane Abbey, County Kerry, home of Daniel O'Connell, MP (1775–1847) with O'Connell and friends in foreground' by Havell & Havell after an original painting by John Fogarty. By kind permission of the National Library of Ireland.

potato crop failed and Ireland faced a challenge of unimaginable proportions, especially along the western seaboard. From 1845–50, with serious
after-effects continuing until 1852, the Great Famine scoured the country,
resulting in a decline in population of almost two million people from famine-
related mortality and emigration. Although on the face of it not the most
obvious spur, the famine years saw significant numbers of travellers visit
the country, with the more traditional scenic tourists displaced by increasing
numbers of social observers, religious figures, and journalists, many of whom
specifically journeyed to witness misery at first-hand. Texts such as William
Bennett's *Narrative of a Recent Journey of Six Weeks* (1847) and James Hack
Tuke's *A Visit to Connaught in the Autumn of 1847* (1847) told much of
the hardship endured by the Irish peasantry during these years, and are lit-
tered with stories of poorhouses, famine roads, and soup kitchens, as well
as the physical appearance of the Irish themselves: as victims of opthalmia,
malnutrition, dysentry, fever, and cholera:

> A little further, in a cask, placed like a dog-kennel, was a poor boy, who had lain
> there some time, in high fever, without friends or relatives. I proceeded down
> the main street... The town [Kenmare] itself is overwhelmed with poverty;

and the swollen limbs, emaciated countenances, and other hideous forms of disease to be seen about, were innumerable. In no other part of Ireland had I seen people falling on their knees to beg. It was difficult to sit over breakfast after this.[19]

The immediate post-famine years, however, witnessed an even more bizarre phenomenon: the promotion of Ireland as a place of settlement for thrifty English and Scotch farmers. How, after so much trauma and misery, could this unexpected turn of events take place? Quite simply, as the decline in the population was increasingly emphasised by British newspapers and magazines, the sense of a newly available terrain, much closer to Britain than many of its other colonies, swiftly emerged. Where the Irish landscape was traditionally seen as a place of poverty and dereliction, it was now promoted as a place where, if not fortunes, then considerable sums could be made, a space where British capitalists and industrialists could re-invent the landscape (political and literal) as well as themselves:

> The lands around [Westport] were manifestly in a state of transition, and I could not but admire the persevering industry that was converting one of the most impracticable slopes I ever saw into a creditable farm ... As I saw all this enacting before me, I fancied that I could read my own history.[20]

Significantly strengthened by the publication of the 1851 census, these post-famine texts, or at least those that were compiled at the tail-end of the calamity, represented Ireland in a brighter light. John Ashworth, for example, remarked on how 'the ample resources, [and] the immense capabilities, of the Sister Isle are beginning to attract attention in England', and perhaps more importantly – given the constituency to whom he was appealing – that 'Ireland has seen her worst days' (p. 43). Moreover, writers such as Ashworth, as well as figures like Harriet Martineau (*Letters From Ireland*, 1852) and John Forbes (*Memorandums Made in Ireland*, 1852), shored up this emerging orthodoxy, and fuelled the notion of political stability, cheap lands, and even cheaper labour for potential English and Scots investors. While the numbers of intending emigrants from Britain to Ireland were not as extensive as initially anticipated, the post-famine euphoria enjoyed by at least some travel writers revealed a hope that not only the economic, but also the political misfortunes of Ireland, could be finally alleviated.[21]

Not surprisingly, the post-famine excitement over the potentially lucrative nature of Ireland died down within a relatively short period, and by the 1870s and 1880s, as land agitation and a more volatile politics re-emerged, the optimism that had been shared by a number of post-famine travel writers was effectively extinguished. The country remained a popular destination, though, and a number of notable texts were produced. For example, James Macaulay's *Ireland in 1872* emphasises not merely the virtues of union with Britain, but the inherently superior character of Protestantism. Like Martineau and Forbes before him, Macaulay saw Ireland's salvation, if not in settlement by Protestant Scots and English, then in the elimination of Catholicism, and he points to Ulster as proof that Protestant thrift, resourcefulness, and willingness to work hard, will turn Ireland into a safe and prosperous component of the Empire:

> With one-third of the whole population, Ulster's share of the police, jail, and poor-law expenses is not above one-eighth. Its pauperism, its crime, its poor-rates are all less; its education, its wealth, its industry, its benevolent and religious institutions are all more, in proportion to the numbers of its people. In short, there is a condition of social and moral health, and an atmosphere of prosperity in the north, utterly diverse from the south, with its filthy cabins, swarming beggars, decaying villages, and its Catholic faith.[22]

Yet other travellers found less reason to believe that Ireland was ready to turn towards Protestant sobriety. James Hack Tuke, on a return visit to Ireland, noted widespread support for land reform, and for the radical parliamentarian Charles Stewart Parnell. Tuke's *The Land Question: A Visit to Donegal and Connaught in the Spring of 1880* (1880), describes a country torn by conflict over land rents and rights, and an increasingly disaffected population, and his impression is reinforced in Bernard Becker's self-explanatorily entitled *Disturbed Ireland* (1881), which includes an account of the transportation of Orangemen from Ulster to County Mayo to gather the harvest of the man who had just given his name to the English language: Captain Boycott. Moreover, the tales of disruption and conflict, reflective of political developments in the country generally, continue throughout the 1880s. Titles such as *To and Fro* (1884), *The Eve of Home Rule* (1886), *Ireland's Disease* (1887), *Ireland Under Coercion* (1888), *John Bull and His Other Island* (1890) all reveal the fact that Ireland, and travellers to her, were preoccupied with politics throughout the decade. However, although this remains an intermittent theme in the 1890s, perhaps in response to the death of Parnell, and the rise of cultural as opposed to militant nationalism, many travellers begin to reflect a more benign image of the country. For example, the American traveller, Marietta Lloyd, in *A Trip to Ireland* (1893), brings a strong sense of the domestic to her writing – providing copious detail about furnishings and the comforts of home – but also a sense that political rancour is less evident than was once the case. And in Alfred Austin's *Spring and Autumn in Ireland* (1900), an even more sheltered image of Ireland becomes available. As Britain's Poet Laureate, Austin was in a position greatly to influence the perception of Ireland, especially for British readers, and he declared that he wrote as he did because 'of the love and admiration the author has long felt for Ireland'.[23] Indeed, so enamoured is Austin of the place that he is prepared to put up with a number of inconveniences, not just because he is an agreeable traveller, but because one senses a determination on his part to be favourably disposed towards, even positive about the marriage of Saxon and Celt: 'When going from Galway to Recess by the new light railway, I wanted at Oughterard to look at the river, but feared I should not be able to do so in the time allowed for our halt. "Sure, we'll wait for you," said a porter; and they did. In Ireland people like waiting' (p. 53).

If Austin wrote about the pleasantries of an Irish tour, promoting the place to his English compatriots, while at the same time declaring a specifically English affection for the Irish themselves ('it is part of his [the Celt's] politeness, of his urbanity, to talk; and the taciturnity of the Saxon seems to him inhuman'), such tokens of friendship would be short-lived (p. 60). Only five years after Austin toured Ireland, Matthew Arnold published *The Study of Celtic Literature*, seeking in Celtic culture a revitalising energy with which to counter materialism: 'let it be one of our angelic revenges on the Philistines . . . [and let us] found at Oxford a chair of Celtic, and to send, through the gentle ministration of science, a message of peace to Ireland'.[24] But the die had been cast. In 1913 the UVF (Ulster Volunteer Force) and the Irish Volunteers were both formed, with gun-running to Larne and Howth respectively, taking place the next year. And on 24 April 1916 Irish Volunteers seized central Dublin buildings, initiating the Easter Rising. Between 1916 and 1922 Ireland went from rebellion to war of independence, and from partition to civil war.[25] Of the writers who travelled throughout this period, most were British, indicating that even with the recent history of Anglo-Irish conflict, Ireland retained the fascination she had exerted since the Act of Union. For example, Wilfrid Ewart, author of *A Journey in Ireland, 1921* (1922), fed English curiosity regarding Ireland's turmoil through his accounts of being mistaken for a political agent: 'Everyone seemed to see in an English stranger a potential spy . . . I was openly reviled by an apparently sober and respectable Irishwoman on the railway station platform who evidently took me for a plainclothes Black and Tan.'[26] Ewart's account was serialised in *The Times*, the *Westminster Gazette*, and the *Sunday Times*, continuing a well-established tradition of the journalist as travel writer, and emphasising the sense of drama that developments in Ireland seemed to demand. However, it was not exclusively English writers who saw a certain potential in the Irish situation. In 1920, Ibrahim Rashad published his account of *An Egyptian in Ireland*, and his travels provoked a consideration less of Ireland's future, than of Egypt's, if she should only follow the former's example of liberation through revolution:

In free countries, the ablest are entrusted by the people with the direction of the affairs of the nation, in Egypt it is the weakest that are put into office to carry out the dictates of the English adviser, inspector, master, or whatever he is called, whose interest obviously clashes with our own . . . The fate of tyrants is always the same, it is only a matter of time when they shall disappear.[27]

Irish idylls

The 1930s saw the beginning of a relatively peaceful time in Ireland, despite the Anglo-Irish economic war. It also stimulated a romantic view of the country that endured well into the 1960s, and attracted writers from continental Europe as well as from Britain. County Kerry, the west of Ireland generally, as well as parts of County Antrim, received large numbers of tourists and travel writers. The country had been routinely presented by many – especially throughout the nineteenth century – as a place of poverty and political instability, but another, equally forceful image, was of Ireland as a place of pastoral innocence. And it is this model that became especially dominant in these decades, when Irish neutrality, 'anti-modernity', and a distinct lack of industrialisation made the place seem essentially charming. As early as 1930, when John Gibbons published *Tramping Through Ireland*, even apparently politicised encounters are rendered quaint and harmless by an innate Irish good nature. He recounts an evening in a pub where an elderly man sings 'all about English soldiers being tyrants and despots and things . . . and how we English starved the Irish. The odd thing was that the old man apologised to me before each song, and then went on to sing it.'[28] However, at the end of the entertainment, after Gibbons has stood for the Irish national anthem, the customers seek to return the compliment by singing 'God Save the King':

> And then standing bolt upright with all those kindly people waiting gravely and courteously for me to begin, the awful and almost inconceivable thing came to me. I am an Englishman; I believe with all my heart and soul in 'the King' and all that it stands for; and I would wish the thing to be played all round the world in salute to the Union Jack. But as I stood there the dreadful knowledge suddenly came to me that I do not know the words of it. Except just the opening lines that they play as you leave the theatre. Most fortunately the old man who had sung the rebel-despot songs was able to help me out. But it was an awfully near thing. (p. 99)

This innocuous tale encapsulates English desires regarding Ireland in the early twentieth century. The fantasy of forgiveness, the endurance of good-will, and the suggestion of a sneaking regret at the 'loss' of British identity, revealed in the old man's ability to sing the British anthem, all cast Ireland as a place from which tension and antagonism have been excised. Once again Ireland became a sort of Eden, a place from which the serpent of politics had been banished, and many travel writers confirmed this view of the country – especially the Free State – as not only untouched by war, but by many of the excesses of modernity. Authors such as Kees Van Hoek (*An Irish Panorama*, 1947), Stuart Mais (*I Return to Ireland*, 1948), and Lionel Rolt (*Green and Silver*, 1949), convey a generally favourable impression of the place, showing Ireland to have retained an admirable value system which much of the rest of Europe has lost.

There are a few interesting exceptions to this pattern, however. Cicely Hamilton's *Modern Ireland as Seen by an Englishwoman* (1936) in part explores the border between the two Irish states, and the accord which has arisen between farmers and traders on both sides as a result of their smuggling activities. Written at the height of the Anglo-Irish economic war (1932–8), Hamilton captures the exasperation of those caught by the high tariffs exacted by the two sides, but largely avoids the political implications of the border by reading the situation in a generally comic mode. Acknowledging that much of the smuggling is a natural response to artificially high taxes, she goes on to say 'but there is a further stimulus, and a strong one, in the traditional Irish feud with the law and its minions. Opposition to the police, as representatives of the powers that be, if it is not in the blood of every Irishman, is in that of a fairly high percentage.'[29] A later anecdote, regarding the smuggling of a bull from the South to the North (the drover simply goaded the bull into a gallop, calling meantime to the customs officer to stop it – both bull and smuggler ran safely over the border) is entirely in the tradition of 'Irish Bulls', and indicates a determination on Hamilton's part to maintain a benevolent image of the country, despite partition and its potential for political discord. Nevertheless, the border itself continued to exercise a certain fascination, and in *Ireland Revisited* (1949) Charles Graves described his several crossings (many unwitting, as he travelled on unapproved roads) in a manner that suggested that Ireland's internal border offered chances for illicit thrills, which in contrast to the greater excitement of the just-concluded war, might be enjoyed in relative safety. The predominantly benign image of Ireland presented by these writers continued after the war, and texts such as Olivia Manning's *The Dreaming Shore* (1950) and Oriana Atkinson's *The South and the West of It* (1956) charted the eccentricities of Irish life against dramatic landscapes, showing the country's relatively slow pace of life – which had a genuine appeal after the horrors and frugalities of war-torn Europe – to be its greatest asset. Hardships there undoubtedly were, recounted graphically by writers such as Heinrich Böll in his *Irish Journal* (1957), but the sense in many of these post-war texts is of narrators who have decamped from more demanding environments, and who see Ireland as a strangely liberating, perhaps even mystical venue.

Irish tourism boomed during the 1960s but rapid modernisation – especially in the Republic – led to the island losing some of its appeal to certain travel writers, especially when compounded by the eruption of civil unrest in Northern Ireland from the late 1960s onwards. Ironically, however, the Troubles provoked a renewed interest in Northern Ireland, with texts such as Richard Brown's *The Passion of Richard Brown* (1974) explicitly mixing the travel narrative genre with elements of autobiography and reportage. Indeed, from the early 1970s onwards, a visit to the unsettled streets of Derry and Belfast became *de rigueur* for any travel writer, taking the history of travel accounts on Ireland full-circle, and reinstating politics at its heart. Paul Theroux (*The Kingdom by the Sea*, 1983), Bryce Webster (*In Search of Modern Ireland*, 1986), and Thomas Keneally (*Now and in Time to Be*, 1992), amongst others, have found space for the North, and recent years have seen works which focus principally on that state, even to the exclusion of the Republic. In fact, Martin Fletcher's *Silver Linings: Travels Around Northern Ireland* (2000) is an example of how the part of the island most associated with danger and instability has yet become the most fascinating, while Nick Danziger's *Danziger's Britain* (1997), a devastating study of Britain's social and economic underclass, includes a depressing glance at Belfast. Perhaps as the remainder of the country modernises, and becomes more homogeneously European, the much derided primitivism of Northern Ireland is an increasing draw. This is not to suggest that the South has lost its attraction, only that a certain fascination with the atavism of the North has prompted a fresh round of inquiries, and that 'terror tourism' is a now respected element of the Irish tourist industry. Of course, some texts are still written in a distinctly upbeat mood, by journalists and media figures such as Pete McCarthy, whose *McCarthy's Bar* (2000) largely endorses the continuing appeal of the country, even if the country described is a relatively safe one, far from the streets of Belfast. But perhaps that has always been the real advantage of the travel narrative form anyway: that the slippy unpredictability which sets it off so markedly from many other forms of writing, that allows it so many guises and shifts, makes it the one best suited for such difficult times, and such difficult places.

NOTES

1 See James Buzard's essay (Chapter 2); and Barbara Korte, *English Travel Writing: From Pilgrimages to Postcolonial Explorations* (Basingstoke: Macmillan, 2000), pp. 66–81.

2 For a general discussion of the historical and political background, with particular reference to this chapter's title, see Norman Davies, *The Isles: A History* (London: Macmillan, 1999).

3 Christopher Hussey, *The Picturesque: Studies in a Point of View* (London: Putnam, 1927), pp. 83, 93–4.

4 Malcolm Andrews, *The Search for the Picturesque: Landscape Aesthetics and Tourism in Britain, 1760–1800* (Aldershot: Scolar, 1990), p. 67.

5 William Gilpin, *Observations on the River Wye, and Several Parts of South Wales, Relative Chiefly to Picturesque Beauty: Made in the Summer of the Year 1770* (5th edn, London: Strahan, 1800), p. 1 (italics in original).

6 William Gilpin, *Observations, Made in the Year 1772, On several Parts of England; Particularly the Mountains and Lakes of Cumberland and Westmoreland*, 2 vols. [1786] (Poole: Woodstock, 1996), vol. I, pp. xxiv–xxv.

7 Duncan C. Tovey, ed., *The Letters of Thomas Gray*, cited in Hussey, *The Picturesque*, p. 106.

8 Brian Osborne, ed., *Thomas Pennant, A Tour in Scotland, 1769* (Edinburgh: Birlinn, 2000), pp. xxiii, 78.

9 Linda Colley, *Britons: Forging the Nation 1707–1837* (New Haven: Yale University Press, 1992), p. 101.

10 Peter Levi, ed., *Samuel Johnson, A Journey to the Western Islands* (London: Penguin, 1984), p. 133.

11 J. R. Gold and M. Gold, *Imagining Scotland: Tradition, Representation and Promotion in Scottish Tourism since 1750* (Aldershot: Scolar, 1995), p. 5.

12 Philip Luckombe, *A Tour Through Ireland* (Dublin: Byrn, 1780), p. 25. See also John Bush, *Hibernia Curiosa* (1769), Richard Twiss, *A Tour in Ireland* (1776), and Charles Topham Bowden, *Tour Through Ireland in 1790* (1791).

13 Anne Plumptre, *Narrative of a Residence in Ireland* (London: Colburn, 1817), preface.

14 John Christian Curwen, *Observations on the State of Ireland, Principally Directed to its Agriculture and Rural Population, in a Series of Letters*, 2 vols. (London: Baldwin, 1818), vol. I, p. 186.

15 Thomas Kitson Cromwell, *Historical and Descriptive Sketch of the Past and Present State of Ireland*, 3 vols. (London: Longman, 1820), vol. II, p. 145.

16 Henry D. Inglis, *A Journey Throughout Ireland, During the Spring, Summer and Autumn of 1834*, 2 vols. (London: Whittaker, 1834) vol. I, p. 28.

17 Anon, *Ten Days in Ireland* (Liverpool: Rockliff, 1835), p. 34.

18 James Grant, *Impressions of Ireland and the Irish*, 2 vols. (London: Cunningham, 1844), vol. II, p. 186.

19 William Bennett, *Narrative of a Recent Journey of Six Weeks in Ireland* (London: Gilpin, 1847), p. 128.

20 John Hervey Ashworth, *The Saxon in Ireland: Or the Rambles of an Englishman in Search of a Settlement* (London: Murray, 1851), p. 34.

21 It is difficult to ascertain the extent of British emigration to Ireland after the famine, although considerable numbers, especially around Clifden, County Galway, were noted by several travellers, among them Harriet Martineau in her *Letters From Ireland* (1852).

22 James Macaulay, *Ireland in 1872: A Tour of Observation, with Remarks on Irish Public Questions* (London: King, 1873), p. 157.

23 Alfred Austin, *Spring and Autumn in Ireland* (Edinburgh: Blackwood, 1900), preface.
24 Matthew Arnold, *The Study of Celtic Literature* [1905] (Port Washington: Kennikat Press, 1970), p. 152.
25 See, for example, Douglas Goldring, *An Englishman in Ireland* (1918) and G. K. Chesterton, *Irish Impressions* (1919).
26 Wilfrid Ewart, *A Journey in Ireland, 1921* (London: Putnam, 1922), p. 130.
27 Ibrahim Rashad, *An Egyptian in Ireland* (privately published, 1920), p. 96.
28 John Gibbons, *Tramping Through Ireland* (London: Methuen, 1930), p. 98.
29 Cicely Hamilton, *Modern Ireland as Seen by an Englishwoman* (London: Dent, 1936), p. 4.

II

KATE TELTSCHER

India / Calcutta: city of palaces and dreadful night

How to write about India? The novelist Elizabeth Bruce Elton Smith opens *The East India Sketch-Book* (1832) with this question. Her narrator itemises the tropes and genres available: a land of *Arabian Nights* exoticism, a country unchanged for 3,000 years, or a site to be mined for statistical information. Addressing a companion slumbering on a coach, the narrator reads aloud excerpts from half-written verse dramas, steeped in Romantic Orientalism, followed by entries from a journal of military life ('Twaddle!' comments the friend). Finally the narrator, lacking the necessary 'powers of attention and abstraction' to describe 'the length and breadth and height of mountains and minarets, palaces and pagodas, tanks and mausoleums', also rejects the travel account; 'besides', the narrator adds, 'you can learn all this from the thousand and one veracious *Travels Through Hindostan*'.[1] Smith's introduction both justifies her own choice of the 'sketch-book' form and dramatises the sense of belatedness that haunts the early nineteenth-century travel writer: the conventions for representing India are already fixed, the genres well-worn, and the land over-described.

By the 1830s, India had been subjected to the English gaze for well over two centuries. The foundation of the East India Company in 1600 and subsequent trade missions to the Mughal court gave rise to a number of accounts by captains, merchants, diplomats, and accompanying chaplains (figures like William Hawkins, William Finch, Sir Thomas Roe, and Edward Terry) that were collected by Samuel Purchas in *Purchas his Pilgrimes* (1625). Focusing on the possibilities for trade, the accounts tended to represent India as a land of great wealth and fertility. But until the mid-eighteenth century, it is probably more accurate to speak of a European, rather than an English, tradition of writing about India. Accounts by travellers of other nationalities were promptly translated into English and frequently reissued; particularly popular were François Bernier's Mughal history (translated 1671–2) and Jean-Baptiste Tavernier's *Six Voyages* (translated 1677). During the early eighteenth century, Europeans gleaned most of their information on

India from missionary letters, notably the thirty-four-volume Jesuit *Lettres édifiantes et curieuses* (1702–76). These accounts established many of the enduring Indian travel-writing topoi: an unchanging land where the customs of biblical times persisted, where diabolical idols were worshipped, where men were effeminate and widows followed the rite of *sati*, sacrificing themselves on their husbands' funeral pyres.

By the mid-eighteenth century, a more identifiably British tradition of writing about India emerged. In 1765 the British acceded to *Diwani*, the Mughal grant to collect land revenues and administer civil justice in Bengal, and throughout the second half of the eighteenth century the East India Company expanded its territorial control. Travel writing played its part in the transition from trading partner to ruling power, both promoting the idea of British rule and articulating its attendant anxieties. Texts like Jemima Kindersley's *Letters* (1777) stressed Indian military incompetence, the deficiencies of Mughal government, and the inherent submissiveness of Hindus. The benign nature of British rule was celebrated in narratives such as William Hodges's *Travels in India* (1793) and *The Travels of Dean Mahomet* (1794), the first travel account published by an Indian in English. For much of this period, Company rule in southern India was threatened by the armies of Mysore under Haidar Ali and Tipu Sultan. The four Mysore wars generated a mass of military journals and narratives of captivity which demonised the two sultans and returned insistently to the sufferings of British prisoners forcibly converted to Islam, focussing particularly on the captives' compromised sense of national identity.

The final defeat of Tipu Sultan in 1799 exorcised such anxieties for the first half of the nineteenth century. During this period, a more confident rhetoric of British supremacy emerged. One of the most influential texts of the period was James Mill's *History of British India* (1817) which became a textbook at Haileybury, the training college for Company recruits. Mill attacked the sympathetic response of a previous generation of oriental scholars to Hindu culture and attributed the debased state of Indian society to political and religious tyranny. By mid-century, most of the subcontinent was subjected to British rule, either through conquest or subordination to the 'paramount' British power. Travel writers followed in the wake of conquering armies, documenting the peoples, customs, topography, flora, and fauna of newly acquired territories. After the Gurkha War of 1814–16, for instance, a spate of Himalayan travel narratives appeared. These years also saw an increase in the number of travel texts published by women. To represent India, writers such as Maria Graham, Emma Roberts and Fanny Parks turned to (and at times subverted) the conventions of the picturesque. The country was emptied of political threat through conversion into a series of picturesque set pieces; charming ruins were set in a gently variegated landscape peopled by an array of Indian types.[2]

But this reassuringly familiar scene was shattered by the rebellion of 1857, the Bengal army mutiny that sparked a popular revolt across much of India. Extensively reported, the revolt had its heroes and villains, its sacred sites of suffering and vengeance, of siege and liberation. Almost immediately, 'Mutiny' memoirs, both male- and female-authored, flooded the market: tales of endurance and martyrdom, treachery and selflessness. Following the rebellion, both the Mughal dynasty in Delhi and the East India Company were abolished, and India was placed directly under crown rule. The desire to assert British power gave impetus to a new discipline, closely allied to the genre of travel writing: that of anthropology. Watson and Kaye's eight-volume *People of India* (1868–75), extensively illustrated with photographs, attempted to assign a place and character to every caste and tribe in a great hierarchy of Indian types. This ambitious exercise in surveillance differentiated between martial and indolent races, between criminal and law-abiding tribes. The wish to locate trustworthy Indians also found expression in the publication of Bholanath Chandra's *Travels of a Hindoo to Various Parts of Upper India* (1869) which paid handsome tribute to the benefits of British rule and an English education. Travel writing was inevitably involved in the Victorian project to map, classify, and comprehend the Indian empire, both its present and past. Travel texts increasingly directed their attention to India's history and monuments. Popular tourist texts focused on the monument considered the masterpiece of Mughal architecture, already *the* Indian site: the Taj Mahal. In the Taj, travel writers found classical proportions, grace, sublimity, and *Arabian Nights* romance; in short, an Orientalist dream.

The Victorian ambition to survey the whole of India was rejected by later imperial travelogues. J. R. Ackerley's *Hindoo Holiday* (1932) detailed neither customs nor castes, and ignored sites of architectural or historic importance. The text focused instead on the court of Chhokrapur (a fictionalised version of Chhatarpur) and the narrator's relationship with his employer, the maharajah, and two beguiling youths. Transgressive in form and content – the account charts the narrator's desire to kiss the youths – *Hindoo Holiday* also heavily satirises the British in India. Somewhat less arch in tone is *The Hill of Devi* (1953), E. M. Forster's account of two visits to the court of Dewas Senior, the first in 1912–13, the second in 1921 as private secretary to the rajah. Forster was a friend of Ackerley, and recommended him for the post at Chhatarpur. Both writers were employed by anglophile Indian princes at a time of increasing nationalist activity, but politics are largely absent from Ackerley's account and appear only at the margins of Forster's. Excised too from Forster's published text is a memoir detailing his guilt-ridden sexual encounters with the rajah's servants.[3]

In twentieth-century texts, particularly those published after independence in 1947, India offers a site for the interrogation of the writer's own identity. This is obviously the case with the Trinidad-born, British resident V. S. Naipaul who, over three books and nearly thirty years, chronicled his response to independent India. *An Area of Darkness* (1964) recorded the narrator's first impressions of the subcontinent which his grandfather had left as an indentured labourer: a land of abject poverty, dirt, and defecation. The second book, *India: A Wounded Civilization* (1977), was written during the emergency declared by Indira Gandhi in which civil rights were suspended and political opponents imprisoned. For Naipaul, the emergency exposed the inadequacies of Indian civilisation and the shortcomings of its intellectual resources. But the India encountered in the final book, *India: A Million Mutinies Now* (1990), is in some respects a country renewed. The poverty which had neurotically haunted the narrator was now diminished, and the country which, according to Naipaul's earlier work, had lacked any sense of a past, was awakening to history and self-assertion. This new autonomy was mirrored by a narrative style which allowed individuals to tell their own stories with little apparent mediation.

The turn towards oral history in *A Million Mutinies Now* is uncharacteristic both of Naipaul's oeuvre and, more generally, of contemporary travel writing. With the writer's subjectivity centrestage, India usually serves as a backdrop – be it charming, exotic, infuriating, or comic – to the narrator's travels. The journey is often framed as a quest or a challenge within self-imposed constraints. In Eric Newby's *Slowly Down the Ganges* (1966), the journey is to be exclusively by boat down the course of the (sometimes unnavigable) Ganges; in Dervla Murphy's *On a Shoestring to Coorg* (1976), the narrator is accompanied by her five-year-old daughter; and Mark Shand rides an elephant 600 miles in *Travels with my Elephant* (1991). Robyn Davidson's *Desert Places* (1996) appears to be located firmly within this genre: her task, the completion of a year's migration with the nomadic Rabari of Rajasthan; her accessory, a camel. But Davidson foregrounds the process of producing the text, the demands of magazine sponsorship and the need to stage suitably exotic scenes for the photographer. The search for novel modes of transport reveals the sense of belatedness afflicting contemporary travel writers; of course this is nothing new, we have already noted it in Elizabeth Smith's 1832 introduction. In the case of India, the length of British involvement with the subcontinent and the exhaustive documentation of the encounter makes the burden of the past particularly heavy.

Calcutta

Nowhere is the influence of previous texts more obvious than in the representation of the former imperial capital: Calcutta. Officially now known as Kolkata, the city has long attracted the most contradictory of epithets, ranging from the glamorous 'City of Palaces' to the gruesome 'City of Dreadful Night'. Situated on the banks of the river Hugli (a tributary of the Ganges), Calcutta grew from a cluster of villages into a major port which, by the late eighteenth century, monopolised the East India Company's Bengal trade and dominated Asian seaborne commerce. The city was divided on racial lines between the Black Town of narrow streets and mud huts and the White Town of neo-classical mansions and broad esplanades. It was of course the European quarter which was dubbed 'The City of Palaces', an epithet that can be traced to an 1824 poem by James Atkinson (although descriptions of Calcutta's 'palaces' date from the 1780s).[4] As the capital of British India, Calcutta saw active Bengali-British collaboration in administrative and commercial concerns. The city developed a distinct and lively culture, a synthesis of the Bengali and European.

The interdependence of British and Indians bred mutual attraction and distrust. The early collaboration of Bengalis with the colonial system was succeeded by growing political resistance and economic discontent, particularly following the move of the imperial capital to Delhi in 1911. At its most flourishing, Calcutta became a symbol to travel writers of the immense profits of British rule. But while celebrating the city's grandeur and wealth, travel texts also manifest the anxieties of the coloniser: fear of the people, the place, the possibility of contamination, and disease. These threats find their clearest expression in Rudyard Kipling's narrative, 'The City of Dreadful Night' (1888) whose title – itself borrowed from a poem by James Thomson – had first been used by Kipling for a piece on Lahore, but would remain associated with Calcutta for at least a century.[5] The framing trope of the narrative is a descent into the city's underworld modelled on Dante's *Inferno*. The crowded horrors of this hell haunt subsequent accounts of Calcutta, particularly those produced in the decades following independence and partition. The 1940s brought famine, communal riots, and waves of refugees to Calcutta; in 1971 the city's population was once again swollen by those fleeing war in East Pakistan. For many writers, the ensuing problems of civic disorder and poverty made Calcutta, despite its vigorous intellectual and cultural life, the 'worst, the most irredeemably horrible, vile, and despairing city in the world'.[6]

In tracing a shift in the British representation of Calcutta from the 'City of Palaces' to 'The City of Dreadful Night', I am drawing on the work of the historian S. N. Mukherjee. Calcutta's glamorous image of Palladian grandeur, Mukherjee argues, is succeeded by one of chaos, disease, and death around the 1850s. The change is not related to any actual deterioration in urban conditions, but to the manifestations of popular resistance and nationalist agitation that began in the 1860s.[7] But in locating such an abrupt transition, Mukherjee fails to take into account both the lingering memory of the Black Hole of 1756 and the many anxieties of colonial rule: the dangers of cross-cultural proximity and dependence, the unease generated by the inequalities and excesses of British government.

From the eighteenth century on, Calcutta was a site both of magnificence and menace. Thomas Twining, son of Richard Twining, an East India Company director involved in the tea trade, recalled his arrival in Calcutta as a young Company servant in 1792 in *Travels in India* (published posthumously in 1893). Twining describes the approach to the city by river:

> The situation of the elegant garden houses, as the villas on the left bank were called, surrounded by verdant grounds laid out in the English style, with the Ganges flowing before them, covered with boats and shipping, struck me, as it does everybody who sees it for the first time, as singularly delightful. These charming residences announced our approach to the modern capital of the East, and bespoke the wealth and luxury of its inhabitants. Turning suddenly to the north, at the end of this reach, the 'City of Palaces', with its lofty detached flat-roofed mansions and the masts of its innumerable shipping, appeared before us on the left bank of the Ganges; and on the same side, in the foreground of this beautiful perspective, were the extensive ramparts of Fort William.[8]

Travellers were characteristically charmed and impressed by their first view of Calcutta. The scene of arrival was replayed in many eighteenth- and early nineteenth-century travel texts.[9] The cityscape invariably unites busy activity with architectural elegance; the shipping and mansions together represent the getting and spending of wealth.

But behind the white stucco façades lurks a much darker story. On his first foray into the city, Twining encounters 'an obelisk in a neglected, ruinous state':

> From my very early years few things had filled my mind with more horror than the very name of the Black Hole of Calcutta, although the exact history of its tragic celebrity was unknown to me. With peculiar force was this impression revived, when, on deciphering an almost obliterated inscription, I found that the column which I beheld was the monument which had been erected to the memory of the victims of that horrible massacre. (p. 76)

The obelisk had been raised in 1760 by John Zephaniah Holwell, whose *Genuine Narrative* (1758), which supposedly narrated the events following the attack on the British trading base of Calcutta in June 1756 by Siraj-ud-Daulah, Mughal nawab of Bengal, gave the phrase 'The Black Hole of Calcutta' to the English language. Holwell's *Narrative*, retold by generations of travel writers and historians, quickly assumed the status of a founding myth of empire, although the reliability of the account was repeatedly questioned in the twentieth century. According to Holwell, who was acting governor of Calcutta when the city fell, he and 145 other captives were rounded up and placed in the Black Hole, an eighteen-feet square punishment cell in Fort William. The next morning, only twenty-three of the prisoners remained alive. But as the inscription deciphered by Twining maintains, the suffering was avenged in 1757 by the defeat of the nawab's army at the battle of Plassey (Palashi), and the subsequent death of Siraj-ud-Daulah. Colonial historiography took its cue from Holwell, largely because of the significance which Plassey later acquired as the starting point of British power in India. The Black Hole thus functioned as a justification for British military intervention and colonial rule. But it is a deeply troubling founding myth (as we can see from Twining's terror at the very name); one which locates British helplessness, pain, and death at the start of the story of Empire.

The sack of Calcutta led to the rebuilding of Fort William on a massive scale. When finally completed in 1778, the fort dominated the city and river approach. But although writers note its handsome extent, descriptions of the fort do not generally detain them long. For the most part, the rôle played by military force in maintaining East India Company power is written out of accounts of Calcutta. Rather, the 'City of Palaces' tag, with its aristocratic or regal associations, suggests the legitimacy of the British claim to Bengal. The title also tends to obscure the commercial basis of British rule. From the 1770s on, one of the most frequent accusations made against the East India Company by its critics, including Adam Smith, was that it constituted an unholy alliance of commercial and ruling power. The 'City of Palaces' epithet endows Calcutta with a grandeur that outshines its trading origins. The clearest expression of this desire to impress was the erection of a new Government House by Marquess Wellesley, governor-general from 1798–1805. Conceived on a monumental scale and built at vast expense (without the prior consent and to the considerable anger of the Company's London-based Court of Directors), the new Government House epitomised Wellesley's expansionist policy and imperial ambition.

The palatial splendour of Government House was strikingly recorded by the trader and artist James Baillie Fraser in a series of coloured aquatints issued in London, *Views of Calcutta and its Environs* (1824–6). Fraser took advantage of the fashion for picturesque engravings of Indian scenes set by Thomas and William Daniell, the uncle and nephew team who were the

10. James Baillie Fraser, 'A View of Government House from the Eastward' (1819), coloured aquatint. From his *Views of Calcutta and Its Environs* (1824–6), plate 3. Courtesy of The British Library.

first to publish a series of aquatints of the city, *Views of Calcutta* (1786–8), followed by their much more ambitious *Oriental Scenery* (six parts, 1795–1808). Fraser's 'View of Government House from the Eastward' (1819) shows the extent of the site cleared by Wellesley for his grand design (fig. 10). The gleaming white façade of Government House is set off by the shadowed foreground and flanked by a ceremonial gateway, topped with sphinxes and a lion. The cantering soldiers and coach and four suggest the busy activity of the state and present a marked contrast to the languor of the group of Indians in the foreground. Turning their backs to the viewer, the resting figures provide an audience for the great architectural spectacle of Empire.

The grand pretensions of Government House excited many writers to hyperbole. The poet and journalist, Emma Roberts, included an elaborate Gothic description of the basement entrance to the building in her *Scenes and Characteristics of Hindostan* (1835). On arrival, the stranger could scarcely 'escape the notion that, instead of being the guest of a palace, he is on the point of being conducted to some hideous dungeon, as a prisoner of state'. In the obscurity, he imagines instruments of torture, and the forms of sleeping bearers appear to be 'the dead bodies of the victims to a tyrannical government'.[10] Beneath the humour of the passage lingers the suggestion of coercion, just as the nineteenth-century colonial régime was itself haunted by memories of the activities of early governors of Bengal. The preceding century had seen repeated parliamentary investigations into the methods of government in Bengal with accusations of despotism and violence made against Robert Clive and Warren Hastings.

The anxieties of colonial rule surface frequently in accounts of Calcutta. Foremost among them was the fear of contamination and corruption through contact with Indians. Roberts, for instance, notes the worrying proximity of the huts of Indian servants to the mansions of the British: '[a] mud hut, or rows of native hovels, constructed of mats, thatch, and bamboo, not superior to the rudest wigwam, often rest against the outer walls of palaces' (p. 3).[11] The concerns were not merely aesthetic, for the dwellings of Indians were regarded as the source of dirt and disease. This was particularly the case with the Black Town to the north which suffered from a severe lack of municipal amenities; 'a more wretched place can scarcely be imagined', wrote Roberts, 'dirty, crowded, ill-built, and abounding with beggars and bad smells' (vol. I, p. 3).[12] Wellesley's minute of 1803 on Calcutta's street policy made the connection between lack of regulation and contagion explicit: 'In those quarters of the town occupied principally by the native inhabitants, the houses have been built without order or regularity, and the streets and lanes have been formed without attention to the health, convenience or safety of the inhabitants'.[13] With its crowds threatening civic order and public health, Black Town shadowed White Town menacingly. Its poverty manifested all too clearly the inequalities of colonial rule – although the travel narratives maintain a silence on such matters. From its huts and those abutting the British mansions issued the workforce that serviced the colonisers. One of the common complaints of travellers – particularly women writers – concerned the large number of servants required to run a household in Calcutta. In the long lists of domestic staff and frequently voiced suspicion of servants' honesty, we may detect the anxiety of dependence and the fear of being outnumbered.[14]

From the 1860s on, Calcutta held additional threats for the British; the city had developed into a centre of political activity. Although the rebellion of 1857 had not directly touched the city in a military sense, the following decades saw popular resistance in the form of strikes by Calcutta's sweepers and water-carriers, and the start of nationalist debate in the city. The increase in political activity coincided with the growth of Calcutta into a major commercial and industrial city dealing in jute, tea, and coal. As the city's economy grew, so did its colonial bureaucracy, staffed by a Western-educated élite among the Bengali middle class, the *bhadralok*. It was the *bhadralok* that was largely responsible for the spread of nationalist ideas and activity in the city. This was the class which Kipling satirised in the figure of the babu who 'drops inflammatory hints / In his prints' in the poem 'A Tale of Two Cities', and who makes interminable speeches in the Bengal Legislative Council in the narrative 'The City of Dreadful Night' (1888).

Kipling's journalistic account of Calcutta belongs to the distinctive nineteenth-century genre of the slumming narrative. By day, the narrator of 'The City of Dreadful Night' views the workings of Calcutta local government; by night, he is guided by a police superintendent on a tour of the city's brothels, gambling halls, and opium dens. For Kipling, the Bengal Legislative Council is an exercise in futility. The babu mouths the rhetoric of parliamentary democracy and the proceedings ignore the real affliction of the city, the great 'Calcutta Stink'. Issuing from rubbish heaps and dirty tanks, the odour 'resembles the essence of corruption that has rotted for the second time'.[15] With the Stink permeating the whole city, Kipling blurs the distinction drawn by earlier writers between the elegant White Town and the insalubrious Black Town. The inhabitants and their respective cultures overlap. In a high-class brothel, the narrator discovers babus whose fluent English recalls the debaters in the Council chamber; in a low-class one, a sailor, 'sleeping like a little child . . . a pure-blooded white' (p. 40). But in 'the lowest sink of all . . . the last circle of Inferno', the narrator encounters Mrs D., a Eurasian prostitute, openly soliciting on the street. '[S]he has offended against the white race', the narrator thunders (pp. 40, 41). Incarnating the threat of miscegenation, both in her own mixed blood and her trade, Mrs D. and her fellows are responsible for the collapse of colonial hierarchies: 'the secret of the insolence of Calcutta is made plain. Small wonder the natives fail to respect the Sahib – seeing what they see and knowing what they know' (p. 42).

Later twentieth-century writers do not share Kipling's racial diagnosis of the ills of the city, but the trope of infernal descent recurs repeatedly, and the narrative's title comes to stand for Calcutta's misery and blight. As the journalist James Cameron despairingly observed in the 1970s: '[t]he urban awfulness of Calcutta has become a cliché of such dimensions that one flinches from even trying to say more about it, with such lasting and eloquent disgust has every aspect of the appalling place been described since Kipling called it "the city of dreadful night" ' (p. 178). But despite the dangers of repetition, writers are drawn to the scene of horror. Both Cameron and the German novelist, Günter Grass, write of the compulsion to return to the city. 'Calcutta is obsessive', Cameron asserts (p. 187), and in *Show Your Tongue* (1989), an illustrated journal of a visit to Calcutta, Grass maintains that the 'horrifying city, the terrible goddess within, would not let him go'.[16] Playing Dante to the exiled Bangladeshi poet Daud Haider's Virgil, Grass recapitulates the *Inferno*-esque theme as he is guided to the 'remotest, blackest corners of the city' (p. 32).

The desire to visit Calcutta to indulge in what Cameron terms 'revulsion and recrimination' (p. 187) is evidently transgressive. According to Peter Stallybrass and Allon White, the 'bourgeois subject continuously defined and re-defined itself through the exclusion of what it marked out as "low" – as dirty, repulsive, noisy, contaminating... But disgust always bears the imprint of desire. These low domains, apparently expelled as "Other", return as the object of nostalgia, longing and fascination'.[17] Much as nineteenth-century writers like Dickens, Mayhew, and Engels dwelt on the dirt and degradation of British slums, so twentieth-century authors like Grass, the travel writer Geoffrey Moorhouse, and the French writer of popular histories and 'epics', Dominique Lapierre, return obsessively to the sewers, filth, and disease of Calcutta. Indeed, for Moorhouse, the slums of Calcutta recall 'the stews of Whitechapel early in the nineteenth century' and for Grass, Engels's descriptions of Manchester in *The Condition of the Working Class in England* (1845).[18]

It is Lapierre who most revels in the abjection. The title of *The City of Joy*, both alludes to and inverts Kipling's title and, as David Spurr has pointed out, Lapierre's book is also a quest, if not to *Inferno*, then to *Purgatorio* where souls are purified in preparation for the ascent to heaven.[19] The book, which Lapierre notes was based on three years' research in Calcutta, follows the adventures of a fictitious French priest who discovers true nobility in the depths of poverty. In the course of his attempts to establish a leprosy dispensary, the priest encounters 'the only person in the city who could help him': Mother Teresa.[20] It comes as no surprise that the most famous twentieth-century European resident of the city, an Albanian nun, founder of the order of the Missionaries of Charity, should enter the narrative; indeed Mother Teresa is the presiding genius of this story of self-denying European heroism and the redemptive power of suffering. The people of Calcutta figure primarily as the object of European charity. *The City of Joy* was subsequently filmed in Calcutta by Roland Joffe in the face of opposition from the Government of West Bengal (which banned the film) and the Calcutta press which objected to the representation of the city. Despite such local outcry, both versions of *The City of Joy* became central to the Western construction of the city as *the* site of urban deprivation.[21]

How is it that Calcutta comes to epitomise 'Third World' poverty for the West? In part this may relate to the history of post-colonial Calcutta, a narrative which can be framed as representative of the problems – famine, violence, displacement – besetting newly independent nations. In the final years of the colonial régime, Bengal was devastated by a man-made famine. It has been suggested that the brutalising effects of the 1943 famine, in which over a million people died, paved the way for the communal killings of 1946 that initiated the partition riots of 1946–7.[22] Since independence in 1947, an enormous number of refugees, uprooted by the partition of the province into East Pakistan and West Bengal, flooded into Calcutta in successive waves. In 1969, a peasant uprising in Darjeeling gave rise to the Maoist-inspired Naxalite movement which spread political violence to the city. And in 1971 an already over-crowded Calcutta was placed under further pressure when refugees from East Pakistan fled the war which gave birth to Bangladesh. This massive increase in Calcutta's population, described by Sukanta Chaudhuri as 'arguably the biggest mass migration in the history of man' (vol. II, Introduction), created an immense unofficial slum city alongside the official city; a post-colonial reprise, one might say, of the old White Town/Black Town division. Such squatter settlements, Neera Chandhoke has argued, subvert all notions of urban planning and property rights, and so constitute a challenge to the social order itself.[23]

The crowds of Calcutta became a standard travel-writing topos. Geoffrey Moorhouse's *Calcutta* (1971), often regarded as the definitive work on the city, devotes an entire chapter to 'People, People'. The packed street scene forms one of the set pieces:

> A traffic, too, in people who are hanging on to all forms of public transport, who are squatting cross-legged upon the counters of their shops, who are darting in and out of roadways between the vehicles, who are staggering under enormous loads, who are walking briskly with briefcases, who are lying like dead things on the pavements, who are drenching themselves with muddy water in the gutters, who are arguing, laughing, gesticulating, defecating, and who are sometimes just standing still as though wondering what to do. (pp. 94–5)

The use of the present tense and the ever-extended syntax combine to create a sense of immediacy, activity, and bewildering excess. European notions of 'public' and 'private' are violated by the very visible bodies on the street: sleeping, washing, excreting. Indeed the confusion extends even to the categories 'living' and 'dead', 'human' and 'non-human', in the brutal image of pavement dwellers, 'lying like dead things'. The simile inevitably carries the suggestion of violence, for Calcutta crowd scenes often evoke menace, an echo of the riots and communal killings of 1946–7. Moorhouse even ends his book with an apocalyptic vision of a murderous mass uprising that will destroy Calcutta in the near future; a conclusion which he was obliged to rescind when the book was reissued in 1983 (pp. 370–2, 9).

Death stalks the city. Calcutta's name is most commonly thought to have derived from that of the goddess Kali of Kalighat. Travel texts delight in descriptions of her terrible aspect – devilish eyes, tongue dripping with blood, neck garlanded with snakes or skulls, sickle-wielding arm – and the daily practice of propitiating her with the sacrifice of a live goat or sheep.[24] Her protruding tongue, interpreted as a sign of shame, suggests the title of Grass's journal (and the long narrative poem that concludes the text): *Show Your Tongue*. Indeed Kali haunts Grass's text, appearing at times as the personification of the city, and at others, incarnated as a coconut vendor. In the heaps of discarded coconut husks, Grass sees 'decapitated heads among them, here Hindus, there Moslems, as they were lying piled high – and not only in the year of Independence, beginning, sharp as a machete, with India's partition – on the streets of Calcutta . . . and will be piled again soon enough' (p. 17). For Grass, Calcutta's history of bloodshed is ever-present and, like Moorhouse, he anticipates its imminent return. *Show Your Tongue* is illustrated by Grass's own vigorous pen-and-ink sketches of Calcutta street life. Appropriately enough, the opening plate, redolent with menace, is entitled 'Kali Puja is announced'.

The city is also associated with the diseases of poverty: cholera and leprosy, in particular.[25] Inhabited by diseased beggars and emaciated street dwellers, with its civic services collapsing, its port silting up and industry moribund, Calcutta is often declared dead or dying. In 1964 V. S. Naipaul prematurely pronounced the city dead in *An Area of Darkness*, only to revise his diagnosis in *India: A Million Mutinies Now* (1990) to that of terminal decline.[26] The preoccupation with morbidity and death owes much to the figure of Mother Teresa. Moorhouse visits both Nirmal Hriday, the refuge for terminally ill destitutes, and one of the leper colonies run by the Missionaries of Charity. In graphic and disturbing descriptions that recall a 'particularly hellish production of the witches' scene in *Macbeth*', the account dramatises for a foreign audience the afflictions of poverty (p. 100). As John Hutnyk has argued, it was largely Mother Teresa's international reputation as a modern-day saint that was responsible for turning Calcutta into a stage for the display of poverty. But in a 1992 essay, Christopher Hitchens launched a spirited and controversial attack on Mother Teresa's political sympathies – expanded in *The Missionary Position* (1995) – which recast her (rather than the lepers in her care) as the 'ghoul of Calcutta'.[27]

Among Bengali intellectuals, Mother Teresa had long had her critics, as Bharati Mukherjee discovered when re-visiting the city of her childhood in 1973. Mukherjee herself interprets Mother Teresa not as a European, but as an Indian saint, precisely because 'she had concentrated her efforts, her love, on hopeless cases'.[28] This appropriation of Mother Teresa as specifically Indian is characteristic of a text which foregrounds Calcutta's cultural hybridity. *Days and Nights in Calcutta* is itself a product of two cultures, written by a husband and wife team: the Canadian author, Clark Blaise, and Bharati Mukherjee, the Bengali-born novelist, resident in Canada. The text has two parts, each with its named author, followed by individual epilogues and a jointly written afterword. The sections play off against each other, inviting the reader to compare the ways in which Calcutta is represented by a male, North American, first-time visitor, and a Bengali-Canadian woman, attempting to find a place in her *desh* or homeland.

In some ways, Blaise articulates an entirely standard set of responses to Calcutta: he is initially terrified by the crowd's potential for violence, terms the city 'the world's largest outdoor garbage heap' and finally departs from Howrah station which is 'more like a circle of hell than any place on earth' (pp. 64, 63, 297). But Blaise also celebrates the Bengali capacity for cultural synthesis and devotes much space to a discussion of the work of film-maker Satyajit Ray (the book is itself named in homage to Ray's realist classic, *Days and Nights in the Forest*). Mukherjee's response to the city is more complex and ambivalent. In her account we encounter a new kind of Calcutta, a 'tolerant, open, friendly city' (p. 199). For Mukherjee, Calcutta consists of the upper-class circles of her family and friends; a largely female élite to which other travel writers have little access. Mukherjee finds herself both at home with and excluded from this class, partly through her long use of English rather than Bengali as a first – and literary – language, and partly through her inability to conform to the expected feminine rôle. By interrogating her Bengali origins, the visit to Calcutta helps to clarify questions of gender and cultural identity that have preoccupied Mukherjee throughout her writing career.

Days and Nights in Calcutta, with its engagement with issues of cultural hybridity, its distinct authorial voices, and open-ended structure, challenges many of the travel-writing commonplaces of Calcutta. Although formally less inventive, *Abdul's Taxi to Kalighat* (2000) by the British travel writer Joe Roberts also attempts to rewrite the city. According to Roberts, the event which sparked his account was Mother Teresa's death in 1997. The subsequent obituaries in the British media simply perpetuated the image of Calcutta as the most benighted city on earth.[29] But for Roberts, the demise of Mother Teresa, patron saint of Calcutta's dying, paradoxically freed Calcutta from its association with death. In *Abdul's Taxi*, Calcutta features instead as 'a civilised and charismatic city' (p. x). Other Calcutta myths are also discarded. The Black Hole is debunked with a joke, and Calcutta's municipal chaos is reinterpreted as a political gesture (pp. 27, 64). Questioned, too, is the well-worn identification of the city with Kali. In a parody of Grass, Roberts reworks the Kali parallel as the maudlin outburst of a would-be poet, author of an unpublished (and unpublishable) cultural history of Bengal written in rhyming couplets.

While Roberts refutes received notions of Calcutta, he is clearly located within the tradition of writing about the city. For, as we have seen, images of

Calcutta are endlessly repeated, elaborated, challenged, and revised. The city has for centuries been haunted by an aura of darkness born of racial fear: the horrors of the Black Hole somehow fuse with the shadow of Black Town and the threat of the City of Dreadful Night. Calcutta has long been viewed primarily in economic terms: as the palatial expression of colonial wealth or the epitome of 'Third World' poverty. In recent years, this reputation has attracted what Hutnyk terms 'charity-tourism' (bus tours even include Calcutta's slums) but excluded the city from standard tourist itineraries.[30] Both desired and reviled, visited and shunned, Calcutta's paradoxical status reminds us of the intimate relation between travel texts and the travel industry.

NOTES

1 Elizabeth Bruce Elton Smith, *The East India Sketch-Book* (London, 1832), vol. I, pp. 1–3, 4–21, 25–6.

2 Nigel Leask, *Curiosity and the Aesthetics of Travel Writing 1770–1840: From an Antique Land* (Oxford University Press, 2002), chs. 4, 5.

3 E. M. Forster, *The Hill of Devi and Other Indian Writings*, ed. Elizabeth Heine (London: Edward Arnold, 1983), p. 324. See Revathi Krishnaswamy, *Effeminism: The Economy of Colonial Desire* (Ann Arbor: University of Michigan Press, 1998), pp. 160–1.

4 J. P. Losty, *Calcutta: City of Palaces: A Survey of the City in the Days of the East India Company, 1690–1858* (London: British Library, 1990), pp. 7–8.

5 Gail Ching-Liang Low, *White Skins/Black Masks: Representation and Colonialism* (London: Routledge, 1996), p. 168.

6 James Cameron, *An Indian Summer* (Harmondsworth: Penguin, 1974), p. 178.

7 S. N. Mukherjee, *Calcutta: Essays in Urban History* (Calcutta: Subarnarekha, 1993), pp. 49–69.

8 Thomas Twining, *Travels in India a Hundred Years Ago* (London: James R. Osgood, McIlvaine & Co., 1893), p. 73.

9 See for instance, John Splinter Stavorinus, *Voyages to the East Indies* (London: G. G. & J. Robinson, 1798), vol. I, pp. 122–3; Alfred Spencer, ed., *Memoirs of William Hickey (1749–1775)* (London: Hurst & Blackett, 1913–25), vol. II, p. 120; Eliza Fay, *Original Letters from India (1779–1815)*, ed. E. M. Forster (London: Chatto & Windus, 1986), pp. 171–2; Fanny Parks, *Wanderings of a Pilgrim in Search of the Picturesque*, ed. Esther Chawner (Karachi: Oxford University Press, 1975), vol. II, p. 102.

10 Emma Roberts, *Scenes and Characteristics of Hindostan with Sketches of Anglo-Indian Society*, 3 vols. (London: William H. Allen, 1835), vol. III, pp. 70–1, 71.

11 See also Jemima Kindersley, *Letters From the Island of Teneriffe, Brazil, the Cape of Good Hope and the East Indies* (London: J. Nourse, 1777), pp. 274, 277; Philip Dormer Stanhope, *Genuine Memoirs of Asiaticus*, ed. W. K. Firminger (Hughli: N. L. Chowdhury & Co., 1909), p. 30.

12 See also Reginald Heber, *Narrative of a Journey through the Upper Provinces of India* (London: John Murray, 1828), vol. II, p. 296; George Valentia, Viscount,

Voyages and Travels to India, Ceylon, the Red Sea, Abyssinia, and Egypt (London: William Miller, 1809), vol. I, p. 236.

13 Quoted in Dipesh Chakrabarty, 'Open Space/Public Place: Garbage, Modernity and India', *South Asia*, 14 (1991): 16.

14 Kindersley, *Letters*, pp. 282–8; Fay, *Original Letters*, pp. 179–82; Roberts, *Scenes*, vol. I, p. 4, Parks, *Wanderings*, vol. I, p. 26.

15 Rudyard Kipling, *The City of Dreadful Night & Other Places* (Allahabad & London: A. H. Wheeler, 1891), p. 5.

16 Günter Grass, *Show Your Tongue*, trans. John E. Woods (London: Secker & Warburg, 1989), p. 96.

17 Peter Stallybrass and Allon White, *The Politics and Poetics of Transgression* (London: Methuen, 1986), p. 191.

18 Geoffrey Moorhouse, *Calcutta* [1971] (London: Orion Books, 1998), p. 104; Grass, *Show Your Tongue*, pp. 20–1.

19 David Spurr, *The Rhetoric of Empire: Colonial Discourse in Journalism, Travel Writing, and Imperial Administration* (Durham, N.C.: Duke University Press, 1993), p. 133.

20 Dominique Lapierre, *The City of Joy*, trans. Kathryn Spink (London: Century Hutchinson, 1986), p. 209.

21 John Hutnyk, *The Rumour of Calcutta: Tourism, Charity and the Poverty of Representation* (London: Zed Books, 1996), pp. 96, 187–95.

22 Sukanta Chaudhuri, *Calcutta: The Living City*, 2 vols. (Calcutta: Oxford University Press, 1990), vol. II, p. 17.

23 Neera Chandhoke, 'On the Social Organization of Urban Space – Subversions and Appropriations', *Social Scientist*, 21 (1993): 63, 69.

24 See for instance, Moorhouse, *Calcutta*, pp. 20, 216–17; Cameron, *Indian Summer*, p. 183.

25 See for instance V. S. Naipaul, *An Area of Darkness* (London: Macmillan, 1995), pp. 309–10; Moorhouse, *Calcutta*, p. 100; Lapierre, *City of Joy*, *passim*.

26 Naipaul, *Area of Darkness*, p. 310; Naipaul, *India: A Million Mutinies Now* (London: Heinemann, 1990), p. 347.

27 Hutnyk, *Rumour of Calcutta*, pp. 56, 84.

28 Clark Blaise and Bharati Mukherjee, *Days and Nights in Calcutta* (Harmondsworth: Penguin, 1986), p. 242.

29 Joe Roberts, *Abdul's Taxi to Kalighat* (London: Profile Books, 2000), p. x.

30 Hutnyk, *Rumour of Calcutta*, p. 207.

12

BRUCE GREENFIELD

The West / California: site of the future

When European ships began tracing the west coast of North America, the varied terrain and climate between Mexico and Alaska was home to many different societies. Within what is now California, indigenous peoples took advantage of the seasonal variety of food and climate in the three main geographic zones of coast, central valley, and the Sierra on the eastern side of the central valley. These peoples and their rich environment attracted Spanish missionaries in the late eighteenth century, who sought to convert them to Christianity, and to the rôle of labourers in the stock-raising and agriculture that constituted the economic basis of the missions. These missions notwithstanding, at the beginning of the nineteenth century California was still a remote and mysterious place for most Europeans and Americans, accessible only via the long ocean voyage around Cape Horn. By 1850, however, California, a new state of the USA, was a destination for thousands of immigrants from elsewhere in the USA, from Europe, and from Asia, travelling by land and sea. Twenty years later, railways collapsed the six-month ocean or overland journey into a matter of a few days, and the telegraph and mechanised printing presses rapidly conveyed news of what travellers saw. Travel writing about California reflects the west coast's rapid transformation from a remote non-place to a focal point of a powerful mythology, a development stemming from two centuries of European colonising experience in North America, newly stimulated by the rapid development of mass transportation and communications. The earliest published accounts of California are products of strategic and scientific explorations in the late 1700s, which were imitated by official overland expeditions between 1790 and 1840. But thereafter, we enter an era chronicled in a multitude of narratives of journeys around Cape Horn or across the continent, by trappers, farmers, would-be gold miners, journalists, and writers in search of a subject. California's remoteness, beyond mountains and deserts, and its Mediterranean climate, reinforced the habit of generations of Americans and Europeans who regarded the American West as a land of exceptional promise, a place beyond accustomed limits. Its modern accessibility attracted millions to experiment with their particular versions of this mythology. Much of the travel writing about California both fosters and debunks the idea that it is a special place.

Early California by sea

European settlement in Alta California did not begin until 1769, with the first Spanish mission in San Diego. Sailing northward from Mexico, the Spanish had explored the coast beginning with Juan Cabrillo's voyage of 1542, but accounts of these voyages, and of numerous overland expeditions, were mostly not published until the nineteenth century.[1] Sir Francis Drake's account of his landing near San Francisco was published by Richard Hakluyt in his *Principal Navigations* (1589), but for the next two centuries fogs, storms, coastal mountain ranges, and scarcity of good harbours kept most vessels at a distance. The narratives of Jean François de Lapérouse (1797) and George Vancouver (1798) are the first substantial accounts of Spanish California. In narratives of research voyages of the sort pioneered and epitomised by James Cook, Lapérouse, and Vancouver contribute strategic, scientific, and ethnographic observations to a European knowledge-gathering enterprise.[2]

The arrival and initial reactions to the place recorded in these two narratives initiate a topos of California travel reportage. The long and dangerous journey thither, whether by land across the deserts and mountains or by sea around Cape Horn, made arriving in California inherently dramatic. Lapérouse's Monterey materialises out of the fog, and Vancouver traces his way into magnificent San Francisco Bay along a coast 'presenting a most dreary and barren aspect'.[3] Once on land, both travellers celebrate a climate and landscape that seem settled and that invite repose. On a ride to the mission of Santa Clara, Vancouver sees hillsides of 'luxuriant fertility, interspersed with copses of various forms and magnitude, verdant open spaces'. His party picnics in a grove of trees on an 'enchanting lawn'. The country 'could only be compared to a park..., a scene not inferior to the most studied effect of taste in the disposal of grounds' (vol. II, pp. 717, 718). Lapérouse finds soil that is 'inexpressibly fertile', trees that are 'inhabited by the most charming birds' and that 'stand apart from each other without underwood', and that are surrounded by 'a verdant carpet, over which it is pleasant to walk'.[4] Fairly soon, however, both express disappointment that California society, native or immigrant, seems not to realise the potential of the natural surroundings. Lapérouse blames Spanish policies for the fact that 'California, notwithstanding its fertility, does not yet possess a single European colonist', whereas 'good laws, particularly freedom of trade, would soon procure it a certain number of inhabitants' (vol. I, p. 458). The conditions of the mission Indians remind Lapérouse of a slave plantation at Santo Domingo. Vancouver, too, is surprised by the lack of development: 'Instead of finding a country tolerably well inhabited and far advanced in cultivation ... there is not an object to indicate the most remote connection with any European, or other civilized nation.' All of which conveys 'some idea of the inactive spirit of the people' (vol. II, pp. 710–11). Some forty years later, another English traveller, Sir George Simpson, governor-general of the Hudson's Bay Company Territories, epitomised this topos with what he called 'California in a nutshell': 'Nature doing everything and man doing nothing – a text on which our whole sojourn proved to be little but a running commentary.'[5]

The Spanish settlements attending the missions attracted trading vessels, many of them American, whose captains offered a commentary, often self-interested, on California's present and its prospects. William Schaler's 'Journal of a Voyage from China to the Northwestern Coast of America' (1808), and his supercargo, Richard Cleveland's *Narrative of Voyages and Commercial Enterprises* (1842), both recount the smuggling exploits of the *Leila Byrd* along the California coast. Some traders established themselves in local society, converting to Catholicism and marrying into local families. One such, Alfred Robinson, began as a clerk in 1829, touring the missions in order to buy hides. As a result he was able to render one of the best accounts of the missions before their secularisation.[6]

Richard Henry Dana Jr.'s *Two Years Before the Mast* (1840) was the most influential account of California as viewed through the contacts of this coastal trade. Dana chronicled his experiences in 1834–6 when he enlisted as a common sailor on a voyage around Cape Horn to spend eighteen months loading hides from California ranches. *Two Years* was a bestseller, probably the most widely read book about California up to the gold rush of 1849. The son of a prominent Massachusetts family, Dana sometimes eyes California as raw material for the Boston business élites. Like other travellers before him, he contrasts the good harbours, fine forests, abundant fish, multiplying cattle, mild climate, and rich soil with the ramshackle pueblos: 'In the hands of an enterprising people, what a country this might be!' More often, however, he speaks from his experience as an ordinary seaman who hauled hides from shore to ship, and from this perspective California is a dreary place where men felt they were 'at the ends of the earth'.[7] Dana's juxtaposing of the labourer's experience with the optimistic projections of commerce anticipates an enduring division within California lore, between the bounded world of labourers in the industrial agriculture of the central valley, of immigrant gardeners in Los Angeles, and the expansive aerospace

and computer industries, the glamour of Hollywood, and the natural ease touted in tourist brochures and real estate promotional tracts.[8]

Explorers and mountain men

North of Mexico, the Pacific was first reached over land in 1793 by Alexander Mackenzie, a fur trader from Montreal. From the United States, Lewis and Clark arrived at the mouth of the Columbia River in 1805. The publication of Mackenzie's *Voyages from Montreal . . . to the Frozen and Pacific Oceans, in the years 1789 and 1793* (1801) probably contributed to President Thomas Jefferson's launching of the expedition jointly commanded by Meriwether Lewis and William Clark, which from 1804 through 1806 traversed the country between St Louis and the mouth of the Columbia River and back to St Louis. The first and most significant of American overland military-scientific expeditions was conceived by Jefferson as the land-based equivalent of the circumnavigations of Cook, Lapérouse, and Vancouver. The transcontinental journey engaged landscapes that threatened annihilation – vast plains, fierce deserts, towering mountains – and resulted in experiences that came to be part of what is meant by 'the West'. The scope and detail of Lewis and Clark's journals remain unequalled in the literary tradition of responses to engulfment by a continent that they initiated.[9]

Narratives of subsequent military expeditions in the Far West include those by Zebulon Pike in 1805–7, Stephen Long in 1820, and John Charles Fremont in 1842 and 1843–4. Fremont had the advantage of following the already established wagon road to Oregon, as well as parts of the Spanish trail that ran between Los Angeles and Santa Fe, and he employed well-known 'mountain men' as guides. If he was less radically on his own in the West, compared to Lewis and Clark, his published reports 'introduced a new kind of intelligence from the West: readable narrative combined with competent maps, both produced from personal observation'.[10] His aesthetic responsiveness, coupled with his athleticism, anticipates writers such as John Wesley Powell, Clarence King, and John Muir.

Some of the mountain fur trappers made their way into southern California, beginning with Jedediah Smith in 1826, but few of these men left records of their experiences.[11] A notable exception is James Pattie's vivid account of his trapping expedition with his father Sylvester into New Mexico, down the Colorado River and eventually to San Diego, where they were imprisoned, and where the elder Pattie died in jail.[12] James Pattie spent six years in Spanish territories, learning Spanish, and travelling as far north as San Francisco. His relationship with the authorities was combative, his opinions of the locals rarely flattering; his narrative gives voice to the grassroots

American view that California would be better populated by his Anglo contemporaries.

Washington Irving, perhaps the best-known American writer of the 1830s, picked up the growing interest in the Far West, particularly to do with the trapping and trading in the interior. In addition to *A Tour on the Prairies* (1835), which recounts Irving's own month of travel on the southern plains in the company of a troop of Arkansas Rangers, he wrote two books chronicling the travels and adventures of the trappers and fur traders of the mountain West. *Astoria* (1836) is the story of John Jacob Astor's attempt to establish a fur trade entrepôt on the Pacific that would link the continental fur trade with trans-Pacific shipping; *The Adventures of Captain Bonneville* (1837) develops Benjamin Bonneville's own record of his travels among the native groups and American trappers of the mountain West.

The overland trail

Each year of the 1840s saw a doubling of the numbers of overland emigrants, bound initially for the fertile valleys of Oregon and California, and after 1848 for the mines in California. Many of these kept diaries, some of which were published. An example from the end of the decade is William Lewis Manly's *Death Valley in '49*. Even though Manly composed the account forty years after his journey, it nonetheless vividly evokes each day's sights and sufferings along the trail. An unmarried man of twenty-nine, Manly joined a party that tried to trace, in reverse, Fremont's route between southern California and the Great Salt Lake, only to find themselves stranded in the fierce place they subsequently named Death Valley. Manly and the other single man in the party walked across the Mojave Desert into the San Fernando Valley, where they were aided by the Spanish ranchers. They returned to bring help to the two families waiting for them. His narrative conveys the horrors of their desert experiences, but it also reveals some of the grandeur that would later attract visitors, and the plot of a desert journey ending in a fertile valley evokes the Old Testament narratives that many American emigrants called to mind as they reflected on their experiences. When Manly attains his first glimpse of a green California meadow covered with grazing cattle his 'sick heart' fills with a 'most indescribable joy' at the sight of the animals that 'might be descended directly from Jacob's famous herd, blessed of the Lord'.[13]

The phenomenon of the overland emigrants aroused the interest of professional writers. Kentucky newspaperman, Edwin Bryant, set out in 1846 with the intention of publishing an account of his journey by wagon, and then by mule, from Independence, Missouri to California, and then of his experiences among those engaged in the American conquest of California. He returned to Kentucky in 1847, just missing the discovery of gold. His *What I Saw in California* (1848) offers a day-by-day account of the overland journey, making it seem surprisingly ordinary and practicable, even though emigrant wagons were still finding their way, and many of his travelling companions were wavering between Oregon and California as their destination.

Francis Parkman's *The Oregon Trail* (1849) is another ambitious literary man's response to the phenomenon of the overland emigrants, though Parkman remained aloof from the wagons and mostly professed contempt for long trains of 'emigrants with their heavy wagons ... dragging on in slow procession'. Whereas each wagon was a microcosm of hearth and home, Parkman actively sought the exotic, proposing 'to join a [Dakota] village, and make myself an inmate of their lodges'. He describes Indian villages in vivid detail, and he is excited by rumours of a war between the Dakota and the Snakes, for 'their warlike rites were to be celebrated with more than ordinary solemnity, and a thousand warriors ... were to set out for the enemy's country'. He sketches powerful personalities and all the movement, noise, sights, sounds, and smells that surround him. That Parkman was preparing to write what would become his multi-volume history of France and England in North America when he undertook his summer ramble along the wagon road is evident in the meta-narrative of continental destiny that informs *The Oregon Trail*, dooming what he finds exciting and admirable. The dull emigrants and their descendants 'in the span of a century, are to sweep from the face of the earth' the Indian peoples.[14] Parkman renders the prairie landscape in a similarly conflicted manner, sketching vivid details of rich plant, animal, and human life only to erase the diversity with adjectives like 'barren' applied to the site in general.

After 1849, events in the mining camps and in San Francisco were widely reported in newspapers around the world. The journey to the mines and the life in the camps became a marketable subject attracting professional journalists.[15] Samuel Langhorne Clemens launched his pseudonym, Mark Twain, and his writing career by building on the discourses established in the 1850s by such writers. In 1861, young Twain accompanied his brother to the silver mining districts of Nevada, where after a few semi-serious forays into prospecting, he resumed work he already knew, reporting and writing features for Nevada newspapers. A decade later, when he undertook to write up his western experiences in book form, *Roughing It* (1872) resonated with three decades of popular publications about the Far West. A mere observer in the silver fields, Twain mined the established genres and tropes of writing about the West for their usefulness as satire, burlesque, and parody. Especially in the early sections of the book, Twain's persona itself is the butt of much humour, insofar as his ideas about the West typify current myths and stereotypes. Before he is invited to accompany his brother, for example, Twain imagines him 'on the great plains and deserts, and among the mountains of the Far West', where he would 'have all kinds of adventures, and may be get hanged or scalped, and have ever such a fine time'. The Far West internalised by the young Twain through the popular press is again and again held up to the West the traveller experiences. The 'Moral' with which Twain ends the book resonates throughout and darkens the tone: 'If you are of any account, stay at home and make your way by faithful diligence; but if you are "no account", go away from home, and then you will have to work, whether you want to or not'.[16] The feckless character Twain concocts for the purposes of his story, of 'no account' insofar as his imagination has been colonised by popular myths of easy wealth in the West, ironically finds on western ground the calling that would make him rich and famous. But it is through the 'faithful diligence' of writing, in the east, mainly for an eastern readership, that his western travels yield their rewards.

A new western nature

Western mountain ranges, deserts, and canyons, on a scale and assuming forms that beggared most travellers' experiences, elicited new kinds of descriptive writing. One notable mode invoked the emerging science of geomorphology in order to explain landforms like the Grand Canyon, where layers of sediment a mile thick, exposed to view by flowing water, conjured up processes acting over millions of years. Whereas emigrants in wagons reacted to deserts and canyons as barriers and threats, with an occasional aside about grandeur, geologists like John Wesley Powell and Clarence King made extreme landforms a focus of interest in themselves, developing a vocabulary that would later serve various kinds of tourism focused on nature. That both men began their books as a series of magazine articles indicates their desire to deploy science in an appeal to the general reader's visualisation of the West.

Powell's *Exploration of the Colorado River and Its Canyons* (1875) precedes the narrative of his expedition's boat journey through the Grand Canyon with chapters describing valleys, mesas and buttes, mountains and plateaus, cliffs and terraces, in terms of the processes that produced them – sedimentation, volcanic eruption, uplifting, and erosion. The visual apprehension of such landforms is enabled by this invocation of time on a vast scale: description relies on the narrative of origins. Powell's account renders his remarkable journey along the Colorado River in terms of the paddling and climbing necessary as responses to the force of the water and the height

11. Thomas Moran, 'Cliffs of the Upper Colorado River, Wyoming Territory' (1882).
Courtesy of the Smithsonian American Art Museum, Bequest of Henry Ward Ranger
through the National Academy of Design.

of the walls, but these human actions are situated at the present cutting edge of an ongoing geological process: at the canyon bottom Powell and his men trace water's action on stone, the long-term effects of which tower above them.

Where Powell plumbs the depths, Clarence King's *Mountaineering in the Sierra Nevada* (1872) scales the heights. A series of sketches growing out of his participation in the California Geological Survey and the Fortieth Parallel Survey, *Mountaineering* has little of the formal expeditionary character of Powell's volume. The narrator of various journeys among the valleys and high peaks of the Sierra is light-hearted and youthful, open to chance adventures and alert to the makings of a good story. Even so, the 'student of geology' is sometimes anxious lest he should fall 'to the level of a mere nature-lover', and the explanatory narrative of contemporary geology is ubiquitous. In addition to what an average climber would regard as the 'view' from the top of Mount Shasta, King sees 'volumes of geological history': 'Old mountain uplift; volcanoes built upon the plain of fiery lava; the chill of ice and wearing force of torrent, written in glacier-gorge and water-curved canyon'. The scale of such forces and the time they imply contribute to the sublimity of 'the lifeless region, with its savage elements of sky, ice and rock, [that] grasps one's nature', and from which one is happy to descend 'into softer air, and enter the comforting presence of trees'.[17]

A largely self-taught naturalist and geologist, John Muir invoked and contributed to the scientific discourses of his day, but his writing about the Sierra Nevada is most notable for the passion and completeness with which its speaker centres himself in each environment – high granite peak, lush mountain meadow, sombre, towering forest. Muir arrived in California in 1868, aged thirty, having already walked thousands of miles in the northern forests of the Great Lakes, and having begun the journey that would bring him to California by walking from Indiana to the gulf coast of Florida. He continued to walk, from a base in the Yosemite Valley rambling throughout the high peaks, often alone, with tea and dry bread in his pockets. He had partly shed the constraints of his father's Calvinism by the time he started for Florida, but his first walk from San Francisco across the coast range, the central valley and into the Sierra (eventually recounted in *My First Summer in the Sierra*, 1911) reveals intense religious feelings that permeate his writing. Now evoked by nature, they nonetheless retain something of Calvinism's reverence for the Absolute: 'Perched like a fly on this Yosemite dome, I gaze and sketch and bask, oftentimes settling down into dumb admiration, ... humbly prostrate before the vast display of God's power, and eager to offer self-denial and renunciation with eternal toil to learn any lesson in the divine manuscript.'[18] *The Mountains of California* (1894), organised as a kind of textbook, reflects in the density of its descriptions years of such toil, but at the core of each chapter remain the particular, journal-recorded encounters with squirrels, trees, glaciers, and storms. Muir's descriptions paradoxically evoke the observer through his losing of himself in the particulars of his surroundings. Although he published periodical articles beginning in 1872, Muir's books appeared years later, after his work as a conservation advocate instrumental in the establishment of Yosemite as a national park, and after he founded the Sierra Club. They serve as scriptures to a central branch of American environmentalism, but they also retain the freshness of their writer's youthful responses to the Sierra environment.

As Muir's works helped to popularise the natural wonders of the Sierra Nevada, John C. Van Dyke's *The Desert* (1901) and Mary Austin's *Land of Little Rain* (1903) explored ways to appreciate the deserts of southern California and Arizona. A professor of art history, Van Dyke responds to desert landscapes in aesthetic terms, noting the ennobling simplicity of 'large masses, ... breadth, space and distance', and the restfulness of horizontal lines: 'Things that lie flat are at peace and the mind grows peaceful with them'. He studies the beauty in colour and light, and finds that people who spend time in the desert eventually fall in love with 'the weird solitude, the great silence, the grim desolation'.[19] Austin's account is less purely a matter of aesthetics; her desert of the Owens Valley has a history and current inhabitants – one-time miners, a Shoshone medicine man, a Paiute basket maker – all of which remind one that a given site has been a series of places, that place is a product of culture, even when the current approach is to see it as 'nature'. But like Van Dyke, Austin values the abstraction of the desert, where 'stars move in the wide clear heavens to risings and settings unobscured...Wheeling in their stations in the sky, they make the poor world-fret of no account'.[20]

On the road

Muir and Austin were aware that their preferences for walking, for lingering in particular western places, were acts of resistance to the norm established by their contemporaries, who mostly gazed from moving trains, as the next generation would from automobiles. Already in the 1860s, Twain in his horse-drawn 'cradle' experienced the passivity of mass travel, his journey west framed by a stagecoach window. A few years later, in 1872, Helen Hunt Jackson looked down from her railway car passing high along the side of Echo Canyon, Utah, while below an emigrant party in ox-drawn wagons followed the river. 'I envied them. They would see the canyon and know it. To us it would be only a swift and vanishing dream. Even while we are whirling through, it grows unreal.'[21] A vast railway promotional literature would attempt to stabilise and commodify each sight and wonder along the way, but even the relative independence of the automobile left travellers frustrated with the lubricity of their impressions. Van Dyke's rendering of the desert in terms of line, colour, light, and volume initiates a vocabulary of visual appreciation readily adaptable to the landscapes framed by railway, automobile, and even airliner windows. And yet, as Jackson's comment suggests, dissatisfaction with the superficiality of road views starts early and runs deep. As a symptom of this dissatisfaction, Kris Lackey argues, the automobile road narrative asserts a 'myth of independence' wherein each traveller (recall Jackson's envy of the emigrants' experience) re-enacts 'the discovery and early settlement of the country'.[22] Thus the narrator of William Least Heat-Moon's *Blue Highways* (1982), through his choice of the simplest vehicle and the least modern roads, aspires to contact a United States more authentic than anything seen along interstate freeways. His stops for the remote, the old, the neglected are a reaction to his awareness that his windshield is 'a movie screen'.[23]

Jack Kerouac's *On the Road* (1957), a work of fiction based on the author's own travels, is one of the most vigorous and influential iterations of the 'myth of Independence' that Lackey associates with the automobile road trip in America. Kerouac's book became the authorising scripture of innumerable automobile treks to 'the coast', even though it reveals the limitations of the dream of easy mobility prompted by the post-war ubiquity of the automobile. Unlike the journeys epitomised in John Steinbeck's *Grapes of Wrath* (1939), desperate migrations from the depression-era dust bowl to agricultural labour camps in the central valley, Kerouac's journeys are expressions of youthful wanderlust during a period of prosperity. Sal Paradise, the young narrator, and Dean Moriarty, his heroic companion, enact a series of breakneck road trips back and forth between New York and San Francisco, in which each sunrise, each drunken spree, each girl is an attempt to realise the infinite but unspecified promise vested in a still vast but ostensibly unified 'America'. On his first journey the West is fully identified with the narrator's destiny, unspecified as both remain. Pausing in Iowa, he says, 'I was halfway across America, at the dividing line between the East of my youth and the West of my future.'[24] This conflation of self and symbolic geography reveals its inherent contradictions when the traveller arrives in California and confronts the boundedness of even this very large continent: 'there was nowhere to go but back'. His question – 'Oh where is the girl I love?' – is also his wondering where he belongs in 'the great raw bulge and bulk of my American continent' (pp. 71, 72). Action itself becomes the only way to hold onto possibilities; the 'one noble function of the time, move', realises 'the purity of the road' (pp. 125, 126). But movement as a mode of being also exacts its toll. The continent thus crossed and recrossed is 'groaning', 'awful', the road a 'senseless nightmare' whose internalised reality is 'endless and beginningless emptiness'. Initially invested with infinite promise, the continent comes to seem a vacuum into which all particulars vanish, like the friend who, left behind on the road, 'grew smaller and smaller...till there was nothing but a growing absence in space' (pp. 121, 238, 241).

Revisionist views

One can see Joan Didion's essays of the 1960s and 1970s as acts of resistance to the popularisation of the western road trip and the way it turned California, her birthplace, and the physical limit of the Pacific Ocean into 'the Coast', the last-chance site of every 'dream deferred', no matter how nebulous or improbable. In two essay collections, *Slouching Towards Bethlehem* (1968) and *The White Album* (1979), Didion runs a loving but alienated eye over what California has become in her time, entertaining again the old question of whether California is the future, or whether it is where the dreams of the past reveal their insubstantiality. In part, Didion's perspective is that of a California native with deep roots, a kind of Thoreau, travelling a lot in her own village. 'I come from California', she says, 'come from a family...that has always been in the Sacramento Valley'. But the uneasiness with which she regards the present infects the past she somewhat hyperbolically claims: 'All that is constant about the California of my childhood is the rate at which it disappears'. She flaunts her westerner's belief that visitors from 'the East' remain encapsulated in popular myth, that they 'have not in fact been [to California], and they probably never will be, for it is a longer and in many ways a more difficult trip than they might want to undertake'.[25] Meanwhile, her own encounters with her state undermine her sense that she knows where she comes from. In the title essay of *The White Album*, about the period of the Manson murders, she tells us 'about a time when I began to doubt the premises of all the stories I had ever told myself'.[26] Didion wrestles with some of the same anxieties as Kerouac's Beat protagonists, to do with how 'the Coast' figures as a place in her own life and in the life of America. The young Didion recalled in 'Goodbye to All That' also attempts to span a continent, living and working in New York with waning conviction that 'nothing like this, all evidence to the contrary, has ever happened to anyone before'. After eight years, she wearily acknowledges that 'it is distinctly possible to stay too long at the fair'. Despair yields to marriage and a move to Los Angeles, whence she looks back on her New York years as 'years when I called Los Angeles "the Coast"' (*Slouching*, pp. 226, 236, 238). Encountering her own limits, she reconceives California as a finite place with a particular history, but in so doing she also confronts the social phenomena that stem from California's functioning as the sign of infinite hope in the American mythology. The brilliant 'Slouching Towards Bethlehem' observes with dumb horror the inarticulate floundering of teenage hippies who have found their way to the Haight district of San Francisco. The aimless round of drugs and sex that Didion describes is for her a symptom of a failure 'to tell these children the rules of the game we happened to be playing'. These are the children of movement, 'cut loose from the web' of families and neighbours. They have no words – 'they do not believe in words' – whereas Didion is 'still committed to the idea that the ability to think for one's self depends upon one's mastery of the language', and she is 'not optimistic' about 'an army of children waiting to be given the words' (*Slouching*, p. 123). There is nothing to discover in one's deracinated self come to rest above the high water mark on the Pacific shore. One needs to claim one's place, one's language, one's history. We are reminded of the first travellers' dissatisfaction with the level of civilisation of California. But whereas these observers would contrast human mediocrity with a California climate and topography that seemed to offer a helping hand to human potential, a new nature evoking a new human nature, Didion sees an indifferent nature of hot winds, fires, earthquakes, and floods, from which she turns soberly to the limited human 'ability to think'.

A poet who immigrated to California in middle life, Polish-born Czeslaw Milosz, like the native Didion, seeks rooted particulars amidst the swirl of myth. Milosz sees a California that is an aspect of the 'America' that Europeans have seen for centuries, remote yet full of promise, a site of the future. *Visions from San Francisco Bay* (1975), written from his new home in Berkeley, laments his loss of the human scale of European streets and country landscapes, as he zooms 'down three hundred miles of California freeways situated amid menacing, monstrous vistas', but when Milosz revisits western Europe he finds signs that Europe is participating in a process the advance guard of which is California.[27] In the midst of personal and historical change, Milosz brings to bear an acute sense of the specificity of place, and of the importance of place to human individuality. He sees an America that has developed through 'automatic, unplanned movement', and which 'has lost its ability to maintain direction' (p. 182). Rather than take to the road himself, however, Milosz offers his own limited and particular perspective, that of an exile, putting down new roots. Confronting the seemingly limitless mobility of American society, Milosz holds that 'total deracination, uprootedness, is contrary to our nature'. Because we are physical beings we cannot be located nowhere. 'The human plant once plucked from the ground tries to sink roots into the ground onto which it was thrown.' We live in space, 'bounded by the surface of our skin', and our imagination 'extends us, establishing a sensory and visual relationship between us and a street, a town, a district, and a country'. Hardly an optimist, he nonetheless responds to the banality of the restless, commercial society around him with a faith that the essential individuality of men and women is liberated in new forms as time passes and circumstances change: 'By changing civilizations, time continually liberates new souls and bodies in man, and thus time is not a serpent devouring its own tail' (pp. 203, 183).

An America founded on mobility, which seems tragic to Sal Paradise, inarticulate to Didion, and directionless to Milosz, is embraced with a kind of post-modern, stoic joy by French sociologist and philosopher, Jean Baudrillard, in his *America* (1989). Like Kerouac's narrator, but with little sense of trauma, Baudrillard arrives at his own theory of 'a trip without any objective and which is, as a result, endless'. The round-the-clock circulation of cars on Los Angeles freeways is 'the only real society or warmth here', so that to obey the 'right lane must exit' sign is 'to expel myself from paradise, leave this providential highway which leads nowhere, but keeps me in touch with everyone'. Baudrillard sites this community of the road in a culture that is a 'marvellously affectless succession of signs', where the view from behind the windshield is one with the film screen and the television, and where there is little material civilization rooted in history. To understand this post-modern America 'you have to take to the road'.[28] Thus, in language that recalls Kerouac, and before him Whitman, Baudrillard poses as his own kind of easy rider: 'Where the others spend their time in libraries, I spend mine in the deserts and on the roads... My hunting grounds are the deserts, the mountains, Los Angeles, the freeways, the Safeways, the ghost towns, or the downtowns, not lectures at the university.' Baudrillard is careful, however, to disavow the romantic elan that this language betrays. Kerouac's youth-ful Eros will not pierce any of the screens on which Baudrillard's American world of signs is projected. Where Kerouac's hero launches himself into a pin-ball machine of possible contacts along the road, Baudrillard simply drives, seeing in the 'abstraction of the desert' an ultimate 'deliverance from the organic... into that dry, luminous phase of death in which the corruption of the body reaches completion' (pp. 63, 71).

From the beginning a land and climate that inspired desire, California has become a palimpsest of inscribed wishes, to the point that Baudrillard understands California in terms of pure signification and dispenses with ideas of history or place. As the essays of Didion and Milosz suggest, however, not everyone is happy in a desert of detached signifiers. The contemporary environment of projected desires fosters the will to understand the forces that give wishes their shape. To this end, Mike Davis's City of Quartz connects the observable reality of Los Angeles with the economic and political institutions that shape it. But even as he analyses causes, Davis knows that Los Angeles functions symbolically as a destination conflating individual journeys and western history. Los Angeles plays 'the double role of utopia and dystopia for advanced capitalism... [I]t is the essential destination on the itinerary of any late-twentieth-century intellectual, who must eventually come to take a peep and render some opinion on whether "Los Angeles Brings It All Together" (official slogan), or is, rather, the nightmare at the terminus of American history'.[29]

NOTES

1 For texts of the earliest voyages see David B. Quinn, ed., New American World: A Documentary History of North America to 1612, 5 vols. (New York: Arno, 1979).

2 For a discussion of the rôle of science in eighteenth-century travel writing see Mary Louise Pratt, Imperial Eyes: Travel Writing and Transculturation (London: Routledge, 1992), pp. 15–37.

3 George Vancouver, A Voyage of Discovery to the North Pacific Ocean and Round the World, 1791–1795, W. Kaye Lamb, ed., 4 vols. (London: Hakluyt Society, 1984), vol. II, p. 701.

4 Jean François de Lapérouse, *Voyage Round the World, Performed in the Years 1785, 1786, 1787, and 1788*, 2 vols. (London: A. Hamilton, 1799), vol. I, pp. 441–2, 458, 447.

5 George Simpson, *A Journey Round the World*, 2 vols. (London: Henry Colburn, 1847), vol. I, p. 274.

6 Franklin Walker, *A Literary History of Southern California* (Berkeley: University of California Press, 1950), calls Robinson's *Life in California* (1846) 'one of the most reliable and interesting documents dealing with Spanish California' (p. 36).

7 Richard Henry Dana Jr., *Two Years Before the Mast* (New York: P. F. Collier and Son, 1909), pp. 170, 92.

8 For other accounts contemporary with Dana's, see Kevin Starr, *Americans and the California Dream, 1850–1915* (New York: Oxford University Press, 1973).

9 Lewis was charged with preparing the expedition records for publication, but he died before completing the task. The *History of the Lewis and Clark Expedition* (1814) was Nicolas Biddle's collation and abridgement of the two commanders' records; it remained the basis of subsequent accounts of the expedition until Reuben Gold Thwaites's *The Original Journals of the Lewis and Clark Expedition*, 8 vols. (New York: Dodd, Mead, 1904–5). Thwaite's edition has been superseded by Gary E. Moulton, ed., *The Journals of the Lewis and Clark Expedition*, 13 vols. (Lincoln: University of Nebraska Press, 1983–2002).

10 Jackson and Mary Lee Spence, eds., *The Expeditions of John Charles Fremont*, 2 vols. (Urbana: University of Illinois Press, 1970), vol. I, p. xix.

11 See Maurice S. Sullivan, *The Travels of Jedediah Smith, a Documentary Outline Including the Journal of the Great American Pathfinder* (Santa Ana: Fine Arts Press, 1934).

12 *The Personal Narrative of James Ohio Pattie*, ed. Timothy Flint (Cincinnati: John H. Wood, 1831).

13 William Lewis Manly, *Death Valley in '49* [1894] (Ann Arbor: University Microfilms, 1966), pp. 174–5.

14 Francis Parkman, *The Oregon Trail* (New York: Heritage Press, 1943), pp. 80, 97–8, 97, 80.

15 Among the best of these were Bayard Taylor, *Eldorado, or, Adventures on the Path of Empire* (1850); Louise Amelia Knapp Smith Clappe (Dame Shirley), *The Shirley Letters...from the California Mines, 1851–1852* (1949); and J. D. Borthwick, *Three Years in California* (1857).

16 Mark Twain, *Roughing It* (New York: Penguin, 1981), pp. 49, 562.

17 Clarence King, *Mountaineering in the Sierra Nevada* (Philadelphia: J. B. Lippincott, 1963), pp. 178, 238, 245. Among the heirs of these geologist-writers are the modern geologists who guide John McPhee along his own fortieth-parallel journey across the American landscape rendered in his monumental series of essays recently collected as *Annals of the Former World* (1998), but previously published as separate volumes: *Basin and Range* (1981); *In Suspect Terrain* (1983); *Rising from the Plains* (1986); *Assembling California* (1993); *Crossing the Craton* appears for the first time in *Annals*.

18 John Muir, *My First Summer in the Sierra* (New York: Penguin, 1987), p. 132.

19 John C. Van Dyke, *The Desert: Further Studies in Natural Appearances* (Baltimore: Johns Hopkins University Press, 1999), p. 19.

20 Mary Austin, *The Land of Little Rain* (Albuquerque: University of New Mexico Press, 1974), pp. 13–14.

21 Helen Hunt Jackson, *Bits of Travel at Home* (Boston: Roberts Brothers, 1878), p. 15.

22 Kris Lackey, *Road Frames: The American Highway Narrative* (Lincoln: University of Nebraska Press, 1997), p. 42.

23 William Least Heat-Moon, *A Journey into America: Blue Highways* (Boston: Little, Brown, 1982), p. 188. See also Robert Pirsig's resort to the motorcycle in *Zen and the Art of Motorcycle Maintenance* (1974).

24 Jack Kerouac, *On the Road* (New York: Penguin, 1999), p. 14.

25 Joan Didion, *Slouching Towards Bethlehem* (New York: Farrar, Straus, Giroux, 1968), pp. 172, 177, 171.

26 Joan Didion, *The White Album* (New York: Simon and Schuster, 1979), p. 11.

27 Czeslaw Milosz, *Visions from San Francisco Bay*, trans. Richard Lourie (New York: Farrar, Straus, Giroux, 1982), pp. 38, 39.

28 Jean Baudrillard, *America*, trans. Chris Turner (London: Verso, 1989), pp. 9, 53, 5,

29 Mike Davis, *City of Quartz: Excavating the Future of Los Angeles* (New York: Vintage, 1992), pp. 18–20.

III
TOPICS

13

SUSAN BASSNETT

Travel writing and gender

The essence of adventure lies in taking risks and exploring the unknown, so it is hardly surprising to find that early travel accounts tended for the most part to be written by men, who moved more freely in the public sphere. The great European sagas of knightly questing (such as *The Norse Sagas* and *The Arthurian Cycle*) or seafaring exploration (such as *The Odyssey* and *The Lusiads*) are also male narratives with women the objects of desire or destination points rather than active co-travellers, though the figure of the warrior-princess roaming the world in search of adventure was popular in Renaissance epics like *Orlando furioso* and *Gerusalemme liberata*. The adventure quest in the sixteenth and seventeenth centuries, when men journeyed in search of fortune and renown to the new worlds that were opening up beyond the frontiers of Europe, was explicitly gendered, since the idea of man as heroic risk-taking traveller underpinned not only the great travel narratives of the next centuries, but much of the travel writing of the twentieth century also.[1]

Alongside the myths of the heroic explorer, however, are other kinds of narrative, some of which have been produced by women. The travel text as ethnography or social commentary transcends gender boundaries and, increasingly in the twentieth century, male and female travellers have written self-reflexive texts that defy easy categorisation as autobiography, memoir, or travel account. There is also, in British travel writing, a tendency to self-deprecation and irony, a style of writing that has both Henry Fielding and Jane Austen as its antecedents, despite the fact that the latter did not move beyond the confines of southern England. Contemporary writers like Redmond O'Hanlon and Eric Newby subvert or satirise the image of the explorer-hero, turning themselves into anti-heroes in their narratives, a comic reversal of the dominant image of the male traveller who seeks to boldly go where no man has gone before.

Rediscovering women travellers

The feminist revival of the early 1970s had, as part of its intellectual agenda, a conscious revision of what was perceived as male-authored history. One strand in this process of rediscovery was an interest in women travellers. Though some of the nineteenth-century women's travel accounts had reached a substantial reading public and twentieth-century travellers such as Rosita Forbes, Freya Stark, Gertrude Bell, and Rebecca West also had a strong following, by the 1970s their work was out of print and respect for their achievements had declined. In Paul Fussell's study of travel writing, *Abroad: British Literary Traveling Between the Wars* (1980) women are non-existent. The first stages of the revival were therefore to make available works that had all but disappeared and to remind readers of the number of women travellers who had written about their journeys. The UK feminist publishing house, Virago, reprinted classic travel books by women such as Isabella Bird and Mary Kingsley, while a number of anthologies and studies of Victorian women travellers began to appear.[2]

The titles of some of these studies reflect a particular way of looking at women travellers. Though praising their efforts and achievements, the authors hint nevertheless that they are slightly eccentric, and introduce a comic note that can easily be interpreted as mocking. So we find *Ladies on the Loose, The Blessings of a Good, Thick Skirt*, and *Spinsters Abroad*, all of which focus on the unusual life stories of women travellers, on their originality, and on their refusal to conform to social norms of the day.[3] Women travellers are therefore categorised as doubly different: they differ from other, more orthodox, socially conformist women, and from male travellers who use the journey as a means of discovering more about their own masculinity. The underlying impression gained from these volumes is that the woman traveller was somehow in flight from something, seeking to escape from the constraints of her family or her society.

In 1990, Jane Robinson published *Wayward Women*, which provides useful bibliographical information and short, potted biographies of women travellers.[4] The organisation of the volume is idiosyncratic, as are some of the editor's trenchant opinions, but it nevertheless remains a basic source of information on some 400 women travellers writing in English. Robinson also edited an anthology of extracts from travel writing by women, *Unsuitable for Ladies*, where she endeavours to distinguish how women wrote as opposed to their male counterparts by stressing differences of style and emphasis. Women, she argues, 'have rarely been *commissioned* to travel', hence in the absence of a patron or authority figure 'women can afford to be more discursive, more impressionable, more *ordinary*'.[5]

In her pioneering study of women's travel writing and colonialism, *Discourses of Difference*, Sara Mills similarly notes the stress that women lay on the personal and on relationships in general. She also points to what she calls 'the less authoritarian stance they take vis-à-vis narrative voice'.[6] Although Robinson and Mills approach women travel writers from very different perspectives, both emphasise the wealth of detail in women's travel accounts, along with a tendency to write about relationships, and both contrast this with the more public discourse of male travellers. There is the danger of essentialism in this argument, and much early feminist scholarship suffered from a tendency to see 'woman' as a unitary category, and to make assumptions based on that undifferentiated categorisation. Nevertheless, the basic questions remain: do women's travel accounts differ from those written by men in any fundamental way, and is there a way in which travel writing is inherently gendered? These questions continue to preoccupy feminist scholars, and have been made more complex by postcolonial perspectives, which raise issues about the role and status of white women travellers in the age of imperialism. A text like May French-Sheldon's *Sultan to Sultan. Adventures Among the Masai and Other Tribes of East Africa* (1892) demonstrates the unquestioned confidence of a woman who saw herself as a member of a superior culture, though a US and not a British citizen. Meeting Sultan Mireali (she had purposely taken full evening dress and a blonde wig to wear for ceremonial occasions), she describes her shock at finding him dressed 'like a clown' in assorted European clothing. Determined to express her opinion, she is introduced and immediately informs him that he would be better wearing his native dress. French-Sheldon's book is a fascinating combination of imperious behaviour and social conscience. In her Foreword to the volume, she shares with her readers the news of her wealthy husband's unexpected death during the production of the book, then makes a polemical point about the iniquities of colonialism:

> ... it has been with an aching heart I have completed the work, endeavoring with fortitude to do my best to make my readers better acquainted with the possibilities of the natural primitives whom I am proud to call my friends and be called friend by, and to demonstrate that if a woman could journey a thousand and more miles in East Africa, among some hostile tribes, unattended by other than Zanzibari mercenaries, without bloodshed, the extreme measures employed by some would-be colonizers are unnecessary, atrocious, and without the pale of humanity.[7]

This kind of text reflects the contradictions inherent in some of the books produced by nineteenth-century travellers, both male and female. On the one hand, they moved secure in the knowledge of their own superiority, quick to patronise or mock, yet on the other hand, they were ready to bear witness to what they saw as exploitation and cruelty by fellow Europeans and North Americans. It is debatable whether this tendency is more marked in women's travel writing than in texts by men, though on balance the nineteenth-century travel texts by men tend towards a greater scientificity, while much of the women's writing reflects an interest in philanthropic activities, characteristic of early feminism. The extent to which women (the missionary Mary Slessor is a case in point) campaigned actively against twin murder reflects the kind of activism that motivated many European and US female reformers to denounce slavery, exploitative working conditions for women, and children and human rights abuses generally.

Diversity of women's travel accounts

In her study of Victorian women travellers in East Africa, Cheryl McEwan discusses the diversity of women travellers and the variations in their writing styles:

> Travel writings by white women were positioned geographically, metaphorically and metaphysically between the dominant culture and the 'wild zone'. While both men and women have occupied these margins in literary production, they have been positioned there in very different ways. In addition, there were differences between women in how they occupied these margins, which in turn produced significant variations in their texts.[8]

Such variations derive from differences of social class, age, and religion, from shifts in time, from journeys to different parts of the world. McEwan sees women's travel writing as much more complex than previous studies have suggested, and argues convincingly for the need to recognise diversity. Not all women travellers were middle class, not all shared the same ideological standpoint, though clearly those women who travelled under the umbrella of the British Empire were, albeit unconsciously, colluding with the colonial enterprise. McEwan's book shows how far feminist thinking has travelled in thirty years, from conceptualising woman as a single category to acknowledging patterns of diversity that reflect broader social and cultural differences.

One consistent line through discussions of women travellers is the notion that they were somehow exceptional. The theory of the exceptional woman who is somehow different from other women and therefore empowered to perform feats no normal woman would be capable of carrying out has been one of the classic ways of marginalising women's achievements. The problem here is the setting of a benchmark against which women can be measured. Hence in an age when relatively few people travelled at all, the idea of a woman traveller was something of a novelty. Writers like French-Sheldon exploited that novelty value, making claims for their own exceptionality, but others, such as Mary Kingsley, were much more reticent. Isabella Bird, for example, was immensely concerned about how she might be judged by public opinion, and anxious to have credibility with the male-only Royal Geographical Society.

Documenting the everyday

It was certainly true that if a woman traveller expressed opinions that were controversial, the chorus of dismissive voices would be so much louder. Hence the contempt with which Lady Mary Wortley Montagu was treated when she travelled to Constantinople in 1716 to join her husband, who had been appointed ambassador to Turkey. Her *Letters*, written after she returned to England and published after her death in 1762, were widely circulated in manuscript during her lifetime, and reveal the lively, forthright voice of a woman who described herself as 'a traveller' and who experimented with smallpox vaccination by allowing her children to be immunised in Turkey. Significantly, however, her *Letters* challenge the tendency of many European travellers to exoticise the Orient. George Sandys's 1652 account of his travels in the Turkish Empire and Monsieur de Thevenot's *Relation d'un voyage fait au Levant* (1665) are typical of texts that describe the laziness of oriental women and their supposedly 'natural' tendency to lasciviousness. Sandys goes so far as to inform his readers that 'much unnatural and filthy lust is said to be committed daily in the remote closets of these darksome Bannias' (public baths).[9] But Montagu gives a very different account of Turkish women in the bath-house and wittily criticises the stupidity of those writers whose erotic fantasies have led them to distort the more domesticated reality that she finds operating in a community of women. A century later, in her *Letters from Egypt* (1865) Lucie Duff Gordon was to make a similar point, describing the daily lives of Egyptian women in terms that contested the fantasising of her male contemporaries. Far from being exceptional, both these aristocratic women travellers wrote about the experiences of the women they encountered, and in so doing refuted the growing tendency towards eroticisation of the unfamiliar that characterises so many texts by male travellers.

Both these women had access to women's society, and as a result were able to describe daily life in the harem in terms of the normality of women's customs and practices, rebutting male-inspired fantasies about harems as places of highly charged sexuality. Their down-to-earth accounts of the living conditions of Turkish and Egyptian women respectively are in sharp contrast to the more fantastical accounts of veiled women, repressed sexuality, and deviance that appear in many male writers' accounts of their travels in the Orient.

Some works by women travellers provide serious, detailed social documentation. Lady Elizabeth Eastlake's *Letters from the Shores of the Baltic*, another example of the epistolary form popular among women writers especially, was published in 1842. Eastlake uses the format of twenty-five letters to give an account of a journey to visit her sister, married to a local aristocrat and living in Reval, now known as Tallinn in Estonia. Eastlake provides detailed descriptions of diet, childcare, the education of girls in imperial Russia, and even has a chapter about a smuggling expedition, when the upper classes of Reval sail over to Finland for the day to shop for tax-free goods. Although there is a strong authorial presence in this text, there is no self-dramatising, no desire to reinvent herself as someone else and certainly no desire to see travel as a means of escape from the reality of home. Eastlake's account opens with her journey out and ends with her return journey.

The importance of the everyday for women writers has often been noted. In her study *Feminism and Geography*, Gillian Rose examines the distinction between public and private spaces for women, and discusses the importance of what she calls 'time-geography', which focuses on examining the complexity of networks and patterns in everyday life.[10] She argues that the belief that everything is knowable and mappable is fundamentally a patriarchal concept: there is no part of the planet, no society so distant that it cannot be mapped, described and hence contained. But a feminist concept of geography sees the world differently: here the goal is not to map every detail, but to reinsert a physical dimension into the discourse, to engage with the everyday as an end in itself, not as a means to a different end.

Rose draws upon French feminist theory to introduce the notion of the female body into her argument. The fluidity and viscosity of the female body is contrasted with the linearity and solidity of the male body; while the latter results in a vision of the world that creates and controls a set of power relations, the former is less tangible, more flexible, and infinitely varied. Traditional mapping is therefore perceived as an inherently male act, since the intention is to circumscribe, define, and hence control the world. For feminists, an alternative mapping consists of tracing patterns from the most banal and trivial everyday events so as to create a completely different set of identifiable structures outside patriarchal control.

Searching for a rôle

The history of travel writing is linked to the history of mapping and surveying. Nor was mapping restricted to geographical features: the process of mapping the natural world, of labelling flora and fauna, ran parallel to the process of mapping territories. Naming the new and labelling it became a means of marking ownership, in both physical and intellectual terms. As Europe acquired colonies, maps establishing the precise boundaries between disputed claims became vital. Moreover, the early history of colonialism is one in which new territories were metaphorised as female, as virgin lands waiting to be penetrated, ploughed, and husbanded by male explorers. The overt sexualisation of the language of territorial expansion quickly became commonplace.

Women travellers had, then, to write about their experiences from within a tradition that denied them a rôle, for if the image of the coloniser is sexualised as a man bent on raping virgin lands, then a woman from the colonising culture is effectively erased. Yet women did travel in all kinds of rôles – as wives, sisters, daughters of missionaries, diplomats or envoys, as scientists or naturalists, as explorers seeking to prove something to themselves, as individuals in search of the unexpected, or of leisure or instruction, alone or accompanied, for personal or professional reasons. These women have not been silenced, but have chosen to write about their experiences in full knowledge of the absence of a tradition into which they could insert themselves with any degree of comfort or familiarity. One of the effects of this breaking-through can be discerned in the clarity of some of the voices that speak from women's texts and the strong emphasis on the personal. It is rare to find the kind of serious, anthropological monograph with extended footnotes like those produced by many male writers, which may be due to the exclusion of women from scientific professions in the nineteenth century. So French-Sheldon's book, for example, runs to 429 pages, but offers the reader photographs, ink drawings, conversations, and chatty accounts of incidents involving people she meets on her journey rather than scientific analysis. Clearly the method of approaching other cultures is very different from that of her contemporaries such as Richard Burton.

The discursive presence of women travellers in their texts raises some interesting questions. On the one hand, it may be that their reluctance to use footnotes derives from a sense of intellectual insecurity caused by their marginalisation in the newly developing field of anthropology. On the other hand, the excessive use of footnotes by writers such as Burton raises the issue of the function of the footnote, particularly in Orientalist texts. Burton, for example, uses footnotes for comments on sexual practices often bordering on the pornographic in their detail. Here it could be argued that the supposedly scientific served as a screen for material that would otherwise never have found its way into print.

It is important also to note that not all the writings by women travellers were intended from the outset for publication. Male writers for the most part appear, at least from the way in which their texts are presented, to have had publication in mind from the outset. This difference reflects the difference in social terms between men and women in the nineteenth century, with men occupying a far more public rôle and women only assuming a public rôle in particular circumstances. Some pieces of writing were clearly conceived as monographs, others written in the form of letters, diaries, or sketches and then assembled into book form: Isabella Bird's *A Lady's Life in the Rocky Mountains* is composed of seventeen letters to her sister, and is prefaced by a note which points out that the letters 'as their style indicates, were written without the remotest idea of publication'.[11]

The case of the diaries of Margaret Fountaine, not published until 1980, forty years after her death, provides another interesting example of a text written for private purposes but then made public. Fountaine travelled the world in pursuit of her hobby, butterfly-collecting, keeping a diary from the age of sixteen that recorded not only her travels but also her love affairs. Her diaries were locked in a trunk with a note forbidding anyone to read them until 15 April 1978, exactly 100 years from her first entry. Fountaine effectively constructed her own posthumous myth and wrote her own autobiography. As her editor, W. F. Cater points out in his introduction to an edited version of the diaries, rather tweely entitled *Love Among the Butterflies*, the diaries cover her life from her teens to her late seventies, and open in the style of a schoolroom essay: 'The following is an account of all that happened to me, Margaret Elizabeth Fountaine, on the fifteenth day of April, 1878'.[12] Fountaine's writing is an example of the way in which a Victorian woman's private account of her own life has, with the assistance of a posthumous edition, been transformed into popular text. Isabella Bird's books, on the other hand, show the gradual process whereby a writer moved from amateur to professional writer status, for although her early work was not intended for publication, by the time she wrote her accounts of journeys to China, Japan, and Kurdistan, she had a definite reading public in mind. In 1892 she became the first woman to address a meeting of the Royal Geographical Society and was elected to a fellowship shortly afterwards. Her reputation as a serious traveller was one that she guarded jealously, furiously refuting suggestions that she might have dressed improperly in mannish clothing.

Mrs Alec-Tweedie (Ethel Brilliana) is another kind of woman travel writer, who wrote for the growing tourist public at the turn of the nineteenth century, providing chatty accounts of journeys all over the world. The titles of some of her more successful books give a sense of her style and her audience: *A Winter Jaunt to Norway: With Accounts of Nansen, Ibsen, Björnson, Brandes, and Many Others* (1894), *Sunny Sicily: Its Rustics and its Ruins* (1904), *Tight Corners of my Adventurous Life* (1933). One of her most interesting books is her account of a journey across Russia, Siberia, and China, undertaken in the early 1920s when the impact of the Russian Revolution of 1917 was at its height. Clearly horrified by some of the sights she witnessed, Mrs Alec-Tweedie wrote a polemic against Bolshevism, at a time when other Western travellers were producing admiring accounts of the new Soviet order. She combines descriptions of squalid hotels, inadequate public transport, uneatable food, and desperate poverty with rants about the hellishness of life in Russia and Siberia. That the book is anti-Soviet propaganda is obvious, but there are moments when the public mask drops, and she writes about her genuine feelings. The shock for the contemporary reader comes at the end of the book. After 284 pages Mrs Alec-Tweedie moves to a conclusion, informing us that after a hundred thousand miles of travelling since the end of the war in 1918 she came back to London:

> Before I was even settled in my little flat my second, and last son, was killed – for the Country. For two whole years I only went outside the four mile London radius half-a-dozen times, and never slept one single night away. That shows what the strain and discomfort coupled with the ceaseless work of all those adventures really had meant.[13]

Here, for a moment, is the authentic voice of grief, a personal statement by a writer who had built her reputation on appearing to be indomitable. It is merely a moment: the concluding paragraph is a paean of praise for the British Empire, a reassurance to readers that they are fortunate indeed to be privileged enough to be citizens of 'the Greatest Power on God's Earth'. But what the moment shows is a great gap: between public performance and private anguish, between the ideal of home as a safe space and the reality of home as emptiness, between myth and reality. It also provides an insight into another problematic area of debate about women's travel writing: the relationship between narratives of travel and some of the women travellers' search for identity.

Inventing an identity

One of the themes running through many popular studies of women travellers is the difference between their lives at home and life on the road. Women travellers are often presented as having been somehow able to break free of the constraints of contemporary society, realising their potential once outside the boundaries of a restrictive social order. Such a reading proposes that women who chafed at the constraints of domesticity could find escape through travel. So it is often pointed out that Isabella Bird famously suffered from what may have been psychosomatic illness until, in her mid-forties after the death of her parents, she was sent abroad for her health. This provided the excuse she had seemingly been waiting for, and her career as an international traveller began. When she died at seventy-three she was in the process of packing for yet another journey. Similarly, Mary Kingsley kept house for her parents like a dutiful spinster daughter, until their deaths in 1892 enabled her to indulge a dream and travel to West Africa. Perhaps the most famous of all is Lady Hester Stanhope, who left the stifling atmosphere of English society life and in 1810 set out for Turkey and the Middle East, never to return. Her love affairs, her scandalous cross-dressing in Turkish male costume and her (for Victorian codes of conduct) shameless exhibitionism made her a figure of notoriety, but subsequent generations have tended to see her rather as an example of a woman who bravely sought to establish her independence by choosing to move in different cultures.[14] Travel for some women, it seems, may have offered a means of redefining themselves, assuming a different persona and becoming someone who did not exist at home.

Sara Mills is troubled by this kind of interpretation, and asks some important questions in a section of her book that investigates how feminists read women's travel writing. She points out that there are attempts to see some of these women as 'proto-feminists' or precursors, and that the texts can be read to provide examples of strong rôle models. But she also warns against romanticised readings in which assumptions are made that the texts are simply autobiographical. In fact many of the works by women travellers are self-conscious fictions, and the persona who emerges from the pages is as much a character as a woman in a novel. Isabella Bird, for example, stresses the hardships she endures during her travels, as though to reinforce the difference between Isabella the semi-invalid at home and Miss Bird the intrepid explorer who is able to endure hardships that other women cannot.

Isabella Bird's accounts of uncomfortable, dangerous situations run through all her writings. The tone of slightly ironic boastfulness was established in her American book and became her hallmark. So she recounts how, in the company of her admirer, the one-eyed alcoholic Rocky Mountain Jim, she narrowly missed death on a mountain path overhanging a precipice, transforming herself into a heroine capable of extraordinary physical feats. In her account of her relationship with Jim, we enter into the realms of Victorian melodrama. Though she may have claimed that publication was not her intention, nevertheless Bird was crafting a travel book that had woven into it a love story between a respectable lady and a gentleman turned wild, calculated to appeal to a broad audience. However seriously we may take her descriptions of mountain landscapes, it is impossible not to recognise the fictionalising process that she is engaged in throughout this book.

Despite her eventual recognition by the Royal Geographical Society, Bird's writings show how carefully she invented a new persona for herself. Many travel writers, men and women, have reinvented themselves in similar ways, always claiming to be writing in a spirit of 'authenticity' yet fictionalising their experiences by writing themselves as a character into the account of their travels. There is an evident tension between this process of self-fictionalising and the travel writer's claims to veracity.

Fictionalising processes

In the twentieth century, evidence of a change in the construction of travel narratives can clearly be seen in stylistic terms. Though the I-narrator still occupies a dominant position, the increasing use of dialogue in travel writing has further closed the gap between travel account and fiction, making the travel text resemble the novel much more closely. The protagonist engages in conversations that introduce a range of other characters into the narrative, and the reader is expected to believe that such conversations which apparently transcend any language barrier are recorded rather than invented.

The highly successful, though now forgotten travel writer, Rosita Forbes, offers a clear example of the tension between claims to offer an objective account of her travels in many countries and relentless self-dramatisation. Forbes even rechristened herself 'Rosita', abandoning her given name, the much more banal 'Joan'. Her books and articles were extremely popular in the inter-war years, and she produced a number of colourfully titled accounts of her journeys, including *Adventure: Being a Gypsy Salad: Some Incidents, Excitements and Impressions of Twelve Highly-Seasoned Years* (1923). She established herself as a travel writer with *The Secret of the Sahara: Kufara* (1921), an account of a journey through the Libyan desert to the forbidden city of Kufara. Her book struck a chord with readers increasingly fascinated with images of the desert as a place of mystery, sensuality and freedom: Rudolph Valentino's hugely successful film, *The Sheik*, was released in the same year as Forbes's book. Forbes seems to have had a good sense of commercial appeal, and as the vogue for desert books waned, she turned her attention to another popular myth, that of the glamorous gypsy, publishing the first volume of her autobiography, *Gypsy in the Sun*, in 1944. Forbes cultivated her gypsy image, not only by changing her name to the more exotic Rosita, but also by devising a multi-cultural family history, claiming to be related to Royalist aristocrats and Peruvian dancers. She wrote in a gossip-columnist style, dropping names with the panache of someone who today would be contributing to *Hello* magazine. Always elegantly turned out, she travelled sometimes with a husband or a cameraman or another male companion, and her books are richly illustrated with photographs of her in smart outfits or with famous people.

One explanation of Forbes's success must surely be that she appealed to a particular image of woman between the wars, a cross between the gutsiness of a Claudette Colbert and the English superiority of a Celia Johnson. The image of herself that she created was of an elegantly dressed woman, able to endure unpleasantness with affability, socially skilled – she was always dropping names of members of royal houses on whom she could rely for hospitality wherever she went – and with just the right amount of political awareness.

Forbes's image is in marked contrast to that of her contemporaries, Gertrude Bell and Freya Stark, probably the best-known women travel writers of the century. Both Bell and Stark were fascinated with the Arab world, a fascination that derived not only from a great deal of experience travelling in the Middle East, but also from a sound intellectual base. Gertrude Bell was the first woman to obtain a first-class degree in history from Oxford, in 1888, and worked for a time as an archaeologist, learning both Arabic and Persian. In 1914 she became the first woman to travel into the uncharted heart of the Arabian peninsula. Her books include scholarly studies on archaeological sites and Byzantine architecture and her expertise was taken sufficiently seriously by the British government for her to be appointed as a political adviser in Mesopotamia. By the time of her death in 1926, she had acquired a reputation as a serious figure in Middle Eastern politics.[15]

Similarly, Freya Stark also used her knowledge of ancient languages and experience of travel in the region to assist the British government during the Second World War. Stark was a far more prolific writer than Gertrude Bell, and books such as *The Southern Gates of Arabia: A Journey in the Hadhramat* (1934), *Letters from Syria* (1942), and *Riding to the Tigris* (1959) reflect a wealth of scholarly knowledge, combined with a keen eye for detail, a great deal of empathy, and an ability to write beautiful, often lyrical descriptive prose. For both Gertrude Bell and Freya Stark, the Arab world held an appeal comparable to that which motivated T. E. Lawrence or Wilfred Thesiger. For them, travelling and writing about their travels was not prompted by the kind of populist journalistic motivation that drove Rosita Forbes round the world, but seems to have arisen from a dual process of self-exploration and a desire to inform Anglo-Saxon readers of the wonders of the Arab and Persian worlds.

Journeys to self-awareness

Despite reducing everything to the same level of gossip, banter, and mildly comic anecdote, Rosita Forbes won awards for her travel writing and was elected to a Fellowship of the Royal Geographical Society. She is a very different kind of writer from her contemporary, the Swiss Ella Maillart whose books reflect both physical strength (not for her an elegant outfit and a hired driver, she was an Olympic athlete and unconcerned about her appearance) and an absence of sentimentality. Maillart produced a series of books, from an account of her travels in Russian Turkestan in 1934 to the much more spiritual *The Land of the Sherpas* (1955). Her best-known work is *Forbidden Journey: From Peking to Kashmir* (1937), an account of her journey through the wastes of Chinese Turkestan with the English traveller, Peter Fleming. Maillart and Fleming met by chance in China and decided to travel together. Fleming's version of the journey appeared as *News from Tartary* (1936). His very English book, self-deprecatory and ironic, acts in counterpoint to Maillart's unsentimental version, and taken together, the two books illustrate differences of culture, personality, and gender. Fleming writes as a narrative journalist, commenting wryly on the difficulties of the journey, offering thumbnail sketches of people and places and concluding his book with an ironic anecdote about the snobbery of the British in India. Maillart, on the contrary, is more concerned with writing an account of the cultures through which they travelled, always motivated by a strong sense of curiosity and willing to learn from her experiences.

Women's travel writing in the late twentieth century tends to focus more on the relationship between the individual and the societies through which she travels. Ecological questions, world poverty, and the future of the planet occupy writers such as Dervla Murphy, the seriousness of whose books is belied by the triteness of titles such as *In Ethiopia with a Mule* (1968), *On a Shoestring to Coorg* (1976) or *Muddling Through in Madagascar* (1991). *The Ukimwi Road* (1993), though ostensibly an account of her 3,000-mile journey on a bicycle from Kenya to Zimbabwe, offers a searing indictment of the world's failure to recognise the AIDS epidemic in Central Africa. In 1993 her book on Romania, *Transylvania and Beyond*, exposed the difficulties of a society coming to terms with the end of decades of repressive dictatorship.

Powerful and original voices emerged during the 1990s. Sara Wheeler's *Terra Incognita: Travels in Antarctica* (1997) represents another strand of women's travel writing that has grown in importance in the twentieth century: the journey that leads to greater self-awareness and takes the reader simultaneously on that journey. What characterises writers like Isabella Bird or Rosita Forbes or Fanny Bullock – author of such epic works as *Algerian*

Memories: A Bicycle Tour over the Atlas to the Sahara (1895) and *Through Town and Jungle: Fourteen Thousand Miles A-Wheel Among the Temples and People of the Indian Plain* (1904) – is that despite their enthusiasm and their prolificity, there is very little sense of them growing and developing over the years. The works of Gertrude Bell or Freya Stark, in contrast, reflect personal, social, and political changes, so that the journeys they recount are both inner and outer journeys, towards greater self-awareness as well as greater knowledge gained through experience. Sara Wheeler's book goes a stage further, and recounts a journey not only in terms of time and place, but also in terms of gender relations. She charts the months she spent as a writer in residence on different bases in Antarctica, moving between bases staffed by scientists (most of them male) from different countries. In her account, Antarctica, with its history as the site on which men tested their endurance skills to the limit, offers a particular challenge to a woman. With great skill and elegance, through reported conversations and occasional authorial reflection, Wheeler looks at how different groups stationed on Antarctica reflect the social attitudes of men towards women in different cultures today. Her account of her arrival on the British base, described with irony but also with anger, shows the extent to which she felt unwelcome, in contrast to the warm response from US and European men on other bases: 'Men were coming and going along the corridors, engaged in a variety of activities but united by the fact that they all ignored me. Short of erecting a sign outside the base saying "GO AWAY" they couldn't have made it clearer that I was unwelcome.'[16]

Wheeler's book balances social comment with lyrical description, combined with an awareness of the history of expeditions to the places through which she travels. The mixture of erudition, wit, and personal expression gives her book great power. It is a similar power to that found in probably the greatest woman travel writer of the twentieth century, Jan Morris. It is in the work of Morris that assumptions about travel writing and gender are perhaps most seriously challenged, for Jan Morris began her writing career as James. After publishing a series of successful books between 1956 and 1972, she underwent a sex-change operation and has since published as Jan Morris. Reading the books written before and after 1972 it is impossible to distinguish markers of gender other than occasional references to clothing. What Morris does not do, however, is use the journey as a pretext for reinventing herself or for writing autobiography. In the Foreword to the 1974 edition of her book on Venice that had first appeared in 1960, she explains why she has not felt the need to make changes. She acknowledges that Venice has altered as the world has changed and questions what rôle the city will have in the future. 'I have changed,' she writes, and the full impact of that statement is left to her readers to comprehend. Yet she refuses to rewrite her earlier book:

To refurbish my Venice would be false; to rejuvenate myself would be prepos-
terous. The inessentials of this new edition – the facts and figures, that is – have
been amended. The essentials – the spirit, the feel, the dream of it – I have left
unchanged.[17]

Morris's writing challenges the idea of binary oppositions – between home
and other, present and past, masculine and feminine. She focuses on the
spirit, the feel of a place as she puts it; in other words on the relationship
between the travel writer as individual and the space in which she moves.
Everything else is inessential.

Conclusion

The nineteenth century saw a proliferation of travel accounts by male writers
that overtly sexualised whole areas of the globe, contrasting the 'masculine'
northern regions with the softer, eroticised, feminine Orient. This distinction
is less apparent in women travel writers. Although many strove to create an
image of themselves that emphasised their physical stamina and emulated the
endurance of male counterparts, there is a clear assertion of femininity, either
through attention to details of clothing, accounts of domestic life, or the
inclusion of romantic episodes. The ambiguous attitudes and complex self-
representation reflected in the works of Isabella Bird, May French-Sheldon,
Mrs Alec-Tweedie and countless others mirror the difficulties for women
generally of manoeuvring between the public and private spheres in the age
of empire.

Travel writing is always necessarily a product of a particular time and a
particular culture: the women travellers of the eighteenth century, deemed
to be exceptional, reflected social attitudes towards women's mobility, just
as the need for so many women travel writers to reinvent themselves in the
age of empire derived from their reactions to their position in a hierarchical
society of unequal opportunity. The restlessness of women like Ella Maillart
or Gertrude Bell in the more violent decades of the twentieth century mirrors
the struggle of modernist women trying to find a way of realising themselves
in a changing world.

Yet the sheer diversity of women's travel writing resists simple categorisation. Patterns can be traced: the epistolary travel account, which tends
to be more frequently produced by women, gave way to books targeted at
a specific readership and lines became blurred between the autobiographical,
the anecdotal, and the ethnographic. The search for self-expression and the
reformulation of identity are common elements in the work of many of the
travellers discussed in this essay, but processes of fictionalisation are also

common in the work of many male travel writers. In terms of stylistic features, there is no way that women's travel writing can be differentiated from that of male writers, though a case could perhaps be made for differences in emphasis, in selection of material, in the relationship between the traveller and the putative reader.

As travel writing has increased in popularity, so distinctive sub-genres have emerged. We still have texts that present the narrator as an all-action, heroic figure, though there are also ironic texts narrated by anti-heroes, there are texts full of scholarly detail, and texts consisting of superficial anecdotes and casual conversations, texts retracing the steps of previous travellers, and texts recounting spiritual or mystical experiences. Some of the more successful writers like Colin Thubron or Bruce Chatwin have produced works that are at the same time self-questioning and lyricising, writing in a way often described as 'feminine' that transcends the boundaries between fact and fiction and presents a world coloured by nostalgia for another, imaginary time. Sara Wheeler's books, in contrast, or Dervla Murphy's, are firmly rooted in everyday experience and offer down-to-earth portraits of how they as individuals dealt both with physical hardship and social conscience. Although self-reflexively asserting their gender identity, neither lays any claim to special status or exceptionality. Significantly, in her book about a journey through Chile, *Travels in a Thin Country* (1994), Sara Wheeler pays homage not to earlier women travellers, but to Peter Fleming as her rôle model. Murphy and Wheeler are but two of the women travellers who do not merely look at the places they visit, but are engaged in active exploration on many levels.

Travel writers today are producing texts for an age characterised by increasing interest in concepts of hybridity, an age in which theories of race and ethnicity, once used as means of dividing peoples, are starting to crumble under the pressure of the millions in movement around the world. Once the gaze of the traveller reflected the singularity of a dominant culture; today, the gaze is more likely to be multi-focal, reflecting the demise of a world-view that separated *us* from *them*, and the rôle of women in adjusting perspectives is immense.

NOTES

1 See Graham Dawson, *Soldier Heroes: British Adventure, Empire and the Imagining of Masculinities* (London: Routledge, 1994).

2 The Virago reprints include Isabella Bird, *Journeys in Persia and Kurdistan* (1989), and *A Lady's Life in the Rocky Mountains* (1991); Lucie Duff Gordon, *Letters from Egypt* (1983); Edith Oenone Somerville and Violet Martin Ross, *Through Connemara in a Governess Cart* (1990); Lady Mary Wortley Montagu, *Turkish*

Embassy Letters (1994); and *The Virago Book of Women Travellers*, ed. Mary Morris and Larry O'Connor (1996).

3 Dea Birkett, *Spinsters Abroad. Victorian Lady Explorers* (Oxford: Blackwell, 1989); Leo Hamalian, *Ladies on the Loose: Women Travellers of the Eighteenth and Nineteenth Centuries* (London: Dodd, Mead and Co., 1981); Mary Russell, *The Blessings of a Good, Thick Skirt* (London: Collins, 1988).

4 Jane Robinson, *Wayward Women. A Guide to Women Travellers* (Oxford University Press, 1990).

5 Jane Robinson, *Unsuitable for Ladies. An Anthology of Women Travellers* (Oxford University Press, 1994), p. xii.

6 Sara Mills, *Discourses of Difference* (London: Routledge, 1991), p. 21.

7 See the new edition, Tracey Jean Boisseau, ed., *Sultan to Sultan: Adventures Among the Masai and Other Tribes of East Africa by May French-Sheldon, Bebe Bwana* (Manchester University Press, 1999), p. 59.

8 Cheryl McEwan, *Gender, Geography and Empire: Victorian Women Travellers in East Africa* (Aldershot: Ashgate, 2000), p. 9.

9 George Sandys, *Sandys Travails Containing a History of the Originall and Present State of the Turkish Empire: Their Laws, Government Policy, Military Force, Courts of Justice, and Commerce* (London: Printed by Richard Cotes for John Sweeting, 1652), p. 54.

10 Gillian Rose, *Feminism and Geography: The Limits of Geographical Knowledge* (Oxford: Polity Press, 1993).

11 Isabella Bird, *A Lady's Life in the Rocky Mountains* (London: John Murray, 1879), prefatory note.

12 W. F. Cater, ed., *Love Among the Butterflies. The Travels and Adventures of a Victorian Lady, Margaret Fountaine* (London: Collins, 1980), p. 21.

13 Mrs Alec-Tweedie, *An Adventurous Journey (Russia-Siberia-China)* (London: Hutchinson, 1928), p. 284.

14 Charles Lewis Meryon, ed., *Memoirs of Lady Hester Stanhope...* (1845), 3 vols.

15 Gertrude Bell, *The Desert and the Sown* (1907) and *Amurath to Amurath* (1911). See also Billie Melman's essay (Chapter 6).

16 Sara Wheeler, *Terra Incognita: Travels in Antarctica* (London: Cape, 1996), p. 195.

17 Jan Morris, *Venice* (London: Faber and Faber, 1974), p. 12.

14

JOAN PAU RUBIÉS

Travel writing and ethnography

The ethnographic impulse

The description of peoples, their nature, customs, religion, forms of government, and language, is so embedded in the travel writing produced in Europe after the sixteenth century that one assumes ethnography to be essential to the genre. In England this assumption became part of the justification for the most representative form of this writing, the travel collections published from the sixteenth to the nineteenth centuries. Already in 1577 one of the first of these collectors, Richard Willes, had announced that all branches of learning have their 'special times' of flourishing, and 'now' was the time of geography. In Renaissance learning geography, or cosmography, acted as an encyclopaedic synthesis for the description of the world. Therefore, the description of peoples became the empirical foundation for a general rewriting of 'natural and moral history' within a new cosmography made possible by the navigations of the period. As Awnsham and John Churchill wrote in the preface to their 1704 *Collection of Voyages and Travels*:

> What was Cosmography before these discoveries, but an imperfect fragment of science, scarce deserving so good a name? ... But now Geography and Hydrography have received some perfection by the pains of so many mariners and travellers ... Natural and Moral History is embellished with the most beneficial increase of so many thousands of plants ... drugs and spices ... beasts, birds and fishes ... minerals, mountains and waters ... [and] such unaccountable diversities of climates and men, and in them complexions, tempers, habits, manners, politicks and religions ...[1]

The concept of a 'moral' history (moral as involving human rational capacities) had been clearly defined in the sixteenth century by writers like the Spanish Jesuit José de Acosta, in the title of his influential *Natural and Moral History of the Indies* (1590, translated into English in 1604). Although Acosta was a missionary working within the Spanish Empire, his American scientific project had humanist roots and could therefore cut across the growing national or religious divisions within Europe, informing, for example, Samuel Purchas, the most influential English travel collector of the seventeenth century. In the preface to *Purchas his Pilgrimes* (1625) he explained that, amongst the vast material of natural and human history he had omitted the most common and dry, selecting either 'rarities of nature' or accounts of non-European (and 'remote' European) peoples. It was the moral element, 'things humane', and in particular 'varieties of men and humane affaires', which he emphasised.[2]

The description of peoples in their variety was one of the most valued parts of the narratives of travel that proliferated after the Renaissance, both for the entertainment value of the depiction of curious behaviour, and for the philosophical issues which this evidence for variety raised about the existence, or not, of universal human traits. However, not all historical forms of territorial imperialism, or trade-related colonialism, have created such a corpus of descriptive accounts. The European ethnographic impulse was the product of a unique combination of colonial expansion and intellectual transformation. Although the emergence of an academic discourse based on comparison, classification, and historical lineage called ethnology is a nineteenth-century phenomenon, in reality both ethnography and ethnology existed within the humanistic disciplines of early modern Europe in the primary forms of travel writing, cosmography, and history, which often informed specific debates – about the capabilities and origins of the American Indians, the definition of 'natural man', the influence of climate on national characteristics, or the existence of stages in the history of civilisation. On the back of the growth of travel writing both ethnography and ethnology were, in fact, crucial to the Enlightenment project of a world-historical science of mankind. However, in the earlier centuries of European expansion, travel writing generated ethnography as a matter of course, quite independently from any specific intellectual agenda (although, arguably, from the end of the sixteenth century, ethnological concerns sometimes lay behind the ethnographic impulse). Despite the variety of forms of travel writing, it may be possible to generalise that the desire for information, for mainly practical purposes, lies behind the growth of the European genre of non-fictional travel writing throughout the Renaissance. The problem of the nature of ethnographic knowledge, so important for modern anthropology, did not often seem crucial to its earlier European practitioners, who simply went ahead with descriptions of varying levels of quality and originality, but the question remains central to any critical discussion of the historical growth of ethnography.

Ethnography and the genres of travel writing

Travel writing, the varied body of writing that takes travel as an essential condition of its production, appears in so many forms that it is best defined in its plurality. Ethnography is central to some forms, clearly secondary to others, and sometimes entirely absent. For example, in accounts of Francis Drake's voyages, English attacks on the Spanish colonies were the main issue, and occasional encounters with Indians are scarcely mentioned. By contrast, the merchants who as factors were responsible for the earlier activities of the East India Company were encouraged to keep a diary in which the events of the journey were often interspersed with passages describing the lands and peoples encountered. In some cases this kind of description written by merchants abandoned its narrow commercial focus and grew to become an entire treatise, roughly systematic, on a country and its inhabitants. Two notable early examples are Edmund Scott's description of Java (1606), appended to the journal of his sojourn in Bantam, and the 'relation' of Golconda written by William Methwold for Samuel Purchas (1626). For some of the better educated observers who wrote for their own purposes, curiosity was paramount, and their accounts, in their depiction of foreign nations, or of the remains of past civilisations, were shaped by the new antiquarian scholarship of the seventeenth century.

There is of course a rationale behind different levels of ethnographic focus. Whilst there was much ethnography in travel journals or in personal narratives of adventurous journeys, perhaps the most fundamental form was the 'relation', a synthetic descriptive account which could be narrative or analytical and which throughout the sixteenth century was widely used by Iberian and Italian writers as a vehicle for geographical (and occasionally historical) information concerning their discoveries in Africa, America, and Asia. The genre had its origin in the 'relations' written by Venetian ambassadors, and was also adopted by the Monarchy of Spain for its colonial administration and by the Jesuits in their far-flung missions. It became the foundation stone for the great cosmographies of the period, from Giovanni Botero's *Relationi Universali* in the 1590s (soon translated into English as *The Traveller's Breviat*) to Purchas, Botero's English-Protestant counterpart, who titled his first work *Purchas his Pilgrimage, or Relations of the World and the Religions Observed in all Ages and Places* (1613).

William Methwold's account of Golconda can stand as an example of how a relation could constitute a vehicle for a traveller's ethnography. It dissociated his observations from the account of his journey, and sought to provide a systematic treatment of a kingdom. The relation is organised geographically, following the coast of the Bay of Bengal to identify each kingdom or port of interest.[3] Focusing on Golconda (in modern Andhra Pradesh), Methwold first describes the king, his religion and customs, enemies, revenues, castles, and captains. This description is noteworthy for introducing the idea of royal dominion over the whole country, 'for this king, as all others in India, is the only free-holder', with a pyramidal system of prebendalism which resulted in enormous fiscal oppression for 'the countrey people'. Effectively, we have here the seed of the idea of oriental despotism. Methwold continues then by distinguishing the religion of the dominant élite (Muslim) and that of the people ('gentiles or heathens', that is Hindu), noting especially the principle of religious tolerance which prevailed: 'religion is heere free, and no man's conscience oppressed with ceremony or observance' (p. 12). The description of 'gentile' religion is full and includes comments on morality and a detailed description of the caste system. The relation then continues with social aspects like marriages, satis, children, and birth, finally to mention the dress and physical features of the natives. This is completed by some economic information. Methwold's account is not particularly orderly, but as it was written specifically for Purchas's collection by a merchant with many years of experience in India, it offers an excellent example of the thematic variety that a geographical 'relation' was understood to encompass, even by someone not formally educated at university.

Methwold described a kingdom as an alternative system of civilisation and religion, not 'savages' without 'law or religion'. The description of uncivilised barbarians was however important for the English colonial enterprise in modern North America. This took place relatively late if we consider earlier Spanish, Portuguese, or even some French material, and this belatedness in some ways facilitated the integration of ethnography with humanist training. An influential example is the *Briefe and True Report of the New Found Land of Virginia* (1590) by Thomas Harriot, a tutor in mathematical sciences under Ralegh's patronage, who worked together with the artist John White to produce an ethnography which was as visual as it was literary.[4] The report (equivalent to a 'relation') was meant to be an initial sketch only, in fact a promotional tract extracted from a more ambitious natural-historical survey of the colony planned in Virginia. This coloured the positive image which it offered of both the land and the Algonquian tribes which inhabited it. Despite its brevity, Harriot's report displayed an unusual ethnological depth.

In effect the genre of travel writing moved from the primary account of the traveller (a journal, a synthetic relation, or another document) written for a variety of practical purposes, to the more elaborate versions of the historian or cosmographer, dealing, respectively, with an account of particular events organised chronologically, or with the description of the world organised geographically. As can be gathered, history and cosmography were not entirely

12. 'A cheiff Lorde of Roanoac'. Perhaps the most interesting aspect of Thomas Harriot's *Briefe and True Report of the New Found Land of Virginia* as published by Theodor de Bry (1590), and featuring engravings based on John White's original drawings, was the attempt 'to showe how that the inhabitants of the great Bretannie have bin in times past as savage as those of Virginia' by offering images of ancient Picts alongside those of the Indians. The idea, implying not only the full human capacity of the natives, however savage, but also the actuality of a historical process of ascent to civilisation, was soon dominant in European ethnology, since it fitted with the biblical assumption that all men descended from Adam. What we see here is how already in the early reports ethnography sometimes became ethnology.

separate genres. From Peter Martyr and Oviedo in the sixteenth century to William Robertson and Abbé Raynal in the eighteenth, quite often the classi-cally educated historians of navigation, conquest, or colonisation (including Jesuit missionaries like Acosta) conceived their task comprehensively, includ-ing a geographical, economic, and ethnographic summary as part of their work. Indeed, education in the humanist disciplines provided a fundamen-tal resource for the transformation of practical descriptions into a variety of more philosophically oriented discourses. One could in fact interpret the development of scientific ethnology as the consequence of an intense and sustained interaction between these two kinds of ethnographic practitioners, popular and erudite. Between the primary accounts of travel and the more elaborate productions of cosmographers and historians, other sub-genres

13. 'The trvve picture of one Picte', from *Briefe and True Report of the New Found Land of Virginia* (1590).

flourished, like the letter, often adopted by the more erudite travellers (used by Lady Montagu when describing the Ottomans), or even the dialogue, which allowed for a reasoned consideration of debatable issues (such as when Edmund Spenser offered his views about the best policy to follow with the 'wild' Irish). At its most extreme, the systematic traveller-ethnographer published 'researches' about a contentious issue, be it the origin and nature of the American Indians, the existence or not of oriental despotism, or the explanation for cultural diversity.

A fruitful way of approaching the issue of the rôle of ethnography within the plurality of travel writing is to consider a variety of 'types of traveller', as they developed in Europe from the Middle Ages to modern times. Many of the earlier travel accounts were written by pilgrims, and although the re-ligious aims of the genre did not in principle seem to give much scope for ethnographic curiosity, from the late Middle Ages the Middle Eastern back-ground to the Holy Sites often displaced pure religious contemplation as the main focus of the narrative. For example, Mandeville's highly influential compilation was a cosmographical pilgrimage, in which the contemplation of the marvels of the world, with strange races of men, fabulous kings, and religious diversity, served as rhetorical counterpoint to the need for spiritual reform within Latin Christianity. The strategy of turning pilgrimage into cosmography was not confined to fictionalised works, but reflected a deep trend towards empirical curiosity within European travel writing, so that, for example, many of the educated gentlemen writers of the seventeenth cen-tury – writers like George Sandys in his *A Relation of a Journey . . .* (1615) – in effect transformed a pilgrimage to the Holy Sites into a 'Grand Tour' of the East, often combining ethnography with antiquarianism.

Whilst pilgrimage was thus transformed, missionaries grew in importance, and some of the earliest, more solid ethnographies were written by men whose main purpose was the conversion of gentiles to Christianity. Whilst a trader could make do with a minimal amount of cultural curiosity, for a missionary it was necessary to learn languages and interpret the roots of various systems of belief and behaviour. The suppression of religious orders within the Protestant churches often meant that English missionary labours lagged behind Catholic initiatives, spectacularly active in the early phases of the expansion of Europe, but Hakluyt and Purchas were both clerics, and English Protestants did play a rôle in a variety of attempts to convert, or at least to interpret, religious diversity. An example is Henry Lord's *Display of Two Forraigne Sects in the East Indies* (1630), one of the earliest accounts of the 'gentile' religions of Asia. To supplement these sparse efforts, quite often the British relied for their religious ethnography on foreign translations, like Abbé Dubois's *Description of the Character, Manners and Customs of the*

People of India (1817), in reality based on Jesuit materials. In addition, many Anglican clerics, as chaplains, recorded the activities of overseas trading and even corsair expeditions, like the immensely popular account (for essentially nationalistic reasons) of *A Voyage Round the World in the Years 1740–4 by George Anson* (1748), compiled by Richard Walter as the 'official' version of this late incursion against Spanish colonial trade. It was, however, in the nineteenth century that missionary societies had the strongest impact, both in the shaping of how the British Empire dealt with natives in Africa, Asia, and the Pacific, and in the production of travel accounts based on years of intimate contact. Thus some of the best ethnographic descriptions of, for example, the Polynesian islanders, are the work of missionaries like William Ellis (*Polynesian Researches*, 1829) or Thomas Williams (*Fiji and the Fijians*, 1858) in the Pacific.

Compared with these 'religious' travellers, merchants and sailors – writers like William Methwold – produced many more accounts, although they were often superficial. At his most systematic, however, a writer like Jan Huyghen van Linschoten (writing in Dutch but translated into English as early as 1598) could be extremely informative. His *Discours of Voyages into the East and West Indies* offered a fairly comprehensive picture of the Portuguese East as it stood in the 1580s, with a great deal of native ethnography as well as a sharp image of Indo-Portuguese society. It is striking that by the end of the sixteenth century a Catholic, European-dominated society in India could be a primary focus of ethnographic attention, acting as 'other' to non-Portuguese observers alongside more exotic 'natives'.

Successive British imperial projects would produce generations of explorers and surveyors with aims both commercial and scientific, including Cook's Pacific journeys and the great Victorian expeditions to Africa. The quality of ethnographic research, however, remained variable. For all its claims to precision and unprejudiced observation, the naturalist science of the eighteenth century was often conditioned by ideological debates in which scientific and philosophical pretensions seemed to work against common sense, so that native peoples may emerge as carefree noble savages or childish, sexually weak American Indians, often unrecognisable to more experienced observers.[5] In some cases it is possible to separate the sober description of the sailor from the elaboration of the professional writer, as when Hawkesworth undertook to 'write up' the official account of Cook's first voyage, often rationalising the audience's responses to the evidence of, for example, an alternative sexual moral code in the islands of Tahiti.[6] But even Cook himself, despite his care to record details when describing rituals he knew he did not quite understand, was conditioned, in his occasional judgements, by a mild, pragmatic humanitarianism. Thus his sympathy for the natives went only as far as the 'friendly' Tahitians lived up to certain European assumptions about what nature would dictate to morality – perhaps some promiscuity amongst the young, but certainly not when transformed into a religious ethos and (even worse) combined with systematic infanticide.[7]

The emergence of 'scientific ethnology' under the impact of evolutionary theories in the nineteenth century did not seem to help either. Arguably in this latter phase of European imperialism, the active ideology of geographical discovery – a genuine passion for filling blank spaces in an ever more de-tailed map of the world, exemplified by travel writers like Richard Burton – coexisted with the formation of increasingly contemptuous and rigid racial stereotypes. For a naturalist like Alfred Russel Wallace, who to his credit spent eight years in the Malay islands attempting to classify natives (along-side plants and animals) by learning languages and through direct observa-tion, there was no doubt that a very interventionist colonial paternalism was the only means by which the various 'races of savages', by themselves unin-terested in progress, could be prompted to cover the necessary stages between 'barbarism and civilisation'. Paradoxically, Wallace's method of classification in *The Malay Archipelago* (1869) of what he saw as profound racial differ-ences was highly subjective – not according to language families, the more usual cultural marker, but rather through the identification of two synthetic types, the 'impassive Malay' and the 'impulsive Papuan', which distributed themselves alongside geo-zoological lines. Thus the lower human races were so temperamentally rather than physically. Through natural selection, oper-ating at the level of culture, the more savage and independent-minded would inevitably become extinct after being colonised by the superior white races.

The blatantly imperialistic assumptions of many nineteenth-century travel writers stand in contrast with the nuanced portrayal of native courts often displayed by early modern ambassadors. For writers like Thomas Roe in India, there could have been a sense in which Christianity was assumed as the only true religion, oriental kings were somewhat despotic, and European navigation and firearms seemed superior, but there was no overall sense of an overwhelming European cultural, let alone ethnic, superiority domi-nating their narratives. Rather, the Muslim and gentile civilisations of the East represented highly sophisticated and often admirable systems of power with which the British Crown, on behalf of its subjects, sought peaceful trade agreements from a position of relative vulnerability. A similar set of assumptions – the existence of various degrees of civilisation, in which Europeans found some things to admire from foreign nations – underlay the intense curiosity towards the variety of human customs, religions, and sys-tems of government of the most influential observers which emerged in the seventeenth century, those independent travellers with antiquarian interests who toured the more distant regions of the world with sometimes genuine cosmopolitan passion.

The last type of traveller-ethnographer to be considered is the modern professional anthropologist, particularly important in the first decades of the twentieth century, as the scientific enterprise of understanding the, by then fast-fading, native cultures became an academic discipline in the twilight of European imperialism. In fact anthropology derived much of its ethnographic tradition from the work of naturalists, missionaries, and independent travellers of the previous three centuries. Bronislaw Malinowski's claim that scientific ethnography had only begun recently with professionals who, like himself, combined the direct collection of evidence with personal inferences about the hidden rules of social behaviour, is highly unfair to many earlier writers, whose explanations might have been simpler, but not so the methods.[8] From the perspective of a history of travel writing the importance of the idea of ethnographic fieldwork is, more modestly, that it regularised under a scientific ideal many of the circumstances and attitudes which had determined the quality of earlier observations. Linguistic competence, years of intimate interaction, and the need to accept a local system of power which was largely beyond the observer's control, were requisites for good ethnography, sometimes quite independently of theoretical sophistication. This is why many of the earlier travel accounts of men who resided overseas for many years could contain valid ethnography: not for the implicit and often derogatory assumptions they made about other religions, but for the often surprising capacity to describe empirically a functioning social and political system with its hidden rules and agendas, without necessarily passing judgement.

Ethnographic rhetoric and cultural translation

The history of ethnography in travel writing can thus be written as the history of the emergence of a basic set of analytical categories, expressed in different genres and languages, and of the changes in emphasis and assumptions within those languages. An example of continuity is the recurrent interest shown by various writers in topics like political order, including kingship, aristocracies, warfare, and justice; national, or racial, temperaments; economic activities, including (when applicable) cities and trade; religion, in particular the more exoteric aspects (rituals, festivals, idols and temples, religious élites); marriage, women, and sexuality; dress, or nudity, and ornamentation; habits of eating and hygiene; language and oral rhetoric; literature and science; technology, navigation, and other arts. The presence or not of each one of these particular categories of course varied, in part because not all were equally applicable to different societies, but it is remarkable that many were already present in Marco Polo's descriptions of Asia, and would continue to dominate the ethnography of travel writing until the twentieth century.

Significant changes had less to do with 'what to describe' than with emphases of interpretation and the emergence of newly dominant scientific concepts and ideological paradigms. We may, for example, contrast the priority of religious classifications for much of the early modern period, and the concomitant emphasis on anthropological monogenism and cultural diffusionism that Christian theology encouraged, with the emergence of racial theories in the nineteenth century; or the prevalence of climatic over genetic interpretations of national temperament (but not necessarily of physical diversity) also in the early modern period. We may also note the growth of the idea of natural religion between 1650 and 1750, and the parallel strengthening of the secular concept of civilisation, from the rather vaguely defined assumption of sixteenth-century writers to the sophisticated, historically informed theories of the Enlightenment. Finally, the concept of 'barbarism', or 'savagism', changed considerably, as the idea of man living innocently 'in a state of nature' rose and fell not once, but many times, variously informed by a Christian humanist nostalgia for a golden age, antiquarian curiosity for the remote past of mankind, sceptical and enlightened criticisms of the arrogance and corruption of European civilisation, theories about the origins and legitimacy of the state, utopian thought, romantic relativism, and various forms of imperialism and counter-imperialism.

A fundamental task in the analysis of the evolution of the genre is explaining the relationship between the 'spontaneous ethnographies' of ill-educated observers and the complex theories of more educated writers engaged in moral, philosophical, or scientific debate. The observations of Robert Knox, a sailor of the East India Company captive for almost twenty years in the kingdom of Kandy, may never have amounted to much, had he not been stimulated to write his *Historical Relation of the Island of Ceylon* (1681) by men like Robert Hooke, secretary of the Royal Society, and assisted in 'methodising' (that is to say, organising) his information around a number of conventional thematic categories by his cousin John Strype, a cleric with antiquarian interests.[9] One of the most striking sub-genres of the early modern period were sets of instructions for travellers to record what they saw in a methodical fashion, through a number of 'heads' which could vary in emphasis but which tended to reflect those same categories already present in the most systematic travel narratives of the period. These 'methods' for travellers emerged in the late sixteenth century as an expression of the new naturalistic emphasis which dominated humanist, post-Aristotelian dialectics.

They were applied to the Grand Tour no less than to colonial ventures, and although often conceived as politically useful in both European and colonial settings, they also soon came to provide the fundamental intellectual tool that allowed men of science to enlist the help of a multitude of observers in the creation of a fresh universal encyclopaedia. Thus methods for travellers were behind much of Hakluyt's rôle in advising voyages of discovery, appeared central to Francis Bacon's vision for a new, thorough, inductive scientific enterprise, and eventually became one of the characteristic concerns of the Royal Society, from its inception to the great 'scientific' voyages of the eighteenth century.[10] It was in fact in England where these methods (originally a continental idea) were elaborated and published more consistently.

These methods did not always change the common language of ethnography, which remained largely spontaneous, but they contributed to generalising a desire for systematicity and precision. Above all, they inscribed the travel narrative within a scientific project in which more theoretical issues could be discussed. However, the possible superficiality of travellers when describing other cultures was rarely seen as an issue. The very structure of these methods encouraged touching upon all relevant subjects and perhaps taking account of previous narratives, but not addressing 'cultural interpretation' as a problem. It was therefore up to individual observers to bring their own education, experience, and intelligence to their ethnographic practices. The problem here is less any lack of desire for scientific objectivity than the difficulty and sometimes the reluctance of many travellers to engage with native languages, belief systems, and literary traditions. For those with a long experience living overseas amongst non-Europeans, typically missionaries like William Ellis, ideological commitments (in his case religious) could block the possibility of a sensitive interpretation of the cultural logic underlying customs and ways of life which could otherwise be described (often within the same narrative) with extreme care and even a tone of detached neutrality.[11] For less committed observers, the challenge was obtaining the intimate familiarity with another culture which only odd contexts (like a long captivity) could provide. Europeans living abroad as Europeans, especially if in a dominant position in relation to natives, were unlikely to become great cultural decoders unless motivated by a particular scientific passion. Even then, given that the categories of analysis, with the language of the narratives, were defined in a European setting, it was unlikely that many observers would find ways of letting the 'native voice' be heard.

Despite these difficulties, there is evidence of a variety of efforts of 'cultural translation' through comparative analogies (however misleading on many occasions), by the use of native sources for historical antiquarian research, or through linguistically sensitive research.[12] For example, a number of travellers noted that many of the languages spoken by illiterate natives (like Ellis's Polynesians) were of great complexity, often in ways that defied categorisation in European languages, and the importance of oral rhetoric amongst 'barbarians' was repeatedly noted and emphasised. An example of the way language could become central to ethnography is Roger Williams, whose *A Key into the Language of America* (1643), in effect an account of the Algonquian language of the Narragansett Indians (of modern Rhode Island), appears remarkably self-reflective within the context of New England. Although committed like his contemporaries to bringing 'civilitie' and 'Christianitie' to the natives of America, the radical Protestant Williams offered an ethnographic approach which did not see native culture from outside, as an object of study, but rather offered evidence of conversation and dialogue, letting Indian voices, with their questions as well as their beliefs, come across. He made it clear that there were two perspectives on the encounter:

> Their names are of two sorts: first, those of the English giving, as Natives, Salvages, Indians, Wildmen (so the Dutch call them Wilden), Abergeny men, Pagans, Barbarians, Heathen. Secondly, their names which they give themselves. I cannot observe that they ever had, before the coming of the English, French or Dutch amongst them, any names to difference themselves from strangers, for they knew none; but two sorts of names they had, and have amongst themselves. First general, belonging to all natives, as Nínnuock, Ninnimissinnúwock, Eniskeetompaúwog, which signifies men, folke, or people; secondly, particular names, peculiar to severall nations...[13]

In Williams's *Key* a vocabulary organised ethnography, whilst systematic ethnological analysis was treated summarily and rather inconclusively in a few heads, by way of prologue. Although this linguistic key was conceived as a flexible tool, for the practical needs of the English traveller and colonist, as trader, missionary, or in any other capacity, it also echoed a serious concern with the uncertain possibility of conversion. Williams's unusual intimacy with the Indians was in reality a consequence of his profound discomfort with the lack of religious authenticity and moral coherence of his own society, which had led to his voluntary 'exile' into wilderness.

Perhaps the more interesting case of 'native voice' is when the non-European became sufficiently anglicised to write his own travel narrative. In some cases, like the abolitionist autobiography *The Interesting Narrative of the Life of Olaudah Equiano, or Gustavus Vassa the African, Written by Himself* (1789), the vision of a remote childhood in Africa, was inevitably quite fictionalised. In other cases, like the former Indian sepoy's *Travels of*

Dean Mahomet (1794), the native (a Bengali Muslim) who once served the East India Company and now has successfully settled in Britain, travels back, with his pen, to his original country. Mahomet, writing conventional letters in exquisite English for a British audience, observes the Gangetic plain, or more accurately 'remembers' it, with European-like eyes, as a retainer and then officer in a British army. Even though the traveller is at root an insider (at least within his Muslim military socio-professional group, less so when describing Hindus), the ethnographic genre is here more European than oriental, not relying on the existence of an independent tradition of Arabic-Persian ethnography in India, but adopting European literary conventions and leaning on British Orientalist scholarship and other travel accounts to complement his own memories. Dean Mahomet can of course be very sympathetic to the virtues of Indian Muslims, and insightful about their beliefs, but he seems fully to share the imperial vision of his British patrons and describes the army's brutal exactions on a resistant countryside without flinching – he was himself in charge of provisioning the troops and dispersing 'unruly natives'. It was thus the culture of the Company's army which shaped his vision. The identity of the 'voice' of the traveller is for all these reasons complex – the result of a cross-over in which the Indian traveller, to Europe and then back to his memories, has made the European discourse his own.[14]

Ethnography and politics

The fundamental issue about the political dimension of the description of other peoples in travel writing is determining the extent to which ethnography and ethnology were essentially a justification, or a tool, for empire. In some cases the evidence is clear enough. When Edmund Spenser argues through his mouthpiece Irenius in *A View of the State of Ireland* (c.1597) that a number of Irish customs are 'repugnant to the good government of the realme', it is obvious that it was mainly for the benefit of an English dominion of dubious legitimacy that this 'good government' was being defined, since the Irish did not clearly wish to be brought by force and through loss of liberty from 'licentious barbarisme' to 'the love of goodnes and civilitie'. Thus the Irish traditional means of clothing, the mantle, is 'a fit house for an outlaw, a meet bed for a rebel, and an apt cloke for a theife' – that is, it empowers the Irish against the English and thus must be forbidden.[15]

But to reduce ethnography to this kind of imperialism would be crude and misleading. As we have seen, many travel writers engaged in ethnography for other purposes. Even ethnographic works clearly written under the shadow of growing British imperialism could be impressively systematic and neutral, or even sympathetic, in tone. Finally, the considerable evidence of imperialist uses and assumptions within the ethnographic discourse of travel writing must be set against not a small number of ethnographies which were anti-imperialist in general intent. Some of these romanticised natives, others deplored their fate after contact with Europeans, others finally, without necessarily admiring 'the other', stressed the profound differences, perhaps even the incommensurability, between different cultural systems. The classic example of romanticisation is the image of the 'noble savage' which dominated debate amongst 'philosophes' for much of the eighteenth century, and which in the English experience found its most significant expression in accounts of the Pacific Islanders. In French writers like Montaigne, Rousseau, and Diderot the positive image of the savage as natural man, although based on the evidence of actual travel writers, and even personal interviews with natives taken to Europe, was largely rhetorical or at most speculative. The case of Rousseau is the most revealing, since in his *Discourse on the Origins of Inequality* (1755) he misunderstood or neglected many of his sources so as to draw a simple, anti-ethnographic distinction between happy savages and corrupt civilisation. It was indeed the criticism of the costs and limitations of civilisation, and of European civilisation in particular, which motivated these authors. This does not however mean that the love of the 'uncontaminated' native – that is, the love of the other as pure other – could not have some basis in genuine admiration for concrete forms of observed behaviour. When the American painter George Catlin wrote of the wild and warlike Indians of the plains, with whom he spent so many years, that their high ideals of pride and honour were pursued through extreme prudence and self-denial, he was not simply projecting the desire for 'otherness' of the civilised man sitting in his study.[16] If from a modern, globalised perspective the desire for cultural purity seems to imply a romantic reification of non-European cultures as static, isolated systems, it is also the case that actual historical distances were all too real when, for over more than three centuries, Europeans encountered peoples with whom no direct contact had previously been possible.

It is therefore important not to reduce the terms of the analysis to the dichotomy between a European ethnography assuming cultural superiority and a variety of 'barbarians'. Images of civilised non-Europeans are of particular importance in this respect. A good example of 'orientalist denigration' is the way the account of Anson's voyage depicted the Chinese as deceitful, cowardly, and corrupted by an innate addiction to lucre, in an almost literary caricature of national temperament which served to present the intrusive English in an heroic light.[17] But equally significant is the way travel writing in the same century generated a debate about non-European, non-Christian civilisation. Anson's image of China inaugurated in fact a negative phase in European attitudes towards the Chinese, which must be set against the more positive image offered by Jesuit missionaries in previous years. Montesquieu used the evidence of Anson's voyage to elaborate his concept of oriental despotism in *The Spirit of the Laws* (1748), specifically including the Chinese within the model of a system of stifling arbitrary rule opposed to the more admirable European principles of political liberty, private property, and civil law. But of course not all participants in the Enlightenment agreed with Montesquieu's idea of a general system of oriental despotism, and further debate ensued. The French antiquarian Anquetil-Duperron thus travelled to the East to demolish Montesquieu (*Législation Orientale*, 1778).

What this shows is that the existence of a debate about the nature of non-European (and European) politics is a more relevant fact than any one particular view. It also shows that the relationship between the traveller's observations abroad and the use made of these in Europe by theologians, political scientists, and ethnologists was not one of simple identity, nor always one of manipulation and adulteration, but rather one of interaction. Montesquieu not only relied on travellers' accounts as sources of evidence: he also found in writers like François Bernier sophisticated arguments comparing the political, economic, and religious systems of Europe and Asia, which contained the seeds of the theory of despotism. If, therefore, the traveller was not simply a source of information, but also of analytical developments, it is not sufficient to look at how 'spontaneous ethnographies' informed the work of European writers: we must also consider how, increasingly, travellers departed Europe with a sense of the existence of debates to which they could contribute.

Ethnography as science

Whilst the importance of political concerns in shaping ethnography seems clear enough, it is perhaps the scientific ideal which in retrospect seems more crucial in determining the ethnographic impulse. European travellers, by recording their observations of other lands and peoples, became essential contributors to the growth of a new, empirically informed discourse about both man and nature. The institutionalisation of this new science through books and reviews, learned academies and journals, and at the universities, owed a great deal to the world of travellers and travel writing. The Royal Society of London offers many examples of interest in travel accounts as part of its promotion of natural knowledge. The crucial distinction is that between the practical ethnographical 'science' of merchants, navigators, missionaries, and colonial administrators, on the one hand, and the emergence of an academic discipline of scientific anthropology, on the other.

The first preceded the other, accompanied it, and was finally buried by it. The story is worth summing up. First, spontaneous ethnographers like William Methwold, Roger Williams, or Robert Knox, originally aiming at the needs of traders and colonisers, were seen to contribute, or even asked to contribute by men like Purchas or Hooke, to the emergence of a new history of man. They offered the bricks with which cosmographers and historians would build their intellectual edifices. Then traveller-philosophers like Bernier, or naturalists like Joseph Banks and Alexander von Humboldt, undertook to travel mainly to satisfy intellectual needs, sometimes simply carrying along their own education and curiosity, but often also taking abroad precise intellectual aims backed with systematic readings and carefully drawn instructions. The great romantic traveller-scientists who followed were benevolent gentlemen-imperialists like Thomas Raffles, using a combination of power and erudition to rationally 'improve' the lot of lower civilisations, or heroic adventurers like Burton or Wallace, casting away the security of bourgeois conventions and stepping beyond the boundaries of European dominion in order to search for the remotest manifestations of human and natural diversity, the most savage peoples, or the source of the Nile. Finally, as ethnography became a branch of an academic discipline, the observations of merchants or gentlemen-travellers could be dismissed as superficial or irrelevant. The gaze deepened, the field narrowed, the traveller was left alone.

An interesting and early example of this shift is Robert Louis Stevenson's *In the South Seas* (1896), written when the basic task of compiling the ethnography of the Pacific had already been accomplished. Stevenson no longer depicted natives as 'natural men' in a state of careless happiness, or even as 'men to be converted and civilised', but rather as peoples in irreversible decline: 'change of habit is bloodier than bombardment'.[18] However, more symptomatic (and disturbing) than Stevenson's need to transcend the ethnography of the native as 'pure other' is the reaction of the public, which expected Stevenson's book to be about romance and personal feelings, rather than a moralistic ethnography of native transformation. It is as if, having conquered with the ship, the gun, and the mind the most remote regions and peoples of the world, European curiosity had begun to die, requesting instead pure entertainment, in the form of identifiable passions, from the travel account.

Up to the period between the two World Wars there was a steady increase in ethnographic curiosity and standards, as part of a process of expansion which saw also the creation of a Western identity centred on the idea of modernity. This process seems to have reached a breaking point with the twentieth-century split between the 'professional' ethnography of the anthropologist and the literary late-romantic or post-romantic travel writer, given to subjective musings rather than to conventional and systematic observation. In the latter decades of the century, however, both, well established in their separate posts, seemed to find themselves in a deep crisis. As the encyclopaedia of natural and human history was being completed and, through decolonisation, formal empire shrank, the period following the Second World War generated a new condition which seriously affected the role of ethnography within travel writing. In some ways ethnography has been made increasingly irrelevant, although it may be more precise to say that its focus has changed. Globalisation, and the gradual extinction of the privileged field for the anthropologist, the pure, uncontaminated primitive tribe, has created a blurring of cultural traditions which requires redefining the whole enterprise as, precisely, a description of this blurring and annihilation. There is therefore much potential for the ethnographic analysis of varieties of cultural hybridisation, under the umbrella of a process of globalisation largely defined in Western terms. Those travellers who still care to be traditional ethnographers, on the other hand, may need to seek the remotest parts in a late-romantic quest in which the native can still be inserted as an 'other', object of scrutiny and self-reflection, horror and admiration, and ultimately as a mirror of our own humanity. But for how long, we must ask ourselves, will this be possible?

NOTES

1 A. and J. Churchill, eds., *A Collection of Voyages and Travels* ... (London, 1704), p. lxxiii.
2 *Purchas his Pilgrimes* (London: W. Stansby, for H. Fetherstone, 1625), 'To the reader'.
3 Methwold's account, originally published by Purchas in 1626, was edited by W. H. Moreland, *Relations of Golconda in the Early Seventeenth Century* (London: Hakluyt Society, 1931).
4 Although Harriot's report was published in English in 1588, the 1590 Latin edition by De Bry was the first to include the engravings based on White's pictures. The originals have been edited by Paul Hulton and David B. Quinn, *The American Drawings of John White*, 2 vols. (London: British Museum, 1964).
5 Famously, Thomas Jefferson's views on the 'normality' of the Virginian Indians (including the size of genitals), against the views of 'natural inferiority' expressed by Buffon. See Antonello Gerbi, *The Dispute of the New World. The History of a Polemic 1750–1900* trans. Jeremy Moyle (Pittsburgh University Press, 1973), pp. 252–61.
6 See Neil Rennie, 'The Point Venus Scene', in *Science and Exploration in the Pacific. European Voyages to the Southern Oceans in the Eighteenth Century*, ed. Margarette Lincoln (Woodbridge: Boydell, 1998), pp. 135–46.
7 See Cook's comments in 1769 on the customs of *airoi* of Tahiti, defined as 'inhuman and contrary to the first principles of human nature', in J. C. Beaglehole, ed., *The Journals of Captain Cook* (Cambridge: Hakluyt Society, 1955–67), vol. I, p. 126.

8 Bronislaw Malinowski, *Argonauts of the Western Pacific* (London: Routledge & Kegan Paul, 1922), p. 12. Of course he was reacting to many nineteenth-century armchair ethnologists.

9 Robert Knox, *An Historical Relation of Ceylon*, ed. S. D. Saparadamu, *Ceylon Historical Journal*, 5 (1958): li. Knox, however, was of middle-class origins (his father was the captain of the ship in which he travelled when captured), and received some education in a boarding school when young.

10 See Justin Stagl, 'The Methodising of Travel in the 16th Century: a Tale of Three Cities', *History and Anthropology*, 4 (1990): 303–38, and Joan Pau Rubiés, 'Instructions for Travellers: Teaching the Eye to See', *History and Anthropology*, 9 (1996): 139–90.

11 As noted by Rod Edmond, 'Translating Cultures: William Ellis and Missionary Writing', in *Science and Exploration*, ed. Lincoln, pp. 149–61.

12 In this respect it is of particular importance to study the histories and ethnographies which incorporated material directly from native informants, in some cases literary texts and chronicles. These, however, were usually heavily interpreted and edited, especially accounts of non-Christian traditions by missionaries.

13 Roger Williams, *A Key into the Language of America* (London: printed by Gregory Dexter, 1643), ff. A3r–v.

14 *The Travels of Dean Mahomet. An Eighteenth Century Journey Through India*, ed. Michael Fisher (Berkeley: California University Press, 1997).

15 Edmund Spenser, *A View of the State of Ireland*, ed. A. Hadfield and W. Maley (Oxford: Blackwell, 1997), pp. 20–1, 56–8.

16 George Catlin, *Letters and Notes on the Manners, Customs and Conditions of the North American Indians* (London: Tosswill & Myers, 1841). See letter 17, describing the Mandans.

17 George Anson, *A Voyage Round the World in the Years 1740–4* (London, 1748), book III, chs. 9–10.

18 R. L. Stevenson, *In the South Seas*, ed. Neil Rennie (Harmondsworth: Penguin, 1998).

15

MARY BAINE CAMPBELL

Travel writing and its theory

Introduction

'Travel literature' is the significantly *generic* descriptor that has succeeded the Modern Language Association Bibliography's pre-1980s 'travel, treatment of'. But as a tool it cannot complete a search for relevant critical and theoretical materials. Very early in the contemporary resurgence of interest in travel writing, relations with the analysis of ethnography, thus with the history and function (and future) of anthropology in the West, and with postcolonial theory generally, became vital and generative. The interest in travel writing – across a wide political spectrum – was part of the necessary reimagining of the world first occasioned by the post-World War Two resistance movements and wars of liberation in the former European colonies, as well as by the waves of immigration that followed. It is a vivid shock to walk into the room-sized stained glass globe of the world (1935) suspended in the Mother Church of the Christian Scientists in Boston. Not only because, with loud metaphorical resonance, you can hear the whispers of people on the far side of the glass world as if they were speaking in your own ear, but also because the various pieces, each a different jewelled colour, belong to a world on the point of explosion. Much of the work of observing, interpreting, articulating the explosion of that world, as well as the historical development of the imperialised world that led to it, was done through recovery and analysis of people's writings about 'foreign' and especially 'exotic' places in which they had travelled and lived: as colonial masters, pilgrims, explorers, ambassadors, ambivalent wives, roving soldiers, ecstatic cross-dressers, conquistadores, missionaries, merchants, escaped slaves, idle students of the gentry and aristocracy, 'adventurers', and alienated modern artists.

During the same period theoretical models were developing which would help to launch illuminating readings of texts once considered 'subliterary', of mainly archival use for narrative history, or just boring. These models came mostly from France (including *départementes* such as Jacques Derrida's Algeria and Frantz Fanon's Martinique), Eastern Europe, Britain, and the United States, increasingly since 1980 enriched and sometimes transformed by work from South Asia, the Caribbean, and Africa. These readings in turn fed back into theory, producing unexpectedly out of what at first, in the 1970s, was mainly rhetorical, semiotic, deconstructive, and even psycho-analytical forms of attention, the more *engagé* programme of postcolonial theory. From formalist beginnings came a technique of close but 'suspicious' reading ideally suited to texts that were, in another sense of the word, notably suspicious themselves. From the 'close reading' championed especially by the American New Critics and the rhetorical analysis invigorated in the 1950s and 1960s by the widely read work of Kenneth Burke and the linguist Émile Benveniste emerged, by way of Michel Foucault, the practice of discourse analysis: this aimed, not at the individual productions of a single canonical author, but at the collectively produced 'discourse' surrounding and constituting a particular matter of social interest or action (and not necessarily limited to written or even verbal texts). Hayden White's *Tropics of Discourse: Essays in Cultural Criticism* (1984), aimed more at historiography than at travel writing, was a milestone in theorising and modelling the analysis of both 'discourse' and specific examples of non-fictional representation.[1]

One result of academic attention to travel writing in recent decades has been the wider dissemination among the political classes of critical views of colonialism and the imperial powers, once of Europe, more recently of the United States, Russia, and China. History, including ancient history, composes itself now from different images, different facts, and most importantly, different and multiple points of view. Students in most English-speaking countries are asked to read against the grain of what they are now regularly taught to see, at least at the post-secondary level, as situated and ideological texts, and they are also enabled to study a wider range of texts, produced by a wider range of authors and 'cultures', than they had before.

But much is left to be done in the realm of engaged criticism and theory. Recent attention to globalisation, diaspora, 'nomadism', and cyberspace is showing us the need for new and powerful theoretical work to replace, rather than simply supplement, the polemics and models produced by an academic collectivity concerned mostly with locatable cultures, bounded nations, and the imperial past.[2] Where *is* 'India', now that it is divided into three hostile states, and has produced a huge diaspora mostly of educated professionals with access to public speech? Where is 'Kurdistan'? How do we talk about the Jews as a nation, very few of whose members live in the state of Israel – and some of whom are Arabs? What does 'Chinese' mean? What is the percentage of 'Americans' in California? Where do the people of the Philippines live?

The Cubans? What is the USA to resident Puerto Ricans? What was London in the eyes of its nineteenth-century Irish immigrants? What is '*English* literature'? Questions of travel, as the American poet Elizabeth Bishop titled her famous book, and even of 'space', but not so much of place.[3] The old motifs of the journey – home, departure, destination, the liminal space between – have lost their reference in the lived experience of most people who are not tourists.[4]

Literary critical work on travel writing, or relevant to the reading of it, has continued along with and sometimes between the same covers as the work of historical and cultural revision. As a kind of writing, 'travel writing' provokes certain kinds of essentially literary questions and formulations. Most interesting here are works of literary criticism that find themselves directly facing issues of power, knowledge, and identity as a consequence of the very nature of the formal matters raised.[5] Formal issues that have been fully explored with relation to travel writing in recent decades include the nature and function of the stereotype, lexical matters such as the hidden etymologies so well excavated in Peter Hulme's *Colonial Encounters* or William Pietz's papers on 'fetish', the subjective presence of the author(s) in texts of knowledge, truth value in narrative writing, the independent or hard-wired shape of narrative itself, the rhetorical nature of 'fact', 'identification' in reading (with its consequences in social and political life), the representation of time, inter-cultural 'translation', and the function of metaphor and other figures.[6]

A text that generically proffers itself as 'true', as a representation of unaltered 'reality', makes a perfect test case for analytical work that tries to posit or explain the fundamental fictionality of all representation. Considerable relevant work on our topic, then, is to be found in the pages of *Representations*, a journal started by literary critic Stephen Greenblatt and art historian Svetlana Alpers at Berkeley in the early 1980s. Other interdisciplinary journals whose origins can be traced to the theoretical movements and mergers referred to, and which are particularly fruitful with papers on topics related to travel, travel writing and ethnography, include *Ariel*; *Diaspora*; *Gender, Place, and Culture*; *Journeys*; *Studies in Travel Writing*, as well as (less regularly) the various volumes and collections that issued from, especially, the Essex conferences and symposia on the sociology of literature, the Centre for Contemporary Cultural Studies in Birmingham, the School of American Research in Santa Fe, and anthropologist George Marcus's series *Late Editions*.[7]

A major source of information and theory related to travel writing and its valences with colonial and post-colonial history and geography, not to mention literary concerns with subjectivity and authorial perspective, has been the diverse work of feminist theorists and historians. Many travel texts were discovered, rediscovered, or revisited in the course of bringing back into print and public discourse the European and American women writers of the last three or four centuries, so many of whom wrote autobiographically, whether at home, abroad, or on the frontiers of expanding nations like Canada or the United States. Some of the most celebrated of the non-English include the fourth-century Galician pilgrim Egeria, the sixteenth-century Spanish transvestite Catalina de Erauso, French feminist Flora Tristan in Peru, Swiss adventurer Isabelle Eberhardt (who lived and travelled as a man in North Africa), and the Danish writer Isak Dinesen, sometime wife of a plantation owner and author of *Out of Africa*: since 1980 especially, their writing has been republished and much discussed, even made into movies.[8] Their works have also served as case studies, first in the production of an alternative history of free and mobile female actors, as well as later in their problematic relation to 'colonial discourse', a wake-up call to the initially androcentric assumptions of postcolonial theory. Imperial women travellers such as Lady Mary Wortley Montagu and Mary Kingsley offered particularly provocative occasions for the complication of women's history during the period in which gender studies was coming to the foreground as a more rigorously theorised branch of the wider cultural study of 'difference' than was women's studies per se.[9]

The works of the women and cross-gendered writers above, and those of countless more obscure writers – diarists of the Raj, of the American frontiers, of pilgrimage, of diplomatic and sometimes military and maritime life, as well as contemporary ethnographers and memoirists of the cultures of diaspora and war – have also helped critics of literature and of culture to open up the complexities of the master-slave paradigm, which at first dominated critical discussion of modern travel writing in a crude form: the West vs. the Rest.[10] It has been an important advance to realise that 'the Rest' had its own various power politics and forms of observation, into which usually oblivious Western desires could be plugged, and that the power of colonial masters was not as absolute or deracinating as the masters themselves, or even some of their guilty descendants, believed.[11] The shock with which people began to realise that travelling or displaced women did not comfortably fit the profile of 'Western oppressor' being so subtly and powerfully constructed by postcolonial theory seems peculiar now (which is not to say that women did not have various uses in turn for the structure of colonial oppression in which they had some power, privilege, and mobility). And the study of their work as writing, as records, as narratives, has provided considerable material for discussion of the gendered nature of subjectivity and the positionality or 'situatedness' of all knowledge.[12]

Texts and topics

The rest of this chapter will discuss, briefly, some major works in different parts of our collective field, along with a few individual topics and terms of critical-theoretical import. In the scholarly literature related to these topics and terms students can find formative discussions of the literature of travel and ethnography and its interpretation by contemporary intellectual culture. The academic disciplines that have had most to say or made most cogent use of the recent flowering of interest in the large corpus surveyed in this book are literary and cultural studies, history (including art history and history of science), anthropology, geography, and area studies, as well as various interdisciplinary alliances and projects among them. So many disciplines provide an inconveniently large number of subtopics and key themes for consideration, and I will pay particular attention mostly to the fields and inter-fields in which I am at home: literary and cultural studies, particularly pre-modern, in relation to the histories of anthropology and geography.[13]

Though such statements are never absolutely true, the 1978 publication of Palestinian literary critic Edward Said's starkly titled *Orientalism* – almost contemporaneous with Arab anthropologist Talal Asad's edited volume *Anthropology and the Colonial Encounter* and American feminist philosophers Sandra Harding's and Helen Longino's first papers on 'standpoint epistemology' – initiated for the English-reading public an epistemological shift that would transform the study of culture and cultures.[14] Said had been reading Foucault, and found in the concept of 'discourse' a magic key to the problem of Western imperial domination of 'the East':

> My contention is that without examining Orientalism as discourse one cannot possibly understand the enormously systematic discipline by which European culture was able to manage – even to produce – the Orient politically, sociologically, militarily, ideologically, scientifically, and imaginatively during the post-Enlightenment period.[15]

It is certainly not the case that those interested in travel writing jumped immediately on the bandwagon of Foucault (as modulated in those days by critics familiar with such Marxist thinkers as Antonio Gramsci, Louis Althusser, and Pierre Macherey). But even quite traditional and empirical studies of sub- or non-literary writing that represented places not-home, 'elsewhere', foreign, and exotic, began to proliferate in indirect relation to a new programme of thought whose outlines were emerging from works such as Said's. The study of what we know and how we know it – not to mention who 'we' are – broke loose from its somewhat rarified moorings in philosophy departments and became a vital task for all disciplines as the experiment of empire came to be seen as failing, and indeed the centre did not hold – if it had ever existed.

Said's main target was a kind of multi-disciplinary area studies that included the region of his birth and upbringing (in Palestine and Egypt) among its objects of authoritative knowledge. (It is hard now to remember that the word 'orientalist' was once quite neutral in connotation for most Western European and North American academics.) But of course many of these late eighteenth- and nineteenth-century orientalist texts were composed 'in the field', or as a result of intensive foreign travel, and are what we now call travel writing as well as academic contributions to geography, linguistics, and anthropology. Not only did those who wrote and critiqued ethnography take note of Said's and Asad's interventions, but so did those of us whose discipline at the time was understood to be the re-presentation of texts with occult meaning: 'doing readings of' mainly 'great' (hence intentionally complex) works of literary art or at least of rhetorical intricacy. Said took sophisticated hermeneutic methods normally used to approach the high literary texts he taught in the department of English and Comparative Literature at Columbia University and applied them to non-poetic and non-fictional works, helping to open up the field of literary studies to an apparently endless supply of new and socially salient texts. Among the most interesting and fruitful of these newly approachable corpuses was that loosely gathered under the name of 'travel writing'.

Much early work, both before and after the new spotlights were first shone on the imperial texts of information, was given to traditionally literary questions of genre and tradition, voice and fictionality.[16] Although these topics may seem quaint from the point of view of the highly articulated theoretical advances of the 1990s, they were useful to the theoreticians who began the construction of our current methods of reading – useful not as mere objects of conceptual repudiation but in fact as minesweeping tools and empirical groundwork for the development of reception histories (important to a discourse analysis that presumes to historical illumination). An early and widely cited essay by Jenny Mezciems, "'Tis not to divert the Reader": Moral and Literary Determinants in Some Early Travel Narratives', by its very title instructs social scientists and theoreticians about what they require from literary historians and critics.[17] The sense of travel writing as a genre was, where it manifested itself, often crude and restrictive, but the articulated concept of a corpus or 'tradition' was in fact useful, especially to social historians, in showing contemporary readers how to be proficient at reading *with* the grain of older accounts. Without that we cannot do the 'deeper' work of reading against it. Ambivalent texts of 'false consciousness', or political 'unconsciousness' have much of the complexity of modernist art itself, though it is not aesthetic complexity, and Anglo-American literary criticism was by the late 1970s a highly developed tool for responding to complexity.[18] Literary criticism, one could say, mapped out the textual terrain more cogently represented by discourse analysts and postcolonial theorists. Foucault's complaint that criticism was 'commentary' and that commentary merely repeated a text was perhaps insufficiently grateful to the patient work of discovery performed in many a deconstruction or rhetorical analysis. The discomfort prestigious theory feels in relation to 'empirical' or descriptive critical work with texts is not unrelated to the discomfort felt for so long by critics in relation to subliterary texts, texts that seem – as colonial travel writing does to its feminist theoriser Sara Mills – 'all surface'.[19] That they can seem that way now is a mark of the field's achievement: early readings of individual texts were often laughed out of court for their level of detail and their apparently paranoid decoding of imperialist rhetoric and its key tropes.

One very influential work of what could be called rhetorical criticism, by the French classicist François Hartog, was translated into English in 1988 as *The Mirror of Herodotus: The Representation of the Other in the Writing of History*. Although it took the form of a scrupulously close reading of a single *logos* in Herodotus's *Histories*, its method and some of its terminology were to become widespread, disseminated in North America particularly by the editorial and critical work of the dean of New Historicism, Stephen Greenblatt. His series for the University of California Press, 'The New Historicism: Studies in Cultural Poetics', brought out this translation of Hartog's book as one of its first volumes. Herodotus, 'Father of History' and 'Father of Lies', whose first books are accounts of mostly Mediterranean and Eastern European geography composed from the authority of the writer as traveller, is to the philosophically minded historian a fascinating scandal at the historical root of his vocation. Issues that haunt discussion of travel writing in evolving forms, in particular the truth value of representations, inexpressibility and 'translation', and the difficulty of imagining or representing the Other, are central to this consideration of the urban Greek writer's discussion of the nomadic Scythians – who share the same 'oriental' enemy with the cosmopolitan Greeks, and with Darius's and Xerxes's Persians.

Hartog points to Herodotus's uses of the strategies of negation and, more importantly, inversion, to handle the problem of the inexpressibility of the Other – in this case the nomadic other, the person who is by negation just unimaginably *apolis* (cityless), but seen through the lens of inversion is a nomad whose *aporia*, or disconnectedness – spatially but also, Hartog implies, in terms of representation – is a strategy for survival: 'the Scythians' only advantage is their *aporia*, the fact that there is no *poros* (bridge) by which to reach them, so they remain impossible to seize' (p. 199). In Hartog's words,

'It is not hard to see why travellers' tales and utopias frequently resort to this method [of inversion], since it constructs an otherness that is transparent for the listener or reader: it is no longer a matter of *a* and *b*, simply of *a* and the converse of *a*' (p. 213).

Although Hartog's Scythians are presented as simply an example of the functioning of inversion and of a submerged structure of cultural symmetry in the *Histories*, he has in fact chosen for his study sample the most basic form of cultural otherness represented in Western ethnographic writing: that of the non-agricultural, and therefore spatially unfixed or unlocatable people. Herodotus's Greece saw the nomad (in this case Scythian) as 'primitive', just as Shakespeare's England saw the Algonquians (actually farmers of both crops and fish as well as hunters) and as high modernists saw, with detached approbation, the Bedouin of North Africa. In anthropologist Hugh Brody's widely read experimental ethnography of the Inuit people of northern British Columbia, *Maps and Dreams*, he describes himself during a mapping and ethnographic research expedition commissioned by the government discovering that these supposedly illiterate and nomadic hunting people did indeed have maps and a definite sense of, as well as knowledge of, 'territory'.[20] But this knowledge was as narrative as it was spatial, and indeed was hard to reduce to graphic signs, because of its fluidity and temporality, and the irrelevance to it of what literate peoples think of as 'borders'. Brody reproduces some survey maps on which hunters have drawn lines representing their various routes in different seasons and over time, and also transcribes part of a conversation in which he is told about a kind of map-dreaming, in which the maps show the trails to heaven. The white European academic deals with the difference of the nomadic by, apparently, loosening his own psychic borders and being voluntarily indoctrinated into a different and more narrative form of spatial knowledge. He 'goes primitive', to use Marianna Torgovnick's phrase from her discussion of the function of travel and the exotic in modernism, but in the interests of knowledge and translation, rather than in pursuit of strangeness and aesthetic shock.[21]

'Nomad' became a more and more important – and metaphorical – term in French post-structuralist theory (especially in the work of Gilles Deleuze and Paul Virilio), as well as a persistent source of connection between travel texts and such canonical texts of Western culture as Exodus, the *Odyssey*, the *Aeneid* and other culture-founding Euro-Asian narratives of homeless wandering – in which civilisation is always represented as the end and salvation of the nomadic life. (The one non-indigenous American 'nation' included in Laguna Indian Leslie Marmon Silko's anti-epic novel *Almanac of the Dead*, among the gathering masses of newly awakened peoples repressed and oppressed for so long by European invasions of the Americas, is 'the homeless'. Ironically, this nation is largely made up of veterans of the last great US imperial adventure, the war – 'police action' – in Vietnam.[22]) The post-modern concept, and fact, of 'displacement' has brought the attention of critics and theorists in the 1990s back with a vengeance to questions Hartog handled in almost structuralist fashion in his treatment of the foundational Western case of representing the – nomadic, inexpressible, elusive – Other.[23]

This nomadism may involve some projection: a lost traveller's feel for the locational structure of the space he or she negotiates without real language skills or shared experience is easy to imagine as sliding towards the sense that his or her hosts, too, are lost, excessively unpinned. But it is also true that the Western sense of property and sovereignty – some of it in fact first articulated in early American encounters – is far from universal, and rooted in the historically specific circumstances of late medieval Europe, when for a number of reasons (including climate) agriculture finally began to produce surplus, and with it the bureaucratics of finance and property. The written archives modern historiography depends upon are of relatively recent vintage in European cultural history, but they have made it difficult for Euro-American historians to produce historiography that is *not* adapted to archival sources. Representation of the nomadic is a fundamental limit case for cultures shaped by agriculture, writing, bureaucracy, and the archive. Thus its riveting interest for contemporary theory, in a globalised world where tens of millions of people are officially 'displaced persons' travelling without will, desire, or intention – without the (perhaps imaginary) emotional bedrock, then, of the earlier subjects of travel: the exile, the pilgrim, and the (pre-Second World War) immigrant.

Much of the theoretically informed writing on travel and travel writing has had to do with imperial periods of the later eighteenth, nineteenth, and early twentieth centuries, in which the geographical surveying of the globe as well as the anthropological investigation of its non-metropolitan or 'cityless' (*aporoi*) peoples produced so much knowledge in the service of so much desire for power and wealth. Historians and historicist literary critics, like Francis Jennings and Michael Nerlich, as well as historical anthropologists and ethnohistorians such as James Axtell and Marshall Sahlins, concentrated also on the early, pre-imperial formation of ideas of European hegemony and the development of venture capitalism.[24] Columbus imagined colonial exploitation of labour and resources before he ran into a single actual resource in the Caribbean, and wrote his first report on the voyage – from shipboard – to Queen Isabella's Keeper of the Purse, extolling the benefits of such exploitation for funding a new Castilian offensive against Muslim control of the Holy Land. Pope Alexander VI was soon to divide the globe between Spanish and Portuguese sovereignty, in a move codified by the Treaty of Tordesillas (1494), and the push to empire was in the making. Dutch jurist Hugo Grotius and others were developing the field of international law, in part to decide issues of sovereignty and property rights in places subject to the Pope's treaty.[25]

This early period of imperial aspiration on the part of nations themselves only barely established enough to expand is important to the understanding of the colonial world, even to its dissolution and neo-colonial reconstitution, but difficult to work into social and cultural theory which must explicate a model in its state of function rather than its early stages of development. Marxist theory is the least impeded by the diachronic dimension of the problem, and some literary Marxists have done helpful work that includes the corpus of travel writing in its narratives: I am thinking especially of East German critic Michael Nerlich, author of *The Ideology of Adventure: Studies in Modern Consciousness, 1100–1750*, an account of the combined development of 'adventure capitalism', colonialism, and literary romance, and the literary historian Michael McKeon's *Origins of the English Novel, 1660–1740*, which represents the novel as a mediator of social and epistemological tensions in the world of a newly mobile and acquisitive bourgeoisie and a newly empirical science.[26] A new genre for a new historical phase, the early novel – in McKeon's account – combines the features and content of such emergent factual genres or modes as travel writing, criminal biography, and 'natural philosophy' with older romance and religious narrative forms to produce its 'power both to formulate, and to explain, a set of problems...central to early modern experience' (p. 20). McKeon's narrative, like Nerlich's, takes him back to the twelfth century, a period in which, as I have mentioned, Western European lordships began dealing with the problem and opportunity of surplus, and politically unified regions to develop agricultural markets and, by the fourteenth century, money economies based on gold.

A number of influential works on travel writing or (proto-)ethnography in the special situation of Europe in the so-called Age of Discovery appeared in the 1980s, importing post-structuralist and cultural materialist thinking into the increasingly dense context of travel writing as a literary or at any rate textual phenomenon. Essays by New Historicists Stephen Greenblatt and Louis Montrose in the United States, among others, set the stage for considerable work, still ongoing, with the texts of English explorers in North America, as well as canonical English writers' use of them in the nation-building project under way at home.[27] Their initial interest in historicising and materialising the referents and contexts of Shakespeare's plays and Spenser's *Faerie Queene* gave way quickly to an interest in the exploration texts themselves. Greenblatt's *Marvelous Possessions*, a reading of a number of late medieval and early modern works of travel and acquisition in exotically distant places, marked a climax of this kind of work, which on a Foucauldian ground and fortified with the insights of anthropological theorist Pierre Bourdieu, studies cultural 'moments', events, and documents as if they were literary texts, and with the same tools.[28]

Greenblatt and New Historicism owe a great deal to the impressionistic but extraordinarily sensitive work of the French historian and post-structuralist Michel de Certeau, who from a more Lacanian angle composed a couple of essays that arrived in English translation in the later 1980s: 'Montaigne's "Of Cannibals": The Savage "I"' and 'Ethno-Graphy: Speech, or the Space of the Other', a reading of Jean de Léry's seventeenth-century travel report on his journey to French Brazil with the colonial entrepreneur, Villegagnon. These, along with an essay on the early eighteenth-century anthropological theorist and Jesuit missionary Father Joseph Lafitau, combine rhetorical, linguistic, and psychoanalytically inflected forms of attention to produce – in the unclaimed lineage of Frantz Fanon – a historical psychology of alterity, for early modern and modern Europeans in the process of creating what the historian refers to as ethnology. 'What travel literature really fabricates is the primitive as *a body of pleasure* ... At the same time that it creates a profit, the voyage creates a lost paradise relative to a body-object, to an erotic body. This figure of the other has no doubt played a role in the modern Western *episteme*, more crucial than that of the critical ideas circulated through Europe by travel literature'.[29]

Historians have repeatedly questioned the thinness of empirical research in American New Historicist work, which operates by close readings, or what anthropologist Clifford Geertz calls 'thick description', of fragments and individual moments or events – biopsies, as it were. But the work is compelling for students and readers of the literary (not necessarily the High Literary) in the depths it opens up, and its unusual ability to make connections across scales and registers, between social realms and discourses normally not thought about in the same breath. New Historicist work 'travels'. A rich, even climactic gathering of papers in this vein came out in a special issue of *Representations* (Winter 1991) entitled 'The New World', since reissued as a book, *New World Encounters*.[30] It is dedicated to de Certeau, and concludes with a translation of the late historian's research proposal with regard to travel literature, made to the Centre national de la recherche scientifique in 1978, from which the essays mentioned above are offshoots (though the proposal was rejected!).

Somewhat less problematic to most historians has been the work of European professors of literature who work mainly or partly with factual or information-bearing texts: Peter Hulme and Frank Lestringant offer a number of particularly good examples of theoretically informed and interdisciplinary handling of such texts, from the earliest period of exploration to, in the case of Hulme's *Colonial Encounters*, the last days of the Enlightenment. Hulme's treatment of cannibalism, one of the most frequent and telling motifs of exotic travel writing (from early Greek texts to nineteenth- and even twentieth-century ethnography), has helped engender a great deal of thinking and analysis, from the very literary – Philip Boucher's *Cannibal Encounters* (1992) – to the anthropological – William Arens's recent 'Rethinking Anthropophagy' (1998).[31] Lestringant has written several trenchant articles on the topic himself, especially in its configuration with eucharistic symbolism and the religious wars of Reformation and Counter-Reformation Europe, and a monograph titled simply *Cannibals*.[32] It is a topic that invites analysis of the rôle of the imaginary (including Lacan's Imaginary) in the production of knowledge, even strategic knowledge, and more broadly, of discourse. Arens's case is that cannibalism is simply imaginary in the standard sense of the word, that it has almost never been practised by anyone, only narrated of 'foreigners'. Lestringant takes no position at all – the 'reality' quotient of the practice is not once broached in his book-length treatment of the topic. For Hulme, introducing the collection, it most pertinently 'exists as a term within colonial discourse'. 'For us, the overriding questions remain, why were Europeans so desirous of finding confirmation of their suspicions of cannibalism? and why does cannibalism feature so insistently as a contemporary trope in different kinds of writing?'[33]

The pressures that hold in place such a persistently flamboyant image of 'otherness' are clarified to some degree through a discourse analysis touched by the psychoanalytic theorising of Frantz Fanon, and less directly but perhaps as deeply by Jacques Lacan's model of object relations as well as his linguistically oriented analysis of the 'language' of the unconscious. Feminist refinements and challenges to Lacanian thinking have helped make its valences with the social and collective more available (as in Jane Gallup's *Reading Lacan*[34]), and a number of postcolonial social and literary theorists have taken the matter of encounter with a sentient Other as ground for far-reaching theoretical models of historical action, for example Gayatri Spivak ('Can the Subaltern Speak?' among much other work), and Homi Bhabha.[35] However nervously we might encounter explanations of history that are located too firmly in individual psyches or the fuzzy notion of 'culture(s)', they are a good approach for the unravelling of travel writing, which is produced not only by the culture or society of the person who writes it and the situation which gives her the authority to speak but also by the writer, *a writer*, someone who does indeed have a psyche (whether that amounts to a Self or a 'unified subject' is not the issue), and whose book is constructed to make its effects through an impact on other (culturally or socially produced) psyches. The job of postcolonial theory has been in part to get us to see how those effects are made, especially where they are produced and/or operate unconsciously, and to provide a picture or pictures of the particular, historicised, unconscious within and without them.

The linguistic turn within anthropology led to the famous editing collaboration of critic James Clifford and anthropologist George Marcus, *Writing Culture: The Poetics and Politics of Ethnography*.[36] Along with Mary Louise Pratt's later book, *Imperial Eyes*, Clifford and Marcus's *Writing Culture* has become a kind of textbook in how, and for what purposes, to analyse accounts of foreign or 'exotic' places written by people, especially of the West or 'developed world', who have some kind of authority of speech. Like the projects of the New Historicism, this collection, the ultimate result of an Advanced Seminar at the School of American Research in 1984, is concerned with the loss of 'unchallenged authority' in a once-authoritative anthropological canon and its genres. Its essays set out to dissect ethnographic texts and the situations of their production with the fine tools of literary and rhetorical analysis: the consequences, it would be safe to say, have helped to unsettle the classic account of modernism in the arts as well as the scientific confidence of ethnography. The very fact that rhetorical tropes and allegorical structures can be uncovered or simply pointed out in ethnographic texts has revealed to two generations of scholars and social scientists that ethnographic writing was a kind of representation as wedded to an inherited medium and the associative rip tides of the unconscious as is poetry or political propaganda. Johannes Fabian's searing, almost melodramatic *Of Time and the Other* put a similarly rhetorical-allegorical approach to ethnography to work for a polemic – centred on the ahistoricity with which 'Other' cultures are represented in ethnography – that seemed to leave no morally imaginable future for anthropology at all.[37] A more contemporary and upbeat approach to that despair has been to turn the lenses of anthropology back towards 'home', wherever that may be for the anthropologist or her institution. London novelist Iain Sinclair's finely detailed and historically dense account of his V-shaped traverse of London, *Lights Out for the Territory*,[38] is both a literary masterpiece Sinclair considers a novel and a case of post-modern, one might almost say reverse, ethnography that points to a future for the social science of the Other after all: we have met the Other and – as usual, but now we admit it – s/he is Us. And who might that be? Even the past is still unwritten.

NOTES

1 Hayden White, *Tropics of Discourse* (Baltimore: Johns Hopkins University Press, 1984). See also Michel Foucault, 'The Order of Discourse', in *Untying the Text: A Post-Structuralist Reader*, ed. Robert Young (London: Routledge and Kegan Paul, 1981), pp. 48–79; Kenneth Burke, *A Rhetoric of Motives* (New York: Prentice-Hall, 1950) and *A Grammar of Motives* (New York: Prentice-Hall, 1954); Émile Benveniste, *Problems in General Linguistics*, trans. Mary Elizabeth Meek (Coral Gables: University of Miami Press, 1971). An early master of close reading in cultural as opposed to exclusively written 'texts' is Roland Barthes in his *Mythologies* (1957), trans. Annette Lavers (New York: Hill and Wang, 1972). (Barthes's own travel book 'about' Japan, *Empire of Signs*, trans. Richard Howard (New York: Hill and Wang, 1982), is readable as an explanatory critique of the quasi-genre, especially in its classically Orientalist form.)

2 For early stirrings see, for example, Arjun Appadurai, 'Global Ethnoscapes: Notes and Queries for a Transnational Anthropology', in *Recapturing Anthropology: Working in the Present*, ed. Richard G. Fox (Sante Fe: School of American Research Press, 1991), pp. 93–114; and Caren Kaplan, 'Deterritorializations: The Rewriting of Home and Exile in Western Feminist Discourse', *Cultural Critique*, 6 (Spring 1987): 187–98, as well as many of her subsequent articles. More recently see Françoise Lionnet and Ronnie Scharfman, eds., *Yale French Studies*, 82/83 (1993), special issue: 'Post/Colonial Conditions: Exile, Migrations, Nomadism', and Gayatri Spivak's update on gender in this context, 'Diasporas Old and New: Women in the Transnational World', *Textual Practice*, 10:2 (Summer, 1996): 245–69. On cyberspace, see Christopher Pinney, 'Future Travel: Anthropology and Cultural Distance in an Age of Virtual Reality', *Visual Anthropology Review*, 8:1 (1992): 38–55.

3 Although, see Susan Morgan's *Place Matters: Gendered Geography in Victorian Women's Travel Books about Southeast Asia* (New Brunswick, N.J.: Rutgers University Press, 1996); or Lisa Bloom's *Gender on Ice: American Ideologies of Polar Expeditions* (Minneapolis: University of Minnesota Press, 1993). Place *does* matter still to cultural critics, but not as sovereign, with political boundaries presumed in mainstream culture to reflect long-standing ethnic homogeneity. For early and influential work concentrating on the placelessness of travel, see Victor Turner and Edith Turner's writings on liminality, for example, *Image and Pilgrimage in Christian Culture: Anthropological Perspectives* (New York: Columbia University Press, 1978).

4 Tourism is one of several forms of travel insufficiently represented in this chapter: see also Ross Chambers, 'Strolling, Touring, Cruising: Counter-Disciplinary Narrative and the Literature of Travel', in *Understanding Narrative*, ed. James Phelan and Peter Rabinowitz (Columbus: Ohio State University Press, 1994), pp. 17–42; Patrick Holland and Graham Huggan, *Tourists with Typewriters* (Ann Arbor: University of Michigan Press, 1998); although not a theoretical work, Jamaica Kincaid's *A Small Place* (New York: Farrar, Straus, Giroux, 1981), a description of her home island of Antigua as seen through both the eyes of the tourist ('you') and the knowledge of the native (Kincaid), is a richly suggestive critique.

5 See, for example, Robert Buckeye, 'Form as the Extension of Content: "Their existence in my eyes"', *Review of Contemporary Fiction*, 3:1 (December 1983): 192–5. The works that come first to mind here are Michel Butor's 'Travel and Writing', *Mosaic*, 8:1 (1974): 1–12; Charles Batten Jr.'s *Pleasurable Instruction: Form and Convention in Eighteenth-Century Travel Literature* (Berkeley: University of California Press, 1978); Percy Adams's *Travel Literature and the Development of the Novel* (Lexington: University Press of Kentucky, 1983); Tzvetan Todorov's *Conquest of America*, trans. Richard Howard (New York: Harper and Row, 1984); Peter Hulme's *Colonial Encounters* (London: Methuen, 1986); Patricia Parker's *Literary Fat Ladies: Rhetoric, Gender, Property* (London: Methuen, 1987); François Hartog's *The Mirror of Herodotus*, trans. Janet Lloyd (Berkeley: University of California Press, 1988); Dennis Porter's *Haunted Journeys: Desire and Transgression in European Travel Writing* (Princeton University Press, 1991); Mary Louise Pratt's exemplary discourse analysis *Imperial Eyes: Travel Writing and Transculturation* (London: Routledge, 1992); Tim Youngs's *Travellers in Africa: British Travelogues, 1850–1900* (Manchester University Press, 1994); Paul Zumthor, 'The Medieval Travel Narrative', *New Literary History*, 25 (1994): 809–24; and I will mention here my own *The Witness and the Other World: Exotic European Travel Writing, 400–1600* (Ithaca: Cornell University Press, 1988), as well as chapters on travel books and early anthropology in my *Wonder and Science: Imagining Worlds in Early Modern Europe* (Ithaca: Cornell University Press, 1999). See also the yet untranslated articles in *Littérales*, 7 (1990), special issue: 'Les Modèles du récit de voyage'.

6 See William Pietz's articles on 'The Problem of the Fetish', published in *Res* in issues 9, 13, and 16, especially 'The Problem of the Fetish II: The Origin of the Fetish' (Spring 1987): 23–45.

7 See also *Cultural Critique, Cultural Anthropology, Cultural Studies, Ethnohistory, Inscriptions, L'Homme, New Formations, Public Culture, Semiotext(e)*, and *Social Text*.

8 Nineteenth-century British women are especially well documented and frequently discussed. See Chapter 13 for bibliographical suggestions beyond those scattered throughout these notes.

9 See the Introduction and first chapter of Alison Blunt's *Travel, Gender, and Imperialism: Mary Kingsley and West Africa* (London: Guilford Press, 1994).

10 Edward Said's groundbreaking *Orientalism* (New York: Pantheon Books, 1978) is also a textbook case of this sociological crudity. An early case of looking at who writes back or lives/lived without the presence of the Master is the work of Gordon Brotherston, some of which came out of the Essex conferences: see *Image of the New World: The American Continent Portrayed in Native Texts* (London: Thames and Hudson, 1979), and his essay 'Towards a Grammatology of America: Lévi-Strauss, Derrida, and the Native New World' in *Europe and Its Others*, ed. Francis Barker *et al.* (Colchester: University of Essex, 1985), vol. 1, pp. 61–77, which blisteringly exposed the common assumption (by those who could know better) that the peoples of the New World were 'people without writing'.

11 A major example is Gananath Obeyesekere's *Apotheosis of Captain Cook: Myth-Making in the Pacific* (Princeton University Press, 1992).

12 Contemporary interdisciplinary work on travel, space, geography, and 'situated knowledge' from feminist positions includes Sara Mills's *Discourses of Difference: An Analysis of Women's Travel Writing and Colonialism* (London: Routledge, 1991), Donna Haraway's *Simians, Cyborgs and Women* (New York: Routledge, 1991) and *Modest_Witness@Second_Millennium* (New York: Routledge, 1997); Andrew Parker, Mary Russo et al., eds., *Nationalisms and Sexualities* (New York: Routledge, 1992); Gillian Rose's *Feminism and Geography: The Limits of Geographical Knowledge* (Minneapolis: University of Minnesota Press, 1993) and Rose and Alison Blunt's *Writing Women and Space: Colonial and Postcolonial Geographies* (New York: Guilford Press, 1994); the articles collected in Elizabeth Grosz's *Space, Time, and Perversion: Essays on the Politics of Bodies* (New York: Routledge, 1995); Caren Kaplan's *Questions of Travel: Postmodern Discourses of Displacement* (Durham: Duke University Press, 1996) (especially the introduction and final chapter), and Inderpal Grewal's *Home and Harem: Imperialism, Nationalism, and the Culture of Travel* (Durham: Duke University Press, 1996). On 'situated knowledge' generally see, in addition to Haraway and the work of feminist philosophers Sandra Harding and Helen Longino (see note 14), essays in Linda Alcoff and Elizabeth Potter, eds., *Feminist Epistemologies* (London: Routledge, 1993).

13 I will not be dealing here with imaginary travels, science fiction, metaphorics of travel, or utopias – all materials of real and directly related interest. On relations between real and imaginary travels in the early modern period, see Mary B. Campbell, 'Impossible Voyages: Seventeenth-Century Space Travel and the Impulse of Ethnology', *Literature and History*, special issue 'Placing Travel', ed. Tim Youngs, third series, 6:2 (Autumn 1997): 1–17; on metaphorics, see Caren Kaplan's introduction to *Questions of Travel*; on utopias, Frank and Fritzie Manuel, *Utopias of the Western World* (Cambridge, Mass.: Belknap Press, 1979); Louis Marin, *Utopics: Spatial Play*, trans. Robert A. Vollrath (Atlantic Heights, New Jersey: Humanities Press, 1984); and recently a post-Marxist feminist reading, particularly attentive to science fiction utopics: Jennifer Burwell, *Notes on Nowhere: Feminism, Utopian Logic, and Social Transformation*, *American Culture* vol. XIII (Minneapolis: University of Minnesota Press, 1997).

14 See Talal Asad, ed., *Anthropology and the Colonial Encounter* (London: Ithaca Press, 1973); Sandra Harding, 'The Norms of Inquiry and Masculine Experience', in *PSA 1980*, ed. Peter Asquith and Ronald Giere pp. 305–24; Helen Longino, 'Scientific Objectivity and Feminist Theorising', in *Liberal Education*, 67 (1981): 187–95; as well as Harding's and Longino's subsequent work.

15 Said, *Orientalism*, p. 3. See also by Said, 'Orientalism Reconsidered', in *Europe and Its Others*, ed. Francis Barker et al., vol. 1, pp. 14–27.

16 Some random examples: Charles D. Harrington, 'Self-Definition in Literature of Exploration', *Exploration*, 3 (1975): 1–12; J. K. Hyde, 'Real and Imaginary Journeys in the Later Middle Ages', *Bulletin of the John Rylands University Library*, 65:1 (Autumn 1982): 125–47; Stephen William Foster, 'Deconstructing a Text on North Africa: Ricoeur and Post-Structuralism', *Pre/Text*, 4:3 (Fall–Winter 1983): 295–315; Gregory Dickson, 'Lawrence Durrell and the Tradition of Travel Literature', *Deus Loci: The Lawrence Durrell Quarterly*, 7:5 (1984): 175–95; Cynthia Huff, 'Writer at Large: Culture and Self in Victorian Women's Travel Diaries', *A/B: Auto/Biography Studies*, 4:2 (Winter 1988): 118–29; Christopher

Mulvey, 'Anglo-American Fictions: National Characteristics in Nineteenth-Century Travel Literature', in *American Literary Landscapes: The Fiction and the Fact*, ed. F. A. Bell and D. K. Adams (New York: St. Martin's Press, 1988), pp. 61–77.

17 Jenny Mezciems, "'Tis not to divert the Reader": Moral and Literary Determinants in Some Early Travel Narratives', *Prose Studies*, 5:1 (May 1982), special issue: 'The Art of Travel': 1–19; see also Valerie Wheeler, 'Travelers' Tales: Observations on the Travel Book and Ethnography', *Anthropological Quarterly*, 59:2 (April 1986): 52–63.

18 On political 'unconsciousness', see Fredric Jameson, *The Political Unconscious: Narrative as a Socially Symbolic Act* (Ithaca: Cornell University Press, 1981).

19 Mills, *Discourses of Difference*, p. 11.

20 Hugh Brody, *Maps and Dreams* (New York: Pantheon Books, 1982).

21 Marianna Torgovnick, *Gone Primitive: Savage Intellects, Modern Lives* (University of Chicago Press, 1990).

22 Leslie Marmon Silko, *Almanac of the Dead* (New York: Simon and Schuster, 1991).

23 See George Robertson, Melinda Mash *et al.*, eds., *Travellers' Tales: Narratives of Home and Displacement* (London: Routledge, 1994). Also, Gayatri Spivak, 'Displacement and the Discourse of Woman', in *Feminist Interpretations of Jacques Derrida*, ed. Nancy J. Holland (University Park: Pennsylvania State University Press, 1997), pp. 43–71.

24 See Francis Jennings, *The Invasion of America: Indians, Colonialism, and the Cant of Conquest* (Chapel Hill: University of North Carolina Press, 1975); James Axtell, *The Invasion Within: The Contest of Cultures in Colonial North America* (New York: Oxford University Press, 1985); Michael Nerlich, *Ideology of Adventure: Studies in Modern Consciousness, 1100–1750*, vol. I, trans. Ruth Crowley [1977] (Minneapolis: University of Minnesota Press, 1987); Marshall Sahlins, *Historical Metaphors and Mythical Realities: Structure in the Early History of the Sandwich Islands Kingdom*, ASAO Special Publications no. 1 (Ann Arbor: University of Michigan Press, 1980). For traces of the theoretical storm that followed, with a time lag, see Sahlins's subsequent work on Cook, especially *Islands of History* (University of Chicago Press, 1985) and Gananath Obeyesekere's polemic, *The Apotheosis of Captain Cook: European Mythmaking in the Pacific* (Princeton University Press, 1992).

25 On these juridical and legal formations see Olive Dickason and L. C. Green, *The Law of Nations and the New World* (Edmonton: University of Alberta Press, 1989); James Muldoon, *Popes, Lawyers, and Infidels: The Church and the Non-Christian World, 1250–1550* (Philadelphia: University of Pennsylvania Press, 1979) and subsequent work; Karen Ordahl Kupperman, *Settling with the Indians: The Meetings of English and American Cultures in America* (Totowa, N.J.: Rowman and Littlefield, 1980).

26 Nerlich, *The Ideology of Adventure*; McKeon, *Origins of the English Novel, 1660–1740* (Baltimore: Johns Hopkins University Press, 1987).

27 Of particular interest in this lineage is literary critic Mary C. Fuller's book *Voyages in Print: English Travel to America, 1576–1624* (Baltimore: Johns Hopkins University Press, 1995), on Richard Hakluyt's fundamental Renaissance collection, *Principal Navigations* (1598–1600). See anthropologist Neil L. Whitehead's

spirited rebuttals of these very literary responses to texts of great potential
usefulness to ethno-historians and social historians, most comprehensive in the
introduction to his annotated edition of Walter Ralegh's *Discoverie of the Large,
Rich, and Bewtiful Empyre of Guiana* (Manchester University Press, 1997).

28 Stephen Greenblatt, *Marvelous Possessions: The Wonder of the New World*
(University of Chicago Press, 1991).
29 Michel de Certeau, 'Ethno-Graphy: Speech, or the Space of the Other: Jean
de Léry', in *The Writing of History* (New York: Columbia University Press),
pp. 226–7.
30 Stephen Greenblatt, ed., *New World Encounters* (Berkeley: University of
California Press, 1993).
31 For Arens's essay, see *Cannibalism and the Colonial World*, ed. Francis Barker,
Peter Hulme and Margeret Iversen (Cambridge University Press, 1998),
pp. 39–62.
32 Frank Lestringant, *Cannibals: The Discovery and Representation of the Cannibal
from Columbus to Jules Verne*, trans. Rosemarie Morris (Berkeley: University of
California Press, 1997).
33 Hulme, 'Introduction: The Cannibal Scene', *Cannibalism and the Colonial World*,
p. 4. This term has provoked remarkable work in (ex)anthropologist Michael
Taussig, especially in *The Devil and Commodity Fetishism in South America*
(Chapel Hill: University of North Carolina Press, 1980) and *Shamanism,
Colonialism, and the Wild Man: A Study in Terror and Healing* (University of
Chicago Press, 1987).
34 Jane Gallup, *Reading Lacan* (Ithaca: Cornell University Press, 1985).
35 Spivak's 'Can the Subaltern Speak?', originally published in 1988, is most readily
accessible in *Colonial Discourse and Post-Colonial Theory: A Reader*, ed. Patrick
Williams and Laura Chrisman (New York: Columbia University Press, 1994),
pp. 66–111. Homi K. Bhabha's early essays of the 1980s are reprinted in his *The
Location of Culture* (London: Routledge, 1994).
36 George E. Marcus and James Clifford, eds., *Writing Culture: The Politics and
Poetics of Ethnography* (Berkeley: University of California Press, 1986).
37 Johannes Fabian, *Of Time and the Other: How Anthropology Makes Its Object*
(New York: Columbia University Press, 1983).
38 Iain Sinclair, *Lights out for the Territory* (London: Granta Books, 1997).

The right-hand column lists travel writing, with a generous definition of the genre as long as the text recounts actual travels undertaken. The list is far from comprehensive, but indicates what the Companion's contributors regard as some of the more significant or influential examples of travel writing. The left-hand column mixes events from world and national history, events within travel and transportation history, voyages and explorations, and other travel-related texts, mostly fictional and theoretical.

1492 Columbus's first voyage to America	
1496 Henry VII's patent to John Cabot and sons to explore New World	
1497 Vasco da Gama's voyage to India	
1499 1st English edn of John Mandeville, *Mandeville's Travels* (written in mid-fourteenth century)	
1500 First Portuguese voyage to Brazil	
1503	1st English edn of Marco Polo's *Il Milione*
1507	Montalboddo, *Paesi novamenti retrovati*, early account in Italian of Spanish and Portuguese voyages
1516 Thomas More, *Utopia* (Lat edn, English 1551)	
1519 Beginning of the first voyage of circumnavigation, commanded by Magellan,	

	who died on the voyage, the survivors returning to Spain in 1522	
	Hernán Cortés invades Mexico	
1543	Copernicus, *De revolutionibus*, key text of the scientific revolution arguing that Earth is not the centre of the universe	
1544		Sebastian Munster, *Cosmographia Universalis*, early German account incorporating New World discoveries
1550		Giovanni Battista Ramusio, *Navigationi et viaggi*, first major collection, in Italian, of first-hand accounts of early modern travel
1555	Muscovy Company chartered	Peter Martyr, *Decades of the New World* (translated from Spanish by Richard Eden)
1557		Hans Staden, *The True History of His Captivity* (German)
1562	First English slave-trading expedition (under John Hawkins)	
1572	Luís de Camões, *The Lusiads*, Portuguese verse epic of voyages to Asia	
1576	First of Martin Frobisher's three NW Passage voyages	Humphrey Gilbert, *Discourse of a Discoverie...to Cataia*
1577	Francis Drake begins circumnavigation (completed 1580)	*The History of Trauayle in the West and East Indies*, Richard Willes's expanded version of Eden's translation of Peter Martyr
1578	Humphrey Gilbert receives patent for exploration / settlement of North America	Jean de Léry', *History of a Voyage to the Land of Brazil* (French)

1579	Merchant Adventurers officially licensed (though trading since late fourteenth century)	
1582		Richard Hakluyt, *Divers Voyages*
1583	Gilbert's second expedition to Newfoundland Bartolomé de Las Casas, *A Short Account of the Destruction of the Indies* (originally in Spanish, 1552)	
1584	Amadas-Barlowe voyage to Virginia	
1585	Drake's West Indian voyage First of John Davis's three NW Passage voyages	
1588	Defeat of Spanish Armada Thomas Cavendish completes circumnavigation Michel de Montaigne, "On the cannibals"	Thomas Harriot, *Briefe and True Report of the New Found Land of Virginia*
1589		Richard Hakluyt, *Principal Navigations*
1590	John White finds Roanoke Colony deserted	José de Acosta, *Natural and Moral History of the Indies* (Spanish) Theodor de Bry begins publication of *America* (or *Grands Voyages*)
1592	Levant Company chartered	
1594	Thomas Nashe, *The Unfortunate Traveller*	
1596	Pedro Fernández de Quirós's voyages in the southern seas (till 1606) Edmund Spenser, *A View of the Present State of Ireland* (published 1633)	Walter Ralegh, *The Discoverie of the Large, Rich and Bewtiful Empyre of Guiana*

1598		2nd edn of Richard Hakluyt, *Principal Navigations* (1598–1600)
1600	East India Company and Virginia Company chartered	
1605	Joseph Hall, *Mundus Alter et Idem* (English edn 1609) Miguel de Cervantes, *Don Quixote* (second part 1615)	
1607	Henry Hudson's first voyage to NW Passage English settlement at Jamestown	
1611	William Shakespeare, *The Tempest*	Thomas Coryat, *Coryat's Crudities*
1612	Michael Drayton, *Poly-Olbion*, massive chorographical poem describing the English nation (completed 1622)	Captain John Smith, *A Map of Virginia* William Strachey, *History of Travel into Virginia*
1613		Samuel Purchas, *Purchas His Pilgrimage*
1615	Bermuda Company chartered	George Sandys, *A Relation of a Journey*
1617	Joseph Hall, *Quo vadis? A Just Censure of Travell...*	Fynes Moryson, *Itinerary*
1620	Plymouth Company chartered Voyage of the *Mayflower*	
1624		Captain John Smith, *General History of Virginia*
1625	Francis Bacon, *Of Travel*	Samuel Purchas, *Hakluytus Posthumus, or Purchas His Pilgrimes* John Norden, *England, An Intended Guyde for English Travaillers*
1628		Francis Drake, *The World Encompassed*
1629	Massachusetts Bay Company chartered	
1636		Henry Blount, *Voyage in the Levant*
1642	English Civil War (to 1651)	

James Howell, *Instructions for Forreine Travell*

Descartes, *Discourse on Method* (French)

1649   Cromwell in Ireland: massacre of garrisons at Drogheda and Wexford

1660   Restoration of the Stuart monarchy

Navigation Act

1666   Great Fire of London   Paul Rycaut, *Present State of the Ottoman Empire*

1670   Hudson's Bay Company chartered   Richard Lassels, *An Italian Voyage, Or, A Compleat Journey Through Italy*

1672   Royal African Company chartered

1678   John Bunyan, *The Pilgrim's Progress*

1681   Robert Knox, *An Historical Relation of Ceylon*

1684   Alexandre Olivier Exquemelin, *The Bucaniers of America*

1688   'Glorious Revolution': accession of William of Orange and beginning of parliamentary monarchy

Henry Neville, *The Isle of Pines*

Aphra Behn, *Oroonoko*

1690   John Locke, *Two Treatises of Government*

1691   John Dunton, *Voyage Round the World*

1693   John Ray, *A Collection of Curious Travels and Voyages*

1697   William Dampier, *A New Voyage Round the World* (supplemented in 1699)

1699   William Hacke, *A Collection of Original Voyages*

		Lionel Wafer, *A New Voyage and Description of the Isthmus of America*
1703		William Dampier, *A Voyage to New Holland*
1704	George Psalmanazar, *An Historical and Geographical Description of Formosa* – a popular account later unveiled as a forgery	Thomas Astley, *A Collection of Voyages and Travels*
1705		Thomas Addison, *Remarks on Several Parts of Italy*
1707	Union of English and Scottish parliaments	William Funnell, *A Voyage Round the World*
1712		Woodes Rogers, *A Cruising Voyage Round the World*
1716		Lady Mary Wortley Montagu, *Embassy Letters* (written 1716–18, published posthumously in 1763)
1719	Daniel Defoe, *Robinson Crusoe*	
1721	Baron de Montesquieu, *Persian Letters* (French)	
1724		Daniel Defoe, *A Tour Through the Whole Island of Great Britain* (first volume; published in 3 volumes, 1726)
1726	Jonathan Swift, *Gulliver's Travels*	
1729		*Madagascar: or, Robert Drury's Journal*
1734		Voltaire, *Letters on the English* (French)
1740	George Anson's circumnavigation, completed 1744: only a third of the 2,000 crewmen survived	
1745		A. & J. Churchill, *A New General Collection of Voyages and Travels*

1746 Stuart uprising finally defeated at
Battle of Culloden

1748 Tobias Smollett, *Roderick Random*
Montesquieu, *The Spirit of Laws* (French)

1749 Thomas Nugent, *Grand Tour* – first major guidebook to European travel

1755   Henry Fielding, *Journal of a Voyage to Lisbon*

1756 Seven Years War (to 1763) severely restricts British access to Continent

1757 Robert Clive defeats Nawab of Bengal at Battle of Plassey

1759 General Wolfe captures Quebec
Voltaire, *Candide*
Samuel Johnson, *Rasselas*

1760 James Macpherson, *Fragments of Ancient Poetry, Collected in the Highlands of Scotland* (first of the so-called Ossian volumes)

1762 Harrison's chronometer: enables shipboard calculation of longitude, a major aid to navigation

1764 Oliver Goldsmith, "The Traveller"
Horace Walpole, *The Castle of Otranto*   James Boswell's journal of his tour in Germany and Switzerland

1766   Tobias Smollett, *Travels Through France and Italy*

1767 European discovery of Tahiti by Capt. Samuel Wallis

1768 Capt. James Cook begins the first of his three voyages, mainly to the Pacific   Philip Thicknesse, *Useful Hints to Those who Make the Tour of France*

		Laurence Sterne, *A Sentimental Journey Through France and Italy*
1769	First Spanish mission in Alta California	Thomas Gray, *Journal in the Lakes*
		Arthur Young, *A Six Weeks Tour Through the Southern Counties of England and Wales*
1771		Louis de Bougainville, *A Voyage Round the World* (French)
1772	James Bruce reaches source of Blue Nile	
	Diderot, *Supplement to the Voyage of Bougainville* (French) (not published until 1796)	
1773		John Hawkesworth, *An Account of the Voyages ... in the Southern Hemisphere*
1775		Samuel Johnson, *A Journey to the Western Islands of Scotland*
1776	American Declaration of Independence	Janet Schaw, *Journal of a Lady of Quality* (not published until 1921)
	Adam Smith, *The Wealth of Nations*	
1777		Capt. James Cook, *A Voyage Towards the South Pole and Round the World*
1778		J. R. Forster, *Observations Made During a Voyage Round the World*
		John Hamilton Moore, *A New and Complete Collection of Voyages and Travels*
1779	Death of Capt. Cook in Hawai'i	
1780	Earliest entry for 'tourist' in *Oxford English Dictionary*	Arthur Young, *A Tour in Ireland*

1782		Jean-Jacques Rousseau, *Solitary Walker* (French)
		William Gilpin, *Observations on the River Wye* (pioneered picturesque sightseeing)
1783	Britain recognises independence of the USA	Anders Sparrman, *Voyage to the Cape of Good Hope*
1786		James Boswell, *The Journal of a Tour to the Hebrides*
1788	First Fleet arrives in Botany Bay, Australia	
	Formation of the African Association to promote the exploration of the interior of northern and western Africa	
1789	Outbreak of French Revolution	Olaudah Equiano, *The Interesting Life of Olaudah Equiano*
	Mutiny on board the *Bounty* leads to establishment of mutineers' colony on Pitcairn Island	
1790		Capt. William Bligh, *A Narrative of the Mutiny on Board His Majesty's Ship the "Bounty"*
		James Bruce, *Travels to Discover the Sources of the Nile, 1768–1773*
		William Beckford, *A Descriptive Account of the Island of Jamaica*
1791		William Bartram, *Travels Through North and South Carolina...*
1792	French Revolutionary Wars begin	Chateaubriand, *Voyage to America* (French)
	William Gilpin, 'On Picturesque Travel'	William Bligh, *A Voyage to the South Sea*

Helen Maria Williams, *Letters
from France* (completed 1796)
William Wordsworth,
  "Descriptive Sketches taken
  during a Pedestrian Tour
  among the Alps"

1793 Lord Macartney's Embassy to
      China

1794 Uvedale Price, *An Essay on the
      Picturesque*
      Ann Radcliffe, *The Mysteries of
      Udolpho*

1795 Napoleonic Wars effectively   Samuel Hearne, *A Journey to
      close the Continent to British   the Northern Ocean*
      travellers until 1815
      Founding of London
      Missionary Society
      Xavier de Maistre, *Voyage
      Around My Room* (French)

1796 Mungo Park travels the course   John Gabriel Stedman,
      of the River Niger   *Narrative of a Five Years
                                           Expedition Against the
                                           Revolted Maroons of Surinam*
                                          Mary Wollstonecraft, *Letters
                                           Written During a Short
                                           Residence in Sweden, Norway,
                                           and Denmark*

1798 Napoleon's fleet defeated by   George Vancouver. *The Voyage
      Nelson at the Battle of the   of Discovery to the Pacific
      Nile; French military and   Ocean and Round the World*
      cultural conquest of Egypt
      comes to an end
      Rebellion of United Irishmen,
      led by Wolfe Tone
      Samuel Taylor Coleridge, "The
      Rime of the Ancyent
      Marinere"

1799 Foundation of the Church   Mungo Park, *Travels in the
      Missionary Society   Interior Districts of Africa*
      Alexander von Humboldt
      explores South America
      (to 1804)

Founding of Church Missionary
Society

1801 Act of Union creating United
Kingdom of Great Britain
and Ireland

Alexander Mackenzie, *Voyages
from Montreal...to the
Frozen and Pacific Oceans,
in the years 1789 and 1793*
John Barrow, *Travels into
the Interior of Southern
Africa*

1804 Lewis and Clark's overland
expedition to the Pacific
(completed 1806)

John Barrow, *Travels in China*

1805 Nelson's victory at the Battle of
Trafalgar

1806 Death of Mungo Park on his
second expedition

1807 British abolition of the slave
trade

1810 William Wordsworth, *Guide to
the Lakes*
Walter Scott, *The Lady of the
Lake*

1811

William Marsden, *The History
of Sumatra*

1812 George Gordon, Lord Byron,
Childe Harold's Pilgrimage
cantos I and II (completed
1818)

1814 Walter Scott, *Waverley, or, 'Tis
Sixty Years Since*
Jane Austen, *Mansfield Park*

Meriwether Lewis and
William Clark, *History of
the Lewis and Clark
Expedition*

1815 Final defeat of Napoleon at
Waterloo

1816 Captain James Tuckey's
expedition to the Congo

1817 James Mill, *The History of
British India*

Mary Shelley and Percy Bysshe
Shelley, *History of a Six
Weeks' Tour*
Thomas Stamford Raffles, *The
History of Java*

1818	First regularly scheduled transatlantic steamer service begins operation Mary Shelley, *Frankenstein*	
1820		William Scoresby, *An Account of the Arctic Regions*
1822		William Hazlitt, 'On Going on a Journey'
1823		John Franklin, *Narrative of a Journey to the Shores of the Polar Sea*
1824	Britain recognises new republics as independent of Spanish rule in South America Byron dies fighting for independence of Greece from Turkey	
1826		William Hazlitt, *Notes of a Journey Through Italy and France* Anna Jameson, *Diary of an Ennuyée*
1829	Catholic Emancipation in Ireland	William Ellis, *Polynesian Researches*
1830	First wholly steam-powered railway, between Manchester and Liverpool, begins operation Formation of the Royal Geographical Society	Samuel Rogers, *Italy: A Poem*
1831		Mary Prince, *The History of Mary Prince, A West Indian Slave*
1832	The Great Reform Act widens the British franchise	Frances Trollope, *Domestic Manners of the Americans*
1834	Abolition of slavery in British Empire begins (completed 1838)	Matthew Lewis, *Journal of a West Indian Proprietor*
1835	Karl Baedeker's first guidebook published in Coblenz	

1836	John Murray's first guidebook published in London Capt. Frederick Marryat, *Mr Midshipman Easy*	Edward Lane, *An Account of the Manners and Customs of the Modern Egyptians* Washington Irving, *Astoria* Frances Trollope, *Paris and the Parisians*
1837	Victoria becomes Queen	
1838	The word 'timetable' coined by the London & Birmingham Railway Edgar Allan Poe, *The Narrative of Arthur Gordon Pym*	Stendhal, *Memoirs of a Tourist* (French)
1839	First Opium War (to 1842)	Charles Darwin, *The Voyage of HMS Beagle*
1840	Treaty of Waitangi establishes British control over New Zealand John Bidwell leads first party of overland immigrants to California	Flora Tristan, *London Journal* Richard Henry Dana, *Two Years Before the Mast*
1841	Thomas Cook's first organised tour of 570 people travels ten miles from Leicester to Loughborough and back by train	
1842	P&O steamship service makes Egypt a fashionable tourist destination Alfred Lord Tennyson, 'Ulysses' Alfred Lord Tennyson, *Morte d'Arthur*	Charles Dickens, *American Notes* Countess of Blessington, *The Idler in France* Frances Trollope, *A Visit to Italy*
1843		William Makepeace Thackeray, *Paris and Irish Sketchbook*
1844		William Makepeace Thackeray, *Notes of a Journey from Cornhill to Grand Cairo* Alexander Kinglake, *Eothen*
1845	Great Famine in Ireland (to 1852): leads to population decline of two million	

	Sir John Franklin's last expedition: proof of his fate not discovered until 1859	John Charles Fremont, *Narrative of the Exploring Expedition to the Rocky Mountains...*
		Edward John Eyre, *Discoveries in Central Australia*
1846	Establishment of the Hakluyt Society	Herman Melville, *Typee*
		Charles Dickens, *Pictures from Italy*
1847	Charlotte Brontë, *Jane Eyre*	
1848	Mexico cedes California to the United States of America	Harriet Martineau, *Eastern Life*
	Gold discovered in California	
	Revolutions in Europe; Britain experiences Chartist agitation	
1849	Thomas Carlyle, 'The Nigger Question'	Francis Parkman, *The Oregon Trail*
1851	Herman Melville, *Moby Dick*	Gérard de Nerval, *Voyage to the Orient* (French)
		Mary Wallis, *Life in Feejee or, Five Years Among the Cannibals*
		William H. Brett, *Indian Missions in Guiana*
1852		Harriet Martineau, *Letters from Ireland*
1853	David Livingstone crosses Africa (to 1856)	Alfred Russel Wallace, *A Narrative of Travels on the Amazon and Rio Negro*
1854	Crimean War (to 1856)	Henry D. Thoreau, *Walden*
1855	Thomas Cook's first Continental tour	Richard Burton, *Personal Narrative of a Pilgrimage to Al-Madinah and Meccah*
	Livingstone visits Victoria Falls	
1856	Second Opium War (to 1858)	
1857	Sepoy Rebellion (Indian Mutiny)	Mary Seacole, *Wonderful Adventures...*
		David Livingstone, *Missionary Travels and Researches in South Africa*

Charles Baudelaire, 'Le Voyage'
Karl Marx, *Capital*

1858   End of Company rule in India
       Richard Burton and J. H. Speke
           reach Lake Tanganyika; Speke
           reaches Lake Victoria
       John Stuart crosses Australia
           from south to north (to 1862)
       R.M. Ballantyne,*Coral Island*

1859   Charles Darwin, *The Origin of*   Anthony Trollope, *The West*
       Species   *Indies and the Spanish Main*

1860   The New Zealand Wars (to 1863)

1862   Anthony Trollope, *North*
                                                America

1863   J. H. Speke, *Journal of the*
                                                Discovery of the Source of
                                                the Nile
                                                Henry Walter Bates, *The*
                                                Naturalist on the River
                                                Amazons

1864   Jules Verne, *Journey to the*
       Centre of the Earth (French)

1865   Morant Bay rebellion in Jamaica
       Lewis Carroll, *Alice's*
       Adventures in Wonderland

1867   Livingstone reaches the
       Zambezi

1869   Completion of the Suez Canal   Mark Twain, *The Innocents*
       allows direct steamship service   *Abroad*
       between Europe and Asia
       Completion of the
       transcontinental railway
       across the USA

1871   Stanley 'finds' Livingstone   Leslie Stephen, *The Playground*
       Edward Tylor, *Primitive Culture*   *of Europe* (on Switzerland
                                                and mountaineering)
                                                Mark Twain, *Roughing It*

1872   Clarence King, *Mountaineering*
                                                in the Sierra Nevada
                                                Henry Morton Stanley, *How I*
                                                Found Livingstone

1873	Death of Livingstone Jules Verne, *Around the World in 80 Days* (French)	Anthony Trollope, *Australia and New Zealand*
1874		John Wesley Powell, *Exploration of the Colorado River and Its Canyons* David Livingstone, *The Last Journals*
1875	Britain buys Suez Canal shares	Henry James, *Transatlantic Sketches*
1877	Henry Morton Stanley reaches the mouth of the Congo river after crossing Africa Queen Victoria proclaimed Empress of India	R. L. Playfair, *Travels in the Footsteps of Bruce*
1878		Henry Morton Stanley, *Through the Dark Continent* R. L. Stevenson, *Travels with a Donkey*
1879	British-Zulu War	
1880		Pierre Loti [JulienViaud], *The Marriage of Loti* (French) Isabella Bird, *Unbeaten Tracks in Japan*
1883	Maiden journey of the *Orient Express*, the train that connected Paris and Constantinople Robert Louis Stevenson, *Treasure Island*	Everard Im Thurn, *Among the Indians of Guiana* Henry James, *Portraits of Places* Isabella Bird, *The Golden Chersonese*
1884	Mark Twain, *Huckleberry Finn*	Henry James, *A Little Tour in France*
1885	Berlin Treaties try to prevent a scramble for Africa Death of General Gordon at Khartoum H. Rider Haggard, *King Solomon's Mines*	Wilfrid Scawen Blunt, *Ideas About India*

1888	Rudyard Kipling, *Plain Tales from the Hills*	James Anthony Froude, *The English in the West Indies*
		Charles Doughty, *Travels in Arabia Deserta*
1890		Lafcadio Hearn, *Two Years in the French West Indies*
		Henry Morton Stanley, *In Darkest Africa*
		William Booth, *In Darkest England and the Way Out*
1891	Paul Gauguin lives and paints in Tahiti and the Marquesas Islands (till death in 1903)	
1892	R. L. Stevenson, 'The Beach of Falesá'	
1894		Lafcadio Hearn, *Glimpses of Unfamiliar Japan*
		John Muir, *The Mountains of California*
1895	H. G. Wells, *The Time Machine*	
1896		R. L. Stevenson, *In the South Seas*
1897	Bram Stoker, *Dracula*	Mary Kingsley, *Travels in West Africa*
1898	Spanish-Cuban-American War leads to US hegemony in the Caribbean	
1899	Second Anglo-Boer War (to 1902) Joseph Conrad, *Heart of Darkness* (published in book form in 1902)	
1900	Boxer Rebellion in China Relief of Mafeking from Boer siege Joseph Conrad, *Lord Jim* Sigmund Freud, *The Interpretation of Dreams* (German)	Joshua Slocum, *Sailing Alone Around the World*
1901	The beginning of fifteen years of British Antarctic expeditions led by Scott and Shackleton	John C. Van Dyke, *The Desert: Further Studies in Natural Appearances*

First transatlantic radio
broadcast
Australian Federation
Rudyard Kipling, *Kim*

1902	Land grant in Kenyan highlands begins large-scale white settlement J. A. Hobson, *Imperialism: A Study*	Hilaire Belloc, *The Path to Rome* Jack London, *People of the Abyss*
1904	Francis Younghusband's expedition to Tibet	Lafcadio Hearn, *Japan: An Attempt at Interpretation*
1905	Japan defeats Russia; attempted revolution in Russia	Henry James, *English Hours* Edith Wharton, *Italian Backgrounds* Robert F. Scott, *The Voyage of the 'Discovery'*
1907		Gertrude Bell, *The Desert and the Sown* Wilfrid Scawen Blunt, *The Secret History of the English Occupation of Egypt* Henry James, *The American Scene* J. M. Synge, *The Arran Isles*
1908	The Congo Free State becomes the Belgian Congo Arnold van Gennep, *The Rites of Passage* – classic sociological study of the crossing of frontiers and boundaries Robert Baden-Powell, *Scouting for Boys*	Jack London, *The Cruise of the Snark*
1909	Robert Edwin Peary reaches North Pole	Henry James, *Italian Hours* Hilaire Belloc, *The Pyrenees*
1910	Mexican Revolution	
1911	Roald Amundsen reaches South Pole	Norman Douglas, *Siren Land* John Muir, *My First Summer in the Sierra* Gertrude Bell, *Amurath to Amurath*

1912	Capt. Scott dies after reaching South Pole	Matthew Henson, *A Negro Explorer at the North Pole*
	Arthur Conan Doyle, *The Lost World*	Ezra Pound, *Patria Mia*
	Émile Durkheim, *The Elementary Forms of the Religious Life* (French)	
1914	First World War (until 1918) Opening of the Panama Canal Edgar Rice Burroughs, *Tarzan of the Apes*	
1915	J. G. Frazer, *The Golden Bough* (completion of the definitive 3rd edn which began to appear in 1906)	Norman Douglas, *Old Calabria*
1916	Easter Rising in Dublin	D. H. Lawrence, *Twilight in Italy*
1917	Russian Revolution: many writers would travel to the Soviet Union during the 1920s and 1930s to report on the social and economic experiment V. I. Lenin, *Imperialism: The Highest Stage of Capitalism*	
1919	Amritsar massacre Anglo-Irish War (to 1921)	Frederick O'Brien, *White Shadows in the South Seas* Ernest Shackleton, *South*
1920	Gandhi wins control of Indian Congress	Edith Wharton, *In Morocco*
1921	Civil War in Ireland (to 1923)	D. H. Lawrence, *Sea and Sardinia*
1922	Bronislaw Malinowski, *Argonauts of the Western Pacific* James Joyce, *Ulysses* T. S. Eliot, *The Waste Land*	Apsley Cherry-Garrard, *The Worst Journey in the World*
1924	E. M. Forster, *A Passage to India*	
1925		Aldous Huxley, *Along the Road*
1926	General Strike in Britain	T. E. Lawrence, *The Seven Pillars of Wisdom* (privately printed)

		Aldous Huxley, *Jesting Pilate*

1927

Aldous Huxley, *Jesting Pilate*
Victoria Sackville-West,
  Passenger to Tehran
André Gide, *Voyage to the
  Congo* (French)
D. H. Lawrence, *Mornings in
  Mexico*
Alexander David-Neel, *My
  Journey to Llasa*
H. V. Morton, *In Search of
  England*

1928 Virginia Woolf, *To The
  Lighthouse*
Margaret Mead, *Coming of
  Age in Samoa*

William Carlos Williams, *A
  Voyage to Pagany*

1929 Wall Street Crash
Claude McKay, *Banjo*
Ernest Hemingway, *A Farewell
  to Arms*

H. V. Morton, *In Search of
  Scotland*

1930

Evelyn Waugh, *Labels: A
  Mediterranean Journey*
Alec Waugh, *Hot Countries*
H. V. Morton, *In Search of
  Ireland*

1931

Evelyn Waugh, *Remote People*

1932 Evelyn Waugh, *Black Mischief*

Ernest Hemingway, *Death in the
  Afternoon*
J. R. Ackerley, *Hindoo Holiday*
Freya Stark, *Baghdad Sketches*
D. H. Lawrence, *Etruscan
  Places*
H. V. Morton, *In Search of Wales*

1933 Hitler comes to power in
  Germany
James Hilton, *Lost Horizon*

George Orwell, *Down and Out
  in Paris and London*
Peter Fleming, *Brazilian
  Adventure*
Robert Byron, *First Russia,
  Then Tibet*

1934 Michel Leiris, *L'Afrique
  Fantôme* (French)

Aldous Huxley, *Beyond the
  Mexique Bay*

1947	India wins independence. The partition of India and the creation of Pakistan Malcolm Lowry, *Under the Volcano*	Edmund Wilson, *Europe Without Baedeker*
1948	*SS Empire Windrush* brings first major wave of Caribbean immigrants to UK	E. Lucas Bridges, *Uttermost Part of the Earth* John Steinbeck, *A Russian Journey*
1949	People's Republic of China proclaimed after Communist takeover Éire becomes Republic of Ireland Simone de Beauvoir, *The Second Sex* (French)	Alec Waugh, *The Sugar Islands*
1950	Korean War (to 1953)	Patrick Leigh Fermor, *The Traveller's Tree* Thor Heyerdahl, *Kon-Tiki*
1951	John Wyndham, *The Day of the Triffids*	Norman Lewis, *A Dragon Apparent*
1952	Mau Mau resistance in Kenya leads to state of emergency William Gaddis, *The Recognitions* Frantz Fanon, *Black Skin, White Masks* (French)	Arthur Grimble, *A Pattern of Islands* Norman Lewis, *Golden Earth*
1953	Hillary and Tenzing climb Mount Everest	P. H. Fawcett, *Operation Fawcett*
1954	Beginnning of nationalist uprising in Algeria William Golding, *Lord of the Flies*	
1955	Bandung conference of independent African and Asian countries	Claude Lévi-Strauss, *Tristes Tropiques*
1956	Suez Crisis: defeat of British and French invasion of Egypt after Nasser nationalised the Suez Canal Soviet invasion of Hungary	James Morris, *Coast to Coast* Eric Newby, *The Last Grain Race*

1957	Ghana and Malaya become independent	Lawrence Durrell, *Bitter Lemons of Cyprus*
	Jack Kerouac, *On the Road*	Patrick Leigh Fermor, *A Time to Keep Silence*
	Roland Barthes, *Mythologies* (French)	Richard Wright, *Pagan Spain*
1958	Chinua Achebe, *Things Fall Apart*	Laurens Van Der Post, *Lost World of the Kalahari*
		Eric Newby, *A Short Walk in the Hindu Kush*
1959	Fidel Castro comes to power in Cuba	Wilfred Thesiger, *Arabian Sands*
		Freya Stark, *Riding to the Tigris*
1961	Building of the Berlin Wall	Peter Matthiessen, *The Cloud Forest: A Chronicle of the South American Wilderness*
	Yuri Gagarin becomes first man to travel in space	
1962	Algeria wins independence	V. S. Naipaul, *The Middle Passage*
	Cuban Missile Crisis	Peter Matthiessen, *Under the Mountain Wall*
1963	Assassination of John F. Kennedy	
1964	Vietnam War breaks out (to 1973)	V. S. Naipaul, *An Area of Darkness*
		Wilfred Thesiger, *The Marsh Arabs*
		Tim Severin, *Tracking Marco Polo*
1965	Che Guevara in Congo (until 1966)	Dervla Murphy, *Full Tilt: Ireland to India with a Bicycle*
1966	Jean Rhys, *Wide Sargasso Sea*	Patrick Leigh Fermor, *Roumeli*
		Eric Newby, *Slowly Down the Ganges*
1967	Secession of Biafra and outbreak of Nigerian civil war (to 1970)	Colin Thubron, *Mirror to Damascus*
	Six-day War between Israel and neighbouring Arab states	
	Che Guevara captured and killed in Bolivia	
	Posthumous publication of Bronislaw Malinowski's *Diary in the Strict Sense of the Term* initiates debate	

about the ethics of
anthropological fieldwork

<table>
<tr><td>1968</td><td>Student uprising in Paris.
'Prague Spring' uprising
Murder of Martin Luther King</td><td>Joan Didion, Slouching
Towards Bethlehem
Dervla Murphy, In Ethiopia
with a Mule</td></tr>
<tr><td>1969</td><td>British Troops arrive in
Northern Ireland
First manned moonlanding</td><td>Laurie Lee, As I Walked Out
One Midsummer Morning</td></tr>
<tr><td>1970</td><td></td><td>Roland Barthes, Empire of
Signs (French)</td></tr>
<tr><td>1971</td><td>Civil war in East Pakistan leads
to creation of Bangladesh</td><td></td></tr>
<tr><td>1972</td><td>Italo Calvino, Invisible Cities
(Italian)</td><td>V. S. Naipaul, Among the
Believers</td></tr>
<tr><td>1973</td><td>CIA help overthrow President
Allende in Chile</td><td></td></tr>
<tr><td>1974</td><td></td><td>Geoffrey Moorhouse, The
Fearful Void
Robert Pirsig, Zen and the Art
of Motorcycle Maintenance</td></tr>
<tr><td>1975</td><td>State of emergency in India (to
1977)</td><td>Paul Theroux, The Great
Railway Bazaar</td></tr>
<tr><td>1977</td><td></td><td>Bruce Chatwin, In Patagonia
Patrick Leigh Fermor, A Time
of Gifts
Dervla Murphy, Where the
Indus is Young</td></tr>
<tr><td>1978</td><td>Edward Said, Orientalism</td><td>Eric Newby, The Big Red Train
Ride
Peter Matthiessen, The Snow
Leopard
Martha Gellhorn, Travels with
Myself and Another</td></tr>
<tr><td>1979</td><td>Iranian revolution
Nicaraguan revolution</td><td>Paul Theroux, The Old
Patagonian Express
Jonathan Raban, Arabia
Through the Looking Glass
Joan Didion, The White
Album</td></tr>
</table>

1980	Zimbabwe gains independence	Robyn Davidson, *Tracks*
	Paul Fussell, *Abroad: British Literary Traveling Between the Wars*	Edmund White, *States of Desire: Travels in Gay America*
1981		Jonathan Raban, *Old Glory: An American Voyage*
		Gavin Young, *Slow Boats to China*
		Hugh Brody, *Maps and Dreams*
1982	The Falklands / Malvinas War	William Least Heat-Moon, *Blue Highways*
		Czeslaw Milosz, *Visions from San Francisco Bay*
1983	Miners' strike in UK (to 1985)	Paul Theroux, *The Kingdom by the Sea*
		Colin Thubron, *Among the Russians*
		Dervla Murphy, *Eight Feet in the Andes*
		Michael Ondaatje, *Running in the Family*
1984		Ronald Wright, *Cut Stones and Crossroads*
		Redmond O'Hanlon, *Into the Heart of Borneo*
		Peter Matthiessen, *Indian Country*
1985	*Rainbow Warrior* sunk by French secret service in New Zealand	Jan Morris, *Among the Cities*
		Christina Dodwell, *A Traveller in China*
1986	Explosion of Chernobyl nuclear power station	Barry Lopez, *Arctic Dreams*
	Umberto Eco, *Travels in Hyperreality*	Patrick Leigh Fermor, *Between the Woods and the Water*
		Ronald Wright, *On Fiji Islands*
		Jonathan Raban, *Coasting*
1987	V. S. Naipaul, *The Enigma of Arrival*	Colin Thubron, *Behind the Wall: A Journey Through China*
		Bruce Chatwin, *The Songlines*
		Salman Rushdie, *The Jaguar Smile*

		Caryl Phillips, *The European Tribe*
1988	Jamaica Kincaid, *A Small Place*	Jean Baudrillard, *America*
		Redmond O'Hanlon, *In Trouble Again*
		Pico Iyer, *Video Night in Kathmandu*
		P. J. O'Rourke, *Holidays in Hell*
1989	Fall of the Berlin Wall	William Dalrymple, *In Xanadu*
	Ayatollah Khomeini pronounces *fatwa* on Salman Rushdie	Ronald Wright, *Time Among the Maya*
		Sara Suleri, *Meatless Days*
		V. S. Naipaul, *A Turn in the South*
1990	Nelson Mandela freed from prison in South Africa	Jonathan Raban, *Hunting Mister Heartbreak*
	Iraqi occupation of Kuwait leads to Gulf War	Scott Malcolmson, *Tuturani*
		Geoffrey Moorhouse, *Apples in the Snow: A Journey to Samarkand*
1991	Start of Balkan Wars in former Yugoslavia (to 1999)	Pico Iyer, *The Lady and the Monk*
	Sara Mills, *Discourses of Difference*	William Least Heat-Moon, *PrairyErth*
1992	Mary Louise Pratt, *Imperial Eyes*	Amitav Ghosh, *In an Antique Land*
		Paul Theroux, *The Happy Isles of Oceania*
		Sven Lindqvist, *'Exterminate All the Brutes'* (Swedish)
1993	Paul Gilroy, *The Black Atlantic*	
1994	Genocide in Rwanda	Colin Thubron, *The Lost Heart of Asia*
	IRA ceasefire announced: beginning of peace process in Northern Ireland	Gavin Bell, *In Search of Tusitala*
		Rebecca Solnit, *Savage Dreams*
1995		Norman Lewis, *An Empire of the East: Travels in Indonesia*
		W. G. Sebald, *The Rings of Saturn* (translated from German)

		Paul Theroux, *The Pillars of Hercules*
1996		Redmond O'Hanlon, *Congo Journey*
		Peter Robb, *Midnight in Sicily*
		Sara Wheeler, *Terra Incognita: Travels in Antarctica*
		Edward Marriott, *The Lost Tribe*
		Bill Bryson, *Notes from a Small Island*
		Robyn Davidson, *Desert Places*
1997	James Clifford, *Routes: Travel and Translation in the Late Twentieth Century*	Jon Krakauer, *Into the Wild*
		Dea Birkett, *Serpent in Paradise*
		William Dalrymple, *From the Holy Mountain*
1998		Mary Morris, *Nothing to Declare*
		Philip Gourevitch, *We Wish to Inform You That Tomorrow We Will Be Killed With Our Families: Stories from Rwanda*
1999	UN involvement in Kosovo	Jonathan Raban, *Passage to Juneau*
		Charles Nicholl, *Somebody Else*
		Colin Thubron, *In Siberia*
		Rob Nixon, *Dreambirds*
		Patrick Keiller, *Robinson in Space*
2000		Edward Marriott, *Wild Shore: Life and Death with Nicaragua's Last Shark Hunters*
		Caryl Phillips, *The Atlantic Sound*
2001	Terrorist attack on New York and Washington War in Afghanistan V. S. Naipaul wins Nobel Prize for Literature	Stefan Hertmans, *Intercities*

FURTHER READING

This bibliography offers a list of general books about different aspects of travel, followed by a few key secondary texts for each of the Companion's chapters, and then by a note on other relevant resources.

Anthologies of travel writing

Bassett, Jan, ed., *Great Southern Landings: An Anthology of Antipodean Travel*, Melbourne: Oxford University Press, 1995.

Birkett, Dea and Sara Wheeler, eds., *Amazonians: The Penguin Book of Women's New Travel Writing*, London: Penguin, 1998.

Bryant, William C., ed., *Colonial Travelers in Latin America*, compiled and introduced by Irving A. Leonard, Newark: Juan de la Cuesta, 1986.

Fish, Cheryl J. and Farah J. Griffin, eds., *A Stranger in the Village: Two Centuries of African-American Travel Writing*, Boston: Beacon Press, 1998.

Fussell, Paul, ed., *The Norton Book of Travel*, New York: W. W. Norton & Co., 1987.

Ghose, Indira, *Memsahibs Abroad: Writings by Women Travellers in Nineteenth Century India*, New Delhi: Oxford University Press, 1998.

Hadfield, Andrew, ed., *Amazons, Savages, and Machiavels: Travel and Colonial Writing in English, 1550–1630: An Anthology*, Oxford University Press, 2001.

Hahner, June E., ed., *Women Through Women's Eyes: Latin American Women in Nineteenth-Century Travel Accounts*, Wilmington: Scholarly Resources, Inc., 1998.

Hanbury-Tenison, Robin, *The Oxford Book of Exploration*, Oxford University Press, 1993.

Kaul, H. H., *Travellers' India*, New Delhi: Oxford University Press, 1997.

Morris, Mary, ed., *The Virago Book of Women Travellers*, London: Virago, 1994.

Parker, Kenneth, ed., *Early Modern Tales of Orient*, London: Routledge, 1999.

Pesman, Ros, David Walker, and Richard White, eds., *The Oxford Book of Australian Travel Writing*, Melbourne: Oxford University Press, 1996.

Pettinger, Alasdair, ed., *Always Elsewhere: Travels of the Black Atlantic*, London: Cassell, 1999.

Quinn, David B., ed., *New American World: A Documentary History of North America to 1612*, 5 vols., New York: Arno, 1979.

Robinson, Jane, ed., *Unsuitable for Ladies: An Anthology of Women Travellers*, Oxford University Press, 1995.
Walsh, Alison, ed., *Nothing Ventured: Disabled People Travel the World*, Bromley: Harrap Columbus, 1991.

On ancient and medieval travel writing

Campbell, Mary B., *The Witness and the Other World: Exotic European Travel Writing, 400–1600*, Ithaca: Cornell University Press, 1988.
Casson, Lionel, *Travel in the Ancient World*, London: George Allen & Unwin, 1974.
Friedman, John Block and Kristen Mossler Figg, eds., *Trade, Travel and Exploration in the Middle Ages: An Encyclopedia*, New York: Garland, 2000.
Helms, Mary W., *Ulysses' Sail: An Ethnographic Odyssey of Power, Knowledge, and Geographical Distance*, Princeton University Press, 1988.
Howard, Donald R., *Writers and Pilgrims: Medieval Pilgrimage Narratives and Their Posterity*, Berkeley: University of California Press, 1980.
Sargent-Bau, Barbara N., ed., *Journeys Toward God: Pilgrimage and Crusade*, Kalamazoo, Mich.: Medieval Institute Publications, Western Michigan University, 1992.
Zacher, Christian K., *Curiosity and Pilgrimage: The Literature of Discovery in Fourteenth-Century England*, Baltimore: Johns Hopkins University Press, 1976.

On the history and sociology of travel and tourism

Abram, Simon, Jacqueline D. Waldren, and Donald V. L. Macleod, *Tourists and Tourism: Identifying with People and Places*, Oxford: Berg, 1997.
Chambers, Iain, *Migrancy, Culture, Identity*, London: Routledge, 1994.
Edensor, Tim, *Tourists at the Taj: Performance and Meaning at a Symbolic Site*, London: Routledge, 1998.
Feifer, Maxine, *Tourism in History: From Imperial Rome to the Present*, New York: Stein and Day, 1985.
Glage, Liselotte, ed., *Being/s in Transit: Travelling* Migration* Dislocation*. Amsterdam: Rodopi, 2000.
MacCannell, Dean, *The Tourist: A New Theory of the Leisure Class*, New York: Schocken Books, 1976.
Empty Meeting Grounds: The Tourist Papers, New York: Routledge, 1992.
Moir, Esther, *The Discovery of Britain: The English Tourists*, London: Routledge & Kegan Paul, 1964.
Ousby, Ian, *The Englishman's England: Taste, Travel and the Rise of Tourism*, Cambridge University Press, 1990.
Robinson, Mike, and Hans-Christian Anderson, eds., *Tourism and Literature: Explorations of Tourism, Writers and Writings*, London: Continuum, 2001.
Rojek, Chris and John Urry, eds., *Touring Cultures: Transformations of Travel and Theory*, London: Routledge, 1997.
Schivelbusch, Wolfgang, *The Railway Journey: The Industrialization of Time and Space in the Nineteenth Century*, Berkeley: University of California Press, 1986.
Solnit, Rebecca, *Wanderlust: A History of Walking*, New York: Viking, 2000.

Towner, John, *An Historical Geography of Recreation and Tourism in the Western World, 1540–1940*, London: John Wiley & Sons, 1996.

Urry, John, *The Tourist Gaze: Leisure and Travel in Contemporary Societies*, London: Sage, 1990.

Withey, Lynne, *Grand Tours and Cook's Tours: A History of Leisure Travel, 1750 to 1915*, New York: William Morrow and Co., 1997.

Critical studies of travel writing

Adams, Percy G., *Travelers and Travel Liars, 1660–1800*, Berkeley: University of California Press, 1962.

Bishop, Peter. *The Myth of Shangri-La. Tibet, Travel Writing and the Western Creation of Sacred Landscape*, London: Athlone, 1989.

Bloom, Lisa, *Gender on Ice: American Ideologies of Polar Expeditions*, Minneapolis: University of Minnesota Press, 1993.

Carter, Paul, *The Road to Botany Bay: An Essay in Spatial History*, London: Faber and Faber, 1987.

Chard, Chloe, and Helen Langdon, eds., *Transports: Travel, Pleasure, and Imaginative Geography, 1600–1830*, New Haven: Yale University Press, 1996.

Clark, Steve, ed., *Travel Writing and Empire: Postcolonial Theory in Transit*, London: Zed Books, 1999.

Cronin, Michael, *Across the Lines: Travel, Language, Translation*, Cork University Press, 2000.

Dodd, Philip, ed., *The Art of Travel: Essays on Travel Writing*, London: Frank Cass, 1982.

Duncan, James, and Derek Gregory, eds., *Writes of Passage: Reading Travel Writing*, London: Routledge, 1999.

Dunlop, M. H., *Sixty Miles from Contentment: Traveling the Nineteenth-Century American Interior*, Boulder: Westview Press, 1998.

Edwards, Justin D., *Exploring the Erotics of U. S. Travel Literature, 1840–1930* Lebanon, New Hampshire: University Press of New England, 2001.

Elsner, Jaś, and Joan-Pau Rubiés, eds., *Voyages and Visions: Towards a Cultural History of Travel*, London: Reaktion Books, 1999.

Fausett, David, *Writing the New World: Imaginary Voyages and Utopias of the Great Southern Land*, University of Syracuse Press, 1993.

Fogel, Joshua A. *The Literature of Travel in the Japanese Rediscovery of China 1862–1945*, Stanford University Press, 1996.

Forsdick, Charles, *Victor Segalen and the Aesthetics of Diversity: Journeys between Cultures*, Oxford University Press, 2000.

Gilroy, Amanda, ed., *Romantic Geographies: Discourses of Travel, 1775–1844*, Manchester University Press, 2000.

Goodman, Jennifer R., *Chivalry and Exploration, 1298–1630*, Woodbridge: The Boydell Press, 1998.

Islam, Syed Manzurul, *The Ethics of Travel: From Marco Polo to Kafka*, Manchester University Press, 1996.

Jarvis, Robin, *Romantic Writing and Pedestrian Travel*, London: Macmillan, 1997.

Korte, Barbara, *English Travel Writing: From Pilgrimages to Postcolonial Explorations*, trans. Catherine Matthias, Basingstoke: Palgrave, 2000.

Kowaleski, Michael, ed., *Temperamental Journeys: Essays on the Modern Literature of Travel*, Athens: University of Georgia Press, 1992.

Leask, Nigel, *Curiosity and the Aesthetics of Travel Writing 1770–1840: From an Antique Land*, Oxford University Press, 2002.

Leed, Eric J., *The Mind of the Traveller: From Gilgamesh to Global Tourism*, New York: Basic Books, 1991.

Low, Gail Ching-Liang, *White Skins/Black Masks: Representation and Colonialism*, London: Routledge, 1996.

Mulvey, Christopher, *Anglo-American Landscapes: A Study of Nineteenth-Century Anglo-American Travel Literature*, London: Cambridge University Press, 1983.

Transatlantic Manners: Social Patterns in Nineteenth-Century Anglo-American Travel Literature, London: Cambridge University Press, 1990.

Porter, Dennis, *Haunted Journeys: Desire and Transgression in European Travel Writing*, Princeton University Press, 1991.

Pratt, Mary Louise, *Imperial Eyes: Travel Writing and Transculturation*, London: Routledge, 1992.

Sharpe, Jenny, *Allegories of Empire: The Figure of Woman in the Colonial Text*, Minneapolis: University of Minnesota Press, 1993.

Spufford, Francis, *I May Be Some Time: Ice and the English Imagination*, London: Faber and Faber, 1996.

Spurr, David, *The Rhetoric of Empire: Colonial Discourse in Journalism, Travel Writing, and Imperial Administration*, Durham: Duke University Press, 1993.

Stafford, Barbara Maria, *Voyage into Substance: Art, Science, Nature, and the Illustrated Travel Account, 1760–1840*, Cambridge, Mass.: MIT Press, 1984.

Urbain, Jean-Didier, *L'idiot du voyage*, Paris: Éditions Payot & Rivages, 1993.

Secrets de voyage: menteurs, imposteurs et autres voyageurs, Paris: Payot, 1998.

Von Martels, Zweder, ed., *Travel Fact and Travel Fiction: Studies on Fiction, Literary Tradition, Scholarly Discovery and Observation in Travel Writing*, Leiden: E. J. Brill, 1994.

Wallace, Anne D., *Walking, Literature, and English Culture: The Origins and Uses of the Peripatetic in the Nineteenth Century*, Oxford University Press, 1993.

Williams, Glyndwr, *The Great South Sea: English Voyages and Encounters, 1570–1750*, New Haven: Yale University Press, 1997.

1 Stirrings and searchings (1500–1720)

Andrews, Kenneth R., *Trade, Plunder, and Settlement: Maritime Enterprise and the Genesis of the British Empire, 1480–1630*, Cambridge University Press, 1984.

Bradley, Peter T., *British Maritime Enterprise in the New World, from the Late Fifteenth to the Mid-Eighteenth Century*, Lewiston: Edwin Mellen, 1999.

Campbell, Mary Baine, *Wonder & Science: Imagining Worlds in Early Modern Europe*, Ithaca: Cornell University Press, 1999.

Ceard, Jean, and Jean-Claude Margolin, eds., *Voyager à la Renaissance*, Paris: Éditions Maisonneuve et Larose, 1987.

Edwards, Philip, *Last Voyages: Cavendish, Hudson, Ralegh*, Oxford: Clarendon Press, 1988.

The Story of the Voyage: Sea-Narratives in Eighteenth-Century England, Cambridge University Press, 1994.

Foss, Michael, *Undreamed Shores: England's Wasted Empire in America*, New York: Charles Scribner's Sons, 1974.

Frantz, R. W., *The English Traveller and the Movement of Ideas: 1660–1732*, Lincoln: University of Nebraska Press, 1934.

Fuller, Mary C., *Voyages in Print: English Travel to America, 1576–1624*, Cambridge University Press, 1995.

Hadfield, Andrew, *Literature, Travel, and Colonial Writing in the English Renaissance, 1545–1625*, Oxford: Clarendon Press, 1998.

Knapp, Jeffrey, *An Empire Nowhere: England, America, and Literature from Utopia to 'The Tempest'*, Berkeley: University of California Press, 1992.

Matar, Nabil, *Turks, Moors, and Englishmen in the Age of Discovery*, New York: Columbia University Press, 1999.

Munter, Robert, and Clyde L. Grose, eds., *Englishmen Abroad*, Lewiston: Edwin Mellen, 1986.

Penrose, Boies, *Travel and Discovery in the Renaissance*, Cambridge, Mass.: Harvard University Press, 1952.

2 The Grand Tour and after (1660–1840)

Andrews, Malcolm, *In Search of the Picturesque: Landscape Aesthetics and Tourism in Britain, 1760–1800*, Stanford University Press, 1989.

Batten, Charles L., Jr., *Pleasurable Instruction: Form and Convention in Eighteenth Century Travel Literature*, Berkeley: University of California Press, 1978.

Black, Jeremy, *The British Abroad: The Grand Tour in the Eighteenth Century*, London: Macmillan, 1992.

Brewer, John, *The Pleasures of the Imagination: English Culture in the Eighteenth Century*, New York: Farrar, Straus, Giroux, 1997.

Buzard, James, *The Beaten Track: European Tourism, Literature, and the Ways to 'Culture,' 1800–1918*, Oxford: Clarendon Press, 1993.

Chaney, Edward P., *Richard Lassels and the Establishment of the Grand Tour: Catholic Cosmopolitans in Exile, 1630–1660*, London: Warburg Institute – University of London, 1982.

The Evolution of the Grand Tour: Anglo-Italian Cultural Relations since the Renaissance, London: Frank Cass, 1998.

Chard, Chloe, *Pleasure and Guilt on the Grand Tour: Travel Writing and Imaginative Geography 1600–1830*, Manchester University Press, 1999.

Ferguson, Frances, *Solitude and the Sublime: Romanticism and the Aesthetics of Individuation*, London: Routledge, 1992.

Pemble, John, *The Mediterranean Passion: Victorians and Edwardians in the South*, Oxford University Press, 1988.

Redford, Bruce, *Venice and the Grand Tour*, New Haven: Yale University Press, 1996.

Trease, Robert G., *The Grand Tour*, London: Heinemann, 1967.

3 Exploration and travel outside Europe (1720–1914)

Bayly, C. A., *Empire and Information: Intelligence Gathering and Social Communication in India, 1780–1870*, Cambridge University Press, 1996.

Brantlinger, Patrick, *Rule of Darkness. British Literature and Imperialism, 1830–1914*, Ithaca: Cornell University Press, 1988.

Bridges, Roy, 'Towards the Prelude to the Partition of East Africa', in *Imperialism, Decolonization and Africa*, ed. Roy Bridges, Basingstoke: Macmillan, 2000, pp. 65–113.

Cain, Peter J., and Antony G. Hopkins, *British Imperialism: Innovation and Expansion 1688–1914*, London: Longman, 1993.

Cohn, Bernard S., *Colonialism and its Forms of Knowledge: The British in India*, Princeton University Press, 1996.

Curtin, Philip D., *The Image of Africa. British Ideas and Action, 1780–1850*, London: Macmillan, 1965.

Drayton, Richard, *Nature's Government: Science, British Imperialism and the 'Improvement' of the World*, New Haven: Yale University Press, 2000.

Driver, Felix, *Geography Militant. Cultures of Exploration and Empire*, Oxford: Blackwell, 2001.

Edney, Matthew H., *Mapping an Empire: The Geographical Construction of British India, 1765–1843*, University of Chicago Press, 1997.

Kiernan, Victor Gordon, *Lords of Human Kind: European Attitudes to the Outside World in the Imperial Age*, London: Weidenfeld, 1969.

Marshall, Peter J., and Glyndwr Williams, *The Great Map of Mankind. British Perceptions of the World in the Age of the Enlightenment*, London: Dent, 1982.

Metcalf, Thomas R., *Ideologies of the Raj (New Cambridge History of India: III.4)*, Cambridge University Press, 1995.

Rotberg, Robert, ed., *Africa and Its Explorers. Motives, Methods and Impact*, Cambridge, Mass.: Harvard University Press, 1970.

Stafford, Robert A., *Scientist of Empire. Sir Roderick Murchison, Scientific Exploration and Victorian Imperialism*, Cambridge University Press, 1989.

4 Modernism and travel (1880–1940)

Bierman, John, *Dark Safari: The Life Behind the Legend of Henry Morton Stanley*, London: Hodder & Stoughton, 1990.

Birkett, Dea, *Mary Kingsley: Imperial Adventuress*, Basingstoke: Macmillan, 1992.

Booth, Howard, and Nigel Rigby, eds., *Modernism and Empire*, Manchester University Press, 2000.

Fussell, Paul, *Abroad: British Literary Traveling Between the Wars*, Oxford University Press, 1980.

Hobsbawm, Eric, *The Age of Empire 1875–1914*, London: Cardinal, 1987.

Kern, Stephen, *The Culture of Time and Space, 1880–1918*, Cambridge, Mass.: Harvard University Press, 1983.

Schweizer, Bernard, *Radicals on the Road: The Politics of English Travel Writing in the 1930s*, Richmond: University Press of Virginia, 2001.

Thomas, Nicholas, *Colonialism's Culture: Anthropology, Travel & Government*, Cambridge: Polity Press, 1994.

5 Travelling to write (1940–2000)

Cocker, Mark, *Loneliness and Travel: British Travel Writing in the Twentieth Century*, London: Secker and Warburg, 1992.

Holland, Patrick, and Graham Huggan, *Tourists with Typewriters: Critical Reflections on Contemporary Travel Writing*, Ann Arbor: University of Michigan Press, 1998.

Kaplan, Caren, *Questions of Travel: Postmodern Discourses of Displacement*, Durham: Duke University Press, 1996.

Kaur, Raminder, and John Hutnyk, eds., *Travel Worlds: Journeys in Contemporary Cultural Politics*, London: Zed Books, 1999.

Russell, Alison, *Crossing Boundaries: Postmodern Travel Literature*, London: Palgrave, 2000.

Shakespeare, Nicholas, *Bruce Chatwin*, London: The Harvill Press, 1999.

6 The Middle East / Arabia: 'the cradle of Islam'

Assad, Thomas, *Three Victorian Travellers, Burton, Blunt, Doughty*, London: Routledge and Kegan Paul, 1964.

Behdad, Ali, *Belated Travelers: Orientalism in the Age of Colonial Dissolution*, Durham: Duke University Press, 1994.

Daniel, Norman, *Islam and the West: The Making of an Image*, Edinburgh University Press, 1960.

Freedgood, Elizabeth, *Victorian Writing about Risk: Imagining a Safe England in a Dangerous World*, Cambridge University Press, 2000.

Hourani, Albert, *Islam and the West*, London: Macmillan, 1980.

Kabbani, Rana, *Europe's Myths of Orient: Devise and Rule*, London: Macmillan, 1986.

Leask, Nigel, *British Romantic Writers and the East: Anxieties of Empire*, Cambridge University Press, 1992.

Melman, Billie, *Women's Orients: English Women and the Middle East, 1718–1918: Sexuality, Religion and Work*, 2nd edn, London: Macmillan, 1995.

Schiffer, Reinhold, *Oriental Panorama: British Travellers in 19th Century Turkey*, Amsterdam: Rodopi, 1999.

Schwab, Raymond, *The Oriental Renaissance: Europe's Discovery of India and the East 1680–1880*, trans. G. Patterson-Black and V. Reiking, New York: Columbia University Press, 1984.

Sheppard, Naomi, *The Zealous Intruders: The Western Discovery of Palestine*, London: Collins, 1987.

Southern, R. W., *Western Views of Islam in the Middle Ages*, Cambridge, Mass.: Harvard University Press, 1980.

Tidrick, Kathryn, *Heart Beguiling Araby*, Cambridge University Press, 1981.

7 South America / Amazonia: the forest of marvels

Botting, Douglas, *Humboldt and the Cosmos*, London: Michael Joseph, 1973.

Burnett, D. Graham, *Masters of All They Surveyed: Exploration, Geography, and a British El Dorado*, University of Chicago Press, 2000.

Price, Richard, and Sally Price, 'Introduction', to John Gabriel Stedman, *Narrative of a Five Years Expedition Against the Revolted Negroes of Surinam*, ed. Richard and Sally Price, Baltimore: Johns Hopkins University Press, 1988, pp. xiii–xcvii.

Rivière, Peter, *Absent Minded Imperialism*, London: Taurus, 1995.

Stepan, Nancy Leys, *Picturing Tropical Nature*, London: Reaktion Books, 2001.

Whitehead, Neil L., 'Introduction', to *The Discoverie of the Large, Rich and Bewtiful Empyre of Guiana*, ed. Neil L. Whitehead, Manchester University Press, 1997, pp. 1–116.

8 The Pacific / Tahiti: queen of the South Sea isles

Bongie, Chris, *Exotic Memories: Literature, Colonialism, and the Fin de Siècle*, Stanford University Press, 1991.

Daws, Gavan, *A Dream of Islands: Voyages of Self-Discovery in the South Seas*, New York: W. W. Norton and Company, 1980.

Dening, Greg, *Mr Bligh's Bad Language: Passion, Power and Theatre on the Bounty*, Cambridge University Press, 1992.

Denoon, Donald, ed., with Stewart Firth, Jocelyn Linnekin, Malama Meleisea, and Karen Nero, *The Cambridge History of the Pacific Islanders*, Cambridge University Press, 1997.

Edmond, Rod, *Representing the South Pacific: Colonial Discourse from Cook to Gauguin*, Cambridge University Press, 1997.

Lamb, Jonathan, *Preserving the Self in the South Seas 1680–1840*, University of Chicago Press, 2001.

Lamb, Jonathan, Vanessa Smith, and Nicholas Thomas, eds., *Exploration and Exchange: A South Seas Anthology*, University of Chicago Press, 2000.

Lincoln, Margarette, ed., *Science and Exploration in the Pacific: European Voyages to the Southern Oceans in the 18th Century*, Suffolk: The Boydell Press / National Maritime Museum, 1998.

Rennie, Neil, *Far-Fetched Facts: The Literature of Travel and the Idea of The South Seas*, Oxford: Clarendon Press, 1995.

Smith, Bernard, *European Vision and the South Pacific*, New Haven: Yale University Press, 1985.

Imagining the Pacific: In the Wake of the Cook Voyages, New Haven: Yale University Press, 1992.

Smith, Vanessa, *Literary Culture and the Pacific: Nineteenth-Century Textual Encounters*, Cambridge University Press, 1998.

Spate, O. H. K., *Paradise Found and Lost*, London: Routledge, 1988.

9 Africa / The Congo: the politics of darkness

Blunt, Alison, *Travel, Gender, and Imperialism. Mary Kingsley and West Africa*, New York: The Guilford Press, 1994.

Cairns, H. Alan C., *Prelude to Imperialism: British Reactions to Central African Society 1840–1890*, London: Routledge & Kegan Paul, 1965.

Coombes, Annie E., *Reinventing Africa: Museums, Material Culture and Popular Imagination in Late Victorian and Edwardian England*, New Haven: Yale University Press, 1994.

David Livingstone and the Victorian Encounter with Africa, London: National Portrait Gallery, 1996.

Fabian, Johannes, *Out of Our Minds: Reason and Madness in the Exploration of Central Africa*, Berkeley: University of California Press, 2000.

Hammond, Dorothy, and Alta Jablow, *The Africa that Never Was: Four Centuries of British Writing about Africa*, New York: Twayne Publishers, 1970.

Hochschild, Adam, *King Leopold's Ghost: A Story of Greed, Terror, and Heroism in Colonial Africa*, London: Macmillan, 2000.

McLynn, Frank, *Hearts of Darkness: The European Exploration of Africa*, London: Hutchinson, 1992.

Nederveen Pieterse, Jan, *White on Black: Images of Africa and Blacks in Western Popular Culture*, New Haven: Yale University Press, 1992.

Youngs, Tim, *Travellers in Africa: British Travelogues 1850–1900*, Manchester University Press, 1994.

10 The Isles / Ireland: the wilder shore

Andrews, Malcolm, *The Search for the Picturesque: Landscape Aesthetics and Tourism in Britain, 1760–1800*, Aldershot: Scolar, 1990.

Brady, Ciaran, ed., *Interpreting Irish History: the Debate on Historical Revisionism*, Dublin: Irish Academic Press, 1994.

Brown, Terence, *Ireland: A Social and Cultural History, 1922–79*, London: Fontana, 1981.

Colley, Linda, *Britons: Forging the Nation 1707–1837*, New Haven: Yale University Press, 1992.

Davies, Norman, *The Isles: A History*, London: Macmillan, 1999.

Glendening, John, *The High Road: Romantic Tourism, Scotland, and Literature, 1720–1820*, London: Macmillan, 1997.

Gold, J. R., and M. Gold, *Imagining Scotland: Tradition, Representation and Promotion in Scottish Tourism since 1750*, Aldershot: Scolar, 1995.

Hadfield, Andrew, and J. McVeagh, eds., *Strangers to that Land: British Perceptions of Ireland from the Reformation to the Famine*, Gerrards Cross: Colin Smythe, 1994.

Harkness, David, *Ireland in the Twentieth Century: Divided Island*, London: Macmillan, 1996.

Harrington, John. ed., *The English Traveller in Ireland*, Dublin: Wolfhound, 1991.

Howe, Stephen, *Ireland and Empire: Colonial Legacies in Irish History and Culture*, Oxford University Press, 2000.

Leerssen, Joep, *Mere Irish and Fíor-Ghael: Studies in the Idea of Irish Nationality*, Cork University Press, 1996.

Maxwell, Constantia, *The Stranger in Ireland, from the Reign of Elizabeth to the Great Famine*, London: Cape, 1954.

Morgan, Marjorie, *National Identities and Travel in Victorian Britain*, London: Palgrave, 2001.

O'Connor, Barbara, and Michael Cronin, eds., *Tourism in Ireland: A Critical Analysis*, Cork University Press, 1993.

O'Farrell, Patrick, *England and Ireland since 1800*, Oxford University Press, 1975.

Ryle, Martin, *Journeys in Ireland: Literary Travellers, Rural Landscapes, Cultural Relations*, Aldershot: Ashgate, 1999.

Woodham-Smith, Cecil, *The Great Hunger: Ireland, 1845–49*, London: H. Hamilton, 1962.

11 *India / Calcutta: city of palaces and dreadful night*

Bayly, C. A. *The Raj: India and the British 1600–1847*, London: National Portrait Gallery, 1990.
Bhattacharya, Nandini, *Reading the Splendid Body: Gender and Consumerism in Eighteenth-Century British Writing on India*, Newark: University of Delaware Press, 1998.
Chaudhuri, Sukanta, ed., *Calcutta: The Living City*, 2 vols., Calcutta: Oxford University Press, 1990.
Ghose, Indira, *Women Travellers in Colonial India: The Power of the Female Gaze*, New Delhi: Oxford University Press, 1998.
Grewal, Inderpal, *Home and Harem: Nation, Gender, Empire, and the Cultures of Travel*, London: Leicester University Press, 1996.
Hutnyk, John, *The Rumour of Calcutta: Tourism, Charity and the Poverty of Representation*, London: Zed Books, 1996.
Losty, J. P., *Calcutta City of Palaces: A Survey of the City in the Days of the East India Company 1690–1858*, London: The British Library, 1990.
Majeed, Javed, *Ungoverned Imaginings: James Mill's 'The History of British India' and Orientalism*, Oxford University Press, 1992.
Moore-Gilbert, Bart, *Writing India: The Literature of British India*, Manchester University Press, 1996.
Singh, Jyotsna G., *Colonial Narratives/Cultural Dialogues: 'Discoveries' of India in the Language of Colonialism*, London: Routledge, 1996.
Suleri, Sara, *The Rhetoric of English India*, Chicago University Press, 1992.
Teltscher, Kate, *India Inscribed: European and British Writing on India 1600–1800*, New Delhi: Oxford University Press, 1995.

12 *The West / California: site of the future*

Fender, Stephen, *Plotting the Golden West: American Literature and the Rhetoric of the California Trail*, Cambridge University Press, 1981.
Greenfield, Bruce, *Narrating Discovery: The Romantic Explorer in American Literature, 1790–1855*, New York: Columbia University Press, 1992.
Lackey, Kris, *Road Frames: The American Highway Narrative*, Lincoln: University of Nebraska Press, 1997.
Lyon, Thomas J., ed, *A Literary History of the American West*, Fort Worth: Texas Christian University Press, 1987.
Mattes, Merrill J., ed., *Platte River Road Narratives: A Descriptive Bibliography of Travel Over the Great Central Overland Route to Oregon, California, Utah, Colorado, Montana, and Other Western States and Territories, 1812–1866*, Urbana: University of Illinois Press, 1988.
Starr, Kevin, *Americans and the California Dream, 1850–1915*, New York: Oxford University Press, 1973.
Stegner, Wallace, *Where the Bluebird Sings to the Lemonade Springs: Living and Writing in the West*, New York: Random House, 1992.
Stewart, George R., *The California Trail: An Epic With Many Heroes* [1962], Lincoln: University of Nebraska Press, 1983.

Walker, Franklin, *A Literary History of Southern California*, Berkeley: University of California Press, 1950.

San Francisco's Literary Frontier, Seattle: University of Washington Press, 1969.

13 Travel writing and gender

Bohls, Elizabeth A., *Women Travel Writers and the Language of Aesthetics, 1716–1818*, Cambridge University Press, 1995.

Harper, Lila Marz, *Solitary Travelers: Nineteenth-Century Women's Travel Narratives and the Scientific Vocation*, London: Associated University Presses, 2001.

Lawrence, Karen R., *Penelope Voyages: Women and Travel in the British Literary Tradition*, Ithaca: Cornell University Press, 1994.

Lewis, Reina, *Gendering Orientalism: Race, Femininity and Representation*, London: Routledge, 1996.

McEwan, Cheryl, *Gender, Geography and Empire. Victorian Women Travellers in West Africa*, Aldershot: Ashgate, 2000.

Mills, Sara, *Discourses of Difference. An Analysis of Women's Travel Writing and Colonialism*, London: Routledge, 1991.

Morgan, Susan, *Place Matters: Gendered Geography in Victorian Women's Travel Books about Southeast Asia*, New Brunswick: Rutgers University Press, 1996.

Robinson, Jane, *Wayward Women. A Guide to Women Travellers*, Oxford University Press, 1990.

Rose, Gillian, *Feminism and Geography. The Limits of Geographical Knowledge*, Oxford: Polity Press, 1993.

Smith, Sidonie, *Moving Lives: Twentieth-Century Women's Travel Writing*, Minneapolis: University of Minnesota Press, 2001.

14 Travel writing and ethnography

Clifford, James, *Routes: Travel and Translation in the Late Twentieth Century*, Cambridge, Mass.: Harvard University Press, 1997.

The Predicament of Culture: Twentieth-Century Ethnography, Literature, and Art, Cambridge, Mass.: Harvard University Press, 1998.

Gerbi, Antonello, *The Dispute of the New World. The History of a Polemic 1750–1900*, trans. Jeremy Moyle, University of Pittsburgh Press, 1973.

Hodgen, Margaret, *Early Anthropology in the Sixteenth and Seventeenth Centuries*, Philadelphia: University of Pennsylvania Press, 1964.

Lach, Donald F., *Asia in the Making of Europe*, 3 vols., Chicago University Press, 1963–93.

Pagden, Anthony, *The Fall of Natural Man. The American Indian and the Birth of Comparative Ethnology*, Cambridge University Press, 1982.

European Encounters with the New World: from Renaissance to Romanticism, New Haven: Yale University Press, 1993.

Rubiés, Joan Pau, *Travel and Ethnology in the Renaissance. South India Through European Eyes 1250–1625*, Cambridge University Press, 2000.

'Instructions for Travellers: Teaching the Eye to See', *History and Anthropology*, 9 (1996): 139–90.

Stagl, Justin, *A History of Curiosity: The Theory of Travel 1550–1800*, Chur, Switzerland: Harwood Academic Publishers, 1995.
Stocking, George W. Jr., *Victorian Anthropology*, New York: The Free Press, 1987.
Vermeulen, Hans F., and Arturo Alvarez Roldán, eds., *Fieldwork and Footnotes: Studies in the History of European Anthropology*, London: Routledge, 1995.

15 Travel writing and its theory

Asad, Talal, ed., *Anthropology and the Colonial Encounter*, London: Ithaca Press, 1973.
Bhabha, Homi K., *The Location of Culture*, London: Routledge, 1994.
Barker, Francis, Peter Hulme, Margaret Iversen, and Diana Loxley, eds., *Europe and Its Others*, 2 vols., Colchester: University of Essex, 1985.
De Certeau, Michel, *Heterologies: Discourse on the Other*, trans. Brian Massumi, Minneapolis: University of Minnesota Press, 1986.
The Writing of History, trans. Tom Conley, New York: Columbia University Press, 1988.
Clifford, James, and George Marcus, eds., *Writing Culture: The Poetics and Politics of Ethnography*, Berkeley: University of California Press, 1986.
Hartog, François, *The Mirror of Herodotus: The Representation of the Other in the Writing of History*, trans. Janet Lloyd, Berkeley: University of California Press, 1988.
Hulme, Peter, *Colonial Encounters: Europe and the Native Caribbean, 1492–1797*, London: Methuen, 1986.
Said, Edward, *Orientalism*, New York: Pantheon Books, 1978.
Culture & Imperialism, New York: Vintage Books, 1994.
White, Hayden, *Tropics of Discourse: Essays in Cultural Criticism*, Baltimore: Johns Hopkins University Press, 1984.

Resources

Useful reference works are *The Literature of Travel and Exploration: An Encyclopedia*, London: Fitzroy Dearborn, 2002, and Felipe Fernández-Armesto, ed., *The Times Atlas of World Exploration*, London: Harper Collins, 1991; while recent developments in the study of travel writing can be tracked from the *Studies in Travel Writing* home page: http://human.ntu.ac.uk/stw/
Journals dedicated to travel writing are: *Studies in Travel Writing* (from 1997); *Journeys: The International Journal of Travel and Travel Writing* (from 2000); and *The Journal of African Travel Writing* (from 1997). Also relevant are the *Journal of Travel Research* (from 1962); and the *Annals of Tourism Research* (from 1974).
A number of publishers either specialise in travel texts or have dedicated series. John Murray has a long history of publishing travel books. See also Random House's 'Vintage Departures'; Picador Travel Classics; Signal Books's 'Lost and Found: Classic Travel Writing'; Reaktion Books's 'Topographics' series; Continuum's 'The Literature of Travel, Exploration and Empire'; Manchester

University Press's 'Exploring Travel' series; the University of Oklahoma's 'The American Exploration and Travel Series'.

For a full listing of the invaluable Hakluyt Society publications, see R. C. Bridges and P. E. H. Hair, eds., *Compassing the Vaste Globe of the Earth: Studies in the History of the Hakluyt Society 1846–1996*, London: The Hakluyt Society, 1996. A good collection of extracts from the Romantic period is available in *Travels, Explorations and Empires: Writings from the Era of Imperial Expansion 1770–1835*, 2 sets of 4 vols., London: Pickering & Chatto, 2001, vol. I covering North America, the Far East, the North and South Poles, and the Middle East, and vol. II Africa, India, the Caribbean, and the South Seas and Australia. The extracts are produced as facsimiles, but the selections are made with a good eye for illuminating literary connections and the notes and introductions are very useful. (There will be further books in this series.)

An archive of classic Arctic travel writing is available from CD–Academia Book Company (infocd@cd-books.com), while a vast range of travel writing is also available on microfilm: Adam Matthew publications has particularly strong ranges on Western travellers to China and Japan (http://www.adam-matthew-publications.co.uk).

The publisher has used its best endeavours to ensure that the URLs for external websites referred to in this book are correct and active at the time of going to press. However, the publisher has no responsibility for the websites and can make no guarantee that a site will remain live or that the content is or will remain appropriate.

INDEX

Major treatments of a subject are indicated by bold type; illustrations and tables by italics; references to material in notes by an 'n' between the page and note number.

Qatar, 119, 188

Raban, Jonathan, 6, 95–6, 118–19:
    Arabia: A Labyrinth, 118; *Arabia:*
    Through the Looking Glass,
    118–19; *Coasting*, 6; *Passage to*
    Juneau: A Sea and its Meanings,
    95–6, 98
Rabari of Rajasthan, 194
race, 9, 71
    classification of types, 73, 157, 193,
    250
    stereotypes, 165, 250
racism, 66, 73, 75–6, 93, 116, 159, 163,
    200, 240, 252
    anti-racism, 91
Radcliffe, Ann, 44: *The Italian*, 44; *The*
    Mysteries of Udolpho, 44; *The*
    Romance of the Forest, 44
Raffles, Thomas, 258
railways, 38, 47–8, 70, 82, 90, 108–9,
    185, 207
Ralegh Travellers' Club, 61
Ralegh, Sir Walter, 25, 26, 29, 33,
    98, 123, 125, 135, 136, 245:
    Discovery of the Large, Rich, and
    Beautiful Empire of Guiana, 26,
    125
Ramusio, Giovanni Battista, 22:
    Navigationi et viaggi, 22
Rashid, Rehman, 10: *A Malaysian*
    Journey, 10
Rawlinson, Sir Henry, 63
Ray, John, 29
Ray, Satyajit, 204: (film) *Days and*
    Nights in the Forest, 204
Raynal, Abbé, 246
readership, 19–20, 30, 31, 56, 90, 99,
    123, 131, 136, 226, 232, 233, 235,
    236, 239, 249, 255
Red Sea, 112
refugees, 11, 195, 202
religion, 84, 117, 245, 250, 251, 253,
    270, 272; *see also* Calvinism;
    Catholicism; Christianity;
    evangelicals; gentiles; Hinduism;
    Islam; Jesuits; Judaism;

Judeo-Christian; missionaries;
    natural; Protestantism; Wahhabism
Rennell, James, 59: *Memoir of a Map of*
    Hindoostan, 59
reportage, 94, 168, 188, 208; *see also*
    journalism
Reval (Tallinn, Estonia), 230
Rhodesia, 167
Rhys, Jean, 74
Richardson, Robert, 159: *The Story of*
    the Niger, 159
Richburg, Keith B., 168–9: *Out of*
    America: A Black Man Confronts
    Africa, 168–9
Rilke, Rainer Maria, 91
Rimbaud, Arthur, 98
Ringrose, Basil, 28: *The Buccaneers of*
    America, 28
roads, 176, 178, 187, 216–17, 219
Robb, Peter, 97–8: *Midnight in Sicily*,
    97–8
Roberts, Emma, 192, 198–9: *Scenes*
    and Characteristics of Hindostan,
    198–9
Roberts, Joe, 204: *Abdul's Taxi to*
    Kalighat, 204
Roberts, John, 167: *Congo Adventure*,
    167
Robertson, William, 246
Robinson, Alfred, 209
Robinson, Edward, 109–10: *Biblical*
    Researches in Palestine, 109–10
Robinson, Jane, 226, 227: *Unsuitable*
    for Ladies, 226; *Wayward Women*,
    226
Roe, Sir Thomas, 28, 191, 250
Rogers, Mary Eliza, 112
Rogers, Samuel, 49
Rolt, Lionel, 187: *Green and Silver*, 187
Roman Empire, 157
Romania, 237
Romantic Orientalism, 191
Romanticism, 6, 159
    anti-romantic, 82
Rosa, Salvator, 45
Rose, Gillian, 230: *Feminism and*
    Geography, 230

CAMBRIDGE COMPANIONS TO LITERATURE